Gender, Kinship, Power

Gender, Kinship, Power

A Comparative and
Interdisciplinary History

EDITED BY MARY JO MAYNES, ANN WALTNER,
BIRGITTE SOLAND AND ULRIKE STRASSER

Routledge
New York • London

Published in 1996 by

Routledge
29 West 35th Street
New York, NY 10001

Published in Great Britain by

Routledge
11 New Fetter Lane
London EC4P 4EE

Library of Congress Cataloging–in–Publication Data

Gender, kinship, power: an interdisciplinary and comparative history /
    edited by Mary Jo Maynes ... [et al].
      p. cm.
   Includes biliographical references and index.
   ISBN 0–415–91297–0 (hb)—ISBN 0–415–91298-9 (pb)
    1. Kinship—Cross-cultural studies. 2. Sex role—Cross-cultural
studies. 3. Family—Cross-cultural studies. I. Maynes, Mary Jo.
GN480.G46 1995   95–33971
                             CIP

To our four mothers:

Kathryn Maynes (née Price)
Else Soland (née Christensen)
Henrike Strasser (née Wolf)
Nell Waltner (née Laird)

And to:

Elizabeth Maynes-Aminzade

CONTENTS

Part Three: "Fish without Bicycles": Gender and the Paradoxes of Kinship

Part Four: Parents, Breadwinners, Providers: Family Roles between Ideology and Economics

Part Five: Gender and Kinship in Changing Political Economies

Acknowledgments

Conversations across boundaries—geographic and disciplinary—have been at the heart of the intellectual process that has produced this book. The idea of a conference on comparative women's history came from conversations we are able to enjoy at the University of Minnesota because our faculty and graduate student community includes historians of women in different cultures. Our overlapping interests led us to develop a program in Comparative Women's History and also to organize an inaugural conference on a particularly important theme that links historians of women across broad geographic fields—namely, the place of women in kinship systems. The conference, entitled "Matrilineality and Patrilineality in Comparative and Historical Perspective," took place in Minneapolis in May 1992.

This book is based on work originally presented at that conference. We would like to thank the authors and other participants at the conference for taking up the conversation and enriching it. Their contributions to this ambitious editorial project go beyond what is evident in individual essays, for producing the book has relied on their collaboration from the beginning. And although not all of the papers presented at that conference ended up in this collection, the influence of all of them is evident here, as the notes to the introduction and individual essays attest.

We would also like to thank the members of the conference planning board and the conference sponsors. These include, at the University of Minnesota: the Graduate School, the College of Liberal Arts, the Department of Conferences, the Office of International Programs, the Institute for International Studies, the Western European Areas Studies Center, the MacArthur Program, the Department of History, the Center for Advanced Feminist Studies, the African Studies Council and the Center for Early Modern History; and externally: the Social Science Research Council and the Council for European Studies. Of course, the funders made it possible for us to write this book, but they are not responsible for its contents.

Throughout the editorial process we have also relied on research assistance. We would like to express our gratitude to Tim Coates for help with translation and to Eve Dvorak and Jamie McCarthy for their cheerful, energetic and insightful editorial help, as well as for doing their best to keep the sometimes scattered editors in line.

M.J. Maynes
Ann Waltner
Ulrike Strasser
Minneapolis, Minnesota

Birgitte Soland
Columbus, Ohio

December 1, 1994

Introduction: Toward a Comparative History of Gender, Kinship and Power

MARY JO MAYNES, ANN WALTNER, BIRGITTE SOLAND AND ULRIKE STRASSER

Those of us who are heirs to the European cultural legacy have long lived with certain norms and practices regarding kinship that are part of our native view. Many of the technical terms we use to map kinship—like "agnatic" to refer to relations traced through the father's line—come directly from Ancient Roman civil law, which was decidedly patrilineal. That is, it emphasized the kinship relations through the father, and de-emphasized those established by other lines of affiliation. Westerners have lived with these norms for so long that they appear almost natural—as if derived from reproductive biology. The essays in this book make clear, however, that kinship systems are human creations, the product of history and culture rather than simply biology. The historians and anthropologists whose work is represented here contribute to two closely related efforts: historicizing kinship in ethnography, and finding new ways of exploring kinship through historical sources.

Historians of women and the family have already demonstrated the malleability of family and gender roles. We have learned much about family history through demographic studies and research on households and the family economy. We now know, for example, that because of high death rates, single parenting and what we now call blended families were very common in past centuries. We also know that since the late Middle Ages marriage in Europe has taken place at a much later age than in Asia or Africa. Moreover, attitudes about breast-feeding, child labor, disciplining children and the like have varied tremendously from one region to another and over time. In addition, gender divisions of labor within the household, while they exist everywhere, vary from place to place, and both respond and contribute to historical change.

Still, many important manifestations of kinship—the evolution of rules that assign different kinds of family power to men and women, for example, or the functioning of metaphors of kinship like mother tongue or fraternity in broader cultural systems—have only recently received attention from historians.[1] This book will explore many facets of kinship in historical perspective, but our emphasis is on those aspects of kinship systems which affect the intergenerational transfer of resources, nurturance, identities and community. And we are particularly interested in how gender differences structure both kinship relations and the broader ideologies that rest on or support them.

Because the study of kinship is fairly new to history, historians have often turned to anthropology to find ways to analyze the practices, ideals and strategies that constitute a kinship system. Around the same time that historians began to interest themselves in kinship, many anthropologists began to reconsider their discipline's approaches to it. Some anthropologists argued that anthropological accounts were not sensitive enough to the historical character of kinship arrangements, which instead were often treated as permanent. Others noted that early ethnographers whose studies formed the bases of anthropological theory had often unconsciously employed Western categories of kinship as if these were universal.[2] Jane Collier and Sylvia Yanagisako, two anthropologists who specialize in kinship, have called into question some of the fundamental premises of anthropological kinship theory. In their view, there is no indisputable basis in nature or biology for the mother-child bond or for male authority. They also argue for acknowledgment of the role that erroneous assumptions about actual European practices have played in earlier ethnographic observations of other peoples. It is our goal to build on such insights.

The emphasis of this book on the historical evolution of kinship in different cultural areas allows us to address questions about how kinship systems respond to social, economic and political change, as well as to explore the durability and conservatism of kinship relations. A focus on changing understandings of the function and meaning of kinship illustrates the sense in which kinship categories are creations of human history. Juxtaposition of diverse family forms and particular practices that in each social context appear to be "natural" underscores the process of social construction. Our goal is not so much to establish a new general theory of kinship as to find ways of constructing categories of kinship that are sensitive to historical change and cultural variability. We have thus built cross-regional comparison into each section of the book. Moreover, in order to demonstrate historical as well as cross-cultural variation, we have included, in some cases, several essays on the same society at different points in time (two historical and one contemporary analysis centered on Brazil, and four studies of Italy ranging in time from the Roman period to the nineteenth century). This allows for attention to both cross-time and cross-cultural comparison that will encourage more careful and precise construction of analytic categories, and will help us to resist employing conceptual language based on one region or time as the unexamined norm from which other patterns are seen as deviant.

Part One—Kinship Systems: Theories, Practices, Contradictions

The essays in Part I introduce dramatically different systems of kinship in a variety of times and places. Every culture has a system that maps people into networks of near and distant family relationships, and attaches meaning to those relationships. But the particular claims about who is related to whom and what those relationships mean vary tremendously from one culture to the next; moreover, those claims change over time.

Ironically, however, each system of kinship is seen in its own context as the "natural" or "god-given" one. In the case of Ancient Judaic culture, described by Howard Eilberg-Schwartz, or of early modern China, in Ann Waltner's analysis, the rules of kinship are established in the realm of the supernatural, in an exchange between gods or sages and humans. The Romans who are the focus of Gianna Pomata's study root their notions of kinship in medical theories about biological generation. Both kinds of claims have the effect of rendering existing understandings of kin relations sacrosanct.

Yet each of these studies shows that, however kinship rules are legitimized, there are paradoxes, denials and contradictions within them that belie claims that they simply reflect the way things are. The rules are never completely consistent or transparent. For example, Ancient Judaic beliefs rested on a clear patrilineal connection created by a covenant between God and Jewish men. The covenant rested on a notion of God as Father and His promise of plentiful male "seed" that would insure the continuity of the Jewish people. Nevertheless, this complex of beliefs was contradicted and undermined by another tenet of faith—that God had no sex, and therefore could not really be male. In the Chinese case, to offer another example, the catastrophe represented by the failure to produce a male heir—seen as the "most unfilial of all acts"—led families to circumvent the explicit logic of filiation rules. They often adopted seemingly unrelated individuals or took in concubines to mitigate heirlessness. The father-son or mother-child relationship, while normatively seen as biological, could also be generated by legal fictions or social contracts.

Moreover, the ways in which kinship systems organize people into supposedly natural categories generally reinforce social and political hierarchies as well. Men and women, young and old, native and non-native—all of these categories of inequality and many more have often been rooted in the "natural" relations of kinship. One of the recurrent themes in the book is how frequently metaphors and relationships derived from kinship systems spill over into other cultural and social realms, and are used to legitimate and "naturalize" (that is, attribute to nature) inequalities in other spheres.[3] Several of the essays in this section raise very pointedly the question of who naturalizes which relationships and what the stakes are in the act of naturalizing. They point out how difficult it is to reconcile kinship systems with simple notions of biology. For example, Waltner's account of the complicated Chinese rules about different kinds of mothers (birth, adoptive, father's other wives, and so on) suggests just how far a society's rules about relationship could depart from a biological understanding of the mother-child relationship. Pomata's essay explores changing perceptions of the role of the mother and father in procreation as reflected in medical theory and legal arrangements in Roman texts. Her examination of the historical origins of Western European views on kinship reveals a fascinating denial in legal and medical sources of the seemingly evident tie between mother and child. Indeed, it was only in later epochs that brothers and sisters of the same mother but different fathers were seen, in these sources, to "share the same blood." Pomata suggests how this denial of the mother was related to broader gender inequalities in the Roman politico-legal system.

The essays in this part also introduce a series of important methodological issues which will figure prominently throughout the book. Pomata's essay argues that it can be useful for a historian to read historical materials with an anthropologist's eye. Conversely, her analysis helps to historicize the terminology of kinship that Westerners have inherited—a historicization that should discourage the tendency to universalize from one culture's categories. But it is also important to recall that, while the texts she examines may well reveal what were once the "ruling views" on kinship in the West, they were by no means universally held. Here, as always, the analyst remains prisoner of his or her sources. A related methodological issue is raised by Alex Bolyanatz, when he reminds us of the need to differentiate between dominant norms and everyday practices. Bolyanatz begins his paper with a question: "What is matriliny: descent dogma or politico-economic practice?" Distinguishing between the two, his paper shows that "social relations which are seemingly based on matrilineal descent ideology are also informed by cultural understandings which have little or nothing to do with descent."[4] He reminds us, in other words, to be careful not to conceive of kinship in too abstract a fashion. Kinship systems are practices as well as theories, and even though it may be particularly hard to learn about actual practices, especially for the historian, this dimension should never escape our attention. The advantage of the ethnographer, of course, lies in his or her ability to question a variety of people about their beliefs and observe their practices. Bolyanatz's essay and others in the book demonstrate the power of the ethnographic approach directed toward capturing a multiplicity of perspectives on kinship.

Attention to perspective marks all the essays in the collection. The authors are each writing about the perspectives of a particular time and place. And their analyses are based on particular sources. This sensitivity to perspective and context shapes their conclusions and their very language: Pomata deliberately speaks of "us" and "our" system; when she does so she is addressing influential traditions which she sees as reaching down to contemporary Westerners despite the centuries that divide them from the authors of the legal and medical texts Pomata cites. Her essay also underscores the Western construction of the ethnographic "other" as a complex process. Other authors in this section place themselves in varying positions *vis-à-vis* the cultures they study; not all examine their own culture's indigenous views. But in no case do the authors make claims that generalize beyond the bounds of the particular evidence they examine. And in no case is it even argued that all members of a given society shared the same notions of kinship. Notions of kinship are understood to be rooted in time, space and position within society.

Part Two—Women's Perspectives on Kinship

The articles in Part II explore the issue of gender-specific strategies and perspectives in kinship systems that privilege the male line. They all employ sources that allow answers to questions about how kinship systems appear from particular gender positions. Christiane Klapisch-Zuber follows an indirect route as she tracks female perspectives in a strongly patrilineal society—that of Renaissance Florence. She follows the faint trace of a female voice by reading the presence of a mother as informant behind a genealogy written by a man; in so doing she uncovers hints of "a specifically female way of retaining memory of kinship." Lucia Ferrante also studies urban northern Italy, in particular Bologna. In contrast to Klapisch-Zuber, she is able to find more direct evidence of female perspectives and strategies. For in the century between the period of Klapisch-Zuber's study and Ferrante's, the

Catholic Church became increasingly involved in family decisions about marriage. Ferrante's sources—court records concerning cases of marriage litigation—document the clash between the private law enforced by powerful patrilineal clans and ecclesiastical law aimed at asserting church control over marriage. In this situation of contention between competing authorities, women could sometimes find support for their own preferences by appealing to the church against their fathers. In so doing, they also left records of the ways in which daughters' views of kinship prerogatives differed from their fathers'.

Shanti Menon finds both gender and generational variation in perceptions of women's place in twentieth-century Kerala in South India, although her analysis of change over time reminds us that it is never one-dimensional or unidirectional. She employs a primarily ethnographic approach, but historicizes the experience of kinship by drawing on the perspectives of informants from different age groups. Traditional matrilineal practices (that is, those tracing important kinship relations through the maternal line) and more recent patrilineal practices coexist. Menon's sensitivity to generational and class differences illustrates the resilience of older matrilineal practices while revealing their changing meanings in a changing world. In both systems of descent, the situation and experience of women varies according to their kinship position (daughter, wife, mother and so on) and their class.

Gloria Goodwin Raheja's approach to female subjectivity also emphasizes the importance of positionality. In her fieldwork in a patrilineal village in northern India, she collected songs in which women express their awareness of the contradictions of their situations. In them, Raheja tells us, "women speak as differently positioned actors (wife or daughter or sister, or mother-in-law or daughter-in-law, or high caste or low caste) and though their voices may not be unitary, they all articulate an awareness of the contradictions of kinship ideology and their implications for female identity."

Finally, in the last essay in this part, Pamela Feldman-Savelsberg looks for women's perspectives on kinship in the West African country of Cameroon through an analysis of domestic practices and cooking metaphors. The Bangangté women she speaks to must move to their husband's village upon marriage; their children are claimed by the father's line. However, through their command of domestic space and and resources, and by way of metaphors that draw analogies between cooking and procreation, Bangangté women assert their indispensability and maintain their connections to their natal, especially maternal, kin.

Taken as a group, these papers call attention to the problem of how to find more concealed or suppressed views about kinship, especially those suppressed by power imbalances between the sexes. As we mentioned earlier, sensitive ethnographers are attuned to any informant's position in the system he or she describes. These essays all ask how women or men view the kinship systems in which they occupy varying positions. Raheja's data collection shows one approach to this problem: she turned to where women expressed themselves as women in particular positions in women's songs. She found that women's perspectives on kinship differed depending on who was singing and who was listening. Menon and Feldman-Savelsberg combine field research about differently positioned actors with creative reading of the historical record. Klapisch-Zuber and Ferrante had to read obliquely from the historical record of institutions that obscured or suppressed female views on kinship arrangements. The authors suggest a variety of ingenious approaches to and assessments of the gendered nature of kinship strategies and subjective experiences of kinship. All of these essays also suggest how the methodological problem of uncovering gendered perspectives on kinship is related to the even broader problem of how kinship affects power relations between the sexes.

Part Three—"Fish Without Bicycles": Gender and the Paradoxes of Kinship

The essays in Part III center on how gender presumptions matter in the transfer of resources through kinship. They call our attention to the frequency with which norms and practices collide. They explore how, despite the presumption of male domination written into many rules, in practice men are unable or unwilling to fill the roles prescribed to them. Our section title alludes to the political slogan: "A woman without a man is like a fish without a bicycle." The point of the slogan, of course, was to suggest that women can do quite well in the absence of men. The essays, however, suggest the difficulties women encounter when they take on the tasks of survival and nurturance in the absence of men, in cultures where norms and institutions presume that men are in charge.

Barbara Hanawalt's study of widows in late medieval London explores the provision for widows and orphans among London's propertied citizenry. Her study demonstrates how a variety of legal and institutional supports protected widows and fatherless children in this setting. Quite central to her analysis are strong legal stipulations that established an economic partnership between spouses. Hanawalt's study of court cases, such as women's claims to their dowries, illustrates the conscientious implementation of the laws. Female independence was rooted in material resources and a legal system which allowed widows access to those resources. Hanawalt argues that framing this relative independence was a milieu-specific kinship system that emphasized concern for the nuclear family over male lineage.

Maura Palazzi's examination of the situation of single women in eighteenth- and nineteenth-century Bologna points to the changing impact of dominant kinship norms on women's options for independence. Her focus is on women's work. She argues that "women alone"[5] can be functional to the operation of a strongly patrilineal system. Still, she found, such women (widows and unmarried or abandoned women) were marginalized in subordinate positions in the economy and in hierarchies of kinship. Palazzi also explores changes over time which, while not removing the persistent subordination of women, nevertheless altered the balance of power between the sexes.

Eni de Mesquita Samara uses census material to uncover a world of female activity even within the "masculine space" of colonial and postcolonial Brazil. Women, she finds, took part in a wide range of economic activities, and functioned in the domestic economy as well as that of the streets. They occupied a variety of positions in the complex class-racial hierarchy of this dynamic society: they were patrons and clients, slaves and slave owners. The important regional and chronological variations de Mesquita Samara has uncovered are also suggestive. Clearly women's abilities to integrate themselves into active roles in the economy differed widely in more settled and frontier situations, and from one local economy to another. Her discovery of women in a wide range of places where, according to dominant norms, they were not supposed to be echoes Palazzi's findings about the economic roles of "women alone" in Bologna.

Part Four—Parents, Breadwinners, Providers: Family Roles between Ideology and Economics

The essays in this part focus explicitly on kinship and domestic roles. They address questions about women's and men's expectations about family formation against a background of ideas about masculinity and femininity, fatherhood and motherhood. Here, we once again encounter the problematic nature of fathering. The essays in the first part introduce contradictions in various understandings of biological generation, especially accounts of the role of the father and the connection between fathering, masculinity and male domination. These contradictions are addressed in several essays in Part I—in the context of Ancient Judaic religious thought, for example, in Eilberg-Schwartz's essay, or Roman law as analyzed by Pomata. They will appear again in the context of contemporary discussions of fatherhood and the conferral of citizenship rights in the British Virgin Islands, the subject Bill Maurer examines in Part V.

In Part IV, however, the essays examine practices associated with a more marginal kind of fatherhood—fatherhood that is in fact tenuous and distant, however patrilineal the dominant norms might be. The situations described here remind us of Carolyn Steedman's autobiographical observations about the psychology of father-child relations among the lower classes in mid–twentieth-century Britain. Her childhood memory of seeing her father humiliated by a park warden ("the scene in the bluebell wood") came to symbolize for her all the ways in which dominant notions of fatherhood were inapplicable to the situation of children like her:

> I…could bring forward incidents of my childhood to question all the official interpretive devices that I encountered. The scene in the bluebell wood with my father, the eruption of the angry keeper…was a way of thinking about the oedipal account…and the whole generalized account of human culture built around the position and role of the father. It was a way of wondering about how the myth works when a father is rendered vulnerable by social relations, when a position in a household is not supported by recognition of social status and power outside it. The scene was a way of saying: no: it wasn't like that; he wasn't important; he didn't matter.[6]

Several of these essays address situations where fathers are similarly "rendered vulnerable by social relations." Parry Scott, for example, asks what men and women among the poor of contemporary urban Brazil gain from setting up households. Scott explores how men's attitudes, expectations and experiences shape their roles as mates and providers. He deals with the gap between an ideology of male dominance and a lived reality of matrifocal households. Men's economic marginality, their inability to be the breadwinners, corrodes patriarchal practice even while leaving the ideology intact. Women see men as a burden; their independence (if that is the right word in this context of economic underprivilege) is the other side of male economic disempowerment. These themes are quite familiar to contemporary North Americans, of course, for they have played a central role in analyses of African-American family formation since the 1960s. They also echo the many situations in the developing world where gender-specific labor migration patterns draw men away from their families.[7]

Scott's analysis raises the larger issue of how "dominant" kinship norms operate within different class milieux, which is the primary focus of Mary Jo Maynes's essay as well. In the European working-class autobiographies she examines, fathers appear as similarly marginal and problematic figures. They and their kin ties play a less central role in memories of childhood than mothers do. Their failure to behave "like a father" casts them as the chief villains of many a life plot, even if the authors' intent was to illustrate the effects of social ills like poverty and unemployment. As in contemporary Brazil, matrifocality may well have empowered women within these European working-class families (relative to upper-class women), but the economic and psychic costs of this form of empowerment hardly recommend it as beneficent for women or children.

Carmen Ramos-Escandon takes on the history of norms about mothering in her study of the social construction of motherhood in turn-of-the century Mexico. By using legal codes and popular literature, Ramos-Escandon shows how changes in family legislation in Mexico served the state policy of promoting a nuclear family ideology and what the author has termed "a renewed submission of women to male authority." Her essay points to a case where there was a deliberate effort to recontruct laws and practices in the face of a popular culture where norms were at odds with the state agenda (in particular, there were very high levels of illegitimacy).

Norbert Ortmayr's explicitly comparative study allows for an assessment of the possibilities and perils of unmarried motherhood in two different contexts. Ortmayr's work is instructive in that it suggests the variety of ways in which a phenomenon like widespread illegitimacy among economically marginal populations can be generated and understood. Even though Ortmayr argues forcefully that illegitimacy of this sort is an unfortunate consequence of poverty and disappears only with regular employment that can in turn provide the material basis for family stability, he evaluates two historical situations in somewhat different terms. The cultural stigma attached to unwed motherhood in Austria, as well as residence and employment patterns that force illegimate children into foster homes, appear in Ortmayr's account to be a far more cruel set of arrangements than the ways that unmarried mothers and their children live in Jamaica. There is no romanticization of the plight of the latter; nevertheless, in Jamaica the psychic and social consequences of fatherlessness seem attentuated in comparison with the Austrian experience.

Part Five—Gender and Kinship in Changing Political Economies

Kinship systems reflect and reinforce gender inequalities, but, as the previous discussion makes clear, they are implicated in other sorts of inequalities as well. Several of the essays in Part V are set in colonial or postcolonial contexts where clashes between divergent kinship systems were part of larger colonial confrontations. More broadly, all of the essays here assess transformations in kinship systems under the impact of sweeping changes in the global political economy.

Jean O'Brien searches through sparse documentation for clues about how Native American women attempted to preserve or reconstruct family economies in colonial New England. The image she presents is that of a "shattered society" in which colonialism and the infringement of the world market wreaked havoc with preexisting social forms. Her essay deals with the range of accommodation strategies employed by Native American women in colonial New England who were losing their traditional economic base—the land—and their traditional support network—their kin. Her essay points to the process of disempowerment of a people, a disempowerment that occurs through demographic catastrophe and land deprivation, the latter affecting women particularly adversely. Ironically, the very scarcity of evidence about Native American understandings of kinship and gender relations, which makes her work so difficult, is itself a product of the colonial assault on indigenous cultures and cultural memory.

Muriel Nazzari's study of colonial Brazil, in contrast, examines changing lineage strategies among the Portuguese colonizers; for them, she suggests, the colonial frontier setting promoted some reshaping of kinship practices—in particular, rules about naming—in the face of changing family strategies. She argues that new naming practices reflected a balance of power that shifted toward women. Her explanation of this change also centers on the encounter between European and indigenous people, but one which took a different form from North America. Early Portuguese settlers intermarried with Native women, thereby creating a racially mixed colonial elite. But European presumptions about racial and color hierarchies led elite families in later generations, at least temporarily, to transgress patrilineal naming practices they might otherwise have subscribed to more rigorously. As Nazzari puts it, "in the face of an exclusively male immigrant flow, it was only daughters who could marry Europeans and whiten the lineage. Thus, the power of the founding families of São Paulo was transmitted especially through daughters" who thus become more prominent in family strategy. Nazzari's work describes "a historical situation in which racial and class strategies in marriage alliances took precedence over the preservation of gender hierarchies, thereby increasing the power and importance...of daughters and wives."

Kiran Cunningham's essay suggests how gender interests affect the ways in which men and women view tradition and change in kinship in a contemporary setting. Her study of postmarital residence patterns among the Mende in Western Africa suggests that "where a married couple resides has tremendous implications for a woman's power, in the context of her relationship with her husband and within the community in general." Recent innovations in postmarital residence (an increasing number of women have begun moving into their husband's village) affect gender relations. The new residential trend is directly related to the collapse of Sierra Leone's mining industry, which has forced men to return to their home villages to set up households, often with women from the outside. In Cunning-ham's words, the "locations of power" are shifting as a result, and she also finds evi-dence of "deliberate attempts on the part of women to locate themselves in their natal communities."

The last essay in the book also looks at how change occurs in a contemporary society. Bill Maurer's study examines how lineality and descent are currently con-structed in law and political discourse in the British Virgin Islands. Maurer sees his essay as "an effort to grapple with the naturalized constructions of 'nature,' 'kin-ship,' 'gender' and 'nation'…in a colonial context." Maurer's essay applies an anthropologist's approach to the compelling political problem of who does and does not "belong" to a nation and how such "belonging" is established through kinship and other means. He shows that even discourses that critique orthodox views often replicate some of their naturalizing presumptions. Virgin Islanders who protest narrow definitions of citizenship based on the citizenship status of fathers still conceive of birthplace as the basis of their alternative notion of nation-al belonging. In Maurer's own words, "what's tricky is that 'we' naturalize power through gender, kinship and other domains such as race and nation; but so, too, do the 'others' we study who have been subjected to Western colonial and capital-ist regimes. If we are not attentive to the usually unexamined grounds of our analyses, we risk a kind of collusion between 'our' categories and those of the peo-ple whose lives we study." Although this case focuses on the twentieth century, we can see the resonance between Maurer's arguments and those made in Part I by Eilberg-Schwartz and Pomata about Ancient Judaic and Roman cultures, respec-tively. All these analyses identify problematic connections among generation, political identity and belonging.

Learning from Comparison, Drawing Conclusions

It might be useful to take on the question of power by starting from two concrete cases. Comparison between the complementary studies of Indian kinship systems by Shanti Menon and Gloria Raheja represents one of many possible starting points from this collection. Menon and Raheja uncover a multifaceted reality of male-female power relations underneath the labels of matrilineality and patrilin-eality. Read together, their essays document that, whether women are central or marginal to definitions of lineage, their centrality or marginality shapes but does not fully determine gender relations. Menon finds strong evidence for male con-trol over women's sexuality even in the matrilineal arrangements of South India. She illustrates how both traditional matrilineality and more recent patrilineality exist in a context of specific male powers over women's bodies. She finds that class differences, more than anything else, attenuate the degree of men's power over women's lives. On yet another level, Menon traces female practices that subvert men's power while nevertheless leaving patriarchal ideology intact. Menon's access to knowledge about these subversive practices stems from that fact that informants see her to be an insider to the culture she analyses. For example, in a discussion about forms of resisting male control that are "shared secrets" among women, an informant tells Menon, "You are a Nayar, you have lived in a *taravad*, do these things have to be spelled out?" Raheja, on the other hand, documents women's resistance and agency in a village in which she is an observer from the outside. Her own status no doubt amplifies her awareness of positionality, and she focuses on how her female informants' positions in the kinship system (as daughters, wives, and so on) shape how they experience male power. Raheja argues that women's critical discourse reveals what she calls "narrative potency" and operates as a vehicle for change, whereas Menon claims that women's private resistance simply helps to perpetuate gender hierarchies.

Such different conclusions about the potential for female subversion raise key questions about power that continually resurface in this book. How should we interpret men's and women's varying understandings of kinship or the diverse and mutable kinship practices these studies keep uncovering? What implications do they have for the changing distribution of power between the sexes? What can we say comparatively about the impact of different ways of mapping kinship on the nature or degree of female versus male power? How should we interpret conflicting views about how kinship works? As we have suggested, even in the case of strongly patrilineal systems, which tend to place men on the center of the stage and grant priority to links among men in drawing intergenerational connections, women often seem to disagree that the men's stage is the one that really matters. Is their disagreement subversive or simply compensatory? How do we observers and theorists of kinship decide on which stage the real action happens? Is this a question of whose side we are on? How are such judgments affected by insider or outsider status?

We cannot, of course, come up with definitive answers to difficult questions about how kinship arrangements affect the balance of power between the genders or about how to understand diverse constructions of kinship. But we would like at least to point out some of the specific connections among gender, kinship and power that we think the essays illuminate. Readers will, we hope, find many more connections and draw their own conclusions.

13

Mapping Kinship: The Power to Name

Naming—perhaps the primal act of culture—is a conceptual act that is central to the mapping of people into kinship relationships. It should therefore not be too surprising to see naming appear in these essays as an important dimension of power. In particular, a cultural association between the recognition of paternity and the dawn of civilization recurs throughout the kinship systems these essays examine. Ann Waltner's essay introduces us to the Ancient Chinese dating of the dawn of civilization to the moment when the sages granted humans patrilineally traced surnames. The connection reverberates in other cultures as well. But if in many cultures recognition of the father-child bond is taken as one sign of civilized human community, anxieties about it permeate many kinship codes and practices around paternity. This anxiety is apparent, beyond the Chinese, in the Judaic, Roman and Mediterranean Christian cultures.

Such associations, emphases and anxieties influence discussions of kinship, and certainly have been a complicating factor in cross-cultural contact. The attempt to prove that kinship rules were a marker of a civilization's level of development colored early Western anthropological theories that argued that human culture had progressed from matrilineal to patrilineal organization. As numerous essays in the collection show, however, such theories reflect Western anxieties and projections more than varied historical experiences. Among the essays in this collection, Alex Bolyanatz is clearest in arguing that the historical evolution of kinship systems can take many directions.[8] Concerns about preserving paternal lineages and the strict control over women that this sometimes entails also contributed to colonial clashes between divergent kinship practices as discussed, for example, by O'Brien, Ramos-Escandon, or Ortmayr. These studies all document the effects of colonial efforts to superimpose European notions about marriage and gender roles on indigenous people who often had very different concepts.

Naming and categorizing in other realms—in important bodies of theoretical knowledge—also frequently mirror kinship mapping. For example, Eilberg-Schwartz draws our attention to the oral communication of sacred knowledge through the male line in Ancient Judaic culture. Women in this culture were thus religiously marginalized in ways that built on and echoed their subordination in kinship. Obviously, we do not have female views on this development. We are reminded of the connections between gender imbalances and the power to name in this larger sense—that is, in the sense of creating the very categories and rules that determine not only who is kin, but also who is powerful in other cultural realms. In this case we have only men's word for it. Presumably some degree of cultural power—the discursive power inherent in what Raheja calls the "strategic use of speech" to name, comment on and criticize subordinate positions—was as available to Ancient Judaic women as it was to the women of Renaissance Florence or contemporary North India whose testimony Klapisch-Zuber and Raheja employ. But even in these better-documented cases, we are still left with differing interpretations of how subversive such feminine redefinitions (largely for female audiences) were.

Kinship rules also affect the power to name in a more literal way—to bestow on a child a name that marks his or her kinship alliances. In addition to its role in ancient Chinese and Judaic traditions, we see this kind of naming appear as an important element of family strategy in colonial Brazil. In the Chinese case, surname is paramount and kinship connections are marked by surname; in the Luso-Brazilian case, the preeminence of transmission of status and property dictated name changes and the adoption of names through the maternal line which would have been unthinkable in China. Naming practices serve and signal strategies for making lineage connections across the generations; as such they comprise another form of discursive power around kinship.

We too, as theorists of kinship, are both fascinated and trapped by the power of naming as reflected in kinship terminology. One clear example of this came up in our effort to choose the best translation for the term "women alone" as used by Maura Palazzi in her essay. The problem is simple but revealing: Palazzi made it clear that she wanted to discuss all women living in households which they headed—therefore including single or never-married women, separated women and widows, however many people lived in their households, as well as women who actually lived alone. For analytic reasons Palazzi wanted to exclude women who were unmarried but living as dependents (for example as servants or dependent relatives). In all of the languages we know we ran up against the double-edged marginality of these "women alone"; they are hard to name and categorize precisely because they are not supposed to be there. To call them, for example, "independent women" would grant them more economic and political security than they usually commanded. To call them "women alone" as we, following Palazzi's lead, have done throughout this introduction, is not quite right either, for it suggests that they were solitary when they in fact often lived quite sociable lives in large households. Finally the English term "single women" is usually taken to mean only the never-married, and does not normally comprise the widowed or separated women Palazzi wanted to include. The existence of such women in Bologna suggests that even in strongly patrilineal societies women could be more independent and powerful than they were supposed to be (a theme echoed strongly in de

Mesquita Samara's essay). At the same time, their marginality meant that they typically survived only very meagerly in the absence of men. This is just one example, but it is a particularly telling one. The fate of such women varies widely in time and space, and might serve as an interesting indicator of change over time and comparative advantage. At the same time, our difficulty in finding just the right term in any language to categorize them reveals how hard it is to separate the power to name from the power-ridden categories of lived experience.

Enforcing Kinship Relations:
The Legal and Political Dimensions

Behind the power to name lurks the power to enforce one system of rules over challengers, a specifically political dimension of kinship. Lucia Ferrante's focus on Bolognese women's uses of the church courts drew our attention to the legal framework within which kinship relations operated there. She describes a classic situation of split sovereignty. Older traditions of private law, whereby the patriarch made decisions for his offspring, coexisted with newer arguments advanced by the Catholic Church that spouses should consent to marriage. Her study demonstrates the impact on kinship of changing political and legal contexts. Indeed, throughout the late medieval and early modern period of European history, the long contest between the church and secular authorities, eventually the centralized state, would continually contribute to the revision of kinship practices and norms.[9] There were several historical moments such as the one described by Ferrante during which a clash between state and church opened up women's possibilities for appeal, even if the eventual evolution of a more collaborative relationship between church and state meant that this particular women's strategy of playing powers off against one another was available only temporarily. Still, this possibility was clearly important for the evolution of kinship in Europe, an observation which can be strengthened by comparison. In particular, in traditional China there was no institution analogous to the church in Europe that successfully competed with the Confucian state; women there never had an alternative power base or legal tradition to which they could appeal.[10] This is one clear example of the interplay between state power, gender and kinship; several other essays—in particular the studies by Pomata, Maurer, Waltner, Ferrante, and Ramos-Escandon—also explore this relationship. In each of these cases, state intervention into kin relations had a gender-specific impact. The political and legal realm, at times underwrote, and at other times undermined, the gender balance of power encoded in kinship.

Transmission through Kinship

One additional way to approach the problem of power relations embedded in kinship systems is to focus on what is transmitted across generations through kinship and to whom: identity and affiliation, nurturance, resources. Human beings reproduce themselves and nurture their offspring within kinship groups, instilling in them their first sense of connectedness and culture. As we have already mentioned, maternal or paternal lineages are called upon in the transmission of names and the larger identities and claims to affiliations and community behind those names. Lineages also transmit material resources such as land or other property along with the status in society such resources often confer.

Nurturance—the reproduction of life from day to day and over the generations—is at the heart of many kinship transfers. Kinship maps indicate who can make what kinds of claims for support and to whom. But many of the essays in this book document situations where such hypothetical claims are either unmet or unspoken. Despite prevailing myths or norms, not all women are equally subjected to male power and not all men are equally powerful: their positionality *vis-à-vis* other hierarchies (such as class and race) always comes into play in kinship practice. Several authors focus on situations of poverty and historical moments of economic restructuring. In all of these essays, placement in economic class hierarchy is a critical variable, and authors pay attention to how kinship is "lived" in highly class-specific ways. The cases range from the European and Latin American historical transition to capitalism (the subject of chapters by Maura Palazzi, M.J. Maynes, Norbert Ortmayr and Eni de Mesquita Samara) through contemporary lower-class family formation in the context of global restructuring (in the chapters by Parry Scott and Norbert Ortmayr). The essays address difficult questions about power and resources differentially available to men and women through kinship, as well as the issue of when and why fathers shun responsibilities *vis-à-vis* the children they help to conceive.

In some nominally patrilineal or bilateral cultures such as the early modern Mediterranean world, Western Europe or contemporary Brazil, poor men could be entirely marginal to the domestic scene. Indeed, as Parry Scott reminds us, the maintenance of patrilineal practices apparently requires strong incentives; in the absence of these, kinship practices often develop a decidedly matrifocal tendency.

And this is not always with the best of consequences for the women and children who are the least subject to male domination and protection. Palazzi, Maynes and Ortmayr suggest that it is the inability of lower-class women to wrest resources from their children's fathers that, in the absence of alternatives to the kin

17

network, contributes to their poverty and its intergenerational replication. These studies de-romanticize the plight of "women alone," and especially unmarried or separated mothers in societies that make no provision for them. The fate of most of the "women alone" in this book suggests that they suffer from their inability to tie the father to his home and heirs. Where patrilineal norms are enforced, fathers are at least constrained to support their progeny to some degree; but in more economically marginal kin groups or, for that matter, in more individualistic cultural milieux and societies, women and children suffer because claims about what kin, especially male lineages, are supposed to provide remain unfulfilled. Our forays into a variety of cultures of fathering suggest that the answer to the question of what keeps fathers tied to their children when the incentives of patrilineally transmitted power are lacking is: not very much. Lower-class women in a number of the cases ranging from Latin America through Europe and southern India seem less restricted by male control than upper-class women, but they are also less likely to be able to command male support, especially from the fathers of their children.

On the surface, ironically, this conclusion is not only bleak, but could be misread as a backhanded defense of patrilineal arrangements. It suggests that men only stay involved with their offspring when they exercise disproportional power in the domestic realm and when there are strong material incentives for persistence. Readers might conclude that this is a prescription for reinforcing patriarchy, a prescription currently offered by antifeminists as a cure for a whole range of deep societal problems. Certainly we do not intend to suggest this, for to do so would not only undermine our quest for more egalitarian gender relations, but would back us into another form of essentialism—one that sees the behavior of men and women as immutable and, irrespective of setting, assigns universal responsibilities to fathers or unchallengeable rights to mothers.

Countering this interpretation is the abundant evidence that there is no one universal or natural way to assure that children are nurtured until adulthood. There is a great deal of variety in how rights, claims and responsibilities are defined *vis-à-vis* mothers and fathers, maternal and paternal kin, and nonkin institutions. We will argue, however, that not all arrangements are equally propitious. Children suffer, of course, from the same inadequacy or maldistribution of resources that their parents do, but beyond this, some cultures seem to handle better than others the intergenerational transmission of resources. For example, the practice of separating daughters from their natal families at marriage, common in patrilineal or virilocal societies (that is, where a newly married couple typically reside with the husband's family) such as early modern Mediterranean Europe, traditional China and contemporary northern India and Sierra Leone, seems to weaken women's position materially, politically and emotionally *vis-à-vis* both their natal and their marital kin. Studies ranging from Klapisch-Zuber's analysis of genealogy to Cunningham's study of residence suggest the costs such daughters bear. To cite another example, children of "women alone" are typically at risk, but the social arrangements that affect such potentially vulnerable children can vary widely as the essays by Hanawalt, Palazzi and Ortmayr suggest. Ortmayr, in particular, contrasts the case of late-nineteenth- and early twentieth-century Austria, where unmarried mothers were more-or-less forced to put their children into foster homes where they were neglected and abused, with contemporary Jamaica where, although such children still often live in poverty, at least they do so in their mother's or grandmother's care. Thus, the material, cultural and psychic consequences of fatherlessness can obviously vary tremendously according to how such a condition is interpreted culturally and how the children are supported materially.

Throughout the essays, in fact, we find demonstrations of the ways kin relations both mediate and are mediated by access to material resources. As we have already seen, notions, strategies and practices of kinship can vary across classes in the same society. Mechanisms for the transfer of resources through the kin group can thus operate quite unevenly. How this happens varies widely. In some societies the kinship group is central in determining access to the use of land. In such societies, kinship norms about the inheritance of such rights as well as patterns of postmarital residence have important effects on the balance of power between men and women. Such effects are apparent in essays like Bolyanatz's study of New Ireland, Cunningham's of the Mende or Maurer's assessment of disputes over the transmission of citizenship in the British Virgin Islands. Divergent understandings of how access to land should be passed along, as well as different notions of residence, were at the heart of the disempowerment of Native American women described by O'Brien.[11]

Another economic dimension of kinship has already come to light in the earlier discussion. In one study after another, it appears that although lower-class women are affected by patrilineal assumptions, they are rarely as rigidly controlled as upper-class women. These studies illustrate the double-edged character of gender prescriptions under male dominance—norms simultaneously restrict and reward, punish and protect subordinates. Such differences have implications for processes of social transformation. For example, Lucia Ferrante finds that daughters and younger sons—that is, the relatively disinherited in the patrilineal culture she studies—seem to be less bound by the rules than their older brothers are. Here we find a tantalizing suggestion about the origins of transformation. Even as the daughters of Bologna were quicker than sons to seize upon the opportunities offered by the Church to intervene in family decisions about marriage, so do we find similar dynamics elsewhere. The essays by Cunningham, Scott, Bolyanatz, Maurer, Raheja and others all intimate that subversion of kinship norms often occurs among people in structurally more subordinate or marginal positions. In historical moments when transformation becomes possible, it may well be the less powerful, those who benefit least from prevailing arrangements, who are freer to assume roles as agents of change. Obviously this is not straightforward, for the marginalized pay a considerable price for their marginality, and can also simply be suppressed. Still, their lesser claim to resources transmitted through kinship may well make people in subordinate positions less rule-bound and more likely to seize opportunities to resist or transform the rules.

We can thus usefully ask, in studying kinship: Who benefits from the rules governing transmission through the various affiliations of lineage? Whose interests are better or worse served? We can ask which arrangements look better or worse from the point of view of individuals in particular kinship locations (such as female children or daughters-in-law). Certainly many of the essays in this collection are doing just that, at least implicitly. As feminists, we do not shy away from making implicit judgments about the situations the authors assess here, even though to do so is to enter very shaky terrain. Our goal of advancing a feminist project—not just to recognize the operation of gender power but to locate the origins of gender inequalities—leads us to reflect on these historical and cross-cultural comparisons in a judgmental way, but, we hope, without simply reflecting and reinscribing the biases of the modern West.

Power and Cross-Cultural Discussion

Along all of these dimensions—the power to map and theorize about kinship, the power to enforce some rules over others, the power to transmit and receive resources through kinship—we find evidence of the operation of gender imbalances and other forms of inequality. Power, of course, operates at many levels. If most of these studies address a particular place and point in time, it is clear that another important dimension of the discussion of kinship, naming, and power is the geopolitical. In our current postcolonial context, there has been an increasing awareness of how Western academic discourses helped create and tend to reinforce the power differential between colonizers and colonized.[12] The scholars whose work is represented here tap into a variety of positions in this matrix, though by no means evenly: we have included, for example, Europeans critically analyzing and historicizing their own "native" culture; Latin Americans, North Americans and Europeans all interested in the study of Latin American cultures; a North American and an Indian native who address questions of lineage in different regions of India. This comparative volume certainly cannot escape or deny its grounding in the perspectives of Western feminism; yet, in presenting various reports from the field, it also highlights the role of perspective in structuring knowledge. We hope that this book will advance cross-cultural conversations that avoid the worst forms of cultural relativism, on the one hand, and the worst forms of ethnocentrism, on the other. As feminists, we recognize our own position and the influence it holds over our understanding of the issues these studies address. We also recognize that we are all to a large extent products of our culture, and we can only reiterate Alex Bolyanatz's observation that "to be human is to be ethnocentric." We nevertheless believe in the possibility of and urgent need for communication, collaboration and respect across our various ethnocentrisms.

Notes

[1] The study of family history emerged as a subfield of European and North American historical scholarship in the 1960s. Pioneering works include: Philippe Ariès, *Centuries of Childhood: A Social History of Family Life* (New York: Vintage, 1962); Michael Gordon, ed., *The American Family in Social-Historical Perspective* (New York: St. Martin's, 1978); Jean-Louis Flandrin, *Families in Former Times* (Cambridge: Cambridge University Press, 1979); and Louise Tilly and Joan Scott, *Women, Work and Family* (New York: Holt, Reinhart & Winston, 1978). For examples of family history centering on kinship, see: Christiane Klapisch-Zuber, *Women, Family and Ritual in Renaissance Florence* (Chicago: University of Chicago Press, 1985) and David W. Sabean, *Property, Production and Family in Neckarshausen, 1700–1870* (Cambridge: Cambridge University Press, 1990). Hans Medick and David Warren Sabean's edited collection, *Interest and Emotion: Essays on the Study of Family and Kinship* (Cambridge: Cambridge University Press, 1984), is a pioneering joint effort by historians and anthropologists.

In the African context, the study of family, gender and household history has since its origins been associated with historical anthropology. Among the influential works have been E.R. Leach, *Rethinking Anthropology* (London: Athlone Press, 1961); J.R. Goody, ed., *Kinship* (Harmondsworth, UK: Penguin, 1971); Henrietta Moore, *Feminism and Anthropology* (Minneapolis: University of Minnesota Press, 1988); Ifi Amadiume, *Male Daughters, Female Husbands: Gender and Sex in an African Society* (London and New Jersey: Zed, 1987); and Christine Oppong, ed., *Female and Male in West Africa* (London and Boston: Allen & Unwin, 1983). For surveys of the fields of family, women and household history, see the special issue on family history of the *Journal of African History*, No. 24 (1983); Jane Guyer, "Household and Community in African Studies," *African Studies Review* (1981) 24:87–139; and Claire Robertson, "Changing Perspectives in Studies of African Women," *Feminist Studies* (1987) 13:87–136.

Important works in English on history of family, gender and kinship in the Latin American context include: Lavrin Asunción, ed. *Sexuality and Marriage in Colonial Latin America* (Lincoln and London: University of Nebraska Press, 1989); Larissa Adler Lomnitz and Marisol Perez-

Lizaur, *A Mexican Elite Family, 1820–1980* (Princeton: Princeton University Press, 1987); Raymond T. Smith, ed., *Kinship Ideology and Practice in Latin America* (Chapel Hill: University of North Carolina Press, 1984); Silvia Arrom, *The Women of Mexico City, 1790–1857* (Stanford, CA: Stanford University Press, 1985); Elizabeth A. Kuznesof, "The Role of the Female-Headed Household in Brazilian Modernization," *Journal of Social History* (1980) 13:589–613; Robert McCaa, "Marriageways in Mexico and Spain, 1500–1900," *Continuity and Change* (1994) 9:11–43; Alida C. Metcalf, *Family and Frontier in Colonial Brazil, 1600–1900* (Berkeley and Los Angeles, CA: University of California Press, 1992).

For the historical study of family, gender and kinship in Asia, see: Ann Waltner, *Getting an Heir: Adoption and the Construction of Kinship in Late Imperial China* (Honolulu: University of Hawaii Press, 1990); Gail Lee Bernstein, ed., *Recreating Japanese Women* (Berkeley and Los Angeles, 1991); Janice Stockard, *Daughters of the Canton Delta* (Stanford, CA: Stanford University Press, 1989). Several papers given at the conference on "Matrilineality and Patrilineality," on which this book is based, are also pertinent: Kathleen Uno, "Adoption and Inheritance in Modern Japan: Questioning Patrilineality"; John Shepard, "Matrifocality and Suitor Service in Taiwan"; and Margery Wolf, "Feminist Theory, Anthropology and Patrilineality." For collaborative work between historians and anthropologists, see: Patricia Ebrey and James Watson, *Kinship Organization in Late Imperial China, 1000–1940* (Berkeley and Los Angeles: University of California Press, 1988) and R.S. Watson and P. Ebrey, *Marriage and Inequality in Chinese Society* (Berkeley and Los Angeles: University of California Press, 1991).

[2] Anthropological works developing historicized approaches to the study of kinship, in addition to the works cited in the previous note, include: David Schneider, *American Kinship: A Cultural Account* (Chicago: University of Chicago Press, 1968); Ronald Inden, *Marriage and Rank in Bengali Culture* (Berkeley and Los Angeles, University of California Press, 1976); Verena Martinez-Alier, *Marriage, Class and Colour in Nineteenth-Century Cuba* (Ann Arbor: University of Michigan Press, 1989); Sylvia Vatuk, *Kinship and Urbanization: White Collar Migrants in Northern India* (Berkeley and Los Angeles: University of California Press, 1972); and Marilyn Strathern, *After Nature: English Kinship in the Late Twentieth Century* (Cambridge: Cambridge University Press, 1992). For works offering gendered perspectives on kinship, see, for example: Margery Wolf, *Women and the Family in Rural Taiwan* (Stanford, CA: Stanford University Press, 1972); Ranajit Guha, "Chandra's Death," in Ranajit Guha, ed., *Writings on South Asian History and Society* (Delhi and New York: Oxford University Press, 1983); Lila Abu-Lughod, *Veiled Sentiments: Honor and Poetry in a Bedouin Society* (Berkeley: University of California Press, 1986); Sylvia J. Yanagisako and Jane F. Collier, *Gender and Kinship; Essays toward a Unified Analysis* (Stanford, CA: Stanford University Press, 1987); Lisette Josephides, "Gendered Discourses of Change in Papua New Guinea," given at the conference "Matrilineality and Patrilineality"; and Doranne Jacobson, *Women in India: Two Perspectives* (New Delhi: Manohar, 1977). For explorations of problems pertinent to the themes of this book, see: Carol Delaney, "The Meaning of Paternity and the Virgin Birth Debate," *Man* 21: 494–513; Mindie Lazarus-Black, "Why Women Take Men to Magistrate's Court: Caribbean Kinship Ideology and Law," *Ethnology* 30: 119–133; and Gloria Goodwin Raheja and Ann Grodzins Gold, *Listen to the Heron's Words: Reimagining Gender and Kinship in North India* (Berkeley: University of California Press, 1994).

[3] Our discussion of the role that kinship plays in naturalizing inequality is informed by the lively discussion on the subject at the conference "Matrilineality and Patrilineality." Especially pertinent papers include: Verena Stolcke, "Marriage, Race and Status in Nineteenth-Century Cuba";

Luise White, "Bleeding Men: Kinship, Relationship, and the Body in Eastern Africa, 1800–1950"; Kath Weston, "Forever is a Long Time: Friendship and Enduring Solidarity in Gay Kinship Ideology"; and Elaine Tyler May, "Infertility, Gender and Medicine in Twentieth-Century America."

[4] The quotations throughout the introduction from various contributors to the book are drawn both from the essays themselves and from helpful correspondence between the editors and the contributors.

[5] See below, pp. 15–16 as well as Palazzi's chapter, for a discussion of the problem of terminology raised here.

[6] Carolyn Steedman, *Landscape for a Good Woman* (New Brunswick, NJ: Rutgers University Press, 1987), p. 72.

[7] For pertinent work on the African-American family, see: Carol Stack, *All Our Kin* (New York: Harper& Row, 1974); Maxine Baca Zinn, "Family, Race and Poverty in the Eighties," *Signs* (1989) 14:856–874; Herbert Gutmann, *The Black Family in Slavery and Freedom* (New York: Pantheon Books, 1976); and Rose Brewer's "Matrilineality and Patrilineality" conference paper, "African-American Family Formation: Adolescent Fathers, Mothers, and Kin."

[8] The issue was addressed directly in the "Matrilineality and Patrilineality" conference paper by Ifi Amadiume, "Kinship Ideologies and Sociocultural Systems in Africa and Europe."

[9] For discussion of aspects of the contest over the family between church and state in Europe, see: Jack Goody, *The Development of the Family and Marriage in Europe* (Cambridge: Cambridge University Press, 1983); Hermann Rebel, *Peasant Classes: The Bureaucratization of Property and Family Relations under Early Habsburg Absolutism* (Princeton: Princeton University Press, 1983);

Thomas Safley, *Let No Man Put Asunder: The Control of Marriage in the German Southwest, a Comparative Study* (Kirksville, MO: Northeast Missouri State University, 1984); Lyndal Roper, *Holy Household: Women and Morals in Reformation Augsburg* (Oxford: Oxford University Press, 1989); and Sarah Hanley, "Engendering the State: Family Formation and State Building in Early Modern Europe," *French Historical Studies* (1989) 16:4–27.

[10] For discussion of authority over marriage in traditional China see Patricia Ebrey, *The Inner Quarters: Women and Marriage in Sung Dynasty China* (Berkeley and Los Angeles: University of California Press, 1993). On the encounter between Chinese and Western notions of marriage, see Ann Waltner, "Demerits and Deadly Sins: Jesuit Moral Tracts in Late Ming China," in Stuart Schwartz, ed., *Implicit Understandings* (Cambridge: Cambridge University Press, 1994).

[11] Another particularly telling analysis of the implications of residence patterns for power in other realms was introduced in the "Matrilineality and Patrilineality" paper by Janice Stockard "New Constructions of Patrilineality: A Comparative Analysis of Chinese and Overseas Chinese Societies." Stockard discusses how, in Taiwan, kinship presumptions fed into the disadvantaged position of women in religious theory, especially regarding relationships to ancestors. Residence and household formation patterns affect the gender balance of power quite independently of access to land, as several essays here suggest (among them, those by Klapisch-Zuber, Cunningham, Menon, Raheja, O'Brien and Scott).

[12] This issue was at the center of Ifi Amadiume's "Matrilineality and Patrilineality" conference paper, cited in note 8.

Part One

KINSHIP SYSTEMS
THEORIES, PRACTICES, CONTRADICTIONS

The first culture this book explores is that of Ancient Judaism. In his analysis of Ancient Judaic religious texts, Howard Eilberg-Schwartz reminds us of the explicitly patrilineal character of the religious covenant between God and Jewish men. The covenant, symbolized by circumcision, rested on a notion of God as Father, and His promise of plentiful male "seed." Nevertheless, the same body of texts suggests that the Judaic God (in contrast with other notions of deity) had no sex, and therefore could not really be male. This problematic character of the deity's sexual nature, and the interconnections between kinship and religious belief, are shown to be at the very center of this ancient and influential cultural tradition.

1

The Father, the Phallus, and the Seminal Word: Dilemmas of Patrilineality in Ancient Judaism

HOWARD EILBERG-SCHWARTZ

In *Moses and Monotheism*, Freud argues that a conceptual, cultural and moral revolution occurred when Moses introduced the Jews to an abstract conception of God. By prohibiting the making of divine images, Moses helped the Jews to triumph over the senses, since they now no longer envisioned God in human form.[1] This triumph of spirituality over the senses was an instinctual renunciation which, like all such renunciations, Freud viewed as a sign of maturation and progress. Moses' prohibition of images was analogous to and further refined other triumphs of spirit that Freud believed occurred earlier in history. It is similar, for example, to the victory of paternity over maternity that Freud believed had occurred in the distant past. Freud assumed that the "turning from the mother to the father...signifies above all a victory of spirituality over the senses—that is to say, a step forward in culture, since maternity is proved by the senses whereas paternity is a surmise based on a deduction and a premise."[2] The Mosaic prohibition on images represents an analogous revolution. It raised God and the Jews to a higher level of spirituality. And like all progress in spirituality, it resulted in increasing self-confidence in making the Jews feel superior to those who have remained in bondage to the senses. Freud thus saw a direct relationship between this tranformation of a people and the renunciations of instinctual gratifications which an individual must accomplish on the way to maturity. Over the course of time, this religion, which began with the Mosaic prohibition, progressively developed into a religion of instinctual renunciation. "Not that it demands sexual abstinence; it is content with a considerable restriction of sexual freedom. God, however, becomes completely withdrawn from sexuality and raised to an ideal of ethical perfection. Ethics, however, means restriction of instinctual gratification."[3]

I enter my subject through these reflections of Freud's because I find them both enormously problematic yet tremendously insightful and interesting. Freud has posed the problem in a way that begins to bring out the relationship between the problem of God's image and the issue of paternity and patrilineality in Ancient Judaism. It is not just the problem of a disembodied, imageless or nonsexual God that is at stake here. For this God is, as Freud well knows, conceptualized as a father. And so Freud's reflections enable us to ask a new and productive question— how can an image of a disembodied and sexless father be connected to patrilineality, a symbolic construction that uses sexual reproduction and continuity through the seed as a basis for intergenerational continuity between men? Patrilineal descent played a crucial role in Israelite religion. Descent through the mother as a criterion of "Jewishness" only developed in the late antique period.[4]

There is, then, a seeming paradox or at least a tension here that needs to be pondered. The father/son relationship and all that it means is at the heart of what patrilineality is all about. Indeed, the very concept of a father already presupposes a notion of continuity of men of two different generations. And it is built around the importance of seed. The child is considered the offspring of the man who has fathered him and given the seed for his creation. To be sure, patrilineality sometimes connects men who have no seed relationship. Boys of other fathers and of other tribes can be adopted into the lineage of a certain man. But even here the system assumes and takes as its founding assumption that men are linked to men of the previous generation through their father's seed. The ideology of the seed provides the general presuppositions and framework around which other kinds of variations and substitutions are tolerated. Patrilineality as a construction of male continuity would thus seem to necessitate and even presuppose the sexuality and procreation of the father. There can be no concept of a father—a human father at least—without a mother and without sexual intercourse. The very notion of a father, and hence of intergenerational continuity between males, would seem to rest on the need for a reproducing and sexually active man.

Yet at the heart of Judaism is a God who, as Freud points out, does not reproduce and has no sex. It is from this seeming tension that the following remarks flow. For what I wish to do is consider how the ideology of the seed fits with the image of the spiritualized father. To ask the questions I am pursuing another way,

I want to consider how central the phallus is in the construction of patrilineality. As I hope to show, the tensions between the spiritualized father and the ideology of the seed come together around the phallus.[5] For the phallus is both the vehicle for the transmission of seed and the symbol of patrilineality *par excellence*. Yet at the same time it is the part of the body necessary for sexuality. As I will suggest, patrilineality is one enormously important yet thoroughly problematic and contested construction of Ancient Judaism. And it reflects a tension that is at the heart of masculinity. These reflections thus refine and carry forward the questions that Freud's work generates but does not pursue.

Judaism and Patrilineality

My attention to the tensions around patrilineality represents a development of my own thinking since writing *The Savage in Judaism: An Anthropology of Israelite Religion and Ancient Judaism*. In that context, I explored the way in which circumcision and menstruation as symbolic constructions were linked to patrilineality. In fact, the first stage of my work involved uncovering the link between circumcision and patrilineality, an association other interpreters had missed. As I argued, modern interpreters of Judaism, both Christian and Jewish, had a variety of motives for wishing to deny the similarities between Ancient Judaism and primitive religions. Circumcision, which was a practice with cross-cultural distribution, was assumed to be different in Judaism from other cultures. According to this argument, circumcision in most cultures symbolizes the sexual maturation of a boy, his newly emerging ability to reproduce and perpetuate his lineage. While interpreters concede that circumcision might have had that meaning when Jews first adopted it, the general consensus is that Jews had spiritualized the practice by rejecting the associations to sexuality, fertility and manhood. Already in Israelite religion, the earliest form of Ancient Judaism, circumcision takes place on the eighth day after birth, and thereby the associations with fertility, sexuality and maturation are lost. Circumcision in Judaism thus become an arbitrary symbol of God's covenant.

Partly because I was suspicious of this attempt to differentiate Judaism from "primitive" traditions, and partly because I was reading ethnographies of circumcision, I began to see that this understanding of circumcision was problematic. Why, after all, did the Jews not cut the earlobe as a sign of their covenant with God? Going back to Genesis 17, the context in which God commands Abraham to circumcise himself and all his male offspring, I noticed—what in hindsight seems self-evident—that the major theme of the covenant is God's promise to multiply the seed of Abraham.

> Walk in My ways and be blameless. I will establish My covenant between Me and you, and I will make you exceedingly numerous....As for Me, this is My covenant with you: You shall be the father of a multitude of nations. And you shall no longer be called Abram, but your name shall be Abraham, for I make you the father of a multitude of nations. I will make you exceedingly fertile and make nations of you and kings shall come forth from you. I will maintain My covenant between Me and you and your offspring to come, as an everlasting covenant throughout the ages, to be God to you and to your offspring to come .(Genesis 17:1–7)[6]

Immediately following this promise, God commands Abraham to circumcise himself and all his male descendants (Gen. 17:9*ff*). Circumcision, then, is a motivated symbol. It is no accident that the sign of the covenant is on the penis. The male organ of reproduction is marked to signify that God promises Abraham genealogical success. That circumcision as a symbol of fertility is further underscored by God's command to Abraham to circumcise his son Ishmael. Ishmael is the first son of Abraham, but God refuses to accede to Abraham's request that Ishmael be heir of the covenant. The covenant will be traced through Abraham's as yet unborn son, Isaac (Gen. 17:18*ff*). But God does make a concession to Abraham. Ishmael will also be a progenitor of multitudes. Ishmael's circumcision, then, is consistent with the associations to fertility. Were circumcision simply a sign of the covenant, Ishmael should not be circumcised, since he is not included in the covenant.

But circumcision is not simply a symbol of fertility. Or rather because of its connection to fertility, circumcision is deeply entangled in patrilineality in several ways. Circumcision is a ritual that helps create and make visible intergenerational continuity between males. It marks all of Abraham's descendants as part of his lineage. As such, it differentiates Abraham's line from competing genealogical lines. The cut of circumcision is thus both a symbol of genealogical continuity and rupture. If Abraham is to be a progenitor of a new lineage upon which his former male kin have no claim, there must be a sharp break between himself and his predecessors. Without such a division it is not clear that this man, rather than his father or grandfather, founded the new line. For people to recognize themselves as "sons of Abraham" rather than "sons of Terah," Abraham's father, there has to be some clear-cut distinction between Abraham and his forebears. Circumcision thus solves a symbolic problem that had not arisen in the case of either Adam or Noah, both of whom are depicted as progenitors of lineages. Since Adam was the original human being, there was no need to separate him from those who came before. As for Noah, the flood separated him from all his ancestors, and marked a new beginning for humankind.

This marking that is performed by circumcision thus binds a particular group of men into an intergenerational community that is clearly differentiated from other lines of men. But at the same time, it obviously differentiates men and women as well. Women cannot bear the symbol of the covenant on their bodies. Just as the genealogies of the Hebrew Bible tend to leave out the names of mothers, circumcision too contributes to the effacement of women in patrilineality.

Indeed, circumcision reinforces this dichotomy between men and women in another way as well. The performance of circumcision occurs at precisely the moment when the boy leaves the state of severe impurity caused during childbirth by the blood of his mother. After the birth of a male child, a woman is in a state of impurity as severe as when she has her menstrual period (Levit. 12:1–2). After seven days have elapsed from the birth of a son, a mother enters a lesser state of impurity. Circumcision occurs on the eighth day, when the son enters a lesser state of impurity and presumably cannot contaminate the circumciser. Circumcision is thus a postpartum ritual associated with the separation of the male child from the impurity of his mother. When the child has recovered from the impurity of his mother's blood, he is brought into the covenant when his own male blood is spilled. His blood is clean, unifying and symbolic of God's covenant. His mother's is filthy, socially disruptive and contaminating. Circumcision is thus a rite of passage from the impurity of being born of woman to the purity of life in a community of men.

As this analysis of circumcision suggests, the penis is made into an important symbol of patrilineality. Its role in reproduction is emphasized and its marking helps to differentiate a particular lineage of men, both from other men and from women whose participation is necessary but ignored. The patrilineality of Ancient Judaism is thus an ideology of the seed, in which the penis and its marking are its most visible expressions.

From my analysis, it would appear that patrilineality is a thoroughly unproblematic and uncontested symbolic construction of Ancient Judaism. And it was here that I left the problem in my previous work. But in leaving it this way I made this construction seem much more stable and unproblematic than I now believe it is. Indeed, already in my earlier work I was becoming aware of another problem beginning to make itself felt at the periphery of my consciousness, a problem that would eventually make me rethink these issues. Specifically, my interest in circumcision, and in the way in which patrilineality etched itself on the male body, led me to think about the relationship between the symbolic construction of masculinity, male sexuality and images of divinity. As my thoughts turned to the image of God in Judaism, I began to be aware of some puzzling tensions that I had not previously considered.

On the one hand, as feminist analyses have shown, the image of the male God legitimated and authorized the social order in which men dominated. The image of God the father reflected and reinforced the authority of the human father. And the male role in procreation paralleled God's role in creation.[7] On the other hand, little attention has been given to the conflicts in which men were placed as a result of this image of a male deity. And in particular this image of a male deity whose body cannot be seen or represented raises some interesting questions about other kinds of symbolic constructions that circulate around, partially support, but also contradict and undercut patrilineality.

To put this issue as starkly as possible, what does it mean for an Israelite male to be told on the one hand that his covenantal responsibility is to take part in reproducing the genealogy of Israel and to celebrate that responsibility with a cut on his penis, yet at the same time be told he is made in the image of a male God, whose form is never seen, and who does not and cannot reproduce? An Israelite male, in a sense, is damned if he does and damned if he doesn't. If he fails to procreate and participate in the genealogical proliferation of Israel, he is not a true heir of the covenant. But if he does have sexual relations and procreate, he is not fully in the image of God.[8] In realizing that these religious representations pull in different directions, I began to think about how religious symbols, particularly symbols of divinity, do not just legitimate, reflect or mirror the social order. And in part this is where feminist analyses of Ancient Judaism, partriarchy and patrilineality have been one-sided and misleading. Religious images are a symbolic domain that operates partially independently of other symbolic domains. While they partially authorize other symbols, such as notions of fatherhood and patrilineality, they also stand in tension with, undermine and generate problems for these other symbolic orders. These sorts of realizations led me back to Freud, to his reflections on the sometimes conflictual relations between fathers and sons and on the consequences of a prohibition on image-making.

In what follows, then, I explore the image of this masculine father deity to show how it is interwoven in and simultaneously at odds with the symbolic construction of patrilineality. My purpose is to suggest that the narrowing of the scholarly gaze to patrilineality without attention to other symbolic domains, such as those of divinity, masculinity and the male body, provides a distorted understanding of patrilineality.[9] To do so, as I did in my earlier work, and as many writers on patriarchy do, is to read cultural systems through the eyes of modern assumptions about biology: that is, it is artificially to sort out and thereby privilege the ideology of reproduction and the ideology of the seed in the shifting, conflictual and multiple symbolic domains that make up the cultural system.

The Disembodied Father

It has been conventional wisdom, since at least the first century BCE, that the Jews believed in an invisible incorporeal God. Thus when Genesis says that humans are created in the image of God (Gen. 1:26–28), it does not mean that the human form is in the image of the divine form. Philo is representative of this understanding of Ancient Judaism when he writes that:

> After all the rest, as I have said, Moses tells us that man was created after the image of God and after His likeness (Gen. 2:26). Right well does he say this, for nothing earth-born is more like God than man. Let no one represent the likeness as one to a bodily form; for neither is God in human form, nor is the human body God-like. No, it is in respect of the Mind, the sovereign element of the soul, that the word "image" is used.[10]

There are various kinds of evidence cited in support of this understanding of Judaism: not only the prohibition on images, which Freud cites, but also the fact that the Hebrew Bible seems to studiously avoid describing the figure of God. For example, when God comes down on Mount Sinai, it is in smoke and fire (Exod. 19:18). And when God speaks to Moses it is through a burning bush (Exod. 3:1–4). It is true that on some occasions a theophany occurs, and Israelites are said to have seen God. But even on those occasions when God appears, there is a circumspection, a hesitation about attributing a human form to this deity. Thus, when Moses and the elders go up to the top of the mountain, they see only what is beneath the deity's feet (Exod. 24:1–4, 9–11). And when Moses requests to see God's Presence, God says that no one may see the divine face and live. Moses is only permitted to see God from behind, as the deity passes by (Exod. 33: 17–23). And Ezekiel, who describes God most explicitly, is careful to pile up qualification upon qualification. Ezekiel sees a throne and:

> on top, upon this semblance of a throne, there was the semblance of a human form. From what appears as his loins up, I saw a gleam as of amber—what looked like a fire encased in a frame; and from what appeared as his loins down, I saw what looked like fire. There was a radiance all about him....That was the appearance of the semblance of the Presence of the Lord. (Ezek. 1:26-28)

33

Thus even in these most incautious passages, there is a hesitation about describing God in human form. There is a sense that the attribution of a human form to God is simply metaphoric, simply a use of the human form to describe what is ultimately unknowable and indescribable.

Or so the argument goes. As I will now suggest, however, this interpretation of Ancient Judaism is problematic. It is no accident that the first most articulate presentation of this view that God is disembodied is by Philo, who gives us the first systematic Hellenistic reading of the Hebrew Bible. Philo is taking a foundational axiom of Greek philosophy—that God is incorporeal—and reading Jewish sources in its light. Those sources that seem to contradict it—by alluding to God in human form—are taken as metaphoric. Now, other interpreters have already questioned this reading of Ancient Judaism, and have in fact suggested that the Jews felt entirely comfortable with the image of God in human form. But it seems to me that this literal reading of the Hebrew Bible, though perhaps correcting this Hellenistic reading of Judaism, in fact oversimplifies the issue as well. For it remains a question why there is hesitation about describing God's body, if in fact this divinity is imagined in human form.

I do not have the space here to develop all the evidence to support my argument, but I suggest that this hesitation about describing God's body stems not from an ambivalence about anthropomorphism, as most interpreters assume, but from the problem of representing this deity's sex. Consider the two myths in which Moses is said to have seen God. In the first, the narrator tells us that Moses and the other elders see a pavement of sapphire under the deity's feet. In the second, Moses is allowed to see God only from behind.

I suggest that the aversion of the gaze in these cases reflects an ambivalence about God's sex. Specifically, the gaze is averted from precisely those parts of the deity's body that would indicate a human figure's sex, namely, the front and face. It is the front of the body, the genitals, the appearance or absence of breasts, and the presence or absence of facial hair, that determines to a large extent to which sex a person is thought to belong.[11] And it is precisely these parts of the deity's body that are veiled. It is as if the whole question of this being's sex posed a fundamental danger that could not be faced. From this perspective, the turning of the divine figure, and the diversion of the gaze from the midsection to the feet, represents an act of modesty, both on the part of the deity who turns away and on the part of those Israelites who avert their eyes.

That is not to say that the divine genitals would actually have been exposed if God had not turned away or the gaze not been diverted to the deity's feet. In Israelite imagination, God was presumably clothed, as is suggested by the robes in the theophany of Isaiah. But it is the front of the body, particularly the groin area, that is ultimately the most important part of the body in determining a person's sex. So the turning of the back, whether or not the being is clothed, symbolically represents a hiding of the very spot in which sexual identification can be confirmed once and for all. This interpretation makes the most sense of the fact that the deity is represented as turning away from Moses. Surely there are easier ways to hide the face than by turning away. Why, then, this elaborate choreography, if not to hide something else? In fact, upon closer inspection the text not only allows but actually encourages this understanding. The word that is rendered as "my face" (*panai*) is more equivocal than translations suggest. "Panai" can also mean "my front side."[12] When God says to Moses: "I will take My hand away and you will see My back (*Ahorai*); but *Panai* must not be seen," (Exod. 33:23) it is certainly plausible to understand the deity to be presenting the backside in order to hide the divine front side. Indeed, it is significant to note that Ezekiel, who has a direct frontal view of the deity, rivets his gaze on God's loins. His description of the deity proceeds from the loins up and the loins down, rather than from one end to another, as if his eyesight is irresistibly drawn back to the midsection of the deity's body. If Ezekiel's description is any indication of what other more circumspect texts dared not imagine, it is the deity's midsection that becomes most prominent on a frontal view.

The hiding of the face, then, serves a double purpose. On the one hand, it is a veiling of God's sex, since the face itself is one of the prominent places in which sexual identity can be displayed. Indeed, it is significant that in none of the God sightings, even those that are graphic about the divine figure, is God explicitly represented with a long flowing beard. We have no indication, then, that God is imagined with facial hair, a prominent characteristic of males and male deities as they are depicted and imagined in the ancient Near East.

On the other hand, the hiding of the face is also a diversion from a more explicit version of the same problem. In other words, the whole question of God's genitals has been deflected to the extremities of the body and replayed there. In serving this double purpose, the hiding of the deity's face is thus a screen. It diverts attention from the question of God's genitals, even as it veils the sexual features of God's face.

The diversion of the gaze to the feet reflects an analogous process. The feet, being at the other extremity of the body, also draw attention away from the deity's midsection. The term "feet" is in fact used on occasion as a euphemism for penis (Ruth 3:7). That is not to say that the reference to the "feet" of God is meant euphemistically in this text. But it does show that the substitution of the feet for the genitals did occur in Israelite imagination and makes more plausible the interpretation offered here.

Thus far I have focused narrowly on the two myths in which Moses is said to have seen God. But as we shall now see, the plausibility of this interpretation is supported by another story whose relevance to this issue has never been appreciated. I refer to the myth of Noah and Ham (Gen. 9:20–25), which may, in fact, belong to the very same early tradition as the story of Moses' sighting God's back. This story tells how, after the flood, Noah became drunk on wine and became indecently exposed. At that point, Noah's son "Ham, the father of Canaan, saw his father's nakedness and told his two brothers outside."

> But Shem and Japheth took a cloth, placed it against both their backs and walking backwards, they covered their father's nakedness; their faces were turned the other way, so that they did not see their father's nakedness. When Noah woke up from his wine and learned what his youngest son had done to him, he said, "Cursed be [Ham's son] Canaan; The lowest of slaves shall he be to his brothers." And he said "Blessed be the Lord, The God of Shem; Let Canaan be a slave to them. (Gen. 9:18–25)

The similarities between this story and the story of God turning the divine back are too striking to be passed over. God turns away so that Moses cannot see what should not be exposed. For their part, Noah's virtuous sons turn their backs and divert their gaze lest they see their father's genitals. In both cases, the turning of the back prevents an exposure of an improper sort. The myth does not say why it is so problematic for sons to gaze on their father's genitals. And it is for this reason that many commentators speculate that Ham has committed a homosexual act.[13] But if the worry of this text is homosexuality alone, why did the other brothers walk backwards and avert their gaze? Their behavior only makes sense if gazing on the father's nakedness is itself considered a sin. The important point is that the myth about Noah's drunkenness provides a very striking parallel to the incident between Moses and God. If this story of Noah's nakedness is permitted to affect the interpretation of the incident with Moses, and I think there are good grounds for seeing the two stories as related, then it strenghtens the interpretation considered above: that the turning away of the divine body is to veil the deity's sex.

What are we to make of this desire to avoid the question of this deity's sex? Given that this deity is generally gendered masculine, as feminist interpreters have rightly emphasized, what should we make of this desire to veil the male's body, indeed to avoid the quesiton of whether He has a phallus? This question of course returns us to the very heart of our inquiry, for we have seen that having a penis and marking it is at the very heart of what it means to be part of the covenant and of taking a part in the lineage of Abraham. Yet this God who authorizes the whole system must turn his back so the question of his genitals cannot be addressed. If this line of reasoning seems strange to some readers, it is important to realize that the question of God's phallus only sounds strange because we have been taught to think of God as lacking a body. But a turn to other religious traditions shows that the genitals of deities are sometimes reasonable matters of speculation. The God Shiva in the Hindu pantheon is an excellent case in point. Shiva is an erotic ascetic, as Wendy Donniger O'Flaherty calls him.[14] And the *lingam* of Shiva is the subject of numerous Hindu myths. The penis of Jesus is the subject and even focal point of Medieval Christian art, as Leo Steinberg has shown.[15] And to bring the matter back closer to the subject at hand, the penis of El, one of Yahweh's precursors, is the subject of Canaanite religious poetry. All of this suggests that the question is a reasonable one: What is it that leads Israelites to avoid the question of their God's sex?

I suggest that there are two different dilemmas that are being dealt with here, both of which are relevant to the issue of patrilineality. The first is what I call the tensions of monotheism. Because this God has no other gods with whom to interact, sexuality and procreation make no sense at the divine level, in any form other than metaphoric.[16] To put it more provocatively, what would a monotheistic male God do with a phallus? The phallus of God is thus the point at which the tensions of monotheism would become most apparent. On the one hand, an Israelite male is expected to have sexual relations and procreate, for this is both the responsibility of humanity in general and the specific obligation of Abraham's descendants. Yet, at the same time, a male is expected to be made in the image of this male God who cannot procreate or have sexual relations. The aversion of the gaze from the deity's body is one of the ways in which this religious system glosses over this contradiction.

But there is another problem at stake here as well. A male deity poses a threat to the basic heterosexual assumptions and practices that structure this religious culture. This threat arises because the divine-human relationship is sometimes couched in erotic and sexual metaphors (for example, God, the husband, marrying or making love to Israel, the wife; Hos. 1–2; Ezek. 16). Yet this heterosexual image of divine husband and human wife actually belies the nature of the relationship in question: it is human males, not females, who are believed to have the most intimate relations with the deity. Individual males have the desire both to know and to be known by God. There is thus potentially a homoerotic relationship at the heart of a culture which regards male-male sexual relationships as an abomination.[17] One way of escaping this dilemma is by feminizing the human male. For example, Moses is veiled like a woman after speaking to God (Exod. 34:33). In this way, the heterosexual commitments are affirmed at the expense of human masculinity. Similar results are achieved by the feminization of Wisdom. The female Wisdom (who stands between men and God) also mediates and deflects the potentially homoerotic associations between God and Israelite men. But the safest way of avoiding the homoerotic dilemma is by veiling the sex of the divine body. Following the insights of recent theorizing in feminist film criticism,[18] I suggest that the aversion of the gaze from the deity in Ancient Judaism reflects this desire to avoid thinking about the divine sex generally and the divine genitals specifically. The Jews (or Semites), then, are expected to be like the descendants of Shem, the virtuous son of Noah who turned his back so as not to gaze on his father's nakedness (Gen. 9:18–26). The veiling of the father's nakedness (both Noah's and God's) is a founding act of culture, which both protects the dignity of the father and proscribes homosexual incest. Herein may lie one of the prime motivations behind the prohibition on making images of God in Israelite religion.[19]

What emerges from my argument is a picture of how a male deity destabilizes a human masculinity that is entangled in notions of compulsory heterosexuality and procreation.[20] Since in Israelite religion being a man means having a wife, reproducing, and having a genealogy, the intimacy between a divine masculine and a human male threatens the very meaning of maleness.

Returning to the question of patrilineality, we see that it is not the only way of figuring masculinity and intergenerational continuity between men. But this ideology of the seed stands in tension with the representation of masculinity that is generated by other kinds of religious reflections. And I suggest that alongside this seed ideology is another equally important notion of continuity, which does not generate tensions with the deity's sex. I refer to the issue of the seminal word which is passed from God to certain privileged Israelite males and then to others of the Israelite community. If the penis is the symbol of the seed ideology, this notion of continuity is inscribed on the male mouth.[21] The male mouth is regarded as the organ for the dissemination and occasionally even the reception of God's word. This function of the mouth is thus responsible for worries about the purity of the mouth in Israelite religion. To cite but one example, when Isaiah is first called by God, he cries out:

> Woe is me; I am lost! For I am a man of unclean lips and I live among a people of unclean lips.... Then one of the seraphs flew over to me with a live coal which he had taken from the altar with a pair of tongs. He touched it to my lips and declared, "Now that it has touched your lips, your guilt shall depart and your sin be purged away." Then I heard the voice of my Lord saying "Whom shall I send?" (Isa. 6:5–8).

Isaiah cannot serve as God's mouthpiece until his mouth has been purified and becomes a pure conduit for the divine word.

What is being represented here is a genealogy of knowledge that prefigures later ideas about the reproduction and dissemination of Torah. Furthermore, we have here an incipient idea of oral Torah, that is, a Torah that is passed from mouth to mouth. Divine knowledge is passed through men, from one mouth to the next. God puts words in Moses' mouth, who gives them to Aaron. And God speaks directly to Moses, who only uncovers his mouth to pass along received knowledge to Israel. This symbolism is given expression in later sources as well: "I am the Lord your God who brought you out of the land of Egypt, open wide your mouth and I will fill it" (Ps. 81:11).

This notion of cultural transmission which is intimately connected to the mouth flows alongside, partially reinforcing and partially contesting, the ideology of the seed. These two notions of transmission and continuity sometimes inter-penetrate. According to Deutero Isaiah, God says, "My spirit which is upon you and my words which I have placed in your mouth shall not be absent from your mouth, nor from the mouth of your seed, nor from the mouth of your seed's seed" (Isa. 59:20–21).

This discussion of God's body may seem to have taken us a long way from the issue of patrilineality. But I hope I have shown that to separate out patrilineality from other symbolic constructions, such as representations of divinity, masculinity and the male body, is to provide a distorted understanding of what patrilineality is and how it works. Patrilineality is only one symbolic construction, and a thoroughly contested one at that. It depends upon a certain image of masculinity and a certain theory of continuity which are themselves at odds with other images of masculinity and other forms of continuity. Men, at least in this system, need to be connected to their sons and their sons' sons. But they also need to be like God and have no sons at all, at least no sons who come from their own seed.

Notes

1 Freud (1939, p. 144).

2 Freud (1939, p. 146). Freud is not the only interpreter to make the assumption that paternity is less obvious than maternity. On the problematic assumptions behind this claim, however, see Delaney (1977, 1986, 1990, 1991).

3 Freud (1939, p. 132).

4 For a discussion of patrilineal and matrilineal descent in Judaism, see Eilberg-Schwartz (1990), Jay (1992) and Cohen (1985).

5 For the purposes of this paper, I am not adopting the Lacanian usage of differentiating the phallus and the penis. In another context, I hope to work through how such a distinction might be thought about in the context of analyzing a specific religious culture like Ancient Judaism.

6 I rely on the translation of the Jewish Publication Society (1985).

7 See, for example, Adler (1977), Daly (1973), Delaney (1991), Gross (1983), Lerner (1986),

Ochs (1977), Plaskow (1990), and Ruether (1983) among others.

[8] I work this out more fully in Eilberg-Schwartz (1990) and in my forthcoming book on the subject.

[9] Delaney has made a similar point in her work, although mine takes this insight in a different direction.

[10] Philo, *On the Creation,* 23.

[11] I am oversimplifying a complex issue here. I do not believe that sex is biologically determined. But we do tend to assign people to sexes on the basis of their anatomy. For a more nuanced presentation of this issue, see Butler (1990).

[12] Noth (1981, p. 258), for example, suggests that "front side" is the primary meaning of *panai* in verse 23. The suggestion of God hiding the face in verse 20 is added by a later writer to imply that no one may see Yahweh's face.

[13] See, for example, Rashi (ad loc), and Leach (1969).

[14] O'Flaherty (1973).

[15] Steinberg (1982).

[16] There is currently archaelogical evidence that some Israelites imagined Yahweh with a consort goddess named Asherah. But the view that dominates the Hebrew Bible presupposes that this God is alone and has no consort.

[17] I am influenced in this line of thinking by Butler (1990).

[18] See, for example, Mulvey (1989), Mayne (1985), Doane (1985), Stacey (1988).

[19] See Eilberg-Schwartz (1990).

[20] On the entanglement of masculinity and compulsory heterosexuality and procreation see Butler (1990), Delaney (1990), Rich (1980).

[21] I work this line of analysis out in more detail in Eilberg-Schwartz, forthcoming.

References

Adler, Rachel. 1977. "'A Mother in Israel': Aspects of the Mother-Role in Jewish Myth," in *Beyond Androcentrism,* ed. Rita Gross. Missoula, Montana: Scholars Press.

Butler, Judith. 1990. *Gender Trouble: Feminism and the Subversion of Identity.* New York: Routledge.

Cohen, Shaye. 1985. "The Origins of the Matrilineal Principle in Rabbinic Law." *AJS Review* 10 (1):19–54.

Daly, Mary. 1973. *Beyond God the Father.* Boston: Beacon.

Delaney, Carol. 1977. "The Legacy of Abraham," in Rita Gross, ed. *Beyond Androcentrism.* Missoula, Montana: Scholars Press.

———. 1986. "The Meaning of Paternity and the Virgin Birth Debate." *Man* 21:3, 494–513.

———. 1990. "Seeds of Honor, Fields of Shame," in *Honor and Shame and the Unity of the Mediterranean,* ed. David Gilmore. American Anthropological Association Special Publications 22.

———. 1991. *The Seed and the Soil: Gender and Cosmology in a Turkish Village Society.* Berkeley: University of California.

Doane, Mary Ann. 1985. "The Clinical Eye: Medical Discourses in the 'Woman's Film' of the 1940s," in *The Female Body in Western Culture,* ed. Susan Rubin Suleiman, pp. 152–174. Cambridge: Harvard.

Eilberg-Schwartz, Howard. 1990. *The Savage in Judaism: An Anthropology of Israelite Religion and Ancient Judaism.* Bloomington: Indiana University Press.

———. 1991. "People of the Body: The Problem of the Body for the People of the Book." *Journal for the History of Sexuality* 2 (1) (1991): 1–24

————. 1994. *God's Phallus and Other Problems for Men and Monotheism.* Boston: Beacon.

————. Forthcoming. "The Nakedness of a Woman's Voice, the Pleasure in a Man's Mouth: An Oral History of Ancient Judaism," in *The Female Head in Myth, Religion and Culture,* ed. Howard Eilberg-Schwartz and Wendy Doniger. New York: Paragon Press.

Freud, Sigmund. 1939. *Moses and Monotheism,* trans. Katherine Jones. New York: Vintage.

Gross, Rita. 1983. "Steps toward Feminine Imagery of Deity in Jewish Theology," in *On Being a Jewish Feminist,* ed. Susannah Heschel, pp. 234-247. New York: Schocken.

Jay, Nancy. 1992. *Throughout Your Generations Forever: Sacrifice, Descent and the Patriarchs.* Chicago: University of Chicago.

Leach, Edmund. 1969. *Genesis as Myth.* London: Jonathan Cape.

Lerner, Gerda. 1986. *The Creation of Patriarchy.* New York: Oxford University.

Mayne, Judith. 1985. "Feminist Film Theory and Criticism: A Review Essay." *Signs* 11:1, 81–99.

Mulvey, Laura. 1989. "Visual Pleasure and Narrative Cinema," in *Visual and Other Pleasures.* Bloomington: Indiana University.

Noth, Martin. 1981. *A History of Pentateuchal Traditions,* trans. Bernhard Anderson. Chico, CA: Scholars Press.

Ochs, Carol. 1977. *Behind the Sex of God.* Boston: Beacon.

O'Flaherty, Wendy Donniger. 1973. *Asceticism and Eroticism in the Mythology of Siva.* London: Oxford University Press.

Plaskow, Judith. 1990. *Standing Again at Sinai.* Harper & Row.

Rich, Adrienne. 1980. "Compulsory Heterosexuality and Lesbian Existence." *Signs* 5(4): 631–660.

Ruether, Rosemary. 1983. *Sexism and God-Talk: Toward a Feminist Theology.* Boston: Beacon.

Stacey, Jackie. 1988. "Desperately Seeking Difference," in *The Female Gaze: Women as Viewers of Popular Culture,* ed. Lorraine Gamman and Margaret Marshment, pp. 112-129. London: The Women's Press.

Steinberg, Leo. 1982. *The Sexuality of Christ in Renaissance Art and in Modern Oblivion.* New York: Pantheon Books.

Wittig, Monique. 1980. "The Straight Mind." *Feminist Issues* 1 (1):103–111.

Gianna Pomata turns to legal and medical texts dating from the Roman Empire. Pomata explores changing perceptions of the role of the mother and the father in procreation as reflected in medical theory and legal arrangements. She notes the consistent tendency throughout both medical and legal theory to elevate the role of the father and minimize the role of the mother, a view consistent with prevailing patrilineal political and family practices. Her work thus highlights the ways in which constructions of kinship can reinforce social and political hierarchies.

2

Blood Ties and Semen Ties: Consanguinity and Agnation in Roman Law

GIANNA POMATA

> Properly speaking, neither a mother nor a grandmother can be called blood-relatives.
>
> (Baldus, *Commentary on the Code of Justinian*, VI, 38, 5)

In 1933 anthropologist E. Evans-Pritchard described blood-brotherhood ties among the Azande.[1] He argued that these ties should not be interpreted as "fictive kinship" because "the Zande does not regard kinship as a community of blood, and hence there is no idea of artificially creating bonds of kinship by transfusion of blood." He particularly stressed this point: "I cannot recall a single occasion during my residence in Zandeland on which I heard kinship spoken of in terms of blood. Azande speak of members of the same clan as having sprung from the same seed, but the filiation is not spoken of as one of blood." He concluded glibly: "If kinship and common blood were synonymous in Zande thought their mode of reckoning descent would be matrilineal, since a child is formed out of its mother's blood."[2]

Permission granted by the board of *Quaderni Storici*.

If Evans-Pritchard had just for a moment looked back home, he would perhaps have been less glib in making this assertion. In European history, kinship and common blood seem to have been largely equivalent. Consanguinity (literally, "the sharing of blood") appears to have been a crucial point in the legal and social definition of kinship since antiquity. But in spite of this recognition of kinship as blood tie, the predominant mode of reckoning descent in European history has certainly not been matrilineal. With due recognition of the bilateral character of European kinship, there is no doubt that descent and succession have most often exhibited a marked patrilineal bias (more or less strong in different times and places, but clearly discernible as the predominant trend).[3] This patrilineal bias, however, appears to have coexisted with a recognition of the ties of consanguinity. The European case seems to show that a notion of kinship as blood tie can be compatible with patrilineal descent.

It is worth exploring this apparent contradiction. I will do so by focusing on the legal system that has exerted considerable influence over the definition of kinship in many European countries: Roman civil law. The concept of *consanguinitas* definitely existed in Roman law and had very significant legal consequences. Still, descent and succession as regulated by Roman law were anything but matrilineal. The very term that anthropologists use to indicate patrilineal kinship (agnation) derives directly from the ancient Roman concept of *agnatio*.

What Evans-Pritchard seemed to imply in his observations on the Azande is that for a patrilineal descent system it makes more sense to represent kinship as a bond created by the father's semen rather than by the more obviously maternal element of blood. So while the patrilineal Azande speak of members of the same clan as having sprung from the same seed, in contrast the matrilineal Ashanti, for instance, say: "We are one blood, we have one mother"; and perceive lineage as "one blood,…transmitted matrilineally from a single common ancestress."[4] And yet the Romans who—like the Nuer, the Tallensi or the Chinese, have been seen as paradigmatic examples of people for whom the principle of patrilineal descent was "the fundamental guide to conduct and belief in all areas of social life"[5]— seem to have had a notion of kinship as blood tie. There is an apparent paradox here that deserves investigation and has not received it as yet.

First of all, the notion of consanguinity in European history has been treated as self-evident and as generally meaning—as it does for us—a blood tie created through either the mother or the father. But *consanguinitas*, as we shall see, had a very specific, technical meaning in Roman legal texts, a meaning which has not been brought into focus. Most importantly, historians have not asked which ideas about blood shaped the legal notion of consanguinity. What was meant by blood in the legal usage of *consanguinitas*? How were blood ties created, according to the law? And whose blood are we talking about? The father's, the mother's, or either's? We need simultaneously to explore medical and juridical sources in this respect, which has seldom been done, because of the mutual isolation of legal and medical history. And I had better add that this is a very broad issue indeed, with a very long history to cover, which this paper will just begin to explore.

Agnation and Consanguinity as Native Categories: Roman Civil Law

First of all, we need to reconstruct the native meaning of kinship categories such as "cognation," "agnation" and "consanguinity" in Roman civil law. A source of confusion about these categories is the fact that nineteenth-century anthropologists borrowed them from the Western legal tradition and applied them to the complex field of kinship studies in non-European cultures.[6] Terms such as "agnation" and "cognation" are still key terms of the anthropological vocabulary today. But did *agnatio* and *cognatio* have the same meaning in Roman law as in contemporary anthropological usage?

The Latin terminology of kinship entered the works of nineteenth-century anthropologists *via* the work of legal historians, such as Sir Henry Maine's *Ancient Law*. It is worth recalling here Maine's often-quoted synthesis of "agnatic" and "cognatic" relationship in Roman Law:

> *Cognatic* relationship is simply the conception of kinship familiar to modern ideas; it is the relationship arising through common descent from the same pair of married persons, whether the descent be traced through males or females.... Cognates then are all those persons who can trace their blood to a single ancestor and ancestress; or, if we take the strict technical meaning of the word in Roman law, they are all who trace their blood to the legitimate marriage of a common pair.... All this is easily understood by a modern; but who are the Agnates? In the first place, they are all the Cognates who trace their connection exclusively through males. A table of Cognates is, of course, formed by taking each lineal ancestor in turn and including all his descendants of both sexes in the tabular view; if then, in tracing the various branches of such a genealogical table or tree, we stop whenever we come to the name of a female and pursue that particular branch or ramification no further, all who remain after the descendants of women have been excluded are Agnates.... I dwell a little on the process which is practically followed in separating them from the Cognates, because it

explains a memorable legal maxim, "*Mulier est finis familiae*"—a
woman is the terminus of the family. A female name closes the branch
or twig of the genealogy in which it occurs.[7]

One point is questionable in Maine's summary. He assumes that the Roman *cognatio* is "the conception of kinship familiar to modern ideas" and clearly identifies it with consanguinity ("connection in blood") in the modern sense, which refers to both the paternal and the maternal bloodline. This assumption has been replicated by contemporary historians: it is often stated that *cognatio* in legal Latin refers to a blood-relationship not embraced by *agnatio* while the expression *cognati* is commonly translated as "blood-relatives."[8] Even standard reference works of Roman history inform the reader that *cognatio* is *Blutsverwandtschaft*, *consanguinité*, "the blood-kinship recognized by the law."[9]

We would assume, then, that *cognatio* and *consanguinitas* were related concepts in Roman law. But let us go directly to the legal sources themselves, the texts collected in the *Corpus juris civilis*. We can start with the definition of *cognatio* and *agnatio* that is offered in the *Digest*:

> The nature of kinship (*cognatio*) among the Romans is understood to be twofold: for some kin relationships (*cognationes*) are derived from the Civil Law, others from Natural Law, and sometimes both laws coincide so that kinship by the Natural Law coincides with kinship by the Civil Law. And indeed natural kinship can exist on its own without the civil one, as in the case of women bearing illegitimate children. On the other hand civil kinship, also called legitimate kinship (*legitima cognatio*), does exist without Natural Law in the case of adoption. There is kinship according to both laws when a union is made by marriage legally contracted. However, natural kinship (*cognatio*) is properly called such, whereas instead civil kinship, although it may very properly be designated by the same name, is more accurately called *agnatio*, that is to say, that kinship which is created through males.[10]

It is quite clear from this passage that *cognatio* is a more generic and comprehensive term than *agnatio*, and that while the first is identified with the natural bond of kinship, the latter refers instead to the kinship that is legally binding and has important legal consequences, especially with respect to succession. It is very important to notice that gender is the key to the distinction between agnation and cognation. While men can simultaneously create both *cognatio* and *agnatio*, kinship by natural law and kinship by civil law,[11] women instead can create only *cognatio*, natural kinship devoid of the privileges attached to legal kinship.[12] Although women cannot create agnation by giving birth because they cannot communicate any rights of agnation to their children, they are themselves included in the agnatic bond. A woman can be *agnata*—in being related by birth to somebody through a man: for instance as *amita* (father's sister) but also, obviously, as a man's daughter or a man's sister by the same father (and the same or different mother: the mother does not make any difference in this respect).

Let us look more closely at the kind of kinship that women *cannot* create: *agnatio*. This concept referred first of all to the bond of dependence between the *paterfamilias*, the male head of the household, and his children: *agnati* were all those who, by reason of birth, were under the *patria potestas*, the paternal authority of a freeborn citizen.[13] In a recent essay on gender in Roman law, Yan Thomas[14] has argued that the concept of *patria potestas* is crucial in order to understand not only the asymmetries between the father's and the mother's legal role but also, more generally, the differences in the legal statuses of women and men. The legal notion of father (*paterfamilias*) referred to a freeborn citizen who was no more under the *potestas* of any male ascendant in the paternal line. A man could be so called even if he had not begotten any children. "Under Roman law, the event that made a man a *pater* was not the birth of his child but the death of his own father; at that moment the son ceased to be a son and came into possession not only of his inheritance but, at the same time, of authority over his offspring."[15] The juridical bond of patrifiliation implied an unbroken link of power between the father and the son. If this link had been broken, as when a father emancipated his son, allowed his adoption by another man, or incurred himself into the loss of civil rights (and therefore of *patria potestas*) the direct line of succession was interrupted. For direct succession to happen, the son ought to have been under the paternal power until the very moment of his father's death. In other words, heirs in the first place and in a true sense were not *any* first descendants of a dead man but only those among his descendants who, at the moment of his death, were still under his authority. Being a "proper heir" (*heres suus*) implied literally taking the place of the dead father and exercising, in turn, the power that had been exercised over oneself. Thus, from a juridical point of view, the essence of the paternal bond was fully realized not in birth but in death, when the decease of the father allowed the son to accede to the rank of paternity, as well as to legal autonomy and to the possession of the patrimony.[16]

Matrifiliation, on the other hand, did not involve any link of power between parent and offspring. According to Thomas, here is the crucial difference between patrifiliation and matrifiliation in Roman law. Patrifiliation implied the exercise and transmission of power; matrifiliation did not. A mother's inability to have power over her children had far-reaching consequences for women's status in Roman law. Throughout the long history of this law, from archaic legislation to the New Constitutions of Justinian in the sixth century, a woman could not have "proper heirs." As the *Digest* says: "No woman can have proper heirs, nor can she cease to have them because of the loss of civil rights."[17] The mother lacked *potestas* and what this power gave: successors through whom one's juridical existence could be prolonged after death. In the legal notion of patrifiliation, each male was a link in an uninterrupted chain that went beyond every separate male individual—a continuous line, as it were, of contiguous paternal powers. Once the paternal authority is dissolved by the father's death—the law says—his children "start to have families of their own." But there is a crucial difference between sons and daughters in this respect. The new family started by a son will still be part of a wider family, formed by the "totality of all the agnates."[18] Begetting children in legitimate marriage, a man's sons reproduce the agnatic chain *in infinitum*. His daughters, instead, are personally included in this chain but cannot extend it beyond themselves. A man's daughter was included in the legitimate kinship bond as *agnata* and, if she had been under the father's *potestas* at the moment of his death, she even had as equal a right to his property as her brothers. But she did not inherit the father's power, and therefore could not transmit it to her own children. A woman could not create a*gnatio* because she did not receive and consequently could not transmit power. Thus a daughter inevitably stopped the agnatic chain. As the third-century jurist Ulpian says tersely, in the aphorism partly quoted by Sir Henry Maine: "A woman is the beginning and the end of her own family."[19]

The agnatic order of succession did give women some rights (as far as inheritance of property went) but radically excluded them from ensuring the family's continuity in time. By transmitting his paternal power to his sons, a man created permanent bonds of kinship and indefinitely perpetuated his legal personhood in his male descendants. Matrifiliation, on the other hand, did not have enduring legal consequences; it was something ephemeral, from the point of view of the law. Women could not perpetuate their social identity through their descendants. When a woman died, nobody would step in her place as "proper heir," to fulfill her legal role afresh, as in the case of the father's role. "Women were deprived of institutional extensions of their singular personhood."[20]

So much for the fundamental legal differences between patrifiliation and matrifiliation that derived from the Roman concept of *agnatio*. What about *consanguinitas*? From all that has been said so far, we would expect to find the legal notion of *consanguinitas* to refer to the physical, natural aspect of filiation, and consequently to belong in the semantic sphere of *cognatio*. This is also, as I have already noted, what modern dictionaries lead us to expect, by translating *cognatio* generically as "blood tie." It comes as a surprise to find out that *consanguinitas* in the legal texts is invariably associated with *agnatio,* not with *cognatio.* Modern translations of *consanguinitas* as cognation are seriously misleading in this respect. As we shall see, the translation is correct for Medieval Latin, but definitely not for Classical legal texts (nor indeed for the whole *Corpus juris* including the Code and the Institutions of Justinian).[21]

First of all, contrary to what several dictionaries tell us, *cognatio* is never defined as relationship by blood but simply as relationship "by birth."[22] For us the two are synonymous, but it was not so in the language of Roman law. In the *Corpus juris civilis, consanguinei* consistently has one specific and precise meaning: it denotes the brothers and sisters born to (or adopted by) a common father.[23] It never means generically "cognates": on the contrary, it refers specifically to the closest of agnatic relationships, that between siblings from the same father. A child promiscuously begotten (*spurius*) cannot by definition have any consanguineous siblings, because his father is unknown. The *Digest* says this very clearly:

> If an illegitimate child (*spurius*) should die intestate, his inheritance will belong to no one by the right of *consanguinitas* or of agnation, because the rights of *consanguinitas* as well as of agnation are derived from the father."[24]

Consanguinitas is related to *agnatio* and not to *cognatio* because it refers to a bond of kinship derived only from the father. There is no consanguinity between a mother and her children,[25] or between the children of the same woman from different men. In the Code of Justinian we are told that, "as a positive rule of law," brothers and sisters share the right of *consanguinitas* when they are born from the same father, even though they do not have the same mother.[26] The law shows no ambiguity on this point. In fact, brothers and sisters from the same mother and different fathers are always called *uterini,* never *consanguinei.*

There is no doubt that in the legal texts *consanguineus,* as a rule, means "sharing the paternal blood," never the maternal. But what about ordinary language? Did the term have this narrow, patrilateral meaning also more generally, in nonlegal Latin sources? The answer is no. As a matter of fact, the meaning of *consanguinei* in classical Latin poetry and prose is significantly wider than the restricted, patrifocal one we find in the language of the law. Most importantly, literary sources show clearly that in common parlance the relationship through the mother was also perceived as mediated by blood (as shown, for instance, by expressions such as *materno a sanguine iunctus:* "related by the maternal blood").[27] General linguistic usage thus seems to indicate that the Romans held a fundamentally bilateral view of blood ties. It is only in the specialized, technical texts of the jurists that *consanguinitas* is narrowed down to indicate patrilateral kinship. In privileging the father's blood, the legal language decisively departed from ordinary usage, giving an agnatic twist, as it were, to the notion of consanguinity.

The semantic association of consanguinity and agnation seems to have been a constant element in Roman legal texts, from the jurists of the classical age, such as Gaius, Paulus and Ulpian (second to third centuries) to the compilers of the *Corpus juris civilis* in the sixth century.[28] It is worth asking at this point: Were *agnatio* and *consanguinitas* perfectly equivalent terms? The law speaks of "rights of *consanguinitas*" mostly to refer to matters of inheritance. In fact, the term *consanguinei* denotes a specific category of heirs, those who, in the order of succession, come immediately after the "proper heirs." The *Digest* tells us that "after the proper heirs, the *consanguinei* are called to the succession; next after the *consanguinei*, agnates are admitted to inherit, when there are no *consanguinei*."[29] From this text we gather that, although *consanguinitas* is definitely related to *agnatio*, still the two categories are not totally coincident. Not all the agnates are called *consanguinei*, but only a specific subgroup among them. This subgroup is that formed by a man's direct offspring. In other words, *consanguinei* refers to the closest link in the agnatic chain, that formed by all the children (male and female) born to the same father.[30]

But since the term *consanguinei* means the children from the same father and since, as we know, a man's "proper heirs" are his own children, why does the law distinguish between *consanguinei* and "proper heirs"? "Proper heirs," as already noted, were not simply a man's children, but those of his children who were still under his *potestas* at the time of his death. As a category of heirship, *consanguinei* are those children who are no more, or never have been, under the paternal power. In the *Digest*, in fact, *consanguinei* are also defined as "those who are related to one another by [paternal] blood, even if they are not the proper heirs of their father, as, for example, when they have been disinherited.... Those also who have never been under paternal authority will be *consanguinei*, as for instance those born after the captivity or death of their father."[31] The text tells us that the "right of *consanguinitas*" is kept by children born after the death of the father, or after his captivity or banishment, therefore after he lost his *patria potestas* over them. This further specification of the concept of *consanguinitas* points out something very important. It tells us that *consanguinitas*, differently from *agnatio*, was not derived from *patria potestas*.

Consanguinitas cannot be derived from *patria potestas* because it is not dissolved by the loss of the latter. Therefore *consanguinitas* must refer to the bond of natural kinship between a father and his children, a bond which, differently from that of legitimate kinship (*agnatio*), can never be dissolved. The notion of *consanguinitas* tells us that the tie between father and children is twofold: part of it derives from the father's power and part of it derives from the father's blood. The two are not coincident, because the loss of the father's power does not entail the dissolution of the tie of blood.

All this is very interesting, because it seems to point out that, differently from what was argued by Thomas, the difference between patrifiliation and matrifiliation in Roman law does not rest exclusively on the category of *patria potestas*. There is apparently a further difference between patrifiliation and matrifiliation, beyond the fact that the first involves power, and the second does not. Another asymmetry between the two is pointed out by the notion of *consanguinitas*. The natural relationship between a father and his children creates *consanguinitas*; that between a mother and her children does not. In other words, children of the same father and different mothers share the same blood; children of the same mother and different fathers do not. Just as a woman interrupts the chain of power, so she also discontinues the transmission of blood. It is only through the male sex—as the Code of Justinian tells us—that "the rights of one and the same blood stay uncorrupted."[32]

All this seems to indicate a perceived difference between the paternal and the maternal role in the physical act of generation. Something must be special about the father's blood. What can be the difference between a father's and a mother's blood? For the Roman jurists this is obviously an implicit assumption: they never tell us directly. For an explicit theory of blood and its role in generation we have to turn to ancient *medical* texts.

Gender in the Blood: The Medical View

A clue to an understanding of the Roman concept of consanguinity comes from the *Etymologies* of the seventh-century scholar Isidore of Seville. While analyzing the derivation of kinship terms, Isidore recalls the distinction of brothers into *consanguinei* and *uterini*. *Uterini*, he tells us, are so called "because they are born from different fathers and from the same uterus: for the uterus is found only in the woman." *Consanguinei*, on the other hand, "are so called because they are derived from one and the same blood, that is to say from the semen of one and the same father. For the semen of the man is the foam of the blood, just like water dashed on the rocks makes a white foam, or as red wine makes a whitish foam when shaken in a cup."[33] The image of semen as the foam of the blood is extremely ancient—

rooted in myth, in fact, as Aristotle recognized when he noted in the *Generation of Animals* how the ancients understood that the nature of semen is foamlike (*aphrōdes*): and in fact "the goddess who is supreme in matters of sexual intercourse was called after foam."[34] This image is developed and variously elaborated in several complex philosophical and medical theories that view semen as derived from blood. Historian of medicine Erna Lesky has called this complex of theories the "hematogenic theory of semen,"[35] and has shown how this view became dominant, after the fourth century BC, in both philosophical and medical discourse, superseding other ancient theories—still current, for example, in the Hippocratic texts—where semen was seen as derived from the brain (via the spinal marrow) or from all the parts of the body. Both Aristotle and Galen adhered to the hematogenic theory (although their views varied significantly on many important points). Through the extraordinary influence of Aristotelian thought on the natural sciences and Galen's no less pervasive influence on medical learning, the hematogenic view was established as the unchallenged theory of semen in European culture long after antiquity: in fact, surprising as it might seem, the theory persisted into the eighteenth century.

The hematogenic view of semen was intimately related to a theory of sexual difference. In ancient medicine, the very notion of bodily difference between man and woman was based on a theory of blood, or more precisely a theory about the different ways in which blood was processed in the body. These differences were seen as gender-specific: blood is converted into semen in male bodies, whereas in female bodies it is transformed into milk (and, according to some variants of the theory, semen, albeit of an inferior quality). For both Aristotle and Galen the definition of what constitutes "male" and "female" in the human species is firmly located in a theory of blood. Much has been written on the differences between the Aristotelian and the Galenic theories of generation,[36] but, for the purpose of this essay, what is worth stressing is the strength of the assumption they shared: production of semen happens in the first place in the blood, not in the organs which we associate with the male reproductive function, the testicles.

For Aristotle, semen is the highest, most perfect result of the "concoction" of blood that happens through the "innate heat" of the body. That which is left over as surplus in the various stages in which nutriment is processed by the body is called by Aristotle "residue." Menstrual blood, milk and semen are all "residues" of the concoction of blood. An empirical proof of the derivation of semen from blood is indicated by Aristotle in the fact that "semen emitted under strain due to excessively frequent intercourse has been known in some cases to have a bloodlike appearance when discharged; and this shows that semen is pretty certainly a residue from that nourishment which is in the form of blood."[37] Aristotle even articulates his theory into an imaginary vascular anatomy. He assumes a direct connection in the epididymis (the glandular structure adherent to the upper part of the testis) between an artery branching from the aorta at the level of the kidneys and the vessel running from the epididymis itself (presumably what we call the vas deferens). In the epididymis, he argues, one can find a fluid still similar to blood, although less similar to blood than the one that can be found in the artery branching from the aorta, while in the prosecution of the vessel that goes to the penis we find a white fluid, that is finally semen.[38]

The same concoction that ensures the processing of blood into semen in the male body takes place also in the female. But since females have a lesser degree of "innate heat," their bodies cannot reach the high level of concoction necessary to produce semen. What they produce are residues that represent lower stages in the concoction of blood: menstrual blood and milk. "The female, in fact, is female on account of inability of a sort, viz., it lacks the power to concoct semen out of the final stage of nourishment (this is either blood, or its counterpart in bloodless animals) because of the coldness of her nature."[39] Milk, however, as its white color shows, represents a higher stage of concoction of blood than the menstrual blood; but this is as far as a woman's body can go in concocting blood.[40] In strong disagreement with the Hippocratic tradition, which had attributed the production of semen to both sexes, Aristotle argues that there is no such thing as female semen: the fluid that sometimes women emit in intercourse is just a local secretion, not "a seminal fluid" (that is to say, transformed blood).[41]

From Aristotle's point of view, sexual difference appears to be simply a matter of degrees in "innate heat": women's bodies have an inferior degree of heat, as proved by their inability to convert blood into semen. But by denying the existence of female semen, Aristotle is also constructing a dichotomy which identifies the female with passive matter and the male with spiritual, form-giving activity. In describing the formation of the embryo, he argues that the mother contributes the raw matter (the menstrual blood), while the father gives, through semen, form and soul, the vital principle that quickens the inert matter into life. A striking consequence of this polarization of the male and female contributions to generation is that Aristotle is led, by the internal logic of his theory, to deny significance to the matter of semen. In a brilliant essay,[42] Giulia Sissa has pointed out this paradoxical aspect of Aristotle's theory. Since one of its basic tenets is the idea that the male is the spiritual, form-giving force in generation, this theory, in order to be internally consistent, has to show that the semen itself does not contribute anything material to the embryo. Since he wants to prove that the father transmits only soul

53

and form (nonmaterial elements) to the fetus, the actual physical existence of semen is an embarrassing, contradictory fact for Aristotle. He solves this difficulty quite radically, by denying that semen has any bodily reality at all when giving form and life to the embryo.[43] The material component of semen, for Aristotle, is merely a dispensable vehicle for its key component, the heavenly element called "pneuma," which is the true principle of generation. Here semen is exalted literally at the price of its physical reality. As a consequence of the hematogenic theory, Aristotle downplays the function of the testicles in the production of semen. Although aware of the consequences of the removal of testicles in castrated men, Aristotle attributes to them a quite limited role in reproduction. According to him, they do not play any role in the actual production of semen, but have a secondary, purely mechanical function: through their weight, they ensure that the seminal passages are kept straight and do not retract as in castrated animals. He actually compares them to the stones that weavers hang from the loom, in order to make sure that the cloth is properly stretched.[44]

The anatomists and physicians of the Alexandrian school criticized several aspects of the Aristotelian theory, but still, as Lesky shows, entirely within the framework of the hematogenic theory of semen.[45] Through dissection (presumably only of animals) these anatomists had discovered what we now call ovaries and what they unhesitatingly identified as "female testicles." The discovery of the female testicles resulted in a new formulation of the hematogenic theory to accommodate the existence of two seeds, male and female. We can follow this new formulation in full detail in the works of Galen. In *De semine* Galen criticizes Aristotle not only for his denial of the existence of female semen but also for his reductive view of the function of the male testicles. Those who, like Aristotle, have argued that the testicles do not contribute to the production of semen, have been misled, Galen argues, by the fact that the vas deferens, which carries semen from the testicle to the penis, starts from the epididymis. But dissection shows that "the (fluid) contained in the epididymis has been transferred to it from testicle, just as (it is transferred) from the epididymis to the spermatic vessel."[46] In other words, contrary to Aristotle's view, semen is contained, and therefore produced, not only in the epididymis but in the testicle itself. The "very great power" of the testicles, Galen argues, has been overlooked by "just about all physicians and natural philosophers" except himself. This organ not only serves the purpose of the production of semen, but also distributes "a certain power" to the whole body. "This power is in males the cause of strength and masculinity; in females it is the cause of their very femininity. And for this reason the female animal whose testicles have been excised becomes similar to the castrated male."[47]

Thus Galen identifies the testicles, male and female, as one important source of sexual difference.[48] Neverthelesss, he does not abandon the Aristotelian assumption that the main cause of sexual difference is the different level of heat in male and female bodies. While stressing the role of testicles in the production of semen, Galen still upholds the hematogenic theory. Semen, he argues, cannot be entirely generated by the testicles. This possibility is barred by empirical observation, namely by the fact that semen can already be seen in the vessels that descend to the testicles from above. "The artery and vein that empty in the head of the testicle are seen already to contain a semen-like fluid."[49]

Like Aristotle, Galen believes that semen is already generated in the blood vessels before reaching the testicles. But much more clearly and precisely than Aristotle, he proceeds to explain how the vascular system converts blood into semen. The novelty of Galen's explanation is that it is based not simply on the metaphysical principle of innate heat, but on a carefully detailed observation of the morphology of the blood vessels. Galen is fascinated by a pattern that emerges most clearly, in his eyes, through anatomical observation: the vessels that run to the testes, in males as well as in females, do not run straight but are extremely twisted and coiled, "like the tendrils of the vine or the ivy."[50] This is already enough to dispose of the Aristotelian theory of the testicles as mere weights. Why would Nature have given these organs the function of stretching the vessels when it is quite clear that, on the contrary, she has shaped the vessels in such a way as to make them as twisted and convoluted as possible?[51] These convolutions must serve a purpose. It is clear that Nature has made these vessels so that they can achieve maximum length,[52] and in this way slow down the blood flow. In the coils of these "vine-like vessels," "the blood and pneuma passing to the testes are very greatly concocted, and it is possible to see clearly that the humor contained in the first coils is still like blood and that in the succeeding coils it keeps getting whiter and whiter until in the very last ones, that end in the testes, it has been made absolutely white."[53]

How does Galen's new formulation of the hematogenic theory affect the definition of sexual difference? Galen rejects the Aristotelian polarization of paternal and maternal principles as form versus matter. For him, the male semen is, to use Aristotelian terms, not only the "efficient cause" of the embryo but also its "material cause": in other words, the male semen contributes materially, not only spiritually, to the formation of the embryo while the female semen, in turn, is seen as having some active, form-giving function. Intermingling, both seeds physically cooperate in the formation of the fetus, although the male semen has a much more important role than the female. When it comes to specifying the functions of the female semen, in fact, Galen's list is pretty scanty. First of all, he tells us, it is need-ed to nourish the male semen because each element is best nourished by what is most similar to it, and of course the female semen is close in substance to the male semen. Also, Galen states that the allantoid membrane of the embryo is formed by the female semen. But the other membranes enveloping the embryo, the chorion and the amnion, are formed out of the male semen, and so are the most impor-tant elements of the fetus's body: arteries and veins, nerves, tendons, cartilage and bones.[54] The contribution of the female semen to the embryo is therefore quite small compared with that of the male semen. The fact is, as Galen tells us, that "the female semen is exceedingly weak and unable to advance to that state of motion in which it could impress an artistic form upon the fetus" because it possesses "pneu-ma," "the principle of motion," in much lesser degree than the male semen.[55]

Thus Galen fully retains and further develops the notion that the key difference between the sexes lies in the different degree of "innate heat" with which they are endowed by Nature. Galen criticizes the philosopher Strato, who argued that male and female bodies differ not only in the genital parts but also in the configuration of the veins and the arteries. He was wrong, Galen states categorically: "Not only the number but the molding and position are the same for all the arteries and veins in the whole body of both males and females."[56] The real difference between male and female bodies is not in the configuration of the vascular system but in what happens inside it: the concoction of blood. The blood in the female body can only be processed into "imperfect semen." It cannot be brought to the "peak of concoc-tion" because of the lack of sufficient vital heat. This lack of heat is also evinced by the difference between male and female testicles. The female "has smaller, less per-fect testes, and the semen generated in them must be scantier, colder, and wetter (for these things follow of necessity from the deficient heat)."[57]

In both the Aristotelian and the Galenic version, the hematogenic theory of semen is so slanted as to prove the preeminence of the male over the female role in generation. But what is more important to notice is that, by locating the reason of this preeminence in the processing of blood, the theory allows male superiori-ty to be persuasively established in an aspect of experience where appearances seem instead to stress the maternal role. The physical tie between the mother and the child is much more obvious to direct sensory experience than that between the father and the child, because of the discontinuity in time between impregnation and birth. What happens at impregnation, when the father-child tie is created, is hidden from view in the darkness of the woman's womb. The hematogenic theo-ry probes into this darkness, trying to see beyond direct sensory experience and in fact significantly correcting mere physical appearances (as theories often do). The theory effectively invalidates the appearance of a stronger physical tie between the mother and the child by showing that in fact, in the mother's womb, the new life is really created foremost by the father.

The difference between maternal and paternal blood plays a crucial role in this respect. The maternal blood can nourish but cannot generate: it can be turned into nourishment, either as menstrual blood (for the fetus) or into milk (for the born baby) but it can never be turned into true, perfect semen, the real agent of generation. It is significant that for Galen the first function of the female semen is to nourish the male semen, assisting it, in this ancillary role, in its labor of creation. The "principle of motion" that connects each generation to the next is truly ensured only by the transformation of blood into perfect semen, which is beyond the ability of the female. Even more effectively than Aristotle's metaphysical definition of the paternal semen as the only active agent of reproduction, Galen's materialism forcefully makes this point when he states that the vascular system of the fetus is developed directly from the father's semen. The very vessels in which the blood of the new being will flow—those vessels that are the main agents of the concocting process—come directly from the paternal semen (that is to say, from the perfectly concocted essence of his blood). This Galenic image graphically demonstrates how the link between the child and the father is literally, materially a tie derived from blood.

We could justifiably say that from the point of view of this theory, a tie of blood is truly a tie of semen. Ancient medicine fully explains to us what the legal texts only imply. Siblings can be said to come from the same blood because (and therefore only if) they have been formed out of the same semen. The tie of consanguinity cannot be derived from the mother because of the crucial difference between paternal and maternal blood. The father's blood generates, the mother's blood does not. The tie of consanguinity can be established only through the agency of what women cannot have, that is to say, blood capable of turning into perfect semen.

The Changing Meaning of Consanguinity: From Roman Law to Canon Law

So Evans-Pritchard was right, after all; or at least, his expectation that a system with a strong agnatic bias would privilege the father's semen over the mother's blood as the main agent of reproduction, seems to be answered by the Roman case. Of course, I do not mean to imply any direct causal link between the medical view of male semen as "perfect blood" and the legal definition of *consanguinitas*. I just want to point out that this specific notion of consanguinity can be properly under-stood only within the context of the concomitant medical ideas on the origin of semen. Galen's work (second century AD) dates from the same period as that of the jurist Gaius, for instance, in whose texts we find the patrilateral definition of con-sanguinity. And there is ample evidence that the hematogenic theory of semen was dominant in medical discourse in the centuries that led to the compilation of the *Corpus juris civilis.*[58]

What seems noteworthy, beyond the issue of the temporal link between the medical doctrine and the legal notion of *consanguinitas*, is the function common to the two theories. They both try to rectify what we could call the prescientific evi-dence of a primary blood tie between mother and child, by showing that the pri-macy belongs instead to the paternal blood. Just as the hematogenic theory argues that, in spite of appearances, the father's blood is the chief agent of generation, so does the language of the law correct the popular, generic notion of consanguinity by rigorously limiting the term's use so that it only applies to the father's side. In denying relevance to the mother's blood, the message of the law is actually more rigid and stringent than that of the medical doctrines. The hematogenic theory, both in the Aristotelian and Galenic version, did not entirely deny the bilateral nature of blood ties: although the paternal blood was given the key role, still the body of the embryo was seen as formed also out of the mother's blood. The med-ical view was in fact less narrowly patrifocal than the legal language.

This greater flexibility (and bilaterality) of the medical discourse accounts per-haps for the different fate that the two theories were going to have in European intellectual history. The hematogenic theory of semen, as I have already hinted, was going to enjoy an extremely long life. Its longevity goes well beyond the Middle Ages[59] into the early modern age. The theory survived even the radical attack on Galenist anatomy which started in the Renaissance and reached its cli-max in the seventeenth century with the discovery of the circulation of the blood. Still in 1720, for example, in a survey of contemporary medical theories on this topic (Martin Schurig's *Spermatologia historico-medica*), semen is defined as derived from blood.[60] Schurig's survey shows that, at the beginning of the eigh-teenth century, the hematogenic theory still kept a firm hold on medical thought, although competing with more recent theories that variously viewed semen as deriving from a hypothetical fluid in the nerves (the *succus nerveus*), or from the nutritive juice carried by the newly discovered "lacteals."

Thus, apparently, medical discourse on semen did not undergo much change in European history up to the early modern age. Did the legal notion of consanguin-ity exhibit a corresponding stability? Not at all. On the contrary, the definition of consanguinity changed dramatically in the centuries after the compilation of the *Corpus juris civilis.*

Before relating what changed in the notion of *consanguinitas*, I should briefly mention an even more dramatic change that happened in the legal definition of kinship in general. This change is registered in what we may call the final act in the long history of Roman law, the Constitutions of Justinian. A Constitution promulgated by this emperor in 543 abolished the privileged rights of agnates in matters of succession. Indeed, it invalidated, in these matters, "all distinctions between agnates and cognates."[61] The privileges of the paternal line over the maternal kin had no legal ground any longer.

This revolution in the legal regulation of kinship had been prepared by many centuries during which the privileged status of *agnatio* over *cognatio* had slowly but surely been eroded. But it was nevertheless a revolution. In the crucial matter of succession, *agnatio* was no more the only "legitimate kinship." *Cognatio*, once mere "natural kinship," was recognized by the law as fully legitimate as well. In fact, legitimate kinship was thus redefined as no more patrilateral but bilateral.[62]

In the centuries following this legal change, we find a radical transformation also in the notion of *consanguinitas*. From being associated with agnation, *consanguinitas* moved into the semantic sphere of cognation. For example, in the *Etymologiae*, although recalling, as we have seen, the legally correct meaning of *consanguinei* as brothers from the same father, Isidore of Seville also uses *consanguinitas* to indicate *cognatio*, apparently unaware of any contradiction in this respect. Isidore equates *consanguinitas* and *cognatio* when discussing the degrees of kinship that involve an impediment to marriage. He explains that this prohibition to marry between cognates stretches only up to the sixth degree because "consanguinity slowly fades generation after generation."[63]

The new notion of *consanguinitas* is especially clear in the texts of the canon law that spell out the rules forbidding marriage between relatives. In striking departure from the use of the term in Roman civil law, Medieval canon law used *consanguinei* to denote all those people related by birth (in the paternal or the maternal line, up to the seventh degree) who were forbidden from intermarrying. The category of *consanguinei* thus expanded dramatically and fully included the matrilateral kin.

It should be noted that not only the meaning but also the context of the term had shifted. In Roman law *consanguinitas* was discussed in relation to matters of inheritance and succession, never in relation to marriage. Discussing the prohibition of marriage among kin, the *Digest* talks exclusively of degrees of *cognatio*, never mentioning *consanguinitas*. In canon law, on the other hand, it is precisely in the context of marriage rules that the two concepts of cognation and consanguinity seem to merge into each other. The table representing the forbidden degrees—often drawn in the form of a cross, with the paternal kin on one side and the maternal kin on the other side—was called indifferently *arbor cognationis* (tree of kinship) or *arbor consanguinitatis* (tree of consanguinity).[64] Theologians retain memory of the original meaning of *consanguinitas* as a bond created by the paternal blood. They even quote the hematogenic theory of semen in order to explain the meaning of the term *consanguinitas*.[65] But there is clearly a new notion that blood is transmitted also on the mother's side. The bilateral concept of *consanguinitas* is fully explicit in the definition that the canonists consistently give us for this term. As the author of a treatise on the *arbor cognationis* puts it:

> Consanguinity is the tie binding those people who descend from the
> same person through the act of carnal propagation.... It is so called, as
> it were, from the unity of blood, for *consanguinei* are those who are
> born from the same blood...and I take this to mean from one blood
> either paternal or maternal, that is to say, coming through the male or
> the female line.[66]

This is also the meaning that *consanguinitas* had in common usage in the Middle Ages.[67] The glossators, the Medieval commentators on the texts of the Roman law, were fully aware of the discrepancy between the meaning of *consanguinitas* in the *Corpus juris civilis* and in the usage of their own times. For instance, the fourteenth-century jurist Baldus, in his comments on the Code of Justinian, raises the question whether "a mother or a grandmother can be called *consanguineae*. He answers: "no, because properly and strictly speaking, a mother and a grandmother do not enjoy the rights of *consanguinitas*; still in the common usage, albeit improperly, we call them so."[68] His contemporary Bartolus of Saxoferrato similarly notes that under the appellation of *consanguinei* come also the relatives on the maternal side, although "this is speaking by the current custom, because according to the true meaning of the word it is otherwise."[69]

The new meaning of *consanguinitas* developed in the canon law seems to have definitely prevailed over the Roman meaning. But in the language of the civil law, a trace of the ancient link between consanguinity and agnation was kept in the nomenclature of brotherhood. As late as the early modern age jurists tell us that brothers can be of three kinds: *consanguinei*, when they have only the father in common, *uterini*, when they share only the mother, and *utrinque coniuncti* (connected on both sides) when they share both parents.[70] Because of the changed meaning of consanguinity, the distinction between *consanguinei* and *uterini* seems to have given rise to some equivocation and puzzlement among the jurists. Sir Henry Maine gives us a remarkable example of this, from the history of English law:

> In Agnation too is to be sought the explanation of that extraordinary rule of English Law, only recently repealed, which prohibited brothers of the half-blood from succeeding to one another's lands. In the Customs of Normandy, the rule applies to *uterine* brothers only, that is, to brothers by the same mother but not by the same father; and, limited in this way, it is a strict deduction from the system of Agnation, under which uterine brothers are no relations at all to one another. When it was transplanted to England, the English judges, who had no clue to its principle, interpreted it as a general prohibition against the succession of the half-blood, and extended it to *consanguineous* brothers, that is to sons of the same father by different wives. In all the literature which enshrines the pretended philosophy of law, there is nothing more curious than the pages of elaborate sophistry in which Blackstone attempts to explain and justify the exclusion of the half-blood.[71]

Of course, in the original meaning of *consanguinitas* in Roman law, there was no such a thing as half-blood. The blood that siblings could be said to share came only from one source. It was exclusively the paternal blood, that is to say, blood perfected into semen, consistently represented, throughout all the variations of medical theories, as the overwhelming protagonist of the act of generation.

Notes

[1] This is a condensed version of "Legami di sangue, legami di seme: consanguineità' e agnazione nel diritto romano": *Quaderni Storici*, 86, Aug. 1994, pp. 299–334. I refer the reader to that essay for a fuller, and more fully referenced version of the argument presented here.

[2] E. Evans-Pritchard, "Zande Blood-Brotherhood," in *Africa*, 6, 4 (Oct. 1933), p. 397; see also, "Heredity and Gestation as the Azande See Them," in E. Evans Pritchard, *Essays in Social Anthropology*, London, 1962.

[3] Jack Goody has argued that in Europe a bilateral notion of kinship was always present at the core of inheritance practices (J. Goody, *The Development of Marriage and the Family in Europe*, Cambridge, 1983, pp. 20–21, 232–233). Historical research, however, has documented that this bilaterality was often heavily limited by patrilineal practices and ideologies, especially in late medieval and early modern Europe. See for instance C. Klapisch-Zuber, *La maison et le nom. Stratégies et rituelles dans l'Italie de la Renaissance*, Paris, 1990.

[4] Meyer Fortes, *Kinship and the Social Order*, Chicago, 1969, pp. 161, 167.

[5] Ibid., pp. 290–291. For a more nuanced view, see M. Bettini, *Antropologia e cultura romana*, Roma 1986, esp. pp. 111–112.

[6] On the borrowing of these categories, see for instance L. Mair, *An Introduction to Social Anthropology*, Oxford, 1965, pp. 20, 63–64, 71–73; and A.R. Radcliffe-Brown, *Structure and Function in Primitive Society*, London, 1952, chaps. 1–2.

[7] H. Sumner Maine, *Ancient Law*, New York, 1874, 2nd ed., pp. 141–143.

[8] For example, D.A. Bullough, "Early Medieval Social Groupings: The Terminology of Kinship," in *Past and Present*, No. 45, 1969, pp. 6–7. F.X. Wahl, *The Matrimonial Impediments of Consanguinity and Affinity*, Washington, D.C., 1934, p. 12, translates *cognatio* from the *Digest* as consanguinity. As we shall see, *cognatio* and *consanguinitas* in the *Digest* were two completely different concepts.

[9] *Paulys Realencyclopädie der classischen Altertumswissenschaft*, Stuttgart, 1893, IV ,1, cc. 204–206 s.v. *cognatio*; Ch. Daremberg and E. Saglio, *Dictionnaire des Antiquités grecques et romaines*, Graz, 1969, vol. I/1, p. 146, s.v. *agnatio*.

[10] *Corpus juris civilis, Digesta*, XXXVIII, 10, 4 (ed. Th. Mommsen, Berlin, 1895). All the translations from the *Corpus juris* are mine; I have consulted the English translations (*The Civil Law*, Cincinnati, 1932, repr. 1973, 17 vol.; and *The Digest of Justinian*, Philadelphia, 1985) but I have decided not to use them in this essay because I found them generally misleading or incorrect in rendering the crucial term *consanguinitas*.

[11] *Digesta*, XXXVIII 10, 10, 6.

[12] *Digesta*, XXXVIII 9, 10.

[13] Cf. *Kleine Pauly*, I, cc. 133–134, s.v. *agnatio*.

[14] Y. Thomas, "The Division of the Sexes in Roman Law," in G. Duby and M. Perrot, eds., *A History of Women*, vol. 1: *From Ancient Goddesses to Christian Saints*, ed. P. Schmitt Pantel, Cambridge, MA, 1992, pp. 83–137.

[15] Ibid., p. 90.

[16] Ibid., p. 121.

[17] *Digesta*, XXXVIII, 16, 13. The loss of civil rights implied, as already said, the loss of *patria potestas*: a woman could not lose it because she could never have it.

[18] *Digesta*, L, 16, 195, 2.

[19] *Digesta*, L, 16, 195, 5.

[20] Thomas, "The Division of the Sexes," p. 98.

[21] My research has been guided by *Vocabularium iurisprudentiae latinae* (Berlin, 1803) that lists most of the uses of *consanguineus/a, consanguinitas, jus consanguinitatis*, etc.; I have also used *Vocabularium Codicis Justiniani*, ed. R. Mayr, Prague 1923, and *Hermanns Handlexicon zu den Quellen des römischen Rechts*, Jena 1907, s. v. *consanguineus* and *consanguinitas*.

[22] *Digesta*, XXXVIII, 8, 2; cf. also *Digesta*, XXXVIII, 10, 4.

[23] Cf. *Paulys Realencyclopädie der classischen Altertumswissenschaft*, IV, 1, cc. 889–891, a.v. "*consanguinei*": "In the speech of Roman jurists, these are the brothers and sisters on the father's side, as contrasted with the *uterini*, brothers and sisters on the mother's side." See also *Kleine Pauly*, vol. I, c. 1277 a.v.; E. Forcellini, *Totius Latinitatis Lexicon*, Prati, 1861, t. II, pp. 400–401, s.v. *consanguineus*; and R. Estienne, *Thesaurus linguae latinae*, Basileae, 1711, t. I, p. 651, s.v.

[24] *Digesta*, XXXVIII, 8, 4. Note that, in the English version of the *Corpus juris*, the translator altered the meaning of this passage by rendering *consanguinitatis itemque adgnationis iura* as "the rights of consanguinity or cognation": an unjustifiable and inexplicable mistake unless, as seems possible, he was misled by the modern meaning of consanguinity as generic bilateral kinship and amended the text in consequence, substituting *cognatio* for *agnatio* (*The Civil Law*, trans. S.P. Scott, vol. VII, p. 262).

[25] Unless the woman has been married *in manum*, in which case, by a fiction of the law, she technically becomes the daughter of her husband and the consanguineous sister of his children as well as of the ones they have together: see Gaius, *Institutiones*, III, 24. Cf. *The Institutes of Gaius*,

trans. and introduced by W.M. Gordon and O.F. Robinson, Ithaca, 1988, p. 130.

26 *Codex* VI, 58, 1, ed. P. Krueger, Berlin, 1877.

27 Cf. the detailed analysis of literary sources in G. Guastella, "La rete del sangue," in *Materiali e discussioni per l'analisi dei testi classici*, 15, 1986, pp. 49–123.

28 See Pomata, "Legami di sangue," pp. 308–309.

29 *Digesta*, XXXVIII, 16, 1.

30 *Digesta*, XXXVIII, 16, 2; cf. also *Codex Iustinianus*, V, 30, 3.

31 *Digesta*, XXXVIII, 16, 1.

32 *Codex Iustinianus*, VI, 58, 14.

33 Isidore of Seville, *Etymologiae*, ed. M. Reydellet, Paris, 1984, IX, 6, p. 202.

34 *Generation of Animals* (from now on, GA) 736 a18 (I have used the text and translation in the Loeb Class. Library, Harvard, 1942).

35 E. Lesky, *Die Zeugungs- und Vererbungslehren der Antike und ihr Nachwirken*, Abhandlungen der Akademie der Wissenschaften und der Literatur, Geist. und soz. Kl., n. 19, Mainz-Wiesbaden, 1950, pp. 1344–1417 (*"die haematogene Samenlehre"*).

36 A. Preus, "Galen's Criticism of Aristotle's Conception Theory," in *Journal of the History of Biology*, 10, 1977, pp. 65–85, and more recently, J. Kollesch, "Galens Auseinandersetzung mit der Aristotelischen Samenlehre," in J. Wiesner, ed., *Aristoteles—Werk und Wirkung*, Berlin-New York 1987, vol. II, pp. 17–26.

37 GA 777 a5; 724 b26; 726 b5.

38 *Researches on Animals*, III 510 a14f.; cf. Lesky, *Die Zeugung*, p. 1356. It should be noted that Aristotle uses the same term for arteries and veins, failing to distinguish between them (see C.R.S. Harris, *The Heart and the Vascular System in Ancient Greek Medicine*, Oxford 1973, p. 121 n. 4).

39 GA 728 a17ff.

40 On milk as "concocted blood": GA 776 a15–777 a27.

41 GA 727 b34.

42 G. Sissa, "Subtle bodies," in M. Feher, ed., *Fragments for a History of the Human Body*, New York, 1989, vol. III, pp. 133–141.

43 GA 737 a8–17.

44 On physical changes after the removal of testicles: GA 716 b5f.; 766 a24f.; 746 b20f.; 787 b19f.; on the metaphor of the testes as stones hung from the loom: GA 717 a11f.; cf. Lesky, *Die Zeugung*, pp. 1352–1353.

45 Lesky, *Die Zeugung*, p. 1384.

46 *De semine*, ed., trans. and comm. by Phillip De Lacy, Berlin, 1992 (CMG V 3, 1), p. 116, p. 134.

47 Ibid., p. 122–124; p. 136.

48 See E. Lesky, "Galen als Vorläufer der Hormonforschung" in *Centaurus*, I, 1950, pp. 156–162.

49 *De semine*, pp. 114, 134.

50 *De semine*, p. 106.

51 Ibid., p. 130.

52 Ibid., p. 116.

53 Galen, *De usu partium*, in *Opera omnia*, ed. C.G. Kuehn, Lipsiae 1822, t.IV, p. 184; *De semine*, p. 134.

54 *De semine*, pp. 78, 96, 102; *De usu partium*, IV, p. 189.

55 *De usu partium*, IV, p. 167.

56 *De semine*, p. 182. The idea of a difference in the configuration of the male and female vascular system apparently survived Galen's criticism. In a text from the School of Salerno (twelfth century) we find the notion that women have one vein more than men—a special female vein called *kiveris*: cf. *Anatomia Magistri Nicolai Physici*, trans. G.W. Corner, *Anatomical Texts of the Earlier Middle Ages*, Washington, 1927, p. 84.

57 *De usu partium*, IV, p. 164 and pp. 184–185.

58 For evidence on this point, see Pomata, "Legami di sangue," pp. 320–321.

59 See D. Jacquart and C. Thomasset, *Sexuality and Medicine in the Middle Ages*, Oxford 1988, pp. 52-60.

60 M. Schurig, *Spermatologia historico-medica seu seminis humani consideratio physico-medico-legalis*, Francofurti ad Moenum, 1720, p. 3.

61 *Novellae*, CXVIII; see K.E. Zacharia von Lingenthal, *Geschichte des griechish-romanischen Rechts*, Berlin, 1892, 3rd ed., pp. 133–141. It should be noted that in the *Novellae* we also find a shift in the use of *consanguineus/a*. Next to the

traditional, technical meaning of "brother/sister from the same father," we also find the term to indicate generically "cognate," for the first time in the history of Roman legal terminology: see *Lessico delle Novelle di Giustiniano*, ed. A.M. Bartoletti Colombo, Roma, 1983, vol. I, s.v.

62 Of course, the legal reforms of Justinian did not mean that the practice of kinship became perfectly bilateral. The legal history of the countries under the influence of Roman law shows that the principle of agnaticism would prove to be extremely resilient. In the Middle Ages, the municipal statutes of most Italian cities, for instance, reintroduced the privileges of the agnatic kin in matters of succession, which had been abolished by Justinian. By the seventeenth century, an influential Italian jurist, G.B. De Luca, could state confidently that the principle of agnaticism (that is to say, the privileging of patrilineal kin) was almost universally followed in European countries in matters of inheritance. See G.B. De Luca, *Commentaria ad Constitutionem Sanctae Mem. Innocentii XI de Statutariis Successionibus; cum Particulis Statutorum, & Legum Excludentium Foeminas propter Masculos, tam intra Statum Ecclesiasticum, quam extra illum*, Venetiis, 1734 (1684), pp. 23–25.

63 *Etymologiae*, XI, 6, p. 217.

64 On the *"arbor consanguinitatis,"* see M. Conrat (Cohn), *Arbor Iuris frueh. mittelalters mit eigenartigen Computation*, Abhdl. k. preuss. Akad. d. Wissensch. Berlins, Phil. Hist. Kl., II, 1909; E. Patlagean, "Une représentation byzantine de la parenté et ses origines occidentales," in *L'Homme*, VI, 1966, pp. 59–81; E. Champeaux, "Jus Sanguinis. Trois façons de calculer la parenté au Moyen Age" in *Revue Historique de Droit Français et Etranger*, 4th ser., XII, 1933, pp. 241–290.

65 See for instance, S. Anthoninus, *Summa Theologica*, Venetiis, 1487, III, 1, 14, who explains the etymology of *consanguinitas* with the argument that "according to physicians, semen is the purest blood."

66 Prosdocimus de Comitibus, *Tractatus de arbore consanguinitatis & affinitatis*, in *Tractatus Universi Juris, duce, et auspice Graegorio XIII in unum congesti*, Venetiis, 1584–1586, T. IX, f. 141r; cfr. H. Mangiaria, *Tractatus solennis super declaratione arboris Consanguinitatis & Affinitatis*, ibid., f. 175v.

67 In Medieval Latin, *consanguinei* seems to have often been used as a synonym for cousins, on both the father's and the mother's side: cf. C. Du Cange, *Glossarium mediae et infimae latinitatis*, Graz, 1954, vol. 2–3, p. 392, col. 2, s.v. *cognatus*; see also the evidence from notarial records in S. Epstein, *Wills and Wealth in Medieval Genoa, 1150–1250*, Cambridge, MA., 1984, p. 118.

68 Baldus, *In sextum codicis librum commentaria*, Venetiis, 1615, f. 134v. It is interesting to note the context in which Baldus discusses this question. He is talking about the Italian city statutes that invalidate a contract signed by a woman without the consent of two of her *consanguinei*. The modern, wider meaning of the term raises the issue whether a contract signed by a woman with the consent of her mother and grandmother can be deemed valid. It is in order to rule out this disturbing possibility of female autonomy that Baldus recalls the original, rigidly patrilateral meaning of the word.

69 Quoted in Laurus de Palatiis, *Tractatus super statuto communiter per Italiam vigente, quod extantibus masculis foeminae non succedant*, in *Tract. Univ. Juris*, T. II, f. 281r.

70 I. Cyntholtz, *Tractatus, sue Commentaria in arborem Consanguinitatis, Affinitatis, Cognationis spiritualis atque legalis*, in *Tr. Univ. Juris*, T. IX, f. 147r.

71 *Ancient Law*, p. 146 (cfr. W. Blackstone, *Commentaries on the Laws of England*, Chicago and London, 1979, facsim. of 1st ed., 1765–69, vol. 2, pp. 224–236, esp. p. 232). See also J.H. Baker, *An Introduction to English Legal History*, London, 1971, p. 145: "If a tenant died without issue having a half-brother, the brother could not inherit because he was only related by half-blood. The reason for this rule was the subject of much speculation and controversy until the rule itself was abolished by the Inheritance Act 1833."

Ann Waltner explores texts alluding to the kinship practices of traditional China. She notes the central role of patrilineally linked surnames and the cross-generational ties that they forge to many aspects of Chinese culture— family and religious practices as well as political theory. But if the celebration of the father-child bond is a prominent feature of Chinese civilization, it nevertheless produced a set of flexible practices. Male heirs were critical, but the need for them led families sometimes to circumvent the explicit logic of kinship rules through adoption or concubinage. In this culture, father-son or mother-child relationships, while normatively seen as biological, could be generated by legal fictions or social contracts as well. As in Ancient Judaic or Roman culture, biological notions and cultural requirements around kinship coexisted with some degree of tension.

3

Kinship Between the Lines:
The Patriline, the Concubine and
the Adopted Son in Late Imperial China

ANN WALTNER

Comparative history clarifies differences as well as illumi-
nates similarities. Chinese patrilineality presents an intriguing case for the comparative study of kinship. Most scholarly observers of Chinese society for at least
the last two thousand years have agreed that Chinese society is patrilineal.
Traditional Chinese social theorists conceptualized descent as an unbroken line
which stretched from ancestors already dead to descendants yet unborn, traced
through a line of men. These ideas are present from the very beginning of recorded Chinese history, in the oracle bone inscriptions dating from the Shang dynasty
(eighteenth century to twelfth century BCE). This of course does not mean that the
Chinese notions of kinship were changeless. For example, beginning in the sixteenth century, Chinese lineages maintained genealogies in which they traced
descent through a line of men back to a common male ancestor.[1] The fact that the
ancestor might be legendary, or the filiation fictive, did not diminish the importance of these documents in establishing the identity of the Chinese lineage. These
lineages were the social enactment of ideas about kinship which are at least as old
as Chinese recorded history. Although there was variation in kinship practice
according to social class, historical period and region, the texts discussed in this
paper represent a common fund of literati attitudes toward kinship.

But saying that Chinese society is patrilineal is the beginning of a discussion,
rather than the end of one. It does not mean that the Chinese system precisely resem-

bles that prescribed by Roman law and described by Gianna Pomata in the previous chapter. There are kin arrangements comfortably embedded in the Chinese system which are absent from other patrilineal systems, and indeed which might seem to work counter to the assumptions of other patrilinealities. Two of the institutions which provide some of the most interesting negotiations of patrilineal ideology in traditional China, concubinage and adoption, are in theory at least predicated on the need for male heirs to continue the patriline. Thus they form an intrinsic part of the Chinese patrilineal system, and suggest ways in which the Chinese system is distinct from other systems which might also be called patrilineal.

The Patriline

In Chinese conceptions of the patriline, the dead and the living are intimately linked, and the primary ritual which articulates this linkage is the ancestral sacrifice.[2] The first mention of ancestral sacrifice appears in the oracle bone inscriptions of the Shang dynasty. Much of the ritual writing of the Chou dynasty (twelfth century to third century BCE) centered on the proper performance of sacrifice, and much later writing elaborated on the theory and practice of the rituals. (Indeed, in one formulation, there are four life-cycle rituals: capping, which is a coming-of-age ceremony, marriage, the rites surrounding death, and ancestral sacrifices. This formulation clearly shows that the dead ancestors are regarded as an age group, who retain a lively and present interest in the world of the living.) In the ritual of ancestral sacrifice, the living provide gifts of food and spirit money to their dead ancestors. An ancestor with no descendants to offer him (or her: women could be ancestors too) sacrifices would become a hungry ghost, with the power to wreak havoc in the world of the living. This is not simply a "folk" belief: it is enshrined in state orthodoxy, as evidenced by the fact that the fourteenth-century Ming state established public sacrificial altars for spirits who had no descendants.[3] A woman would assist her husband in the performance of rituals honoring his ancestors, which was a signifier of her incorporation into the patriline of her husband, rather than that of her father. But a daughter could not be the primary celebrant in ancestral sacrifices: a son was required. Most traditional discussions of the need for a male heir underscore the imperative that a man carry on the ancestral sacrifices. Thus the need for a male heir was not an abstract wish to perpetuate a name or a line: there were specific duties required of an heir (sacrifices) and potentially catastrophic consequences if they were neglected.

Despite the fact that the earliest recorded Chinese societies are patrilineal, ritual texts have historicized the patriline and ascribed mythical significance to its development. The *I-li* (*Book of Rites*), dating from several centuries BCE, is one of the central texts of the ritual tradition. It connects the patriline with the creation of human society when it says that animals recognize their mothers but not their fathers. People of low social status, the text continues, do not understand the importance of knowing who father and mother are. The text asserts that the higher one's social status, the longer the line of ancestors one must acknowledge and hence worship.[4] The notion of a prepatrilineal antiquity was not restricted to Confucians: The Taoist text, *Chuang-tzu,* states that "in the age of the legendary ruler Shen-nung, people knew their mother and not their father."[5] Two other texts dating from before the Han dynasty (206 BCE), the *Lü-shih ch'un-ch'iu* (*Spring and Autumn Annals of Mr. Lü*) and the Legalist *Shang-chün shu* (*Book of the Lord of Shang*) concur in positing a deep antiquity where people in a precivilized state recognized their mothers but not their fathers.[6] The connection between the patriline and political order is made clear in the *Spring and Autumn Annals of Mr. Lü*: in the days of high antiquity, when people recognized their mothers but not their fathers (and, the text tells us, when there were no distinctions between men and women), there were no rulers and no hierarchical distinctions. These texts clearly see gender and politics as linked. Before there were gender distinctions and recognized paternity, political order was not possible.

The mechanics of the transition to patrilineality are not articulated in these texts: the point is simply that they equate patrilineality with civilization.[7] Humankind was brought out of primal prepatrilineal chaos by sage kings: humans who taught agriculture, fire and writing to the rest of the human race. (These culture heroes were not uniformly male: the culture hero who taught sericulture was female.[8]) As part of their civilizing mission, these culture heroes bestowed surnames upon people, which were then transmitted from father to child. The surname was a permanent marker of membership in one's paternal family: a woman did not adopt her husband's surname at marriage.

Later theorists articulated the connections between the sage kings, surnames, civilization and nature. For example, the Sung Neo-Confucian Chang Shih (1133–1180), recounting the foundations of the Chinese family system, wrote that the purpose of the sages in establishing surnames was to distinguish among kin groups. The need to clarify questions of inheritance was also part of their motive. Yet Chang invokes another causal model when he tells us that the principle of distinctions among surname groups was

> in accordance with the properties of man's nature and was simply an
> unalterable principle. If a man forces himself from his natural lineage

69

and unites himself with that which he should not be united, he is surely denying his nature.[9]

Thus, surnames, artifices granted by the sages of antiquity, are by the time of the
Sung dynasty (960–1279) seen as markers of nature; the powerful civilizing
mythologies of the sage kings have been naturalized. What had been in the Chou
period a radical assertion of authority on the part of the rulers (what made people human was the civilizing mission of the sage kings) has some thirteen hundred
years later been naturalized.[10] Surname had become, in the eyes of Chang Shih, a
natural category. Thus according to this formulation, civilization is the natural
state of humankind, and patrilineality its natural mode of organization.

Mothers and Concubines

In spite of the power of the metaphor of an unbroken chain of male ancestors and
descendants and the burden of patrilineal ideology, there have always been other
ways of looking at Chinese kinship. Anthropologists have shown us that Chinese
kinship in practice often looks very different from the idealized and schematized
families that Confucian social theorists describe.[11] And there is a growing recognition among historians of the importance of affinal kin within the general patrilineal kin system of late imperial China, and of the distortions we perpetuate when
we ignore them.[12] One's mother's brothers, or one's wife's father, we are now
beginning to recognize, were crucial to a man's life chances in late traditional
China. Career advice, social and intellectual networks, and even material resources
might be shared along kinship lines created by marriage. But how were those ties
conceptualized? If kinship is transmitted through the surname, then how would a
man in the eighteenth century, for example, have described his kin ties with his sister's son? Ritual needs (and the fact that participation in sacrifices was intimately
linked to access to property) led ritual experts to contemplate such questions, and
in fact much Chinese ritual writing is an attempt to clarify precisely how people
are related to their various kin. Attempts to answer such perplexities can be found,
among other places, in the *Wu-li t'ung-k'ao* (*A Comprehensive Examination of the
Five Rituals*), an enormous ritual compendium in 262 *chüan* compiled in 1761 by
Ch'in Hui-t'ien. The *Wu-li t'ung-k'ao* argues that a man's sister's sons share his *ch'i*,
a word nearly impossible to render into English, which implies both matter and
energy as well as life force.[13] Such a relationship is not necessarily subversive of the
patriline, and in fact serves as the basis for arguing that property should devolve
upon sisters' sons rather than daughters' husbands, whose *ch'i* is from entirely alien
sources. But it does reflect the view that men and their sisters' sons share a com-

mon substance, which is we what might call kinship, and which complicates the picture of kin ties transmitted through the surname.

In order to illuminate the question of how matrilateral and matrilineal kinship ties were conceptualized, let us look at a rather special case of maternal ties: concubinage. Concubinage was legally recognized and was fairly widespread among the upper classes in China during the Ming (1368–1644) and Ch'ing (1644–1911) dynasties. In the Ming, it was legally restricted to men over forty who had no sons, thus making clear the linkage between the institution of concubinage and the provision of heirs. The legal strictures seem to have been largely ignored (suggesting that men acquired concubines for a variety of reasons) and were in fact dropped from the code of the subsequent Ch'ing dynasty.[14] While concubinage was almost certainly restricted to the upper classes, it was a variation in family structure and the marriage system, which was taken as normative. It therefore played a crucial role in the way legal and ritual texts imagined upper-class families.[15] An essay written by Wei Hsi (1624–1680) originates in a context in which men might find themselves fathers of children from more than one mother. Wei writes that brothers who have the same father and different mothers are

> like vegetables of the same seed, some planted in an eastern field, some in a western one. Once they have sprouted, no one can say they are not the same vegetables because they are growing in separate fields. Brothers born to different fathers of the same mother are like seeds of two totally different vegetables growing together in the same field. Once they have sprouted, no one will call them the same name simply because they are growing in the same field.[16]

Thus, according to Wei, the connection between brothers resides in the (male) seed and not in the (female) field. Wei is arguing against the notion that biological motherhood generates kinship. The female contribution to procreation is analogized to that of the field: it is nurturing, it is essential, but it does not determine the fundamental nature of the offspring.

Traditional Chinese concern with ritual provides us with a way of examining ways concubines were incorporated into the family system of their spouses. Mourning regulations, which prescribed in intricate detail the form and duration of the mourning to be undertaken at the death of every possible relative, can be read as a map of kin regulations from a ritual and legal point of view. (Many editions of the Ming and Ch'ing legal codes begin with charts detailing these mourning obligations.) The mourning charts describe eight different kinds of mother (which in itself would render the concept of matrilineality prohibitively complex).

The terms are *yang mu* (a mother who has adopted you), *ti mu* (father's legal wife), *chi mu* (a father's legal wife married after the death or, more rarely, the divorce of the first legal wife, often rendered into English as successor wife), *tz'u mu* (a father's concubine who is not your own birth mother who cares for you after the death of your birth mother), *chia mu* (a mother who has remarried after the death of your father), *ch'u mu* (a mother who has been divorced by your father), *shu mu* (father's concubine who may or may not be your birth mother) and *ju mu* (a father's concubine who has breast-fed you).[17] Note that birth mother (for which there is a perfectly good Ming Chinese term, *sheng mu*) is not one of the eight legal and ritual categories.

A child was legally and ritually the child of the father's principal wife, no matter who the birth mother was. There is a saying which encapsulates the tenuousness of the tie between a concubine and her children: "A concubine has no children and a concubine's children have no mother." One mourned the death of one's father's legal wife as if she were one's own mother, no matter what the biological details might be. A concubine's child mourned the death of his or her birth mother, but to a lesser degree than for the legal wife of the father. Legal and ritual maternity was hence defined by legal status in the patriline. But both law and ritual recognized that there were other kinds of motherhood. There might be a formal mourning relationship between a man's concubines and his children by other women, but only if the concubine had borne him children.[18] Thus what generated kinship ties between a concubine and children born to other women in the household was that the concubine was the mother of a sibling: it was not that she had a legally sanctioned sexual connection with the child's father. But one mourned the death of one's father's legal wife whether or not she had borne children: marriage created kinship in a way that concubinage did not.

Despite the fact that the offspring of a concubine were thoroughly legitimate and were in theory the equivalent of the offspring of the legal wife, there is little doubt that they were socially disadvantaged. Even in the legal codes, there are indications of this. For example, when one was negotiating a marriage for one's child, if one concealed that the child was the child of a concubine, one was punished.[19] This implies both that the information was deemed relevant by the parties to the marriage, and that it was subject to concealment. Fictional and anecdotal evidence richly document the potentially tenuous position of the children of a concubine. The anthropologist Rubie Watson has argued that one source of the difference in treatment accorded to concubines' children is the fact that their mothers had no (or minimal) dowries. She suggests that dowry was a central factor in establishing matrilateral ties: a man whose mother married with no dowry was deficient in matrilateral ties and this was a social disadvantage (especially among social classes, where most men's mothers had dowries.)[20] One can broaden Watson's argument: concubinage did not create kin relations the way marriage did. A child without maternal kin was disadvantaged. So despite a patrilineal structure which argued that it mattered not who your mother was, there are clear indications that it could matter very much. Wei Hsi's pungent metaphor of field and seed was not the only voice in the discussion.

Adoption

Having looked at what is perhaps an extreme case of patrilineal authority—the patriline claiming the right to define motherhood—I would like to turn to an arena where the patriline finds itself on shakier ground, in an explicit consideration of adoption. Much of the Chinese ritual and legal discussion on how people are related and how kin lines are drawn centers on adoption. The stakes are high: the fate of the ancestors and of property depends on the correct selection of an heir. Indeed, the classical writer Mencius wrote in the fourth century BCE, "Of the three unfilial acts, the worst is having no heir." It is an aphorism that was often reiterated. If a man during the Ming and Ch'ing dynasties had no male heir, he was obliged to select a boy of the same surname and adopt him. Property dictates and the ancestors demanded a male heir. But law and ritual both forbade the adoption of an heir of another surname. A statute common to both Ming and Ch'ing legal codes reads:

> He who adopts a child of a different surname, thereby causing chaos in the lineage, is to be beaten sixty strokes. He who gives a person of a different surname as an heir is to suffer the same punishment. The adoption is to be annulled.[21]

The prohibitions seem to have been largely ignored. I have written elsewhere on the complex reasons for both the prohibitions and their contravention. Suffice it to say here that legal codifications followed ritual formulations, which made it clear that the purpose of adoption was to continue the ancestral sacrifices. Ancestors simply refused to accept sacrifices of those who were not of the same surname. Ancestral ghosts are cast in the guise of enforcers of patrilineal ideology.

Let me illustrate this point with a story whose ultimate source is the Han dynasty *Feng-su t'ung-i*. The wife of a man named Chou Pa gave birth to a daughter at the same time and in the same place as a butcher's wife gave birth to a son. (It would be helpful to know more about birthing practices in the Han dynasty. A birthing house where women of differing social status give birth side-by-side seems unlikely, but the text implies such a place.) Chou's wife, mindful of the need to produce a male heir, paid the butcher's wife to exchange babies with her. Chou Pa remained ignorant of the deception for eighteen years, and happily raised his son. But when the son performed sacrifices to Chou Pa's ancestors, an observer, who had the reputation for being able to see ghosts, noted that "he saw a butcher, in tattered clothing, his hair in a spiral knot, sitting crosslegged. He held a knife and was cutting meat." When Chou Pa heard the grim ghost story, he rightly interpreted it as meaning that he was not the father of the boy. The butcher in tattered clothing had come to claim the sacrificial items which were due Chou Pa's ancestors. Chou confronted his wife, armed with a sword, and implied that the son was the child of an adulterous union. When his wife told him the truth, the butcher's son was expelled, the daughter was located and reinstated in the household, and a cousin's son was named heir. The conclusion of the story cites an oft-repeated maxim from the *Tso chuan*: "That the spirits do not enjoy the sacrifices of those who are not their kind is clear. What good does it do to adopt someone else's child?"[22] Chou Pa's wife switched babies with the butcher's wife because she clearly understood the need for a son. What she did not understand was that not any boy baby would do. The ending of the story is instructive: we are told nothing of the fate of the expelled boy. Once the deception was revealed, he was of no more interest to the storyteller. The interests of the text are allied with those of the ghost and the patriline. This story is oft repeated as an example illuminating the ways in which kinship was constructed, and as a warning against cross-surname adoptions.

But there are other interests. Not only were adoptions across surname lines reasonably frequent, there was a structure of metaphor which sanctioned and supported such a practice. A common term for an adopted child is *ming-ling tzu*, which literally means "mulberry insect child." A passage from the *Shih ching*, the *Book of Odes*, one of the most venerable of the Confucian classics, is the source of the nomenclature. The relevant section of the poem reads:

> The mulberry insect has young ones
> The wasp carries them away.
> Teach and train your young ones
> And they will become as good as you are.[23]

A Han dynasty commentary tells us what the first two lines mean:

> The wasp entreats the offspring of the mulberry insect: "Resemble me! Resemble me!" After a while, they take him as a model (*hsiao*). It is like the seventy disciples of Confucius taking him as a model.[24]

The analogy of the disciples of Confucius adds a moral dimension to the metaphor. The transformation of the *ming-ling* into wasps is not merely an anomaly of nature: it is a transformation to which one might aspire. (And in fact the transformation is not an anomaly of nature, but rather an artifact of human misunderstanding. The wasp stings the mulberry insect and lays her eggs in the insect's stunned body. The wasp then later reclaims her young. Thus larvae which then emerge from the caterpillar's body are, and have always been, wasps.) *Ming-ling tzu* is an ordinary term for an adopted child of a different surname, though by no means the only one. It occurs in a wide variety of genres—including fiction, biography, and even legal texts.[25]

The point here is that there is a set of metaphors which show mutability, mediating the starkness of kinship absolutes which express themselves in metaphors of unappeased ghosts. If an insect can change species, then surely a child can change families. The necessity for heirs in the patrilineal system is so strong that people are induced to contravene the rules of that system to obtain heirs.

A final irony: when one looks in detail at adoptions across surname lines as revealed in Ming and Ch'ing records, they are predominately adoptions of relatives through a female line. Thus a considerable portion of kinship practice is at odds with its articulated ideology. Matrilateral kinship ties prove to be useful in recruiting heirs for the patriline.

Conclusions

How does this modify our view of Chinese patrilineality? It is true that most property, surnames and, in the view of men like Wei Hsi, kinship itself passed through the male line. But the patriline is not the sum total of how people thought about kinship: metaphors of insects who change species can be used to construct an alternative ideology, an ideology of kinship which existed between the lines, or perhaps even kinship which was nonlinear.

Concubinage and adoption are two ways in which Chinese patrilineality was negotiated differently from, say, Roman patrilineality. The need to continue the line, expressed in stark metaphors of unappeased ghosts, rendered it necessary for people to continue the line in ways other than a son of the legal wife. Concubinage, though constructed in many genres as if it were primarily for the erotic pleasure of men, was conceived of, at least in legal and ritual texts, as a way of obtaining offspring. But concubinage and adoption represent different kinds of negotiation of the patriline. Concubinage reinforces our impressions of the importance of fatherhood: we have seen how, in the Chinese institution of concubinage, it did not matter so much who the mother was—her status was secondary. What mattered about a child's status was who the father was. The mere facts of biological motherhood were manipulated by legal and ritual status.

Adoption was another kind of negotiation, where the needs of the line to perpetuate itself resulted in the construction of cultural categories which supplemented biology. The needs of the collective patriline for descendants were so pressing that they overrode narrow concerns with paternity. If concubinage complicates theories about maternity, adoption challenges assumptions about both fatherhood and motherhood.

Thus if we remove our eyes from the father, we see the patriline in a different light. By looking at concubines, we see how mothers functioned in a patriline: there are profoundly mixed messages about the legal and ritual status of mothers who are not the legal wives of their children's fathers. By looking at adoption, we also see how obligations to ancestors are more important than the claims of fathers, in theory at least. Absolute needs cause negotiation of absolutes. Thus the Chinese case provides further evidence of the ways in which notions of intergenerational transmissions are translated into action. In this case, fathers and mothers are both subordinate to the ancestors; and it is the ancestors who are at the center of Chinese patrilineal ideology. The image enforcing the ideology is an unappeased ghost: the necessity of producing heirs for that ghost leads families to construct both fatherhood and motherhood in imaginative ways. Despite the historical variations in the conceptions of lineage which we see, the ancestors remain central to the patriline. The lively role the dead ancestors play in the construction of the Chinese patriline is one of its distinguishing characteristics.

Notes

[1] Although there are some genealogies which are earlier than this, it is during this period that lineages become a dominant force in Chinese society.

[2] For a translation of the Sung dynasty Neo-Confucian Chu Hsi's prescriptions on ancestral sacrifices, see Patricia Buckley Ebrey, trans., *Chu Hsi's Family Rituals: Twelfth-Century Chinese Manual for the Performance of Cappings, Weddings, Funerals and Ancestral Rites* (Princeton, NJ: Princeton University Press, 1991), pp. 153–177. Chu Hsi's prescriptions remained the standard for generations to come.

[3] "Chieh-hsing shih-lieh," in *Huang Ming chih-shu* (Tokyo: Koten kenkyukai, 1966–67), p. 288.

[4] *I-li Cheng-chu*, Ssu-pu pei-yao edition, 11/8a.

[5] *Kuo Ching-fan Chuang-tzu chi shih* (Shanghai: Ssu-hsing shu-chü, 1986), 29:81.

Cited by Allen Chun, "Conceptions of Kinship and Kingship in Classical Chou China." *T'oung Pao* 76 (1990), p. 25.

[6] *Lü-shih ch'un-ch'iu chiao-shih* (Taipei: Chung-hua ts'ung-shu wei-yüan-hui, 1958) *chüan* 8, p. 101; *Shang-chün shu chien-cheng* (Taipei: Kuang-wen shu-chü, 1975) 2/10a. See J.J. L. Duyvendak, trans., *The Book of Lord Shang* (London: Arthur Probsthian, 1928), p. 225.

[7] There has been an interesting debate as to whether the Chinese neolithic was matrilineal, which uses the kind of evidence for a prepatrilineal society I have cited here, as well as archaeological and linguistic evidence. See Molly Spitzer Frost, "Chinese Matriarchy: Clues from Legends and Characters," Ph.D. dissertation, Georgetown University, 1982. For a refutation of the archaeological argument, see Wang Ningsheng, "Yangshao Burial Customs and Social Organization: A Comment on the Theory of Yangshao Matrilineal Society and its Methodology," *Early China* 11–12 (1985–87), pp. 6–32. For polemical debates, see Ku Yen, "Chiang Ch'ing's Wolfish Ambitions in Publicizing 'Matrilineal Society'" *Chinese Studies in History* 12.3 (1979), pp. 75–79.

[8] The gender of some of the other heroes is contested. For arguments that Hou Chi (often rendered Lord Millet) is female, see Anne Birrell, *Chinese Mythology: An Introduction* (Baltimore: The Johns Hopkins University Press, 1993), p. 55. And Birrell also suggests that the sericulture deity, Ts'an Ts'ung, is male. See pp. 61–63.

[9] Chang Shih, "I-le t'ang chi," quoted in Asami Keisai, "Yoshi bensho," *Nihon Jurin susho*, ed. Seiki Gichiro (Tokyo: Toyo kenkokai, 1927–29), p. 3. Trans. by I.J. McMullen, "Non-agnatic Adoption: A Confucian Controversy in Seventeenth and Eighteenth Century Japan," *Harvard Journal of Asiatic Studies* 35 (1975), p. 142.

[10] For a discussion of this, see Mark Edward Lewis, *Sanctioned Violence in Early China* (Albany: State University of New York Press, 1990).

[11] I am thinking here particularly of Margery Wolf's *Women and the Family in Rural Taiwan*

(Stanford, CA: Stanford University Press, 1972); and Janice Stockard, *Daughters of the Canton Delta* (Stanford, CA: Stanford University Press, 1989).

[12] See, for example, the discussion in James Watson, "Anthropological Overview: The Development of Chinese Descent Groups," in Patricia Buckley Ebrey and James L. Watson, eds., *Kinship Organization in Late Imperial China* (Berkeley and Los Angeles: University of California Press, 1986), p. 286. Watson is citing scholarship by Jerry Dennerline, David Johnson and Patricia Ebrey.

[13] Ch'in Hui-t'ien, *Wu-li t'ung-k'ao* (Taipei: Hsin-hsing shu-chü, 1971), 147/13a. Tu Wei-ming defines *ch'i* as the "psycho-physiological power associated with breathing and the circulation of blood." He cites several translations: "material force" (Wing-tsit Chan), "matter-energy" (Homer Dubs) and "vital spirit" (Frederic Mote). See "The Idea of the Human in Mencian Thought: An Approach to Chinese Aesthetics," in Susan Bush and Christian Murck, eds., *Theories of the Arts in China* (Princeton, NJ: Princeton University Press, 1981), p. 68.

A *chüan* is a textual divison somewhat longer than a chapter and shorter than a volume.

Ch'eng-k'an pen, ed Hsüeh Yü-sheng (Taipei: Ch'eng-wen Ch'u-pan she, 1970)

[14] *Tu-li ts'un-i*, vol. 2, *chüan* 11, p. 294; *chüng-K'an pen*, ed. Hsüeh Yün-sheng (Taipei: Ch'eng-wen ch'u-pan she, 1970)

[15] There is a growing body of literature on concubines in China. Among the most notable recent works are Rubie S. Watson, "Wives, Concubines and Maids: Servitude in the Hong Kong Region, 1900–1940," in Rubie S. Watson and Patricia B. Ebrey, *Marriage and Inequality in Chinese Society* (Berkeley: University of California Press, 1991), pp. 230–255; Maria Jaschok, *Concubines and Bondservants: The Social History of a Chinese Custom* (London: Zed Press, 1988); Patricia Ebrey, "Women in the Kinship System in the Southern Sung Upper Class," in *Women in China*, ed. Richard W. Guisso and Stanley

Johannsen (Youngstown, NY: Philo Press, 1981), and "Concubines in Sung China," *Journal of Family History,* vol. 11 (1986), pp. 1–24. See also Bau Hwa Sheieh, "Concubines in Chinese Society" from the Fourteenth to the Seventeenth Centuries," Ph.D. dissertation, University of Illinois at Urbana-Champaign, 1992.

[16] Wei Hsi, "Wei Shu-tzu jih-lu," in *Hsün-tzu i-kuei,* in *Wu-chung i-kuei,* Ssu-pu pei-yao edition, vol. 1549, 3/30b. My translation is slightly modified from that of Shiga Shûzô, "Family Property and the Law of Inheritance in Traditional China," in David Buxbaum, ed., *Chinese Family Law and Social Change* (Seattle: University of Washington Press, 1978), p. 123. See the discussion in Ann Waltner, *Getting an Heir: Adoption and the Construction of Kinship in Late Imperial China* (Honolulu: University of Hawaii Press, 1990), p. 30.

[17] This particular list was taken from *Ming tai lü-li hui-pien,* compiled by Huang Chang-chien (Taipei: Academia Sinica, 1979), *chüan shou,* p. 32. Nor is paternity unilineal: there are three kinds of fathers listed: (1) a *chi fu* (stepfather) you live with (and there are subdivisions as to whether or not he has biological sons of his own); (2) a *chi fu* you do not live with; (3) a mother's subsequent husband. But the category of "father" (a biological father with whom one has resided) is absent from this list: that kind of fatherhood is presumably unilineal and not partible. There is no such corresponding unified legal and ritual concept of "mother."

[18] *Ta Ming lü chi-chieh fu-li* (Taipei: T'ai-wan hsüeh-sheng shu-chü, 1970), vol. 1, "Mourning Degrees," p. 76.

[19] *Ming-tai lü-li hui-pien,* vol. 2, p. 499. *Ta Ming lü chi-chieh fu-li,* vol. 2, 6/1a–6a, pp.639–649.

[20] See Rubie Watson, pp. 244–245. Bau Hwa Sheieh has found several fictional cases where Ming concubines married with dowry, though she concedes that this is exceedingly rare (pp. 197–198).

[21] *Ta Ming lü chi-chieh fu-li,* vol. 2, 4/9a, p. 558; *Tu-li ts'un-i ch'ung-k'an pen,* vol. 2, *chüan* 9, p. 249.

[22] *Feng-su t'ung-i* (Peking: Centre Franco-chinois d'études sinologiques, 1943), *chüan* 3, p. 105. The text has been reconstructed from *I-lin,* Ssu-pu pei-yao edition, vol. 1417, 4/36–48, and from the *T'ai-p'ing yü-lan* (Shanghai: Shang-wu yin-shu-kuan, 1935), *chüan* 361 (*Jen shih pu*), p. 6b and *chüan* 883 (*Shen kuei pu*), p. 6b. See the discussion in Ch'u T'ung-tsu, *Law and Society in Traditional China* (Paris: Ecole pratique des hautes études, 1961), p. 19.

[23] *Mao-shih chiang-i,* Ssu-ku ch'üan-shu edition, vol. 236, 6/1a. See the translation in James Legge, *Chinese Classics* (Hong Kong: Hong Kong University Press, n.d), vol. 4, p. 334. Some sources identify the *ming-ling* as *chilo simplex,* others as *helio simplex,* others as *heliothus armigera.*

[24] Yang Hsiung, *Fa yen,* Ssu-pu pei-yao edition, vol. 1419, 1/1b.

[25] See the discussion in *Getting an Heir,* pp. 24–28.

Alex Bolyanatz offers us an ethnographic study set in contemporary Papua New Guinea. His work suggests that previous theory, which regards the mode of transmission of land as central to matrilineal practice, is flawed. Social changes have altered dimensions of land transmission among the Sursurunga without disturbing other aspects of society which he considers to be central to matriliny. He finds, in a way reminiscent of Waltner's findings about China, that social practices can be far more flexible than we might expect if we take normative prescriptions about relationships too literally.

4

Musings on Matriliny: Understandings and Social Relations among the Sursurunga of New Ireland

ALEXANDER BOLYANATZ

To be human is to be ethnocentric.[1] To be sure, scientific understanding of the world around us is hampered—but not made impossible—by ethnocentrism; the progress of knowledge is often made by showing that the native view of social life is not consistent with the nonnative view of social life (for example, it is progress to view headaches and fever as being caused by malaria rather than spirits). Sometimes, however, it is the nonnative view that hinders analytical understanding. In this regard, anthropological understandings about matrilineal descent can be shown to vary from the reasoned behavior informing social life—insiders' points of view[2]—in a society with matrilineal descent groups. In this essay, I provide an example of how matrilineal theory fails to reflect the complex cultural realities of matrilineal descent. My approach is to first discuss the anthropological understanding of matriliny, then turn to ethnographic data from the Sursurunga of southern New Ireland in Papua New Guinea.

Matrilineal Theory in Anthropology

Much of early ethnology consisted of attempts to address the issue of cultural variation: how it is that different people do things differently. Matriliny constituted an easily recognizable (to Victorian sensibilities) difference in social organization and therefore was an early subject of analytical efforts. Matrilineal descent was explained by Lewis Henry Morgan[3] as the cultural elaboration of the biological realities of the mother-child relationship. He imagined that there was a need to delineate between different individuals and groups, and that this need to delineate was where kinship began.

Matrilineal descent also served anthropologists interested in alternatives to Western understandings of how human behavior is shaped. In this regard, Malinowski, for example, argued that matrilineal descent forged a "matrilineal complex" which contrasted with the "European" Oedipus complex.[4] This was, for the most part, the condition of anthropology's interest in matriliny until after World War II: matrilineal descent was more of an evidential means to a theoretical end than something to be investigated in itself.[5] After 1945, however, interest in matriliny was renewed, both historically and structurally.[6]

Matriliny and Social Evolution

In *Social Structure*, George Murdock[7] articulated an evolutionary explanation for matrilineal descent groups. Murdock tied the genesis of matriliny to the development of agriculture as an alternative to hunting and gathering. Murdock argued that males retained their specialization in hunting while foraging—traditionally women's labor—became transformed into the practice of caring for and harvesting crops. With the adaptive advantages of agriculture as a form of food production, women acquired increased economic importance—as did land. Women and land thus became a vital economic combination.

The result of women's increased economic importance and prestige meant increased power, including the power to remain in their natal places at marriage ("uxorilocality"). Uxorilocality and women's economic importance developed into a need to monitor and govern the allotment of women's economic resources, especially land. Matrilineal inheritance, then, provided the basis for matrilineal descent dogma.

Later, Kathleen Gough[8] elaborated on Murdock's scheme, introducing a Marxist perspective, using mode of production as the critical element in the genesis of matriliny. Whereas Murdock suggested that it was women's increased economic importance and accompanying power which allowed more choice in postmarital residence, Gough argued that the exigencies of agricultural food production— women's labor—required sedentary residence. The less women shifted residence, the more (agriculturally) productive they were.

Matriliny and Social Anthropology

In 1950 Audrey Richards[9] initiated another emphasis in the anthropological interest in matriliny. Emphasizing the analysis of the ways in which matrilineal descent groups operated, this new perspective was concerned with the sociology of matriliny. Richards's article comparing matrilineal systems in Central Bantu groups was a systematic comparison of societies labeled "matrilineal," and was the beginning of a trend that attempted to formalize what was known about the structures and functions unique to matrilineal descent groups. David M. Schneider took the development of matrilineal theory a large step forward with his "Introduction" to *Matrilineal Kinship*[10]—a piece still cited as the best description of the standard dynamics of matrilineal descent groups.

At the core of this treatment of matrilineal descent groups was the so-called matrilineal "puzzle": tension/conflict inherent in the relationship between a woman's husband and her brother, ostensibly resulting from the fact that while descent group authority resides with the mother's brother, domestic/household authority resides with the father. Richards, for example, pointed out that "the balance of interest between the two sides of the family is bound to be an uneasy one in the case of matrilineal communities."[11] Richards refers to the conflicting pattern of rights and obligations which crosscut the household and the descent group. Offspring are expected to recognize the authority of both father and mother's brother; men are expected to provide both for the younger members of their descent group as well as for the younger members of their own household.

Concerning marriage, Schneider points out that: "The institutionalization of very strong, lasting, or intense solidarities between husband and wife is not compatible with the maintenance of matrilineal descent groups."[12] Schneider notes the same structural dilemma as Richards: a set of conflicting obligations between members of the conjugal family and the lineage.[13] By around 1970, what could be called Standard Matrilineal Theory was particularly focused on the two institutions in which conflict was seen to inhere: (1) marriage and residence, and (2) inheritance and authority.

In a matrilineal system, marriage is understood to present spouses with an affective dilemma. Men, according to the model, must be oriented either toward their sisters' children (their lineage) or their own children (their wife's lineage). Thus Schneider argues that matrilineal descent and strong bridewealth payments are understood to have at least two functions:[14] (1) to promote solidarity of the lineage as its members work together to pool their resources so that its individual members can marry, and (2) to reinforce the marriage brought about by the

83

bridewealth payment, since the wife-giving group will apply pressure to their "sister" to persevere in the marriage so that they are not obligated to refund the bridewealth.[15] High bridewealth payments, then, can be expected to promote both marriage solidarity and lineage solidarity. The resulting structural paradox is that bridewealth reinforces marriage while simultaneously reinforcing the descent group—which itself is seen to be in structural conflict with marriage.

Bridewealth, whether high or low, in a system of matrilineal descent, seems counter-intuitive. Spouses are required (by the rules of exogamy, or "marrying out," which nearly always apply) to come from other lineages. As a result, a patri-lineage needs women, and a matrilineage needs men. Bridewealth in a patrilineal system seems reasonable enough: there is an exchange, with a woman—and importantly, the rights to her children—going in one direction and wealth in the other.[16] In a matrilineal system, if the focus is on the husband's reproductive capabilities, then the husband's lineage provides the wife's lineage both with a man (and his reproductive capabilities) and with a bridewealth payment, thereby giving up wealth for seemingly nothing (that is, no primary rights to the man's children) other than a man's rights *qua* husband. Since, however, the potential cost to men is vastly different from the cost to women with regard to conception, pregnancy and birth, men, boldly put, must be good for something else; and that something is labor, a discussion to which I shall return later.

A discussion of marriage necessarily leads to a discussion of residence since, after all, the newly established conjugal unit must reside somewhere. Anthropological treatments of residence are often cast in terms of residence "rules." One must, however, be careful about inferring too much information from such "rules." At times, the predominant residential pattern is cited as the "rule" without provision for demographic or sociostructural reasons for any deviation from the "rule." Also, there may be little correspondence between a cultural prescription (which more accurately deserves the label "rule") and actual settlement patterns. Indeed, as Meyer Fortes[17] has pointed out, settlement "rules" are among the most fluid of social patterns.[18] Standard Matrilineal Theory assumes certain intrinsic problems with regard to residence. Murdock[19] argued that both avunculocality (postmarital residence in the husband's mother's brother's home) and uxorilocality are consistent with matrilineal descent, because both of these residential patterns keep members of the descent group together across generations.

An important concern of matrilineal theory was the purported disintegration of matrilineal descent groups.[20] This phenomenon was normally expressed negatively,[21] as a loss, a de-emphasis or a weakening of matrilineal understandings as well as the matrilineal descent group. This perspective derives, as noted earlier, from

Standard Matrilineal Theory, which contained certain assumptions about what matrilineal descent groups *do* (for instance, govern the inheritance of land), what human motivations are (for instance, why men would attend to their sisters' children rather than their own), and intrinsic conflict (for instance, authority in the jural-political realm versus in the domestic realm).

For Gough, the signal of the demise of matriliny was when the inheritance of land ceased to pass exclusively or primarily through the matriline. Gough used the decline of matrilineal inheritance of land as evidence for the disintegration of matriliny among the Tonga, Ashanti and Mayombe.[22] In fact, the matrilineal descent group no longer being exclusively or primarily the basis for the inheritance of land does not constitute the "disintegration" of matrilineal descent, although it was taken to be such by Gough.

When men have access to forms of wealth which are partible and not easily identifiable, then the possibility exists that a man might pass some of his wealth to his own children, rather than to his sister's. Problems occur when a man gives a disproportionate amount of wealth to his own children, leaving an insufficient amount for him to pass to members of his own lineage. The choices facing a father/uncle are not, however, nearly as stark as these sentences would suggest. A man is required, within a social context, to do something with his wealth, and his two most likely choices are to pass it on to his children and his sister's children. To be sure, the possibility of such a conflict does not necessarily constitute a problem, but the ethnographic evidence on this point is quite clear: when such wealth is available (almost always in the form of cash), men do provide their own offspring with much of their profit—especially if a man perceives his own children to have contributed to the acquisition of that wealth (as among the Sursurunga). Indeed, this happens often enough that capitalism is perceived to be the single greatest enemy of matrilineal inheritance ideology.[23]

A Critique of Standard Matrilineal Theory

The prevailing views have not gone unchallenged. Jill Nash[24] showed that matrilineal theory was in need of adjustment by providing evidence that, contrary to what the theory predicted, matrilineal descent among the Nagovisi did not "disintegrate" in the face of cash capitalism. Similarly, Annette Weiner[25] demonstrated that matrilineal descent in the Trobriands was remarkably (given the assumptions about matriliny) intact.

Other weaknesses of matrilineal theory are illuminated by Juliana Flinn[26] and Nancy Levine,[27] each of whom challenges the assumptions about an intrinsic con-

85

flict of interest for men in matrilineal societies. Flinn observed that cooperation, not conflict, characterized the relationship between a woman's husband and her brother—ostensibly an important locus of the matrilineal conflict or matrilineal puzzle. Flinn's research highlights the need to look at the function not only of the matrilineal descent group, but of matrilineal descent understandings. Matriliny *qua* dogma does different things in different societies.

Even the assumption of Standard Matrilineal Theory that men have a uniform set of feelings for their children may be misguided. In this regard, Levine points out that:

> What is of interest here [in traditional matrilineal theory] is the notion that, given a choice, men will turn their backs on their matrilineal kin and use their property for their wives and children instead.[28]

While Levine incautiously suggests an either/or option for men, she does helpfully point out that traditional matrilineal theory's assumption that men are inherently more interested in their own offspring than in their sisters' offspring is contradicted by data she provides from Tibet, in which "men's interests in and relationships with their 'real' children are neither inevitable, nor invariable."[29] Naturally, a father's relationship with and concern for all of his children will never be identical, especially (but not exclusively) if the children are borne by different women. Nevertheless, Levine's cases suggest that the assumption that men would provide succor and support for their own offspring if they were not prevented by the constraints imposed upon them by matrilineal understandings ought to be looked at more closely.

Other evidence indicates that the matrilineal descent group does not necessarily conform to the traditional sorts of functions (for instance, inheritance, succession) assigned it in Standard Matrilineal Theory in order to be retained as a group and in order to retain the principle of matriliny.[30] Glenn Petersen[31] shows that Ponapean matrilineal understandings are not dependent upon a functioning system of matrilineal land tenure or a residence pattern more commonly associated with matriliny. In other words, "traditional" matrilineal understandings can exist where there are no "traditional" matrilineal descent group functions.

To argue that the loss of matrilineal inheritance of land is an index of the disintegration of the matrilineal descent group is tautological, and rests on the notion that the matrilineal descent group—or any unilineal descent group, for that matter—is centrally defined by its ability to pass on important resources to its next generation. While it may be the case that this has been and is an important function of some unilineal descent groups, it is not clear that this feature need be a defining characteristic of unilineal descent groups. The issue is: Does primary attention to rules of inheritance—as a central part of the definition of unilineal descent groups—promote our understanding of these groups? Ethnographic evidence suggest that it does not.

Recall the case of the Mae-Enga in the Highlands of New Guinea.[32] During periods of population pressure on the supply of land, patrilineal understandings "tightened up," and only "true" agnates (relatives through the male line) had full land rights. When the land supply was more plentiful, agnatic group membership was extended to men who were not demonstrably agnates. The point of the case is that the relationship between control over land tenure and descent group understandings is variable, and it is easy to imagine that in an area where there is little or no pressure on land supply, the connection between land tenure and the unilineal descent group might be extremely loose. This is the case among the Sursurunga, for whom descent group understandings are not rooted in the transfer of lineage land through generations; rather, descent group understandings are most clearly evidenced in and seen to have ongoing utility as an important guide to life through choice of marriage partners and the sequence of mortuary feasts.[33]

Data collected among the Sursurunga suggest that the picture of matrilineal descent groups presented by Standard Matrilineal Theory may be inaccurate or incomplete. I arrived on New Ireland looking for, but not finding, the conflict, stress and tension that the theory led me to expect. There was no appreciable added strife in those relationships which should have been affected by the matrilineal puzzle, and when there was conflict, it was not clear that the source of the conflict was overlapping spheres of authority between the mother's brother and father.

The behaviors of social actors which are influenced by descent understandings are not the understandings themselves. What, then, is matriliny: descent dogma or politico-economic praxis? According to Standard Matrilineal Theory, it is both: behavior is the outcome of cultural constructs of descent, and descent constructs can be deduced from the actions of individuals in groups.

Standard Matrilineal Theory relies on a notion that cultural understandings and values can be inferred from behavior. It was for this reason that Gough wrote of the disintegration of matrilineal descent *groups* and derived something about the "survival of the matrilineal *principle*."[34] While inferring understandings from behavior is not wrong, it must be seen only as a beginning point in social analysis, providing a basis for investigating the understandings about descent—and the values connected to those understandings—that people actually have. It is worthwhile to distinguish between matrilineal descent constructs and the functions of the matrilineal group, or what I will call matrilineal social relations; social relations which feature, for example, the jural authority of the mother's brother. In the following section, I discuss matrilineal descent constructs and matrilineal social relations as they exist among the Sursurunga. By so doing, I show that the relationship between descent constructs and social relations is not the direct, lineal relationship that has been articulated.

Standard Matrilineal Theory has been concerned to attend to the sociostructural aspects of matrilineal descent groups and social relations among wives and husbands, brothers and sisters, mothers' brothers and sisters' children. The formulations of Standard Matrilineal Theory do not always look like ethnographic reality: matrilineal dogma exists where the expected clashes of authority do not materialize; it occurs where conflict of interest is absent, and it survives, as in the Sursurunga case, where matrilineal inheritance has been superseded and where uxorilocal residence is not the norm.

The principles of what I am calling Standard Matrilineal Theory are still with us. Recently, Oliver[35] assumed that the matrilineal descent group is paradigmatically a land-transmitting group. In describing father-to-son land transfers among the Siwai of Bourgainville Island, Oliver notes that such a transfer represents the "founding [of] an incipient patrilineage." He gives no indication that patrilineal descent understandings are emerging among the Siwai, and seems to have conflated the father-child link with patrilineal descent.

I suggest that the shortcomings of Standard Matrilineal Theory can be attributed to the unidimensional approach which characterizes it. The theory has failed to take into account the understandings of individuals who comprise matrilineal descent groups. In fact, and this is a point which I will make in detail shortly, matrilineal social relations may be guided by understandings which have nothing to do with descent at all, but which themselves are consistent with and integrated with descent understandings.

Sursurunga Matriliny

Most of the approximately two thousand speakers of Sursurunga live on the east coast of southern New Ireland in Papua New Guinea. Salient social groups among the Sursurunga are matrimoieties, matriclans and matrilineages.[88] Colonial resettlement policies have altered residence patterns, so that most couples reside in the husband's home. This has led to some changes in the processes governing the acquisition of land. In the past, most—but not all—parcels of land were received through the matrilineage. Today, people acknowledge two primary means of acquiring land: inheritance through the matriline, and token purchase from one's father. Informants do not indicate a preference for one method of land acquisition over another; rather, most people use both methods to provide themselves and their children with an adequate economic base—an economic base which relies heavily upon tuber gardens, and cacao and copra as cash crops.

Gough's evidence for the disintegration of matrilineal descent groups centered on the fact that the inheritance of land has shifted away from the matrilineal descent group. Such a shift has also taken place among the Sursurunga,[37] but it cannot be said that this coincides with the disintegration of the matrilineal descent group or of matrilineal understandings. The survival of matriliny among the Sursurunga is evidenced by the fact that ninety percent of all marriage partners come from outside the matrimoiety. Furthermore, mortuary feasting is closely tied to matriliny, and important rights and obligations within the feasting complex are derived from matrilineage, matriclan and matrimoiety membership.

Sursurunga Matriliny: Cultural Constructs

Descent understandings often include the view that something is shared between siblings which comes from the mother. Among the Sursurunga, however, descent is commonly characterized in the idiom of a banana plant. A *kabinun* ("stem of a banana plant") refers to a matriclan (and less often, a matrimoiety). Members of lineages who consider themselves to be part of the same clan, but cannot demonstrate that connection genealogically, are represented by the shoots that grow from a banana plant. Quite often, the actual origin of these shoots is under the ground and therefore unseen. Just as clan members are assumed to be connected with each other, the shoots from the banana plant are known to come from the plant, even though the connection is hidden. A notion of common (maternal) origin rather than shared substance is the Sursurunga basis for shared descent group membership.

A concomitant of shared origin among the Sursurunga, as well as in many other parts of Papua New Guinea, is the restriction placed on intimacy between opposite-sex siblings. "Shame" (Sursurunga: *laes*) is the outcome of even inadvertent interaction between brothers and sisters, and the reason for this moral anxiety is the possibility of brother-sister sexual relations. The Sursurunga view brother-sister incest as heinous, but also altogether too possible; hence the need to carefully guard against even the opportunity. To even know of one's sibling's sexuality is proscribed and generates the experience of *laes*. I was told many times that men who formerly exchanged ribald stories in the men's house cease doing so if they become brothers-in-law. While I never saw it happen, I was told that to discuss a man's sister's sexual behavior in his hearing entails reimbursing that man with a pig for the shame that results. Sursurunga descent understandings connect people who have maternal links, but they also separate people within the descent group who are opposite-sexed.

Sursurunga Matriliny: Social Relations

Matrilineal social relations are those which are normally viewed to be influenced by matrilineal descent understandings. These relations include the authority of the mother's brother, which typically appears in descent group functions such as mortuary feasts. Among the Sursurunga, the actions of members of matrilineal descent groups conform to the expectations of Standard Matrilineal Theory with regard to these feasts, but not to land inheritance practice.

Mortuary feasting among the Sursurunga is an activity which makes salient descent group membership. The economic requirements of feast sponsorship can be substantial for a lineage, and failure to contribute according to the wishes of one's mother's brothers—lineage leaders—is generally avoided. The economic solidarity shown by a lineage within the context of the mortuary feasting complex is unsurpassed in any other area of Sursurunga social life. The social relations involved in mortuary feasting among the Sursurunga are quite consistent with matrilineal descent principles.

In contrast, land inheritance among the Sursurunga has shifted in the past thirty years from a norm of matrilineal inheritance to a norm of patrifilial inheritance. In a majority of cases these days, land is transferred to children—both male and female—in return for a token payment of a few kina.[38] This token payment is to the father as a representative of his land-losing lineage. The practice of making the token payment indicates that matrilineal descent principles are still in place, and that matrilineal inheritance is still the paradigmatic form of inheritance. A preference for virilocal residence has, however, made matrilineal inheritance of land much more awkward than the practice of patrifilial inheritance. Thus even though social relations among the Sursurunga conform very closely to Standard Matrilineal Theory in terms of lineage activity and the mortuary feasting complex, Sursurunga land inheritance does not conform to the theory. The Sursurunga data thus show that Standard Matrilineal Theory is inadequate, because it fails to account for the "inconsistency" between behavior and principle.

According to the theory, the absence of matrilineal social relations—specifically matrilineal inheritance of land—was taken to mean the accompanying decay or absence of matrilineal understandings. But the ethnographic evidence—from Sursurunga and elsewhere—shows that this is not the case: matrilineal social relations can be shown to be absent without the corresponding absence of matrilineal descent dogma. The original formulation—that matrilineal understandings result in particular patterns of behavior known as matrilineal social relations—requires revision. I suggest that matriliny be viewed not as a one-dimensional, understandings-generate-behavior phenomenon, but as a set of understandings which, in conjunction with other understandings, motivate people to behave in certain patterns; patterns of behavior which can be construed as matrilineal social relations.

My argument is that matriliny (*qua* groups as well as *qua* cultural constructs of descent) is intricately linked to other aspects of culture. Behavior patterns which are considered to be part of matrilineal social relations are influenced by different sorts of understandings, not simply, as Standard Matrilineal Theory would suggest, a monolithic matrilineal principle. It is important to take into account the varied assortment of understandings which help to compel an actor conducting matrilineal social relations—behavior which may not be the result of matrilineal descent understandings exclusively, or even mainly, but of actors' reasoned behavior in particular circumstances. That reasoned behavior may include understandings which have nothing to do with matrilineal descent understandings.

Sursurunga Marriage, Matriliny, and Mortuary Activity

Traditional marriage rules among the Sursurunga forbade marriage within the moiety and encouraged marriage outside it; there was a preference for cross-cousin marriage. The moiety "rule" is still in place, and thirty-one out of the thirty-three marriages in Tekedan village conform to this pattern. Those individuals involved in the two anomalous marriages were required to pay a small amount of cash as compensation to their spouse's families, a practice which indicates that the exogamy prescription is still intact.[39]

The two most recent bridewealth exchanges at Tekedan village were for one hundred kina and two strands of reu, shell money valued at thirty kina per strand. The exchange of these resources takes place surreptitiously, usually at night. The de-emphasis on the exchange is bound to be remarkable to anyone who has read Highlands ethnography. One man offered that he knew of an instance in which a man dropped off a bridewealth payment while leaving the motor running in his car. Another individual offered the following explanation for this covert activity:

> If we stand up and make a big deal by giving bridewealth to another
> line, then we are doing the equivalent of shouting, "Our brother want

to screw your sister!" And nobody wants to hear that sort of thing, right?

Contrast this with marriage exchanges in the New Guinea Highlands, in which publicity—even showmanship—is a necessary feature of the exchange. I suggest that patrilineal descent understandings in the Highlands are more consistent with an emphasis on marriage and its concomitant exchanges, and that patrilineal descent and elaborate marriage exchange reinforce each other in the same ways that matrilineal descent and mortuary activity reinforce each other.

As noted earlier, in surrendering bridewealth, a man and/or his group receive rights over the woman's issue in exchange. This explanation is consistent with patrilineal understandings, since bridewealth makes biological paternity less relevant: a child is in the group of the man that surrendered resources for the woman. A woman's reproductive capacities are an important part of the image. But bridewealth in matrilineal societies is not a mirror image. Indeed, were it not for the functions of bridewealth described earlier, there would be no reason to expect the institution in a society with matrilineal descent groups. This, then, is the reason for the relative lack of attention to bridewealth where there is matriliny: there is no resources-for-children exchange.

Mortuary events, on the other hand, in which the descent group of the deceased receives goods from related descent groups, are more understandable. In patriliny, what is needed most is an uncomplicated means of social and biological reproduction for the descent group; this is normally provided by bridewealth. In matriliny, mortuary exchanges also provide for the social and biological reproduction of the matriline—after the fact. It is only after a man dies that his descent group is compensated—after the man has spent his energies providing succor and support for children of another descent group. Among the Sursurunga, this payment takes the form of a presentation of pigs known as *bingbingpul*. *Bingbingpul* pigs are presented by the lineage of the wife and children of a deceased man explicitly for the purpose of compensating the man's lineage for the "use" (my term) of his "strength" (*rakrakai*[40]). A Tekedan big-man provided this narrative:

> They [that is, the widow and her firstborn] provide money in addition [to the *bingbingpul* pig]: two kina for paying back the head of the widow, and two kina for paying back the head of the child. So, the child gets his money and with one shilling [that is, a ten or twenty toea piece] at a time he counts all the things his father has done, because *tata* ("dad") brings sugarcane, because *tata* brought water for my bath, because *tata* brought food from the bush for me to eat, because *tata*

climbed for green coconuts which I ate, because *tata* planted bananas
that I ate, for taro, yams, everything like that. The child hits them all,
and he comes with money equal to ten kina for buying the mouth with.

Why should this compensation take place after a man dies, rather than at marriage? I suggest that what a patriline gets from an incoming woman (rights to her children) is qualitatively different from what a matriline gets from an incoming man (his care for the matriline's children). An aspect of Sursurunga grammar highlights this difference.[41] Sursurunga nouns are classified as alienable or inalienable. Inalienable nouns are those which are intrinsic to other nouns: a person's character (*ninsin*), or an item's seed or insides (*pasin*). Alienable nouns, on the other hand, are those which are not inherently connected to something else: a person's dog (*kan pap*) or house (*kan rum*).

Children are classified by the Sursurunga as an inalienable noun (*natun*). The labor that a man puts forth, on the other hand, is expressed as an alienable noun (*kan him*). Thus, the Sursurunga use a grammatical system which describes the relationship between a woman and her offspring as more closely connected than a man and his labor.

Weiner, in *Inalienable Possessions,*[42] suggests that those resources which are perceived as inalienable[43] are protected and not freely given up to exchange. She notes that pigs used in exchanges such as the *moka* and *te* in the New Guinea Highlands are not seen as inalienable possessions and are therefore easily disbursed for exchange purposes. The point is that what is viewed as inalienable is more difficult to relinquish. For Sursurunga speakers, grammatical inalienability reflects the reality that some "possessions" are less easily surrendered. These less easily surrendered "possessions," being dear to their owners, would naturally require immediate rather than delayed compensation. In the case of (potential) children and labor, the former, being inalienable, exact reciprocation immediately—that is, bridewealth. Labor, distal and alienable, need not be compensated until it has been completed—that is, with mortuary payments.[44]

The foregoing is a description of the activities surrounding the death of a man. The same principles obtain in the case of a woman who dies. Among the Sursurunga—as throughout much of the matrilineal Melanesia—the widower's lineage is responsible to surrender pigs to the lineage of the deceased. Nurture is not a unilaterally masculine characteristic on New Ireland, even where it is emphasized.[45] Husbands also receive care through the labor of their wives; indeed, a Sursurunga idiom used by men for "to get married" is "to have someone cook for me."

CONCLUSION

Mortuary feast obligations, grammar, matrimoiety exogamy, and evaluations about bridewealth together form part—perhaps much—of the logic, the "reasonableness," of individuals' behavior at funerals. This behavior, ethnographically portrayed as a tendency of social institutions—matriliny, an emphasis on mortuary activity, and a de-emphasis on nuptial activity—to cohere, is an unintended sociological consequence of individual actions.

Do the Sursurunga—or anyone else—emphasize mortuary feasting because they have matrilineal descent groups, have a system of alienable and inalienable noun classes, and moiety exogamy? The answer is clearly no. Do grammar and understandings about the meaning of bridewealth combine to reinforce the social institution of mortuary payments? Clearly here, the answer is yes. Matriliny—as descent principle and complex of group actions—is an institution which is integrated culturally and sociologically for the Sursurunga.

I began this essay by suggesting that the nonnative view of matriliny need not be limited to a narrow set of descent understandings and the resulting social relations. I showed that among the Sursurunga, matrilineal social relations such as the authority of the mother's brother over lineage resources are carried on as a result of cultural understandings which, in themselves, are not descent understandings. Mortuary activities are, however, reinforced by matrilineal descent understandings in that the grammatical "rules" used by individual actors are consistent with the notion that deceased fathers' groups need to be compensated. Matrilineal principles are reinforced by mortuary activity which, among other things, distinguishes between mother's group and father's group, and which places children in the mother's group.

It is important to view matriliny as part of a larger cultural and sociological whole. Rather than treating matriliny as a list of features—the presence or absence of which are/might be empirically established—it is necessary to address how matriliny affects—and is affected by—the behavior of individuals.

NOTES

[1] Data in this paper come from research conducted with the support of the Institute for Intercultural Studies. Analysis of the data has been supported by a Kenneth and Dorothy Hill Fellowship. I am grateful to Kevin Birth, Marc Swartz, Elizabeth Throop and Donald Tuzin for their comments on early drafts. I am most indebted to the people in and around Tekedan village, New Ireland, for their hospitality and help.

[2] The plural here is a reminder that cultural systems are not monolithic sets of understandings to which all members of a group subscribe. Rather, members of the same society may share only a limited number of understandings, which makes the idea of a single point of view—native or not—somewhat spurious. See Marc J. Swartz, *The Way the World Is* (Berkeley: University of California, 1991), pp. 1–23, for a discussion of this idea.

[3] Lewis Henry Morgan, *Ancient Society* (Tucson: University of Arizona Press, 1985 [1877]).

[4] See especially chapter 2 of Melford E. Spiro, *Oedipus in the Trobriands* (Chicago: University of Chicago Press, 1982).

[5] I am thinking here especially of A.R. Radcliffe-Brown's essay "The Mother's Brother in South Africa," *South African Journal of Science* 21 (1924): 542–555.

[6] For a discussion about the theoretical implications of matriliny, see A. Bolyanatz, "Matriliny and Revisionist Anthropology," *Anthropos* (forthcoming 1995).

[7] George Peter Murdock, *Social Structure* (New York: The Free Press, 1949). See especially pp. 184–226.

[8] David M. Schneider and Kathleen Gough, *Matrilineal Kinship* (Berkeley: University of California Press, 1961). See especially Part 2; cf. also David F. Aberle, "Matrilineal Descent in Cross-Cultural Perspective," in Schneider and Gough, pp. 659–662, for a synopsis of Gough's argument.

[9] Audrey I. Richards, "Some Types of Family Structure Amongst the Central Bantu," in *African Systems of Kinship and Marriage*, A.R. Radcliffe-Brown and D. Forde, eds. (London: Oxford University Press, 1950), pp. 207–251.

[10] Schneider and Gough, op. cit., pp. 1–32.

[11] Richards, op cit., p. 211.

[12] Schneider, "Introduction," in Schneider and Gough, p. 19.

[13] Of course, both types of unilineal systems include structurally induced tensions involving consanguines and affines: marriage is the enemy of unilineal solidarity everywhere. My point here is merely that in matrilineal systems, this tension receives more attention due to its being attributed a greater role in socio-structural stresses.

[14] See Jack Goody and S. Tambiah, *Bridewealth and Dowry* (Cambridge: Cambridge University Press, 1973), pp. 2–17.

[15] It might be expected, given these functions and the incompatibility of strong marriages with matrilineal descent, that matrilineal groups would be unlikely to practice substantial bridewealth payments. The ethnographic evidence fails, however, to confirm that notion, since bridewealth exchanges can be quite prohibitive in a matrilineal society, as on New Ireland among the Barok (several hundred dollars' worth of goods and cash); Roy Wagner, *Asiwinarong* (Rutgers: Rutgers University Press, 1986), pp. 56–57.

[16] Of course, rarely are such payments strictly unilateral. Still, on the whole, wife-givers almost always end up receiving more than they give. The net result in marriage exchanges is therefore what I am referring to by the term "bridewealth."

[17] Meyer Fortes, "Introduction," pp. 1–14 in *The Developmental Cycle of Domestic Groups*, J. Goody, ed. (Cambridge: Cambridge University Press, 1971).

[18] Elsewhere, I have shown that Sursurunga prefer to reside at the husband's place, but that men's reasons for doing so are quite different from women's reasons for doing so. See A.H. Bolyanatz, "The Cultural Construction of Household Membership in Southern New Ireland," an unpublished paper read at the annual meeting of the American Anthropological Association, 1993.

[19] Murdock, op. cit., p. 68.

[20] Kathleen Gough, "The Modern Disintegration of Matrilineal Descent Groups," pp. 631–652 in *Matrilineal Kinship,* op. cit. Much of Gough's article was a discussion of the disintegration of unilineal descent groups in general.

[21] But matriliny is also seen to have some advantages, as Mary Douglas, "Is Matriliny Doomed in Africa?" in *Man in Africa,* M. Douglas and P.M. Kaberry, eds. (London: Tavistock, 1969), pp. 121–136; and Michael Allen, "Rethinking Old Problems: Matriliny, Secret Societies and Political Evolution," in *Vanuatu,* M. Allen, ed. (Sydney: Academic Press, 1981), pp. 9–34; "Elders, Chiefs and Big Men: Authority, Legitimation and Political Evolution in Melanesia," *American Ethnologist,* 11 (1984): 20–41, have pointed out. Still, these advantages are articulated within the approach of Standard Matrilineal Theory.

[22] Gough, op. cit., p. 632. Gough's emphasis on the centrality of land inheritance is probably at least partially due to her Marxist orientation and the concomitant primary of the mode of production. Other evidences that she offers for the decline of matriliny are conflict among the Tonga (ibid., p. 631), and the use of cash within the nuclear family among the Ndembu (ibid., p. 632).

[23] Ibid.; Chie Nakane, *Garo and Khasi: A Comparative Study of Matrilineal Systems* (Paris and The Hague: Mouton, 1967).

[24] Jill Nash, *Matriliny and Modernisation: The Nagovisi of South Bougainville,* The New Guinea Research Bulletin, No. 55 (Canberra: Australia National University Press, 1974).

[25] Annette Weiner, *Women of Value, Men of Reknown* (Austin: University of Texas Press, 1976).

[26] Juliana Flinn, "Matriliny Without Conflict: The Case of the Pulap," *Journal of the Polynesian Society* 95 (1886): 221–238.

[27] Nancy Levine, "Fathers and Sons: Kinship Value and Validation in Tibetan Polyandry," *Man* 22 (N.S.) (1987): 267–286.

[28] Ibid., p. 270.

[29] Ibid., 271. For a sociobiological perspective on patrifiliation and matrilineal descent, see, for example, John Hartung, "Matrilineal Inheritance: New Theory and Analysis," *Behavioral and Brain Sciences* 8 (1985): 661–670; and Arthur M. Diamond and Luis Locay, "Investment in Sister's Children as Behavior Towards Risk," *Economic Inquiry* 27 (1989): 719–732.

[30] Matrilineal understandings have their roots in human physiology in ways that patrilineal understandings do not. While this is not the only reason for the perseverance of matrilineal understandings, I suggest that, *qua* understandings, matriliny will be retained even if a matrilineal descent group finds itself with only few or insignificant sociological functions. In this vein, Allen argued that matrilineal principles are less "flexible" than their patrilineal counterparts (op. cit. [1984]: 27ff.), since agnation is less demonstrable than enation. Part of this "inflexibility," I am arguing, is a perceptual-cognitive resistance to change in descent understandings: people are born of women; that they are no longer to be considered part of their mother's group is counterintuitive.

[31] Glenn Petersen, "Ponapean Matriliny: Production, Exchange, and the Ties That Bind," *American Ethnologist* 9 (1982): 129–144.

[32] Mervyn Meggitt, *The Lineage System of the Mae-Enga* (New York: Barnes & Noble, 1965).

[33] I do not mean to suggest that the matrilineage has nothing to do with the transfer of land. Traditionally, land was passed through the matrilineage. But apparently, land was also at times acquired through other means—*viz.,* from the father's side—without the "disintegration" of the matrilineage or of matrilineal understandings.

[34] Op. cit., p. 638; emphasis added.

[35] Douglas L. Oliver. "Rivers (W.H.R.) Revisited: Matriliny in Southern Bourgainville," *Pacific Studies* 16(3):1–54, 16(4)(1993): 1–40.

[36] A lineage (matri- or patri-) is normally defined as a group of people who can actually trace their genealogical connections to each other: they know who the common ancestor is. A clan is normally defined as a group of people who presume, but cannot demonstrate, the genealogical connection. A moiety is a "half." Many societies break themselves into halves for various purposes. Moieties are not necessarily descent groups, although they often are. A matri- (or patri-) moiety is a descent-based "half" of a society. Normally (as among the Sursurunga) half of the clans are in one moiety and the other half are in the other. Marriage must take place to someone in the other moiety, which is one reason why the moiety distinction is significant.

[37] Among the Sursurunga, the shift from avunculocality to patrivirilocality (accomplished by around 1950) has been accompanied by the possibility and the realization of the acquisition of land and other resources via the patrifilial link.

[38] During the fieldwork period, one Papua New Guinea kina was worth about U.S.$1.05.

[39] Older informants say that before European contact, such marriages, known as *yom*, were punishable by death.

[40] *Rakrakai* is a verb, rather than a noun as I have represented it here. The "use" of a person's *rakrakai* is the best gloss for the expression, "A *rakrakai*," or "he/she/it strongs."

[41] Recent work shows that grammar does have behavioral concomitants. See John Luey, *Grammatical Categories and Cognition: A Case Study of the Linguistic Relativity Hypothesis* (Cambridge: University Press, 1993); *Language Diversity and Thought: A Reformulation of the Linguistic Relativity Hypothesis* (Cambridge University Press, 1993).

[42] Annette Weiner, *Inalienable Possessions* (Berkeley: University of California Press, 1991).

[43] Weiner's use of "inalienable" and "alienable" follows Mauss. She does note Marx's notion of alienation but fails to mention the linguistic classifications noted here. One must be extremely careful not to conflate the terms and assume that Marx, Mauss, and linguists are all referring to the same thing. On the other hand, this homonymic circumstance serves as a reminder that there may be linkages between the concepts, as I shall try to make clear. Unless noted otherwise, my use of "inalienable" and "alienable" will be in their grammatical sense.

[44] Lepowsky argues that this recognition of the father's descent group is the solution to the matrilineal puzzle on Vanatirai (Maria Lepowsky, *Fruit of the Motherland* ([New York: Columbia University Press, 1993, p. 299]). But to the degree that the matrilineal puzzle entails tension and strain it is not clear that such exchanges seem to reduce anxiety.

[45] See, for example, Brenda Johnson Clay, *Pinikindu* (Chicago: University of Chicago Press, 1977).

Part Two

Women's Perspectives on Kinship

Christiane Klapisch-Zuber opens this section with an analysis of a rare and intriguing document—a genealogy dating from fourteenth-century Florence which, although like most such documents from this era was written by a man, bears traces of the influence of a female informant. By comparing this genealogy with those more typical of this strongly patrilineal society, Klapisch-Zuber uncovers clues to gender differences in mental maps of kinship. Her analysis suggests creative ways of using historical documentation to get at questions of women's identities and perspectives even in kinship systems that suppress or subordinate them.

5

Family Trees and the Construction of Kinship in Renaissance Italy

CHRISTIANE KLAPISCH-ZUBER

Historians and ethnographers have long known that a genealogy is a construction, and that what it sets up is a fiction. The fiction, however, is not arbitrary, but rather reveals, through the web of relationships it represents as real, the constraints, exclusions and solidarities of a kinship system that is actually played out on a social stage.

Genealogical works, like all historical works, are influenced by the authors' relationship to their own familial and social contexts. Such "interferences" are particularly evident in genealogy, because the genealogist is intimately involved with the objects of analysis; thus, the genealogist projects onto those described—the living, and, even more, the dead—the affections, tensions and conflicts with which he or she lives in the present. This suggests that the relationships between men and women as they are prescribed, codified and subjectively experienced within a society play a significant role in the elaboration of a genealogy and in the way it depicts kin relationships. In this essay, I attempt to determine whether the way in which genealogists view their universe of kin is influenced by the gender relationships predominant in their society—in this case the Florentine society of the last centuries of the Middle Ages—and also whether this perspective varies significantly with the gender of the author.

Permission to publish granted by the board of *Quaderni storici*.

The Construction of Genealogical Accounts in Fourteenth- and Fifteenth-Century Florence

The image Florentines had of their familial group can be reconstructed through their genealogies, as documented in the so-called *libri di famiglia*.[1] The Florentines to whom I refer here belong to the wealthy, indeed often to the uppermost strata of the urban classes, and the model which I propose is class specific. The genealogical consciousness of the lower urban classes and that of the rural masses is very difficult to determine. The only available sources are testimonies from religious and secular judicial records, and because the genealogical discourse one encounters in such testimonies is cast in the particular framework of the courts, it may not represent how people actually thought about their families and kin networks. In contrast, the *libri di famiglia* were composed by men who spontaneously embarked upon the genealogical adventure. They thus reflect a more or less disinterested concern for recognition, social justification or the transmission of information to descendants. Relying on copious written material preserved in public and private archives, these genealogists also made oral inquiries of the elders of their lineages.[2] The genealogies commonly consisted of a series of male names whose filiation the author indicated through graphic signs—a line or a brace— that together outlined a genealogical diagram of descent or membership within the same group of brothers. These nominal descriptions moved from the common ancestor to a group of descendants. They mapped the transmission of the identity that was the basis of membership in a *casa* (house) and in a lineage through the male line. Kinship thus centered on men linked together by blood and common interest, and it conferred upon them the signs—hereditary name, coats of arms, and so on—of a collective identity.

These particular genealogies included very few, if any, women. When Giovanni Rucellai drew up his account of ancestors in 1457, he cited 149 first names, all male, through eleven generations.[3] Similarly, the genealogists Neri Strinati degli Alfieri, Matteo Palmieri and the anonymous Tornaquinci were also completely silent about the women who were born into or entered their "houses" through marriage.[4]

The rare occasions when women are included in the genealogy suggest reasons for their more usual exclusion. Lapo da Castiglionchio, for example, reported around 1370 the names of two paternal great-great-aunts for the single reason that these women, as heiresses to their father, had transmitted the rights to the patronage of a church to their husbands' families.[5] Similarly, Doffo Spini mentioned two female cousins who belonged to another branch of his lineage; the first, whose name he did not even give, is alluded to because she was the only survivor of a very large family which had at one time numbered twelve sons; the second had a somewhat more controversial legacy. It was noted that she was the heir to her father, "to his own shame and that of his memory, and to the ruin of the house of Spini and in particular of his own (that is, the father's) branch."[6] These examples draw attention to the exceptional character of women as heiresses. Although local statutes severely restricted the naming of female heirs, they did acknowledge it as a legal possibility. Nevertheless, such an act was generally redolent of scandal in a system of succession which reserved the fundamental role in the transmission of patrimony for male agnates. Female heirs aroused the indignation of the men of their family of origin because their marriages posed the risk of alienating the patrimony of the "house." As a result, it is not surprising that most Florentine genealogical reconstructions of this period scarcely concern themselves with the daughters and sisters who left the family in order to marry.

A second group of genealogies was compiled by authors such as Niccolo Busini and Giovanni Corsini, who did not, *a priori*, ignore the women to whom they were related by blood. However, of the total number of individuals whom Busini and Corsini cite as born into their lineage only thirteen to eighteen percent have female names.[7] Giovanni Morelli and Lapo Niccolini named a higher proportion of women, still only twenty-five to twenty-six percent. But neither Morelli nor Niccolini was very informative about the women born into their families prior to their fathers' generation.

Women were less and less visible the further back the generations were traced. Yet they were hardly more noticeable in the generations following that of the narrator, where imbalances existed between recorded numbers of daughters and sons. Giovanni Morelli, for instance, cited only one daughter for every two sons, while Lapo Niccolini "forgot" to mention three of his own daughters in his preliminary genealogical account.[8] The first case suggests the logic of exclusion: once again, due to the probability of their "marrying out," daughters were not integrated into the account.[9] "I will speak of them only when they will have reached the age to be given to a spouse," wrote Morelli, without worrying about the fact that he, like Niccolini, would be likely to forget his daughters by that time because they would have left the "casa."

Women appeared in significant numbers only when the narrator extended his inquiry to marital alliances, that is, when he included daughters and sisters who were given in marriage in addition to wives who were received from other "houses." Among such exceptional narrators were Donato Velluti (around 1370) and Buonaccorso Pitti (of the following generation). Their inclusion of women hinged more on their concern with delineating the role alliances with other houses played in their respective family's fortune than on any desire for genealogical completeness. This, however, did not imply that they devoted equal attention to sons and daughters. Thirty-two percent of the paternal kin Velluti mentioned were women, while Pitti included forty percent.[10] Both displayed a lack of interest in the wives and daughters of slightly more distant ancestors; Velluti's genealogical endeavor, for example, did not include large numbers of female blood relatives until his father's generation, and he could not even determine whether one aunt was a sister of his father or of his grandfather.

The most common attitude among Florentines who otherwise took pride in their ancestry was to throw up their hands when faced with the task of reconstructing the network of kin on the female side. Lapo da Castiglionchio expressed that frustration very vividly when he wrote: "It would now be appropriate to speak about alliances which we have formed by giving some of our women to others. But I see that this work will grow too large; thus, I will move on and will talk only about the rest of us in detail." In effect, he limited his mention to the alliances formed through his four sisters.[11]

Giovanni Rucellai, who returned to his genealogical enterprise twenty years after the compilation of an exclusively male genealogy, attempted a thorough accounting of the daughters "who entered or left the house," and, in so doing, "drew in… half of the town," literally hundreds of affines and kin acquired through marriage alliances.[12] The magnitude of a search of this type intimidated genealogists and contributed to the fact that much genealogical work was schemata where sons and daughters found only paternal ancestors or cousins. These schemata were predominantly male and offered no positive female figures (indeed, the only women mentioned are those who transgressed one or another norm of "the house").[13]

If we concede that in these genealogies, which typically limit themselves to describing the male skeleton of the *casa*, the memory of the women *entrate* or *uscite* (having entered or exited) is neglected and hidden rather than denied or obliterated entirely, it is then very difficult for us to judge from the evidence the extent and consistency of male recollections about wives' ancestors and, even more, about the descendants of their own sisters. While some genealogists indicated that they interviewed elderly female kin—women in their families who had preserved the memory of facts which their male informants had indubitably forgotten or to which they did not attach any importance[14]—they generally refrained from explicitly attributing any such accounts to their female informants. If there was a sort of dormant memory of female kin which passed into written records in only a scanty, indirect and partial fashion, we have lost its origin, restricted as we are to the unilateral and partial reconstructions which the *paters familias* left us in their books.

This type of genealogical reconstruction, then, limited itself to the description of the male lines through which the identity of the lineage was transmitted. Women were excluded from both the process of identity transfer and its documentation. This did not mean, however, that the alliances and the kin acquired through female relatives were of no interest to these men. They were very conscious of the important role women played in the biological and social survival of their kin group. Yet they must have realized—faced with the difficulty of the task at hand— the different quality of the work involved in remembering women.

In sum, we cannot attribute to the citizens of fourteenth- and fifteenth-century Florence an exclusively patrilineal concept of kinship ties. Their awareness of the usefulness and necessity of alliances occasionally involved them in explorations which clearly attest to the contrary. Still, the fact that they could be satisfied with an entirely unilateral presentation must not be underestimated. Such a presentation undoubtedly corresponded to an order of priority in the classification of kinship. The people with whom one was connected through marriage ("affines") had an undeniable effect upon the social and political status and strategies of both individual and kin group; but patrilineal blood relatives remained the mainstay of fundamental identity.

The Da Lutiano Genealogy: An Exceptional Case

Were women confined to a specific vision of their familial attachments? Only one precious text remains which allows us to consider this question. Written shortly after the Black Death, it is the record of a mother's responses to her son's questions about the history and genealogy of their family.[15] In 1366, this son, ser Lorenzo da Lutiano, a notary living in Florence, devoted the beginning of his *breve memoriale* to a description of his family's past. In doing so, he emulated a long-standing Florentine tradition, and the way in which he justified his effort was equally characteristic. Because he had seen "all the elders of [his] house die one after another, and because [he was] not informed about its ancient alliances," he decided to embrace the genealogical task himself.

The Da Lutianos were a family of feudal origin which experienced a rapid decline during the second half of the fourteenth century. Originally from Mugello, in the countryside north of Florence, and claiming themselves united through the ties of *consorteria* (and probably of kinship) with the great Ubaldini family, they were a family loyal to Florence. What is particularly interesting about ser Lorenzo's

105

genealogical account is that he deliberately enlisted and acknowledged the help of his eighty-year-old mother and his elder brother, ser Francesco.

Why, we might ask, did ser Lorenzo turn to his mother for information? Significantly, ser Lorenzo's family could claim a feature that was rather rare in Florence: his mother, Monna Gemma, belonged to the lineage of Da Lutiano by birth as well as marriage. The precise genealogical link between the two branches from which the parents of ser Lorenzo descended cannot be discerned from his *memoriale* but it surely was more distant than the third degree if one computed by canon law. The Da Lutiano lineage on his mother's side could only be traced back two generations before Monna Gemma. On the paternal side, it extended to three generations prior to ser Lorenzo's father. Nevertheless, due to the combined genealogical memory of our three informants, the family lineage could be mapped even further back. While he intermittently acknowledged his inability to specify the genealogical tie, ser Lorenzo at the same time placed this undetermined kinship at the fifth degree, again presumably according to canon law.[16]

As he announced in his preamble, ser Lorenzo intended only to retrieve and record in his book the *parentadi*—that is, the marital alliances of his "house." So exclusive an intention is distinct from the common motivations of his contemporaries or of the genealogists of previous and succeeding generations, who first and foremost wished to establish the blood ties within their *casa*, and only secondarily concerned themselves with relationships acquired through marriage.

About fifteen lineages thus appear in the memoir of our notary. Some recur at several points in his narrative, implying an alliance strategy which privileged only a small number of families. It is not always easy to comprehend the circumvolutions of Monna Gemma's tale. In one place, for example, her son noted that "the Florentine merchant Amadore, son of Nuto, was [the] son of a Da Lutiano, Troppa (paternal great-aunt of ser Lorenzo); his brother-in-law Bizzo the elder, father of Martino, married his sister Tessa with whom he has a son, another Bizzo, himself father of a Tessa, married to Francesco, son of messire Guido dalla Collina." Ten people and no less than four allied families are evoked in this tortured passage, and the reader will notice how the writer (or his female informant) refrained from giving priority to the bonds of paternity over those of marriage.

Given the nature of most Florentine genealogies, the fact that ser Lorenzo compiled information on those families with which the Da Lutiano allied themselves is particularly striking. This choice predictably resulted in an unequal balance between both patrilateral and matrilateral blood relatives on the one hand, and between blood relatives and relations by marriage on the other. Among a total of 133 named persons, the memoir of ser Lorenzo da Lutiano mentions the names of only twenty-eight Da Lutianos; twelve of them in the paternal and maternal lines are women. In contrast, the memoir enumerates a good one hundred relatives by marriage and cousins belonging to other lineages, twenty of whom were women. On Monna Gemma's side of the family, the forty-one people cited include seven women, a distinct minority, but a significant one in view of contemporary genealogical constructs. Gemma remembered parallel patrilateral cousins and their descendants, a female second cousin, some children of paternal aunts and great-aunts, as well as the names of her mother's male and female cousins and their children.

Even more astonishing, we catch ser Lorenzo, captivated by the logic of alliance, giving priority to women over their fathers and spouses. Indeed, in an inversion of the conventional order, his genealogy provides us with information about patrilateral blood relations only when it is required in order to situate the women who were the pivotal figures of the alliances. The enumeration of the groups of blood relations and affines revolved around these women. Ser Lorenzo's genealogical discourse valued them because they served as the nodal points for both sides of the lineage and thus made it possible to understand the web of interrelated families.

Let us take a closer look at this unusual narrative. Even if the rather small number of women mentioned does not wholly contradict the masculine/patrilineal focus of the general corpus of Florentine genealogies, certain aspects of women's position in this particular genealogy are unique. A distinctive aspect of the Da Lutianos' work of memory is that the information transcribed by ser Lorenzo so often mapped the lines of filiation by introducing the female links. Moreover, the exploration proceeded as often from descendants as from ancestors. In general, when genealogists wished to describe an affinal relationship, they began by describing the woman who was the instrument of the matrimonial alliance. This was the case in ser Lorenzo's account, as it was in the memoirs of Velluti, Pitti and Morelli. But, at least as often, ser Lorenzo started from a group of his cousins and then retraced the woman (born a Da Lutiano) who was the basis of their shared kinship. Such a strategy is very rare among the ordinary genealogies of Florentines, which typically proceed from parents to children.

The evidence suggests that maternal kin were of keen interest to ser Lorenzo's female informant. The paternal lineage of such remote cousins as the Bordoni, for example, did not engage his mother's attention. Rather, it was their maternal line, the Signorelli, which she traced back to the important ancestress, Tosa, a Da Lutiano by birth. As for the name of Tosa's husband, Monna Gemma simply left it out. She repeated the slight in the case of two other women, whom she also endowed with anonymous husbands—a scandalous heresy for run-of-the-mill Florentine genealogists!

Worse yet, on one occasion she evoked a line of filiation that was exclusively female. Starting with a certain Giovanni di Donato Albertini dal Borgo, the narrative moves to his mother Ghita, then in turn to her mother Tessa (whose husband Monna Gemma did not even mention) and finally to the great-grandmother Dalagia, who was born a Da Lutiano. The line then descends through Dalagia's husband Rigo to his son, who was also the brother of Tessa. To pursue the series of these three women—members, by marriage, of three different lineages—and then to add the sister of the eldest, several generations back, is an absolutely exceptional approach in Florentine family memoirs.

Two observations need to be made in conclusion. In the Da Lutiano narrative we see pushed to its limit the tendency to fix women as the nodal points of genealogical development. To this end, ser Lorenzo's memoirs employed a technique analogous to that which the church recommended for determining the degree of kinship between potential spouses. Additionally, the memoir's emphasis was not a gendered one: it did not matter so much whether it was men or women who were situated on the line which one traced back to a common ancestor; indeed, the relationship passed as much through the one as through the other. Such an egalitarian approach contrasted with the patrilineal customs more typical of Florentine genealogy.

Gendered Constructions of Kinship?
Discussion and Conclusions

The exceptional character of ser Lorenzo's genealogical strategy raises two sets of problems, one concerning method, the other concerning interpretation. First and foremost, can we attribute these memories and the female focus of the account to Monna Gemma alone? I can draw a few cautious conclusions. Ser Lorenzo also interviewed his older brother, ser Francesco, and we cannot distinguish between the memories of the brother and the mother because the writer did not do so himself. The contributions of the brother and ser Lorenzo himself (who corroborated the maternal tale with his own childhood memories) would surely undermine the conclusion that this text relates an exclusively female memory. Yet the general organization of the narrative and the frequent evocation of Monna Gemma's cousins and those of her mother suggest that the old woman played a key role in the construction of the text. In the very meanderings of the genealogical itinerary laid out by ser Lorenzo, in its reversals of direction, its sudden leaps between generations or lines, and in its lacunae, we can perhaps hear the utterances of a halting memory that sometimes acknowledges its gaps but stubbornly reties the weft threads of a fabric whose design is her own.

Even if we accept the hypothesis of a predominant feminine voice in this memoir, we still need to interpret this difficult text, and determine whether we can speak of a specifically female way of retaining the memory of kinship. Led by her memories and her affections, the eighty-year-old woman pursued the intersecting lines of filiation without letting her genealogical musings be trapped by the rigid form characteristic of male genealogists. The genealogical compilations of a contemporary, such as Donato Velluti, or of a younger man, such as Buonaccorso Pitti, offer rich descriptions of women and marital kin. The genealogy Monna Gemma "dictated" to ser Lorenzo, on the other hand, distinguishes itself from those of Velluti and Pitti in several respects. In the first place, the nodal points are not uniquely comprised of males who belong to the lineage of the genealogist, and whose marriages invite secondary descriptions of wives' kin. Nor are the women in the genealogy limited to daughters or sisters given in marriage: the often remote female kin of the female narrator, descending from or belonging to other lineages, feature prominently. Moreover, the point of departure is frequently a cousin or a group of cousins whose lines are then traced back to a common ancestor. Finally, in following these lines, the genealogy does not eliminate the female ancestors through whom the kinship with the Da Lutianos was passed on. It gives these women a distinct priority over their husbands, whom the narrative order of the tale places in a secondary or subordinate position. The result is an image of an undifferentiated kinship system, of a cognatic group conforming to the teachings of the church.

This information takes on additional importance in the light of evidence from other sources. Contemporary female wills, for example, generally reveal a more open range of relations and illuminate the more varied ways in which a female testator maintained affective bonds with kin of both sexes through her bequests, as opposed to the more restricted legacies of her male counterparts.[17] Memorial masses for the dead requested by women embraced both immediate and more distant relatives, and thus suggested wider ties of kinship than those implied by male requests. Men, in this respect, were loyal only to the ties of conjugality and lineage.[18] Finally, what we know of female patronage (such as that exercised by the spouses of exiled Florentine envoys) reveals that they manipulated kinship ties of all kinds in order to manage complex family life.[19] Why would a woman like Monna Gemma store in her memory information that was erased by men unless because, in everyday life as well as in the representation of her bonds, she must vacillate between two poles—the family of birth and that of marriage—which organize and also disrupt the lives of women? The different perception and usage of kinship relations we see in this text suggest a specific vision of the whole as well as particular cognitive processes in its reconstruction.

Compensating for their precarious situation at the heart of the familial fabric by resorting to a more open and less formal network of kinship than the male network,[20] women experienced and remembered a kinship forming a diffuse whole, indefinite in its contours and different from that which was organized through the agnatic lineages claimed by the men. In short, we find here a set of relations centered on the *ego*, a system which recalls the open bilateral groups of the high Middle Ages, frequently described before the patrilineal lineage was consolidated. A woman certainly did not represent her kin as a matrilineal group in crude opposition to a patrilineal representation characteristic of men. It is clear that our female informant does not reject bonds of blood which derive from birth; but neither does she privilege those put in place by the patrilineal filiation to which the male genealogists confer a sort of permanence in their austere enumerations of ancestors and of kin. The men of the time furthermore feared that a woman might preserve too vivid a memory of her kin by birth and claim it in order to defy her husband. In his *Corbaccio*, Boccaccio elaborates, to the point of caricature, the kin ties about which the abusive wife could brag.[21] In bringing to the surface of consciousness the kin relations and the affections based on kin with and through women, old Monna Gemma deviates noticeably from the unilateral connotations introduced into the genealogies by male solidarities.

I will certainly not conclude from this text that male and female approaches to kinship are radically opposed to one another. Insofar as his book allows us to speculate, ser Lorenzo, the instigator of the memory work of his mother, accepts her propositions and does not claim to have corrected them. On her part, Monna Gemma adopts with a good grace the framework for her recollections which her son proposes to her. She limits herself, for the most part, to detailing the marital alliances undertaken around her and the kin she herself or her children thus acquired. No contradiction between mother and son emerges when it comes to describing marital alliances and affinal kin.

The old woman appears to us, from this point of view, as a good witness of women's appropriation of the mechanisms of marriage alliances. Numerous texts present matrons in the unacknowledged but essential role as advisors in the choice of spouse and throughout the marriage negotiations. While young women remain passive instruments of alliances between families, adult and married women discuss among themselves and with their men not only the technical details pertaining to the constitution of the trousseau and the observation of rituals, but also the qualities and disadvantages of the parties to the marriage, that is to say, all aspects of matrimonial strategies.[22]

Such findings point to the conclusion that women accepted and internalized the rules and constraints which governed Florentine alliances. Indeed, the female parishioners of the Counter-Reformation would be the best guarantors of the Christian institution of marriage, of its virtue as well as its diffusion. From the end of the Middle Ages, urban Italian society carried the seeds of female responsibility for both the sacred and secular bonds of matrimony. Moreover, women's inclination to consider kinship in all its manifold aspects and dimensions may lie in a greater openness towards the teachings of the church. The example of Monna Gemma strongly suggests that women had adopted the church's notion of undifferentiated kinship.

By preserving in written form all the memorable women of her recollections, Monna Gemma offers us a glimpse into a memory of kinship too often concealed. Singular and provocative, this text preserves an engaging and vital counterbalance to male writings. The latter, by far more numerous and confident in their analytical scheme, reflect cohesive familial identities rooted in bonds of prestige and social utility. The former, on the contrary, offers a somewhat shaky image of a universe of divided kinship, balanced between alternating loyalties, constantly reshaped: the world of women for whom birth and alliance not only signified the trappings and benefits of power, but presaged uncertainty and imminent dislocation as well.

Notes

[1] I have provided a list in "Les généalogies florentines du XIVè et du XVè siècle," in G. Delille, ed., *Le modele familial européen. Normes, déviances, contrôle du pouvoir* (Paris, Rome: 1986), pp. 101–131. Reprinted in *La maison et le nom. Stratégies et rituels dans l'Italie de la Renaissance* (Paris: Ed. EHESS, 1990), pp. 37–58. Also "L'aieul des généalogies toscanes," *Annales de démographie historique* (1991): 103–112. F.W. Kent has recently presented an excellent perspective on the problems of the patrician family. F.W. Kent, "La famiglia patrizia fiorentina nel Quattrocento. Nuovi orientamenti nella storiografia recente," in *Palazzo Strozzi. Metà millennio. 1489–1989* (Rome: Istituto della Enciclopedia Italiana, 1991), pp. 70–91. An expanded version of this paper has been published in Italian. See Christiane Klapisch-Zuber, "Albero genealogico e costruzione della parentela nel Rinascimento," *Quaderni storici* 86(2) (1994), pp. 405–420.

[2] Christiane Klapisch-Zuber, "L'invention du passé familial" (1983), in *La maison et le nom*, pp. 19–35.

[3] *Giovanni Rucellai ed il suo Zibaldone*, I: *Il Zibaldone quaresimale*, A. Perosa, ed. (London: The Warburg Institute, 1960), xxi (the genealogy can be found on f lr–2v of the manuscript).

[4] Neri di Alfieri degli Strinati, *Cronichetta* (beginning of the fourteenth century), Florence, 1753. Biblioteca Riccardiana, Florence, Manoscritti 1885, *Memorie della famiglia Tornaquinci* (1376). Archivio di Stato, Florence (ASF), Acquisti e doni 7 (Ricordanze di messer Matteo di Marco Palmieri, 1427–1473).

[5] Lapo da Castiglionchio, *Epistola o sia ragionamento di messer Lapo da C...*, L. Mehus, ed. (Bologna: 1753), p. 53.

[6] *"in verghongna di se e di sua memoria e disfacimento della casa degli Spini et spezialmente del suo lato,"* ASF, *Strozziane*, II, 13, f 16v (1416).

[7] ASF, *Strozz.*, ser. II, 563 et 564 (Ricordanze di Niccolo del Buono di Bese Busini, 1393–1406 and 1400–1413). *Il libro di ricordanze dei Corsini, 1362–1457*, A. Petrucci, ed. (Rome: 1965).

[8] He did, however, register their births and destinies elsewhere in his book. L. Niccolini, *Il libro*, p. 58 and passim.

[9] Giovanni di Pagolo Morelli, *Ricordi*, V. Branca, ed. (Florence: 1956; reedited in *Mercanti scrittori*, V. Branca, ed. [Milan, Rusconi: 1986], pp. 101–339). Lapo di Giovanni Niccolini dei Stirigatti, *Il libro degli affari proprii di casa de...*, Ch. Bec, ed. (Paris: 1969).

[10] Donato Velluti, *La Cronica domestica di messer D.V. scritta fra il 1367 e il 1370, con le addizioni di Paolo Velluti scritte fra il 1555 e il 1560*, I, Del Lungo and G.Volpe, eds. (Florence: 1914), pp. 74–75. Buonaccorso Pitti, *Cronica*, A. Bacchi della Lega, ed. (Bologna, 1905); new edition in *Mercanti scrittori*, Branca, ed., pp. 341–503.

[11] *"Voleva ora dire de' parentadi fatti per noi dando delle nostre donne ad altrui, ma veggio che l'opera cresce troppo: e pero passero, e diro pure di noi propio,"* *Epistola*, p. 57.

[12] F.W. Kent, "The Making of a Renaissance Patron of the Arts," in F. Kent, A. Perosa, et al., *Giovanni Rucellai ed il suo Zibaldone. 2. A Florentine patrician and his palace*, Studies of the Warburg Institute, 24–21 (London: 1981), p. 91. The first genealogy was created in 1457; the first description of alliances—inserted in his only grand-paternal line—was created in 1476.

[13] It is necessary to underscore that the Florentines' procedure of inquiry into the labyrinth of families allied through marriage followed a course entirely analogous to the one they observed when they limited themselves to mentioning the men of the lineage. They always started from a blood relative and his spouse, or from a sister given in marriage and her spouse. After that they moved to the father and mother of the spouse, then to brothers and sisters, and eventually their alliances and descendants. In other words, the genealogist moved down the lines of filiation following the model he adopted for the description of his own "house": he simply added the women to it.

[14] "L'invention du passé familial," p. 22.

[15] *"Cronica ovvero Memorie attenenti alla nobilissima famiglia de' Signori da Lutiano, estratte da un libro manoscritto intitulato Spogli di scritture antiche, esistente appresso i Signori Rosselli giá del Turco, aggiuntevi alcune annotazioni,"* in Giuseppe Maria Brocchi, *Descrizione della provincia del Mugello* (Florence: Albizzini, 1748). The genealogical memories occupy the pages 3–16 in the "Cronica"; diverse accounts follow.

[16] For information on the practice of computing kinship among the fifteenth-century Florentine laity, see my "Kinship and Politics in Fourteenth-Century Florence," in *The Family in Italy from Antiquity to the Present*, ed. David I. Kertzer and Richard P. Saller (New Haven/London: Yale University Press, 1991), pp. 208–228.

[17] See S. Chojnacki's work, in particular "Dowries and Kinsmen in Early Renaissance Venice," *Journal of Interdisciplinary History*, IV (1975), pp. 571–600. Also Heather Gregory, "Daughters, Dowries and the Family in Fifteenth Century Florence," *Rinascimento*, 2e ser., XXVII (1987), pp. 215–237.

[18] Sharon Strocchia, "Remembering the Family: Women, Kin and Commemorative Masses in Renaissance Florence," *Renaissance Quarterly*, XLII (1989), pp. 635–654.

[19] S.K. Foster, *The Ties that Bind: Kinship Association and Marriage in the Alberti Family*,

1378–1428, Ph.D. dissertation, University of Michigan at Ann Arbor, University microfilms, 1985. H. Gregory, *A Florentine Family in Crisis: The Strozzi in the Fifteenth Century*, Ph.D. dissertation, University of London, 1988.

[20] S. Strocchia, "La Famiglia patrizia fiorentina nel secolo XV: la problematica della donna," *Palazzo Strozzi. Metà milennio 1489–1989* (Rome:

Istituto della Enciclopedia Italiana, 1991), pp. 126–137, csp. p. 135.

[21] Giovanni Boccaccio, *Corbaccio*, a c. di P.D. Ricci (Turin, Einaudi, 1977 [Classici Ricciardi]). pp. 46–47, 61–62.

[22] See the works by Foster and Gregory cited above. Also, Lorenzo Fabbri, *Alleanza matrimoniale e patriziato nella Firenze del 400. Studio sulla famiglia Strozzi* (Florence, Olschki, 1991).

Lucia Ferrante's essay works nicely with Christiane Klapisch-Zuber's to highlight the dynamics of changing gender and kinship patterns in a particular region. She also studies urban northern Italy, in particular sixteenth-century Bologna. But in contrast to Klapisch-Zuber, she was able to find relatively direct evidence of female perspectives and strategies regarding marriage. By the period of Ferrante's study, the Catholic Church had begun to intervene more forcefully in family decisions about marriage. Ferrante uses church court records of cases of marriage litigation to document the clash between the private law enforced by powerful patrilineal clans and ecclesiastical law. She finds evidence of women using the church authority and institutions to support their own preferences as opposed to those of their fathers. Read alongside Klapisch-Zuber's essay, Ferrante's study also points to the role of changing political contexts (in this case the centuries-long struggle of the Catholic Church with secular political powers) in the evolution of kinship systems.

6

Marriage and Women's Subjectivity in a Patrilineal System: The Case of Early Modern Bologna

Lucia Ferrante

In a patrilineal society such as that of Bologna in the sixteenth century, marriage occupied a position of fundamental importance. It was the institution which ensured the legitimate transmission of possessions, and thus power, from one generation of males to the next. The entire inheritance went to the sons, minus the considerably smaller share used to endow daughters, either for marriage or the nunnery.[1] Thus choosing a wife for a son was a crucial moment for the entire family, since an error could compromise the destiny of the family both economically and politically. Yet care also had to be taken in choosing a husband for a daughter, because in this case there was the risk of squandering a precious resource, the young woman's reproductive capacity, and creating interfamily relationships which could ruin the family's prestige. In any case, it was necessary to aim for a union between economic and social equals, a need felt by peasants and craftsmen as well as upper-class families.

It is logical to assume that in a period when the recognition of individuality was not very fashionable, family clans paid little attention to their young folks' desires when deciding whom they should marry. On the other hand, the church had for centuries been fighting a battle against the secular conception of matrimony, in the name of values which had nothing to do with questions of succession but instead had the aim of imposing its control on a moment of such importance in the life of the faithful.[2] This struggle was the context for two church regulations, one firmly established in the sixteenth century, whereby matrimony had to be the result of free will of those contracting it, and another according to which so-called clandestine marriages (marriages contracted without "benefit of clergy," with no witnesses or publication of the banns) were considered valid.[3] On the one hand, then, we have strict family control with the unique aim of maintaining a patrilineal society, on the other extremely liberal ecclesiastical regulations. This is the context within which we shall investigate how the subjectivity of individuals came to be expressed, and how gender differences shaped these responses.

Cases of Marital Conflict

The sources used for this study are case records, preserved in the "Matrimonia" (Marriages) section of the Archiepiscopal Archives of Bologna, for approximately twenty years before the Council of Trent in 1563, which promulgated a new discipline regarding matrimony. The records concern the geographical area of jurisdiction of the ecclesiastical tribunal, that is, Bologna and its diocese.[4] The case records in question were unclassified. I had to divide them into categories which I judged would reflect the nature of the conflicts involved and still enable me to group together the greatest number of trials. The four categories I derived are breach of promise to marry, annulment, separation and bigamy.[5]

In my quantitative analysis of the trials I have identified three parties: the plaintiff; the party apparently responsible for the termination of the relationship (sometimes the defendant, sometimes the plaintiff); and the winning party in the lawsuit. I have also attempted to quantify the place of origin of the couple. In every

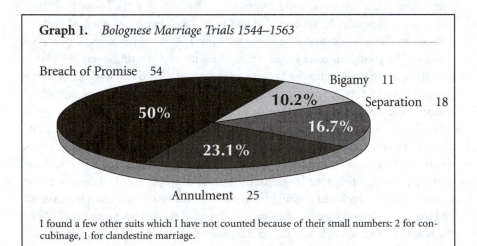

Graph 1. *Bolognese Marriage Trials 1544–1563*

Breach of Promise   54

Bigamy   11

10.2%   Separation   18

50%

16.7%

23.1%

Annulment   25

I found a few other suits which I have not counted because of their small numbers: 2 for concubinage, 1 for clandestine marriage.

Table 1. *Plaintiffs, Party Responsible for Breakdown and Winners According to Gender and Type of Suit (1544–1563)*

		Plaintiff	Party Respons.	Winner
WOMEN	Breach of Promise	29	29	20
	Annulment	11	12	10
	Divorce	11	3	3
	Bigamy	3	7	2
	Total	54 (60%)	51 (54%)	35 (87%)
MEN	Breach of Promise	17	19	2
	Annulment	9	8	2
	Divorce	4	13	1
	Bigamy	5	5	–
	Total	35 (39%)	45 (45%)	5 (13%)

case I have subdivided according to my basic analytic category: gender. (See Tables 1 and 2 and Graphs 1, 2, and 3.)

Graph 1 reveals that half the trials concerned cases of breach of promise to marry, followed at a considerable distance by petitions for annulment, petitions for "*divortium a thoro*"—that is, separation which does not entail dissolution of the bond—and finally cases of bigamy.[6] Table 1 shows a marked overall tendency for women to be protagonists: women took the action that caused the ending of the relationship in fifty-four percent of cases where responsibility can clearly be attributed; it is they who initiated legal action in sixty percent of the cases in which the plaintiff was known; and surprisingly they emerged as the winning party in eighty-seven percent of verdicts. Table 2 shows that the trials concerning couples from rural areas were relatively more numerous. A demographic explanation—

Table 2. *Cases According to the Place of Origin of Couples (1544–1563)*

	Country	Town	Unknown	Total	%
Breach of Promise	30	13	11	54	50.0%
Annulment	11	8	6	25	23.1%
Divorce	3	9	6	18	16.7%
Bigamy	5	3	3	11	10.2%
Total	49 (45.4%)	33 (30.6%)	26 (24.0%)	108	100.0%

I have considered as unknown four couples in which one member came from the town and the other from the country.

Graph 2. *Plaintiffs and Party Responsible for Breakdown in Cases of Breach of Promise According to Gender and Place of Origin (1544–1563)*

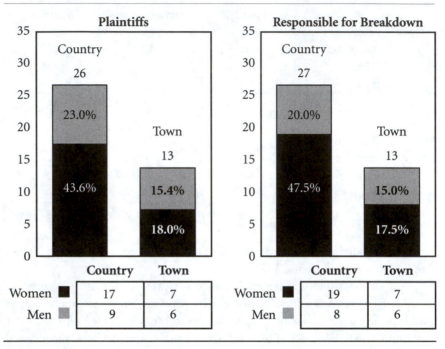

	Country	Town
Women ■	17	7
Men ▨	9	6

	Country	Town
Women ■	19	7
Men ▨	8	6

more people resided in the country than in the town—begs the question, since the geographical distribution of the categories of trials does not always correspond to the distribution of residents between town and country.[7]

To give an example, breach-of-promise-to-marry suits involving rural couples were more than twice as numerous as those involving city couples, but petitions for divorce were three times more numerous from the city than from the country. Moreover, Graphs 2 and 3 show that the protagonists in breach-of-promise suits are rural women, while it is urban men who originate divorce suits. And the difference between rural and urban areas does not stop here. Coercion into an undesired union is the most frequent cause of ending of a relationship in trials that concern breach of promise, annulment and bigamy (thirty-four cases). Of these thirty-four cases, twenty-two (around sixty-five percent) involve rural couples. It seems significant that the only occasion when we hear a father declare explicitly that he does not want to force his daughter into an undesired marriage is in the case of a master craftsman originally from Brescia and residing in Bologna, who was in the habit of visiting craftsmen from other cities.[8]

Graph 3. *Plaintiffs and Party Responsible for Breakdown in Cases of Divorce According to Gender and Place of Origin (1544–1563)*

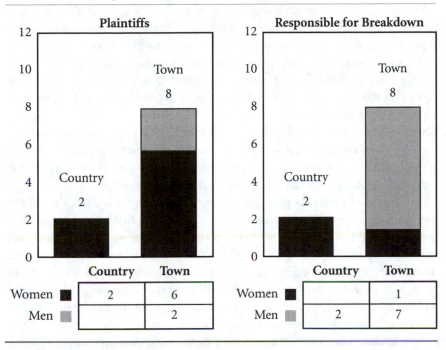

		Country	Town
Women	■	2	6
Men	▨		2

		Country	Town
Women	■		1
Men	▨	2	7

The coercion by family which so often accompanied the formation of the marital bond sometimes took the brutal form of threats and blows, at other times the no less violent psychological pressure: this was exercised on women of all ages, but also on young males and children of both sexes.[9] Violence following the marriage, when a shared life has already begun, was invariably expressed through physical ill-treatment; the psychological torment of adultery was usually exercised by husbands against wives. From the repetitiveness of the petitions of the women's proctors and the replies of the men's, I believe I can advance the hypothesis that women did not feel they could request divorce on the basis of simple ill-treatment, even were it to involve repeated beatings; "marital correction," as the mentality and the law of the time termed it, was perfectly justifiable, since its aim was to educate the wife, who was by nature an inferior being.[10] There is little to be said about these rare divorce cases. I will concentrate on the *other* types of suits. In particular, I will analyze the form and manner of coercion families exercised at the stage of negotiating marriages; in addition, I shall highlight the reactions of the protagonists. It is in fact my belief that the way people reacted to this type of coercion reveals at least some of the features which characterize what it meant to be a man or a woman in and around Bologna in the mid-sixteenth century.

One of the most characteristic elements to emerge from the analysis of these hearings is the coercion exercised on children, despite a lack of evident physical violence. To fully comprehend the significance of coercion it must be borne in mind that marriage was but one part of an overall family strategy aimed at maximizing its reproductive, productive and symbolic resources. In response to the needs of the lay community, the church accepted among justifiable motives for contracting matrimony that of peace between families, that is, a clearly political end in a society where the state was weak and politics a matter for family clans.[11] Children could be promised from the age of seven, and if they did not disavow the pact at a later date, it was considered valid. Marriage "with words of present consent" was admissible for girls from the age of twelve and boys from the age of fourteen.

An example of a marriage pact apparently made with such political aims was the one Ippolito Nanni, father of Diamante, and Vincenzo Totti, father of Alessandro, negotiated.[12] We do not know anything of the events leading up to the betrothal ceremony (*sponsalia*), but it is clear that the two fathers wished to conclude a union with powerful political significance, even though it was not destined to become operative in the short term, since in 1551 Diamante was eight years old and Alessandro, aged twenty, was at the time exiled from the Bolognese area. Yet the two fathers, in conformity with canon law, temporarily took the place of their offspring, concluding on their behalf with all the pomp and ceremony possible a promise to marry.[13] We have the testimony of the parish priest of the church of Saint Mammolo in the village of Medicina: in front of at least six hundred people gathered for the occasion in the church, after the bells had been rung three times and the priest himself had pronounced the "beautiful words" (ritual words), Ippolito and Vincenzo exchanged their promise in "words of future consent" which bound their offspring as if they had been present in person; they touched each other's hands, touched each of the relatives of the other side, and kissed. After the church ceremony, Vincenzo and Ippolito, together with other relations and friends, in an atmosphere of general good cheer, went to the latter's house where "they performed the ceremony with the betrothed one" and celebrated the event. Diamante herself informs us about her participation in this ceremony: "I knew nothing about this promise until the ring was handed over and my sister told me, and one day Vincenzo came to our house with some others including a priest and...he [Vincenzo] touched my hand and we offered him a meal as was the custom."[14] At a later date the ban against Alessandro was revoked, but "on account of certain words spoken" Ippolito himself, with some of his men, murdered Vincenzo—whom he had once embraced in church before a host of people—and another member of the Totti family. The betrothal promise, made with a clear intention of peacemaking, had been in vain, and the bishop's vicar promptly dispensed all concerned from their vows.

For little Diamante, however, this pact had in the interim led to a rather brutal contact with adult life: "Alessandro sent me an invitation to go and visit him in Castelguelfo [where he was hiding out] and I went to see him twice…and each time Alessandro caressed me as if I were his wife, he touched and pawed me all over." When pressed to reveal what exactly had taken place between them, she replied:

> he didn't marry me, nor were there words of present consent to bind us, nor did he ever do anything physical with me, apart from the time Caterina, Piero's wife [and Alessandro's sister-in-law] locked me in a room with Alessandro and he tried a good few times to deflower me, but I wouldn't let him and he dirtied my shirt all over and a white petticoat and Caterina washed it for me so that nobody would find out… the petticoat was only stained and there was no blood on it.[15]

At the time of the hearing, in 1556, Diamante was thirteen years old, and the facts she was describing had taken place within the previous five years. Had Alessandro succeeded in his intent and had the girl been approaching the age of twelve, the incident would not have been rape from a legal point of view, but simply a case of "presumed matrimony," and completely valid. In fact, sexual intercourse that took place following a formal promise to marry was interpreted as "actual consent," equivalent to words of present consent.[16] Everybody therefore would have considered it not a violent act, but a way of expediting the marriage. And that, in all probability, was exactly what Alessandro had in mind when he had himself locked in his sister-in-law's room with Diamante.

In normal situations a girl could be promised in a completely informal manner by her guardian, or else in the traditional manner, with the promised husband touching her hand and pronouncing words of future consent (often apparantly omitted in practice). It was customary for the husband-to-be then to give his future wife presents, shoes, hose always, at times a belt, gloves and jewelry. These gifts often were of material value, but above all they possessed great symbolic meaning: they indicated the girl's state as *sponsa* (betrothed one)—for this reason, on feast days young betrothed girls wore them to Mass and to all the places of social interaction. Making known to the community the betrothal that now bound her was clearly a way of reinforcing that pact, but also a way of discouraging anyone with designs on the girl, since it was a token of her no longer belonging to her original family group, but to a new one.

When the future husband had been imposed under duress, as in the cases of the girls we meet in these hearings, such gifts acquired all the hatefulness of symbols of ownership, and the girls refused to wear them. Taddea Minghini, whose father was dead, had been promised by her brother Giacomo to a certain Galeazzo Vergini, but her aversion toward her husband-to-be was such that "when Galeazzo went to her house to bring her certain gifts as is the custom, she ran away, neither wanting to see Galeazzo nor remain in the same place as him."[17] Asked by the judge whether she had worn the gifts she replied: "that she had worn them only because of the violence and threats of her brother Giacomo, who threatened to beat her and many times had beaten her to make her wear these gifts," and added: "he bashed me once because I didn't want to go the fair so as not to have to wear those things Galeazzo had brought me—shoes, slippers and gloves."[18] In another case from 1550, Minghina, daughter of Giacomo Marchio, says that some eleven months previously, she had been obliged by her father, brothers and other kinsfolk to accept Andrea Serra as her husband-to-be, but that she had never wanted him, so that "she had been beaten and forced to wear the jewelry given her by Andrea," and to move and act in a way befitting a girl whose hand was already promised in marriage.[19]

Scenes of marriages imposed through force on women of all ages—the oldest we know of was forty-five—follow one after the other as we read through the case records with a more or less identical script. The male relatives forcibly drag the wife-to-be before her husband-to-be, while the women of the family try to console her as best they can. The father or the guardian constrains the poor girl, who is crying, struggling and yelling expressions such as "I don't want him!" or "I'm being forced to do this!" The future husband, whose state of mind we can only imagine, slips the ring onto her finger, which is probably purple from the tightness of his grip; she immediately slips it off again and throws it to the floor before leaving the room in despair. One such husband, Ludovico Raspaduro, while opposing his wife Santa Floriani's petition for the annulment of their marriage, was obliged at a certain point to acknowledge that she had never shown much enthusiasm for him, to the extent that "when we were being married Santa did not want to reply [to the priest] but remained seated, and it took two of Ludovico's sisters who were sitting one on either side of Santa, who was crying, to raise her and hold her up" at the moment when, presumably, Ludovico slipped the ring onto her finger.[20]

Because it was possible to contract a valid marriage without the involvement of a priest, it could happen that a suitor, with the aid of complaisant relatives or friends, could force a woman into an undesired marriage. This is what seems to have happened to Camilla Sarti on St. Stephen's Day in 1555:

when [that day] I was at their house, Oliva, Nane's sister, called me into her room and afterwards Nane and Berto Rivani, husband of Oliva came, and when Nane arrived in the room he grabbed my left hand and I tried to take it away and he held it so tight that he scraped away the flesh around my fingernails and in the end he managed to force the ring onto my ring finger, but since the ring was too small, it wouldn't even go further than the first joint and he said nothing at all before marrying me and I kept saying he should leave me alone, that I didn't want him to marry me and therefore he used force to put the ring on my finger…and as soon as he had put the ring on my finger I pulled it off and threw it away… and told him that he had forced me and that I would make him regret it."[21]

Neither in the breach of promise nor the bigamy suits do we find men complaining that they had been obliged by force to accept women they did not want, but there are three men who request the annulment of marriages entered into against their will. There is a glaring disproportion in this respect between males and females, since in these same three types of suits we find a total of thirty-one women claiming to have been coerced. Yet there is no lack of evidence suggesting how strong family influence was even on males, even if less frequently documented. When aged between ten and eleven, Sebastiano Ramenghi had been obliged by his father Battista to marry Nobile, aged ten, the daughter of the father's second wife. But Sebastiano had never wanted anything to do with this union. Once he reached adulthood, and his father and his wife were deceased, Sebastiano took pains not to satisfy his father's wishes. Nobile was extremely poor, homeless, with nowhere to go. Given her uncertain future, the marriage to Sebastiano probably represented her only rescue, so she had no intention of letting him go—quite the contrary. For a time she got relatives and friends to try to convince him, then, probably exasperated by his obstinacy, she applied to the palace guard of the castle under whose jurisdiction they both lived. Under threat of imprisonment, Sebastiano consented to solemnize the marriage vows his father had made him take informally ten years earlier, but he made no secret of his unfriendly intentions toward the girl. The castle official, for the sake of tranquility, had him locked in the cells for an entire week immediately after he had pronounced the fateful words.[22] To his good fortune the bishop's vicar turned out to be more benevolent, and released him from this highly distasteful bond.

Equal social and economic status were fundamental requisites that fathers insisted upon, to the extent of having sons who married women considered unworthy of the family put in prison. Such a case was that of a papermaker, who had the constables apprehend his son, then sent him back to the family's original home, many miles from Bologna. This son was guilty of having married a young woman who belonged to a family of doubtful reputation, as shown by the fact that, among other things, she enjoyed reading epic poetry such as *Orlando Furioso!*[23] But even in cases where the girl's morality provided absolutely no cause for complaint, disparity in economic standing constituted an enormous obstacle, as the story of Caterina Castelvetro illustrates. When Matteo Scarabello made Caterina pregnant, the inhabitants of the village of Calcara, including the parish priest, thought that this was the natural outcome of a love affair between two young people who, apart from this matter, had never given rise to gossip. This is confirmed by all the witnesses' depositions. Caterina's own words reveal her deep feelings, linked to the recollection of meetings and words that had left a mark on her life:

> Matteo was in love with me for two years, always asking me to make love and I kept telling him no and when he saw that I didn't want to give in unless he first took me as his wife he promised me, when we were in our field, about halfway through the period when the wheat starts ripening, to take me as his wife, saying to me: look I promise to take you as my wife if you let me make love to you and I replied that I was poor and not his equal, and he replied that he had belongings enough for both of us and that he accepted me as I was.[24]

However, when Caterina became pregnant, and the judge asked him what his intentions were, Matteo said he preferred to provide her with a dowry rather than marry her—although he would have been happy to do so—because his father "was not content."[25] Behind this acceptance of a father's wishes by his sons there normally lay the fear of disinheritance, which fathers were sure to threaten whenever they saw there was a concrete danger of acquiring a daughter-in-law of inferior social class.[26]

The idea that the ecclesiastical judge was the only person who could intervene to decide on the eventual dissolution of a marriage bond does not seem during this period to have been accepted by the whole population. For example, Ippolita della Magna, already a grown woman, made an attempt to free herself legally from a bond in words of present consent, which from the age of nine had bound her to Annibale Marescotto: but her efforts met with absolutely no success. When she decided to marry Carlo Almerici, he declared that the solution to the problem was an agreement with the previous husband consisting in the payment of a sum of money. The price for Ippolita's freedom was four gold coins.[27] The availability of money enabled women to purchase their freedom in out-of-court settlements. Money also permitted those women to resist their fathers' plans. No doubt Sabatina Marmocchi, betrothed at the age of nine, owed it to her status as heir, along with another sister, to her father's comparatively substantial fortune that she could be the protagonist in breach-of-promise litigation over a four year period. Despite the dogged opposition of her paternal relatives, resentful of her highly unusual opportunity to manage the family resources, and with her mother's decisive support, she succeeded in obtaining a favorable sentence.[28] Sabatina's situation was a lucky exception thanks to the fact that she had no brothers. Normally a girl could not afford Sabatina's legal obstinacy and had to fight against fathers, brothers and uncles who did not disdain heavy-handedness. In this connection it must be said that the paternal family played a preponderant role in the decisions relating to the choice of a marriage partner. There are many indications that point in this direction, and Lucia Cardini, an orphan living through an unhappy love affair, testifies as much explicitly. To the young man who asks her if she wants to marry him she replies: "Yes, but only if my uncles are content, especially the uncles on my father's side."[29]

One highly effective way to escape from a forced marriage, though not without difficulty, was a clandestine marriage with a preferred man. Girls were aware that they had the right to marry in all freedom by means of this not quite orthodox practice, and that the family could not forbid it. Lucia, a sixteen-year-old peasant girl who did not wish to incur the wrath of her paternal uncles, took just this step, because "she knew that her relatives could not prevent it."[30] In the same manner, when Giacoma Mangi's relatives refused to give her in marriage to Simone Brizzi because they had other plans for her, she must have thought that the only remaining solution was to present them with a *fait accompli*. She told the judge, who asked her about her relationship with Simone and that with Cristo Boato, the man foisted on her by the family: "I want the first of the two, Simone, because I believe he's my husband....I believe he's my husband, because when I made my promise to him I wanted in my heart to be his wife and consented to him and made a promise to God."[31] It must be noted that sexual intercourse had not taken place between the two lovers and not even rings had been exchanged, but they had simply said to each other that they wanted to be husband and wife, and they had sealed their pact with a kiss: this had been sufficient for the ecclesiastical judge to acknowledge that, according to the laws of the church, they were validly joined in matrimony. Immediately after the verdict, and in the presence of the archbishop's vicar, their union was solemnized: Simone "of his own free will and greatly moved, married a willing and consenting Giacoma with the ring, and kissed her."[32] However, we do not always find such happy endings. Lisarda da Campeggio found the courage to have her secret pact acknowledged only after her marriage had been publicly celebrated. The proof was in her sudden flight from the dwelling of her still prepubescent husband.[33]

125

At times clandestine marriages could remain secret for months or even years, if the favorable circumstances for them to be revealed and validated did not arise. Particularly significant in this connection is the story of Maria Pagnoni. She lived in Bologna, had two children and had been married for about eleven years to a certain Giovan Maria, a worker at the silk mills. The woman declared that she had two husbands, one she had chosen, the real one, and another imposed on her by her father. With the latter, with whom she had been sharing her life for the last ten or more years, she had never consented to sexual intercourse in spite of sleeping in the same bed, and his trying many times to obtain his rights. The two daughters were the flesh and blood of the one she considered her only real husband, the much older and also much richer Bartolomeo Marzaro. One night, in the house she had lived in when single, Marzaro had married her with a gold ring and taken her adolescent maidenhead. Her daughters had been baptized with the surname of Giovan Maria, who had also found the godparents and claimed paternity. Bartolomeo Marzaro, the true father, "did not want it to be said that they were his children…and did not want it to be said that I was his wife," explained Maria. To the judge who asked her what happened when she went to confession, the women replied that her father confessor, upon hearing that she had had nothing to do with Giovan Maria and had had the daughters by the first, real husband, absolved her with no problems.[34]

Conclusion

From this analysis it seems clear that in the area around Bologna, at least within a section of the population in the mid-sixteenth century, a private law conception of matrimony existed, according to which a bond was created and could also be dissolved through private agreements between the parties, often with little regard for ecclesiastical regulations. The role of the paternal family was preponderant in the choice of spouses, especially husbands, and especially in the rural areas, where extended families were numerous.[35] In this situation the matrimonial policy of the church, as it tended toward the recognition of individual free choice, objectively favored women; perhaps for this very reason they applied to the ecclesiastical court more often than men, and almost always received favorable sentences. Divorce cases, however, were more frequent in town than in the country, and were initiated much more often by husbands than wives, who instead applied to the tribunal to obtain mere separation. Although this was sometimes granted and some cases of reconciliation did happen, the tribunal tended to procrastinate on decisions; sentences rarely provided a definite solution to the problems. Divorcees, who could not remarry, created an element of social instability.

In this context, we find a distinct contrast between male and female behavior regarding the moment of forming the marital bond. Young women rebelled against unions imposed by the family up to the point of taking the case before the tribunal, where often they were victorious and, in some cases, countered with clandestine unions to which they had remained faithful even after having contracted new marriages. This fidelity to their freely chosen man contained a fidelity to themselves, to their own individuality. It was a fidelity tantamount to an affirmation of the self. Men seem to have suffered from a lesser degree of paternal coercion when we compare it with the oppression female offspring suffered. But in the cases where they experienced an alternative love affair they seem to have been less willing than the women to oppose the paternal will. They were, it would seem, successfully blackmailed by the threat of being deprived of their claim—a right by gender privilege—to the inheritance.

Perhaps here we have a possible interpretation of the difference in behavior which characterizes the two genders. The fact of not being the heir to the possessions and the destiny of the family was doubtless a disadvantage to women, but it paradoxically seems to have allowed them to express their individuality with greater determination. The courage shown in these situations is so much greater because there was a concrete risk of losing the dowry.[36] One last element must be underlined: in a period in which, in general, individual rights were not particularly popular and female education received no special attention, a substantial group of young women, often peasants, managed to exploit the opportunities that opened up due to the conflict over the control of matrimony between the secular legal system and that of the church.

Notes

[1] *Statuta Bononiae, Sanctionum ac Provisionum Tomus secundus, Liber IV, De successione liberorum patre vel matre vel aliis ascendentibus morientibus ab intestato rubrica*, Annibale Monterenzi, ed. (Bologna, 1569), p. 162. This collection includes laws promulgated before and during the fifteenth century.

[2] Adhémar Esmein, *Le mariage en droit canonique* (Paris: Larose et Forcel, 1891, tomes I and II); Jean Gaudemet, *Le mariage en Occident. Les moeurs et le droit* (Paris: Les Editions du Cerf, 1987); Gabriel Le Bras, "Mariage," *Dictionnaire de Théologie Catholique* (Paris: Librairie Letouzey et Ané, 1927); Raoul Naz, "Mariage en droit occidental," *Dictionnaire de Droit Canonique* (Paris: Librairie Letouzey et Ané, 1957); Francesco Brandileone, *Saggi sulla storia della celebrazione del matrimonio in Italia* (Milano: Hoepli, 1906); Nino Tamassia, *La famiglia italiana nei secoli decimoquinto e decimosesto* (Milano, Palermo, Napoli: R. Sandron, 1910); George Duby, *Le chevalier, la femme et le prêtre. Le mariage dans la France féodale* (Paris: Hachette, 1981).

[3] John T. Noonan, Jr., "Power to Choose," *Viator* 4 (1973): 419–434; Charles Donahue Jr., "The Policy of Alexander the Third's Consent

Theory of Marriage," *Proceedings of the Fourth International Congress of Medieval Canon Law*, Stephan Kuttner, ed., *Monumenta Juris Canonici* c:5 (Vatican City: Biblioteca Apostolica Vaticana, 1976), pp. 251–281; id., "The Canon Law on the Formation of Marriage and Social Practice in the Later Middle Ages," *Journal of Family History* 1983, pp. 144–158; Michael M. Sheehan, "The Formation and Stability of Marriage in Fourteenth Century England; Evidence of an Ely Register," *Medieval Studies* 33 (1971): 228–263; id., "Marriage Theory and Practice in the Conciliar Legislation and Diocesan Statutes of Medieval England," *Medieval Studies* 40 (1978): 408–460; *Conciliorum Oecumenicorum Decreta*, G. Alberigo, G. Dossetti, P.P. Joannou, C. Leonardi, P. Prodi, eds., and H. Jedin consultant (Bologna: Instituto per le Scienze Religiose, 1973), *Sessio XXIV*, 11 November 1563, *Canones super reformatione circa matrimonium*: 755.

[4] Archivio Arcivescovile di Bologna (A.A.B.), *Cancelleria vecchia, Matrimoni*. This collection contains trials of matrimonial cases, including those relative to dispensations for consanguinity, which I have not utilized. In this collection for the period previous to 1563, I have found no trials earlier than 1546. In another collection, in the Archiepiscopal Court, that is, among the materials produced by the civil tribunal, I found a number of matrimonial trials. In some cases they are just copies of documents from the *Matrimoni* collection, in other cases the documents are original. At the present stage of research, which is rather complex given that the civil cases are extremely numerous and were not ordered or catalogued in any way, I am unable to clarify the archival relationship between records kept in two collections. I intend to deal with this question in a future study, whereas here I shall examine the documents conserved in the *Matrimoni* collection; a brief mention of the others is made in note 26.

[5] For the church, the value of the promise to marry, expressed as "*verba de futuro*" (words of future consent) was relatively limited: real matri-mony is only that in which "actual" consent is expressed, using "*verba de presenti*" (words of present consent), and if a person wished to dishonor a promise which had not been followed by sexual intercourse, they could do so and get away with a penance for perjury and the payment of costs. The Bolognese court condemns the perjurer to take a large white candle into the cathedral. Adhémar Esmein, *op cit.*, I, pp. 139*ff.*

[6] I would like to point out that the overall picture of data which emerges from the Bolognese cases differs considerably from that provided by Richard H. Helmholz, *Marriage Litigation in Medieval England* (London, New York: Cambridge University Press, 1974), pp. 25–33 ,and also from what Michael M. Sheehan writes in "The Formation and Stability of Marriage," *op. cit.*, p. 256. In any case, the distinction proclaimed by the church between words of present consent and words of future consent is a rather complex question, as demonstrated by Antonio Marongiu, "Matrimonio medievale e matrimonio post-medievale," *Rivista di storia del diritto italiano*, 57 (1984), pp. 38*ff.*

[7] Athos Bellettini, *La popolazione di Bologna dal secolo XV all'unificazione italiana* (Bologna: Zanichelli 1961), pp. 39–48. Demographic information for the sixteenth century is rather scarce, especially concerning the diocese of Bologna, but rough calculations enable us to assess the population of the city at around 50,000 toward the middle of the century, and that of the diocese at between 150,000 and 155,000.

[8] A.A.B., *Cancelleria vecchia, Matrimoni 1*, Giulia di Michele da Bergamo vs. Francesco Milani, 1548.

[9] Alessandro III introduced the rule *constans vir, constans mulier* according to which were considered coercion only those behaviors capable of bending the will of a man or a woman endowed with resoluteness and determination (*Corpus Juris Canonici*, Aemilius Friedberg, ed., Leipzig 1881, *Pars Secunda Decretalium Collectiones*, Liber IV, Titulus I, Chapter 15; Adhémar Esmein, *op. cit.*, I, p. 309). For their part, the parties in the

Bolognese lawsuits tend not to distinguish between psychological and physical coercion, while ecclesiastical judges hand down the same type of sentences, dissolving the bond both when they have proof of beatings and when the plaintiff declares initially that she accepted her husband out of "respect" for her father or guardian.

[10] Adhémar Esmein, *op. cit.*, II, p. 94.

[11] Jean Gaudemet, *op. cit.*, pp. 157–158.

[12] A.A.B., *Cancelleria vecchia, Matrimoni 2,* Diamante Nanni vs. Alessandro Totti, 1556.

[13] Adhémar Esmein, *op. cit.*, I, p. 163.

[14] A.A.B., *Cancelleria vecchia, Matrimoni 2,* Diamante Nanni vs. Alessandro Totti, 1556.

[15] Ibid.

[16] Gabriel Le Bras, *op. cit.*, p. 2185.

[17] A.A.B., *Cancelleria vecchia, Matrimoni 3,* Taddea Minghini vs. Galeazzo Vergini, 1561.

[18] Ibid.

[19] A.A.B., *Cancelleria vecchia, Matrimoni 2,* Minghina Marchio vs. Andrea Serra, 1550.

[20] A.A.B., *Cancelleria vecchia, Matrimoni 2,* Santa Floriani vs. Ludovico Raspaduro, 1556.

[21] A.A.B., *Cancelleria vecchia, Matrimoni 2,* Camilla Sarti vs. Nane Merici, 1556.

[22] A.A.B., *Cancelleria vecchia, Matrimoni 3,* Nobile Dini vs. Sebastiano Ramenghi, 1560.

[23] A.A.B., *Cancelleria vecchia, Matrimoni 1,* Angelica Sangiorgio vs. Fabriano Fabriani, 1547.

[24] A.A.B., *Cancelleria vecchia, Matrimoni 2,* Caterina Castelvetro vs. Matteo Scarabello, 1554.

[25] Ibid.

[26] A.A.B., *Archiepiscopal court, Seat II, 5,* Gentile da Savigno vs. Giovan Battista Fulchi, 1545; A.A.B., *Archiepiscopal court, Seat II, 12,* Maddalena Piccinini vs. Marco Antonio Della Moneta, 1559.

[27] A.A.B., *Cancelleria vecchia, Matrimoni 2,* Ippolita Della Magnana vs. Annibale Marescotto, 1544; see also *Matrimoni 3,* Maria della Chelda vs. Girolamo Oliveri, 1559.

[28] A.A.B., *Cancelleria vecchia, Matrimoni 3,* Sabatina Marmocchi vs. Sebastiano Gulini, 1557–1561.

[29] A.A.B., *Cancelleria vecchia, Matrimoni 3,* Lucia Cardini et Alessandro Raimondi, 1562. This is the only case where clandestine marriage figures exclusively. In several other trials which started as breach of promise or bigamy, clandestine marriages are found.

[30] Ibid.

[31] A.A.B., *Cancelleria vecchia, Matrimoni 3,* Giacoma Mangi vs. Cristo Boato 1562.

[32] Ibid.

[33] A.A.B., *Cancelleria vecchia, Matrimoni 2,* Lisarda da Campeggio vs. Simone Rizzardi, 1554.

[34] A.A.B., *Cancelleria vecchia, Matrimoni 3,* Maria Pagnoni vs. Giovan Maria silk worker, no date.

[35] Marzio Barbagli, *Sotto lo stesso tetto. Mutamenti della famiglia in Italia dal XV al XX secolo* (Bologna: Il Mulino 1984), 39 and passim. The most widely used contract in the Bolognese countryside, "*mezzadria*" (tenant farming or sharecropping) favored the presence of extended families.

[36] *Statuta Bononiae, Sanctionum ac Provisionum Tomus II, Liber IV, De dotibus restituendis et ipsarum parte lucranda et fructibus rerum parephernalia rubrica*, Annibale Monterenzi, ed. (Bologna, 1569), p. 270.

Shanti Menon employs a primarily ethnographic approach to study perceptions of women's place in twentieth-century Kerala in South India. She finds that traditional matrilineal practices and more recent patrilineal practices coexist. She is able to historicize women's varied and changing experiences in kinship systems by drawing on the perspectives of informants from different age groups. Menon's sensitivity to generational and class differences illustrates the resilience of older matrilineal practices while revealing their changing meanings in a changing world. In both systems of descent, she finds, the situation and experiences of women vary according to their kinship position (daughter, wife, mother and so on) and their class.

7

Male Authority and Female Autonomy: A Study of the Matrilineal Nayars of Kerala, South India

SHANTI MENON

In the winter of 1990, I was travelling on a train from Trichur to Madras in South India. My travelling companion was a middle-aged Nayar businessman, a widower. We got into a discussion about my research in Kerala. He was surprised that I was even considering studying Nayar women on the subject of female empowerment. "You are wasting your time," he said, with an arrogance that is typical of upper class Nayar men.

> Our women are really very well off, they are treated with great respect and they wield a lot of power. You should be studying the lower castes. Their women are treated like cattle. The men treat them like pieces of property which they own. They are not like us. That is the difference between matrilineality and patrilineality. Our women are in a very fortunate situation.

Later that evening he talked about his attempts to arrange a marriage for his son.

> All we want is a girl with a college degree and from an upper middle-class family. We want a girl who will stay at home and take care of things. I can't believe how difficult that is. Today, the moment a girl has a college degree she wants to go out and work. And once she starts earning some money she becomes very headstrong and self-willed. She

starts placing her interests before that of the men in the household, and that's when the problems start. I know a lot of marriages that are breaking up because of this reason. We want to avoid that. Today girls are very different from what they were when I was young.

I found it interesting that he did not see the contradiction between the two sets of statements that he had made, a tension between beliefs and practices that characterizes the situation of women within the Nayar matrilineal kinship system. In this paper I propose to explore these tensions and the relationship between the dominant discourse on gender and kinship on the one hand and women's agency on the other. As Foucault (1978) states, "where there is power, there is resistance and yet, or rather consequently, this resistence is never in a position of exteriority in relation to power." I argue, through a narration of women's experiences, that Nayar matrilineality, like patrilineal kinship systems, operates within the structures of patriarchy. Nayar women covertly contest and disrupt this script in their everyday lives. They do not, however, openly challenge it.

In the public domain, Nayar women's speech and actions are framed within the terms of the dominant discourse. Scott (1990, p. 4) states that "situations of domination produce a public transcript in close conformity with how the dominant group would wish to have things appear. The dominant never control the stage absolutely, but their wishes normally prevail. In the short run, it is in the interest of the subordinate to produce a more or less credible performance, speaking the lines and making the gestures he knows are expected of him." This is a tactic that Nayar women adopt in their dealings with men. The "hidden transcript" is revealed in their private behavioral practices, at variance with their speech and actions in the public sphere.

In the first section of this article, I will describe the Nayar matrilineal kinship system and the transformation of this institution. In the second section, I will narrate, through Nayar women's "voices," their experiences of living within this kinship system, and what the changes mean in the context of their lives. In the final section, I will analyze women's contestation and disruption of the dominant gender and kinship ideology.

The accounts of women's lives are based on my fieldwork in Alanthara village in Trichur District, Central Kerala. Situated three miles from Trichur town, the district headquarters, Alanthara has expanded considerably over the past thirty years. Traditionally, the village has been an agricultural community. The land reform laws of the 1960s, which included a limit on the size of landholdings and redistribution of excess land among the landless laborers, brought radical changes in the economic pattern in the village. Tenant farming was abolished, and tenants were given the rights to the land that they cultivated. The Nayar households in the village, most of whom were landowners, lost a significant part of their holdings. Today agriculture is no longer a viable primary source of income for most families. Many of the young men work in urban areas, either within the state or outside. The expanding economy in the Middle East, following the oil boom, has provided laboring jobs for several young men in the village. The large sums of money that they send home to their families have drastically affected not only the class structure within the village but also the quality of life that people lead and their expectations and aspirations for the future.

I spent one year living in the village and talking with women from the "old" families. "Old" is a term used by the villagers when speaking of established families who have lived in the village for two generations or more, as opposed to those who have moved into the village in the recent past. In narrating the accounts of Nayar women's lives, I speak from my specific location as a Nayar woman whose family has lived in Alanthara for generations. Though I did not grow up in the village, I have strong ties with the place; it is my "home" in India.

Though the experiences narrated in these accounts are true for many Nayar women living in rural Central Kerala, they cannot be extended to Nayar women living in other regions in the state. Women's experiences within the matrilineal tradition vary across the state depending on socioeconomic and cultural factors.

Nayar Matrilineality in Central Kerala

The Nayars of Central Kerala, a dominant caste group, traditionally "exemplified an extremely matrilineal form of social organization" (Moore 1986, p. 523). This was reflected primarily in their laws of inheritance and marriage systems. The Nayars lived in matrilineal joint families called *taravads*. A traditional *taravad* usually consisted of a set of matrilineally related kin, both male and female. This would include sisters and brothers, the sisters' children and their daughters' children. The property was owned communally by all the members of the family but it was managed by the most senior male member of the family, called the *karanavan*. He had no right to sell or gift the property away; this could only be done with the consent of all the members of the *taravad*, but his authority regarding the management of the property and decisions taken within the *taravad* was absolute. Descent was traced through the female line, and property passed from a mother to her children, both male and female. A son had no right to pass his inheritance on to his children. On his death it reverted back to his *taravad*.

The marriage system (*sambandham*) of the matrilineal Nayars was characterized by loose marital ties, expressed in serial and simultaneous polyandry and polygy-

133

ny and hypergamy, that is to say both men and women had multiple spouses, and women married men of a higher caste or class. Hypergamy was encouraged by the *taravad* because such a union raised its "prestige." The men lived in their own *taravads*, with their mothers and sisters, and visited their wives in the evening. They had no rights or responsibilities over their children. A woman's children were the responsibility of her *taravad.* There were no fathers or in-laws in a *taravad*, and little importance was attached to a relationship between husband and wife or father and children (Mencher 1965).

In the second half of the nineteenth century, the "impact of a cash economy, western style education, improved communication and a British inspired system of law" (Jeffrey 1976, p. xiv) led to major social and political changes. This in turn led to a popular demand for laws changing traditional matrilineal practices. A series of legislative measures stretching from 1896 to 1976, relating to personal and inheritance laws, slowly eroded matrilineal practices in Central Kerala (Jeffrey 1990). The changes were a result of "massive economic, ideological and legislative pressures" (Mies 1980, p. 89) aimed at bringing the group in line with the dominant patrilineal system that existed in the rest of India. This has resulted in a redefinition of Nayar women's positions. In the following section of this paper, I narrate women's accounts of their experiences within this rapidly changing system. In doing so, my intention is not to reproduce the workings of the matrilineal system, but to explore ways in which matrilineality and patrilineality mirror one another. I examine women's locations within matrilineal kinship groups and the implications of these locations for the degree of autonomy that women exercise both within private spaces and in the public domain.

Women's Voices and the "Experience" of Matrilineality.

Though legislation has effectively abolished matrilineal practices in Kerala, the Nayars, like my travelling companion on the train, still regard themselves and are seen by other castes as a matrilineal group. Though they occupy a subordinate position within the kinship group, Nayar women do not experience some of the oppressive situations faced by women in patrilineal kinship groups. Kandiyoti (1988, p. 278) describes the control and manipulation of women under "classic" Indian patriarchy:

> Girls are given away in marriage at a very young age into households
> headed by their husband's father. There, they are subordinate not only
> to all the men but also to the more senior women, especially their

mother-in-law.... The young bride enters her husband's household as an effectively dispossessed individual who can establish her place in the patriliny only by producing male offspring. The patrilineage totally appropriates both women's labor and progeny and renders their work and contribution to production invisible.

Nayar women in Alanthara do not face similar situations. A woman owns property, and is never placed in a subservient position in her husband's home. A girl is not seen as a burden on her family, and there are no social pressures on her to bear sons. Her *taravad* is always her "home," and provides a great deal of security:

It makes a difference when we are living in our own homes, we have greater autonomy because it is our place. The men may have more power than the women, often they only *seem* to take all the decisions in the family. What many people do not realize is that very often it is the women "within" the home who are the real decision makers, the men merely carry them out. But as we all know, it is important to project the men as the "real" figures of authority, to the world at large. This is necessary for the prestige of the *taravad*. However, being on our own ground gives us great strength. We have the freedom to speak freely without bothering about formal niceties. We have to deal with people related to us by blood, our mothers, our brothers, they are all "ours." That is not so with our husband's families. It is easier to deal with our own, to express needs and opinions and take actions that are related to our life. It is different with a set of people who we are connected with by marriage ties. Our strength lies in our own home. (Girija, age twenty-eight)

The *taravad* provides women with a space from which they can challenge the dominant gender ideology and exercise a certain degree of autonomy.

The Nayars are not a homogenous group, and a woman's influence within her kinship group is mediated by the socioeconomic class in which her *taravad* is situated. Women from landowning families are far more dependent on and controlled by the men in their *taravads* than women who are members of less affluent *taravads*. This is often ignored by writers when discussing the situation of Nayar women within the matrilineal kinship system. In 1901, the Cochin Census Commissioner, M. Sankara Menon (a Nayar), wrote:

The condition of women under this complicated system requires to be specially noticed. The two sexes are nearly on a par as to inheritance of

135

> property. Again conjugal freedom also being not all on one side, the relations of the sexes appear to be more rational than amongst most other communities.... Further, the woman is free to enjoy the pleasures of social life, as it seldom falls to her lot to be worried with the miseries of domestic seclusion. (Fuller 1976, p. 6)

This picture was almost never completely accurate. The *karanavan* had considerable authority over all the members of the *taravad,* and women's movements outside the *taravad* and their sexuality were controlled. The extent of autonomy wielded by Nayar women is mediated both by their family organization and by their locations within a hierarchical class structure. Following Dyson and Moore (1983, p. 45) I define female autonomy as women's:

> capacity to manipulate [their] personal environment. Autonomy indicates the ability…to obtain information and to use it as the basis for making decisions about [their] private concerns and those of [their] intimates. Autonomy, in other words, relates directly to human agency.

In the traditional Nayar extended family, like in the patrilineal extended family, the oldest male member, the *karanavan,* was in a position of authority. Upper-class Nayar women, like the women in the other dominant castes and classes in patrilineal India, lived very circumscribed lives, controlled by their male kin. Kalyaniamma, a seventy-three-year-old matriarch of one of the leading *taravads* in Alanthara, described what it was like for her to live and grow up in a rural, landowning, upper-class *taravad*:

> I grew up in a joint family which included my grandmother, my mother, my mother's brother who was the karanavan of the *taravad,* and the five of us children—my four siblings and I. For many years my uncle's wife and their children also lived in our *taravad.* This was very unusual, but then the social practices had slowly begun to change at this time.
>
> My uncle, the *karanavan,* managed all the affairs of the household, including the finances. He would give the women money to run the household, and they were accountable to him for every *paise* that they spent.
>
> Though we women had some degree of freedom within the house, we were in charge of running the household and seeing to it that everything worked smoothly, our lives were very restricted. Most of the time we were confined to the physical space within the *taravad.* We had no access to the front of the house, and as a young girl I was not allowed

to meet with male visitors to the *taravad*. The only time we went out of the *taravad* was to visit the temples, and at this time we were closely supervised by the older women. On rare occasions we visited the homes of other members of the family, but this did not happen often. We did not go to the stores, that was absolutely out. Everything that we wanted, including our clothes, was bought for us by the men. We had no choice but to like the clothes that they bought for us. No one asked us for an opinion anyway, and we never thought to give one. It was not our place. It is so different today. Women move around and there aren't as many restrictions as there were when I was young. My daughters had greater control over their lives when they were young than I ever did. That may have been because the *taravad* had broken up at the time they were growing up, and they lost their father when they were very young. It is easier dealing with a woman than negotiating with an autocratic male. (Kalyaniamma, age seventy-three)

The women in Kalyaniamma's *taravad* had a limited degree of autonomy in the management of "domestic" affairs, but on the whole their lives were controlled by the *karanavan*. The transformation of matrilineality within a brief time span is reflected in her description of the differences between her life and that of her daughters.

Kalyaniamma belongs to an affluent, landowning family in the village, a family that has the financial resources that enables it to seclude its women physically. Her kinswoman, Gowriamma, a member of a distant and less affluent branch of the same *taravad*, had greater autonomy in the management of her affairs. Her relatively lower class status placed far fewer social constraints on her life than that experienced by Kalyaniamma:

My father died when I was around thirteen years old. My mother became mentally unstable, and we were very badly off financially. The *karanavans* in the main *taravad* helped us quite a bit, but there was only so much that they could do, after all they had their own responsibilities. So my brother and I started working. I went out to work. That was quite unusual, in these parts at least. There were very few Nayar women in the job force; it is not like it is today. Today a lot of Nayar women are employed. When I was young only women from poor families went out to work. Families that had some income and could maintain a minimum standard of living, families where the members had something to eat everyday, and clothes to wear, in such families, the women stayed at home, they did not go out to work. I went to work because I had to; I had no choice, but I was an exception. Even many educated Nayar women stayed at home. The families felt that it was a matter of the *taravad* honor, it was a disgrace to send the women out of the home. I have been managing this household from a very young age, after all I helped to raise my siblings. I make all the decisions in this family. I am used to it, I cannot live any other way. (Gowriamma, age sixty-five)

Kalyaniamma and Gowriamma belong to different branches of the same *taravad*. The difference in their class positions influenced the control that each woman had over her life. There were far fewer physical and social constraints in Gowriamma's life than there were in Kalyaniamma's.

Women who lived in small *taravads* where there was no *karanavan* in residence also had a greater degree of autonomy. This fact was alluded to by all the women with whom I spoke:

It is easier for women to live together without men, especially when it is mother and daughters. The house is ours, and it is a very warm and supportive environment. (Janakiamma, age sixty-five)

My father died when I was very young and I lived here with my mother. My uncles did not live with us. We had a very close relationship, I could discuss everything with her. We made all the decisions regarding the household together....There are all the little things that women share with each other, especially mothers and daughters. It is a special relationship. In many respects my life was a lot easier than that of women in some of the other *taravads* where the *karanavans* took all the decisions and the women were expected to follow directions. I had a great deal of freedom. (Sharadaamma, age sixty-five)

Within the matrilineal tradition, the Nayars were both polygynous and polyandrous. Theoretically this meant that a woman could form and break alliances with men. However, in practice this, like the other aspects of her life, was mediated by her class position. For upper-class Nayar women, whose lives were strictly regulated by a set of rigid social codes, the opportunity to form independent relationships with men was practically nonexistent. The *karanavan* controlled the alliances that were formed. It is very likely that, similar to patrilineal kinship systems, women were used in forging male kinship networks and to further the interests of the male members of the *taravad*. The social control of women, through control of their sexuality, differs by class, and has different implications for women depending on their class status. Kalyaniamma describes the situation in her *taravad* in these words:

My mother and my grandmother had *sambandham* relationships. The trend shifted with our generation—we had monogamous marriages. There were monogamous marriages even in my mother's time, but in our *taravad* my mother and grandmother had polyandrous unions....
I have heard it said that after the five of us, my brothers, sister and I, were born our uncles decided that there were enough children in the *taravad*. They felt that the children were depleting the resources of the *taravad*, that they could not afford to economically support any more children. So they stopped the men from visiting my mother. That was the end of her *sambandham* relationships.... Our marriages were all arranged by the family. At this time it had become customary for the boy and girl to meet before the marriage was settled. I remember my husband came to visit us and I did meet with him before we were married. Of course the decision to accept the proposal was taken by the older members of the family, my grandmother and my uncle. I was not asked or expected to express an opinion. (Kalyaniamma, age seventy-three)

In this case, the men in the *taravad* had rights over their female kin, and they exercised these rights to form social links and build power networks. The women had little control over the marriage arrangements, and their dependance on the *taravad* left them with no choices or alternative courses of action.

Gowriamma, on the other hand, was economically independent. She worked to support her siblings, and the absence of a male authority figure gave her greater freedom. She had two children out of wedlock, and has been living with a man whom she has not married. Though this is common knowledge in the village, she is not ostracized, and is accepted by all the Nayar families.

Stolcke (1981) argues that in caste and lineage societies, where members' positions are determined by birth, marriage patterns and rules of inheritance either partially or totally define a person's social condition. Class and caste supremacy is maintained by endogamous marriages and the control of women's sexuality in them. Though the Nayars were hypergamous, marriage between individuals of widely different social classes was frowned upon. For example, Janakiamma, whose family owned a small store in the village, wanted to marry Raghu, a member of one of the landowning families. The idea was met with stiff opposition by both families:

Raghu and I wanted to marry each other but the families were absolutely against it. His family belonged to a higher social class. Even though we are both Nayars, the *karanavan* in his *taravad* made it

> known to the *karanavan* in our *taravad* that they would not accept our marriage. We lived in a joint family at that time, and my uncle made all the decisions in the family. He did not want to do anything that would antagonize Raghu's family, after all their status was higher than ours. So I was married off to a man working in Madras, I suppose they thought that was far enough to keep us apart. (Janakiamma, age sixty-five)

A marriage alliance not only brings two individuals together, but also links families and establishes genealogical status. For a couple to challenge this arrangement would lead to a disruption of class hierarchies, and was therefore actively discouraged.

Janakiamma returned to the village a few years later. Her *taravad* had split up by this time and they were no longer under the control of her uncle. She and Raghu started a relationship that lasted till his death a few years ago. Speaking about this she said:

> I think women today have a lot more freedom than when I was young. I feel that if it had been today, we would not have to go through all that we did, we would have gone ahead and got married, and the families would have eventually come around. My mother was sympathetic but she was powerless, there was little that she could do.... In a way I think the system today is much better. It is easier to talk with and persuade a husband, rather than a brother. I think most women have some degree of power over men in a situation where they are sexually involved, and that is not the case with brothers. There is always a distance and it is impossible to talk with them beyond a point. (Janakiamma, age sixty-five)

It is significant that Janakiamma recognizes that, with the changing times, the control of women has passed from brothers to husbands. Women still do not have the autonomy, within the kinship system, to negotiate relationships for themselves, unless they step out of the sphere of male influence. Today, marriages are still arranged among the Nayars, but many more women have the freedom to refuse a match, and they are no longer governed by a tradition that demanded silence and absolute obedience to the will of the *karanavan*:

> Today marriage proposals are discussed with the young girls, and they have the freedom to turn down an alliance that they do not want. There is a lot of pressure on couples today to make a marriage work, and I think with a little bit of give and take most marriages can be made to work out. There are very few options for women if they walk out of a marriage, it is less socially acceptable to do so. It was easier to walk away

from a marriage when I was young than it is today. (Janakiamma, age sixty-five)

The shift from matrilineality to patrilineality and monogamous marriages has meant that the "ownership" of a woman has passed from her *taravad* to her husband. It has also brought with it social and cultural pressures on women to adapt and conform to the patrilineal and patriarchal image of the "ideal" Indian woman, one who is loyal and submissive to her husband. It is no longer considered "respectable" for a woman to divorce her husband, and it is difficult for a woman to remarry, whether she is divorced or widowed.

Women from lower socioeconomic families are still in a vulnerable position and are often "used" to enhance the status of their *taravads*. Sudha was married at the age of eighteen to a young man in the village who is mentally retarded. She did not want the marriage, but was powerless to do anything about it. With little education and a job as a housemaid, she was pressured by her family to accept the match because:

> My family thought this marriage would get them out of the circle of poverty. Sunil's is an old *taravad,* and the marriage would raise our status. Everyone told me not to be selfish and think only of myself. So my life was sacrificed in the larger interests of the family. (Sudha, age twenty-eight)

The marriage alliance enabled Sudha's family to establish kinship connections that would have been impossible any other way. A few years later, her *taravad* was able to capitalize on this connection when they arranged a marriage for her younger sister to a man who belonged to a higher socioeconomic class. Sudha's better economic situation enabled her to pay some of the wedding expenses.

The shift towards patrilineality and the nuclear family has resulted in a different kind of control over women's sexuality. As Kalyaniamma describes it:

> Today if a woman is widowed, her chances of remarrying are very limited. That was not an issue when I was a child. By the time I was an adolescent there was also a stigma attached to unmarried women who had children. I think it went hand in hand with the spread of monogamous marriages. The women were not ostracized or anything, but people talked about it very disparagingly. Now of course, it is very difficult. It would be really hard on a woman if she has an illegitimate child, no matter to which class she belongs. (Kalyaniamma, age seventy-three)

Janakiamma's relationship with Raghu attracted some comment, but was accepted by the people in the village. Today, a woman in a similar situation would be ostracized irrespective of her caste and class situation.

Today polyandry and polygyny are nonexistent in Kerala. Male role definitions have shifted, and the husband, rather than the brother, is central to a woman's life. With the shift in the location of power, a woman's relationship with her husband and his family has taken on a significance that was absent within the *taravad* system:

> When my daughters come home for the vacations, they spend more time with their husbands' families than they do here. That is a big change in our residence patterns. We do not say anything. Times have changed, and we feel that once the girls are married they ought to follow the wishes of their husbands.... And since the men stay in their homes, they expect their wives to do the same. (Veena, age forty-two)

This change in residence patterns has further weakened the Nayar matrilineal kinship system.

The social and economic changes that have resulted in the slow shift from matriliny to patriliny have also opened up new avenues for women. Today Nayar women are no longer constrained by the rigid traditions and practices that existed in the *taravad*. They have greater access to the world outside the four walls of their home, and increasing numbers are joining the work force.

Male Authority and Female Autonomy

The narratives in the previous section are expressions of the "public" discourse on gender and kinship. They provide only a partial picture of individual women's lives within the matrilineal system. Women's agency and their subversion of the dominant discourse are obscured in this picture. It hides the fact that within their separate sphere women create a space from which they can resist male authority in subtle and silent ways. This resistance is never articulated; it is a shared secret among women. To voice it would be to bring out into the open, to make public the contradictions within which they operate—contradictions which they accept as part of their everyday lives.

The fact that Nayar women lived in *taravads* with related kin made it easy for women to forge bonds and work together to subvert male authority. For example, Janakiamma and Raghu could not influence the *karanavans* in both their *taravads* to arrange their marriage. However, in spite of all the restrictions on her movement,

Janakiamma frequently met with Raghu, and at one time the two of them even contemplated eloping. When I asked her how she did this, she laughed and said:

> There are ways and ways. Do you really believe that the men know everything that goes on in a household? The women do. The women would have liked to arrange this marriage, my mother was sympathetic but there was little that she could do. Marriages are negotiated between two families and the women were helpless.... After my marriage ended, I returned home. My uncles had moved out of the *taravad* by then, and there was only my mother and I. It was easy for Raghu and I to start a relationship. My mother was very supportive, and we did not have to fear anyone. (Janakiamma, age sixty-five)

The strategies women employ to undermine the dominant ideology lurk in the background and are embedded within the contradictions in their narratives. For example, when talking about the control of resources in her *taravad*, Kalyaniamma said:

> In our families it is the men who control the money. They keep the money with them and give it out to the women to run the household. In many instances the women had to account to the men for the money that they spent. My mother did not have to do that. But we had to ask the men for money. (Kalyaniamma, age seventy-three)

Later, when we discussed decision making within the household, she presented a very different picture:

> I am in charge of everything in this household. I control the money, I make the decisions. I think in most *taravads* it is the women who make the decisions. Of course, the men like to think that they do, and we let it seem that way (laughs), but when you get down to the bottom of it, it is the women who are in control. (Kalyaniamma, age seventy-three)

In this instance Kalyaniamma informally subverted the authority of the men in the family. She recognized that this has to be done covertly and within the private space of the family. The men accept this fact, as long as their authority is not publicly challenged and both sides pretend that it is the men who are in charge of affairs. As Scott (1991, p. 779) points out, the fact that women's power can only be exercised within the private domain of the household "reaffirms men's official rule as powerholders [and] is a tribute...to men's continued control of the public transcript."

Women also employ strategies of submission and silence in order to negotiate positions of autonomy for themselves. Neeta, a young woman who works as a clerk in a government office, described the financial arrangements in her family in these words:

> My husband makes almost all the decisions in the household, and I go along with him.... It is not really as difficult as it sounds. I hand my paycheck to him every month, he controls the money and the expenses for the household. I like it that way, it saves me a lot of bother. (Neeta, age twenty-seven)

In this statement she lays out the traditional position that places men in control of household resources. Later, talking about her job, she says:

> I do not think I could ever give up my job. I enjoy the independence it gives me.... I do not have to depend on anyone for money, I do not have to ask someone for every little thing that I need.
>
> I: But you told me earlier that you handed your paycheck to your husband?
>
> N: I do that, but I do not give him everything. I keep some money aside for my use and give him the rest. This money is mine to do with as I please. I do not spend it on the household or on the children; that has to come out of the money in the bank. I am sure that my husband knows that I do not give him all my salary, but he has never asked me about it and I see no need to discuss it with him. There are some things that are best not spoken about, we all know that don't we? (laughs) (Neeta, age twenty-seven)

In this instance Neeta has created a space for herself by not directly confronting her husband's authority. In this situation her submission and silence are temporary holding positions rather than markers of oppression.

My intention in this paper is not to argue that Nayar women are able to resist or counteract all forms of male domination. However, I would like to contradict the suggestion made by some writers (Mies 1980; Liddle and Joshi 1986) that matrilineal kinship systems gave women a considerable degree of autonomy. As these narratives show, women's lives are made up of overlapping and intersecting layers within which they negotiate specific positions, depending on their class locations and the particular historical moment.

Dorothy Smith (1987) argues that our view of the world is not built upon our everyday experiences. Instead it is constructed on the silence of women, by men who occupy positions of power. In this paper, I have attempted to represent the voices of a few Nayar women, to capture some of the tensions of their experiences as they have lived and articulated them. However, "it is not individuals who have experience, but subjects who are constituted through experience" (Scott 1991, p. 779). The evidence presented in these separate yet related narratives offers complex yet partial insights into individual women's lives. Their subversion of the dominant gender and kinship ideology that places them in subordinate positions is embedded in silence and contradictions. They do not offer any critique of their situation or directly challenge male authority. Instead they work around it, and in so doing perpetuate gender hegemonies. In many significant ways, patrilineality and matrilineality, at least as practiced among the Nayars, are two sides of the same coin, particularly with regard to the power relationships within which women are located. Women's resistance to these power relationships may take on new meanings within changing contexts as matrilineality is further transformed and redefined by historical forces and dominant ideologies.

Note

The fieldwork on which this paper is based was carried out in Alanthara village, Trichur District, Kerala during 1990 and 1991. It was supported by a grant from the American Institute of Indian Studies, Chicago. I would like to thank Sari Biklen, Susan Wadley, Jyotsna Singh and Deborah Neff for comments on earlier drafts of this article.

References

Dyson, Tim, and Mick Moore. "On Kinship Structure, Female Autonomy, and Demographic Behavior in India." *Population and Development Review,* Vol. 9, No. 1 (March 1983): 35–60.

Foucault, Michel. *The History of Sexuality Vol. 1: An Introduction.* New York: Random House, 1978.

Fuller, C.J. *The Nayars Today.* Cambridge: Cambridge University Press, 1976.

Jeffrey, Robin. *The Decline of Nayar Dominance.* New York: Holmes & Meier Publishers Inc., 1976.

Jeffrey, Robin. "Matriliny, Women, Development—and a Typographical Error." *Pacific Affairs* 63 (Fall 1990): 373–377.

Kandiyoti, Deniz. "Bargaining with Patriarchy." *Gender and Society,* Vol. 2, No. 3 (September 1988): 274–290.

Liddle, Joanna, and Rama Joshi. *Daughters of Independence.* London: Zed Books Ltd., 1986.

Mencher, Joan P. "The Nayars of South Malabar." In *Comparative Family Systems,* ed. M.F. Nimkoff. Boston: Houghton Mifflin Company, 1965, pp. 163–191.

145

Mies, Maria. *Indian Women and Patriarchy: Conflicts and Dilemmas of Working Women.* New Delhi: Concept Publishing Company, 1980.

Moore, Melinda A. "A New Look at the Nayar Taravad." *Man* (N.S.) 20 (1986): 523–541.

Omvedt, Gail. "'Patriarchy': the Analysis of Women's Oppression," *The Insurgent Sociologist.* Vol. 13, No. 3 (1986): 30–50.

Scott, James C. *Domination and the Art of Resistance.* New Haven: Yale University Press, 1990.

Scott, James W. "A New Look at the Nayar Taravad," *Man* (N.S.) 20 (1986): 523–541.

Scott, Joan W. "The Evidence of Experience." *Critical Inquiry* 17 (1991): 773–797.

Smith, Dorothy. *The Everyday World as Problematic: A Feminist Sociology.* Boston: Northeastern University Press, 1987.

Stolcke, Verena. "Women's Labours: The Naturalisation of Social Inequality and Women's Subordination." In *Of Marriage and the Market: Women's Subordination Internationally and its Lessons* eds. Kate Young, Carol Wolkowitz and Roslyn McCullagh. London and New York: Routledge, 1981, pp. 159–177.

Gloria Raheja's emphasis, in her ethnography of a village in north India, is on the role of positionality in women's experiences of kinship. Raheja's analysis centers on women's songs that mark occasions when women were making transitions from one position to another—in particular at marriage—in a setting where marriage meant that a woman moved from her natal household to her husband's. As we follow her analysis of the texts, we see just how complex a task it is to listen to and interpret these songs in order to understand the various perspectives they reveal. The songs articulate female awareness of the inequities and contradictions inherent in their kinship system and the problems for female identity that kinship practices raise.

8

The Limits of Patriliny:
Kinship, Gender and Women's Speech
Practices in Rural North India

GLORIA GOODWIN RAHEJA

Introduction

> Women's speech practices make visible a crack, a fault line in the dom-
> inant male discourse of gender and power, revealing it to be not mono-
> lithic but contradictory and thus vulnerable. (Gal 1991, p. 196)

As anthropologists began to attend to the contrasting expressive genres in which
men and women construct representations of marriage patterns, sexuality, deference behavior, the "solidarity" of patrilineal kinship groupings, exchange relationships among kinsmen and so forth, diversity within and among gendered
perspectives on such kinship practices became a focus of attention. The critical
theoretical issue however is not simply the discovery of heterogeneous representations, or the recovery of the "female voice." We are faced with the thornier problem of gauging the degree to which women's speech practices not only interrogate
kinship ideologies but also provide alternative moral perspectives in terms of
which women may act to undermine the power of those ideologies.

In this paper, I examine some of the speech practices of rural north Indian
women, focusing on two genres of oral expression in which aspects of patrilineal

---

Permission to publish given by the University of Virginia Press and Bhatkal and Sen.

kinship are critiqued.[1] I suggest that women's ritual songs and proverbial speech make visible the contradictions within dominant north Indian discourses concerning kinship, marriage and gender, and in doing so begin to circumscribe the authority of those discourses. In pointing out the contradictions within north Indian patrilineal kinship that are reflected upon in women's speech genres, I draw attention also to two theoretical issues embedded in analyses of such perspectival multiplicity.

The first of these issues concerns the degree to which the critiques posed in women's verbal practices can be viewed as exemplifying a unitary female voice or a unitary female subjectivity. Gal has taken up this issue in relation to women's use of language, and she has pointed out that the resistance found in women's linguistic genres is often contradictory and ambiguous; but this heterogeneity within women's speech practices does not prevent them from becoming sites of struggle about kinship, gender definitions and power (1991, pp. 176–178, 192–193). The proverbs and songs of rural north Indian women that I examine in this essay are multiply voiced. Women, speaking as daughters or sisters on the one hand, and wives and daughters-in-law on the other, comment differently on the contradictions within north Indian kinship. Yet women's speech practices as a whole differ from men's in that even in their heterogeneity, they nonetheless persist in uncovering the contradictions within the dominant discourse, and thus revealing its vulnerability.

The second issue concerns the nature of such struggles, and the question of whether the alternative representations of gender and kinship embedded in these speech practices constitute a potent challenge to the dominant discourse, or whether they should more properly be viewed as "rituals of rebellion" (Gluckman 1963) that, as Guha puts it, "reinforce authority by feigning defiance" (1983, p. 31) in a temporary, contained and innocuous "reversal" of the otherwise authoritative and unquestioned cultural discourse.

In her review of research on the links between language, gender and power, Gal (1991, p. 177) suggests that women's speech practices may be seen as resistance to a dominant cultural order (rather than mere "rituals of rebellion") when they propose alternative models of the social world, and when these strategies of verbal expression are practiced and valued despite denigration or attempts to suppress them. The active denigration or suppression of these expressive forms might be viewed, then, as an index of the actual threat they pose to the dominant representations of kinship and gender. In northern India, attempts to denigrate or suppress women's expressive forms have surfaced in certain circumstances. There does, minimally, appear to be an ambivalent attitude towards women's songs. On the one hand, songs are viewed as auspicious and necessary to the performance of many rituals; there is a Hindi proverb that, despite its misogyny, counts the singing of auspicious songs as one of the good qualities of women: "Woman, you have four hundred thousand bad attributes, but three good ones: singing auspicious songs, maintaining virtue, and producing sons."[2] Yet in many instances, attempts are made to silence women's song. Songs that redefine women's sexuality in positive and celebratory terms rather than as dangerous to males and to male kinship solidarities (Raheja and Gold 1994) may be viewed by men as "bad songs" that should no longer be sung by "our educated girls" (Flueckiger 1991, pp. 192–193). In the early twentieth century, the singing of such songs was viewed as a serious feminine shortcoming, and women's lack of formal education was the imputed source of this moral failing, in women's didactic literature of the time (Kumar 1991, p. 21). In nineteenth-century Bengal, songs and other forms of women's popular culture were often critical of women's position in Bengali society. "Often stark and bitter in expressing the plight of women in a male-dominated society, the poems and songs popular among the lower social groups were, at the same time, tough, sensuous or bawdy, in an idiom specific to women" (Banerjee 1989, pp. 131–132). From the mid-nineteenth century, however, as Banerjee discovered, Bengali men, influenced both by colonial education and by nationalist politics, attempted to arouse public opinion against these expressive genres, and there were concerted efforts to denigrate and suppress them as "corrupting," indecent, and unworthy of proper Hindu women. Yet rural women all over India continue to sing these songs, despite this widespread opposition.

Gal recognizes that women's responses to powerlessness may sometimes have the effect only of reproducing the forms of their subordination (1991, p. 183), yet she recognizes also the possibility that women's speech genres do not always simply "reflect" or reinforce an already constituted social order; speech genres may function as strategies in ongoing negotiations and contestations of kinship and gender identities.[3] In this paper, I view rural north Indian women's proverbs and songs as potent forms of resistance to dominant cultural representations, which women invoke in their daily lives and ordinary conversations. I do not view them as a "safety valve" that would effectively limit the possibility of actual resistance. With Scott (1990, p. 191), I view such a discourse, and the alternative moral sensibilities encoded within it, as "a condition of practical resistance rather than a substitute for it." Rural women in India do indeed, by their actions as well as their words, undermine patrilineal kinship conventions; in this essay, I delineate the alternative moral codes embedded in song and proverbial speech, in terms of which they understand and value their own defiant acts.[4]

151

Proverbs, Songs and Women's Use of Language

Veena Das has written that very early in their lives, north Indian women learn that their use of language must be different from that of men. While they learn that great circumspection is necessary in using words that reveal the tensions in their experience of kinship relations, or words that undermine the authority of the official discourses of patriliny, they also learn that there are ways in which resistance may be communicated. Das suggests that as a girl reaches sexual maturity, she learns to communicate through nonverbal gestures, through particular speech intonations, and through the reading of subtle metamessages in ordinary language. Mothers admonish their daughters early on to learn the nuances of such communicative practices: "What kind of a daughter are you, if you cannot read the way the eye of the mother points?" (Das 1988, p. 198). In women's songs and proverbs, however, resistance to patrilineal discourses of kinship and gender is not covert, subtle and silent but overt, explicit and articulate.

In rural north India, groups of women sing primarily at the births of sons, at weddings and at various annual festivals. Songs are sung at two different kinds of occasions. Women sing as the ritual events of a wedding unfold, usually in close proximity to the male-dominated formal ceremonies. At these times, women quite literally have to compete to let their voices be heard. At the *pherā*, the climax of the wedding ritual, at which the bride is formally transferred from her natal kin to her husband's family amid ritual acts of deference to the groom's side, women of the bride's side sit just a few feet away in the same courtyard and sing *gālī*, songs abusing the groom's family, in which obscene joking about the sexual proclivities of the groom's family is the most common theme. It is not unusual for the men in the groom's party to become angry at this, to call for a halt, only to be rebuffed and assailed by yet more bawdy abuse. When the bride's mother's brothers come to give gifts just before the wedding is to take place, they stand at the threshold of their sister's husband's house, and behind her the women of the neighborhood sing "songs of the mother's brothers' gifts" in which the brothers' honor and generosity are called into question. Just outside the door, behind the mother's brothers, men of both sides have gathered, and there is among them, inevitably, a raucous band, playing loudly and cacophonously as if to drown out the women's song, stopping only when the women's songs are finished.

At the birth of a son, while a son's marriage party is away at the bride's village, and at the festivals of Holi and Tij, singing and dancing sessions called *khoṛiyās* are held at night in courtyards from which males have been barred. "Dancing songs" or "sitting songs" are sung on these occasions. Unlike other genres of women's

152

songs, both of these take the form of long verse narratives in which the tragic consequences of a husband's failure to transfer his loyalties from his natal kin to his new wife constitute the most frequent theme. At the very time the groom is accepting a bride, a ritual whereby a wife should be assimilated to and demonstrate her deference to the kin of her husband, his own mothers and aunts and sisters are singing of the morally problematic aspects of such a transferal.

The formal structure of the songs likewise highlights the competing voices and multiple perspectives on kinship. As Gold has pointed out, the verses of many north Indian women's songs are "chorused conversations" in which conflicts and opposed perspectives are enacted in alternating question-and-answer conversations among kinsmen (Raheja and Gold 1994). Thus one song may articulate as many as five or six different points of view on a situation or relationship. In the north Indian villages in which I worked, such songs typically depict conversations in which the voices and differing perspectives of husband and wife, the husband's mother and father, his sisters and brothers, and the wives of his brothers may all be heard.

Though they are often interpreted as tokens of an abstract and essentialized "folk mentality," proverbs in northern India, as elsewhere, are strategic speech acts through which speakers comment on recurrent social situations, to persuade others of the salience of their own moral evaluations (Briggs 1988, pp. 101–135; Burke 1973, pp. 291–296; de Certeau 1984, pp. 18–21). Proverbs are used with great frequency in rural north Indian speech. Most are used by both men and women, but many proverbs are used almost exclusively by women (Christian 1891, pp. xxvii–xxix; Fallon 1886, pp. 299–320). Many, though not all, of these proverbs used by women are commentaries on kinship relations, either overtly and explicitly or metaphorically. Such usages occur in ordinary conversations, most frequently among women, though they may also be used in speaking to or in the hearing of men. Women in Pahansu also used proverbial utterances in conversations with me, to draw my attention to particular conventions concerning kinship relationships and to their own perspectives on them.

Proverbs about women and kinship (though not, significantly, those used primarily by women) were sometimes cited in colonial documents as evidence of female passivity and submission to the dictates of "tradition," and of the oppression of women in India. Such citations form part of a larger colonial discourse on women and tradition, a discourse that attempted to provide a moral justification for colonial rule. Colonial reports on the practice of *sati*, for example, often stress women's submissive and unquestioning obedience to the dictates of "religion," and portray them as passive bearers of a fixed, reified and univocal "tradition" (Mani

1984, 1989). Such colonial documents also tend to infantilize women, often speaking of the widow as a "tender child," even though most *satīs* were undertaken by women over the age of forty (Mani 1989, pp. 97–98; Yang 1989). As Partha Chatterjee (1989, p. 622) has pointed out, representing Indian women as voiceless and oppressed provided a rationale for British colonial intervention. Colonial administrators saw themselves as performing a "civilizing mission" as they regarded women's situation as evidence of the moral degradation of Indian culture as a whole. The "protection" of supposedly weak, passive and silent Hindu women became then a justification for colonial domination (Mani 1989; O'Hanlon 1991).

Though colonial proverb compilations often note when a particular proverb is used primarily by women, there is no commentary on the relationship between proverbs about kinship and gender used by men (or perhaps by both men and women) and those used by women. Features of women's speech are thus recorded in the colonial archive, but they are never seen as challenging the supposedly dead weight of the "tradition" that oppresses them.

Like women's songs, however, proverbs used by north Indian women frequently interrogate the dominant discourse by exposing the contradictions in its representations of women in patrilineal kinship. If songs are confined to ritually marked spheres that are somehow set apart from everyday life, proverbs insert those interrogations into everyday life and into the conversations and conflicts in which kinship and gender identities are negotiated.

Proverbs and Songs: Exposing Contradictions

The songs and proverbs that I heard in the north Indian villages of Pahansu and Hathchoya focus attention on three sets of contradictions within north Indian kinship ideologies: those attendant upon a woman's transfer from natal kin to conjugal kin; those attendant upon the conflict between the importance of marriage in this society and the primacy, on the other hand, of preexisting ties among men in the husband's patrilineal unit; and those attendant upon the norm of silent submission to a husband even if he acts in opposition to generally accepted moral codes.[5]

The first of these contradictions concerns the transfer of a woman from natal home to conjugal home in this patrilineal and virilocal milieu in which village exogamy is practiced. In northern India, in other words, significant economic, political, and ritual rights are transmitted only through the male line; married couples live with the husband's family, and spouses come from different villages. Marriage here is spoken of as a *kanyā dān* ("gift of a virgin"), the unreciprocated gifting away of a daughter along with lavish gifts for herself and for the people of her *sasurāl,* her husband's house. She is given away in the course of a complex set of ritual actions designed to effect her transformation from "one's own" (*apnī*) to her natal kin to "other" (*dūsrī*) and "alien" (*parāī*) to them. The woman is often said to undergo a transformation at the wedding, in which she becomes the "half-body" of her husband, of one substance with him. His kinsmen become her kinsmen, and her ties with her own natal kin are transformed as well; people in Pahansu say that unmarried girls share a "bodily connection" (*śarīr kā sambandh*) with their natal kin, but that after the marriage, there is only a "relationship" (*riśtā*).[6] Trautmann has characterized this cultural understanding of marriage and the "gift of a virgin" as a "patrilineal idiom of complete dissimilation of the bride from her family of birth and her complete assimilation to that of her husband" (Trautmann 1981, p. 291).

The present analysis of the commentaries that women compose, in song and proverb, on this patrilineal idiom builds on the observations of Jacobson (1977), Vatuk (1975) and Dube (1988) on this point, and follows their analyses of the limits of "patriliny" in rural north India. Jacobson argued that structural analyses of the patrilineal and patrilocal aspects of north Indian kinship and interpretations that stress the completeness of the transfer of a woman from natal to conjugal kin overlook the complexity of a woman's kinship relations. Though, she argues, much of the ritual and ideology of rural north India does indeed stress patrilineality and the priority of a woman's ties to her husband's kin, many less formalized practices, such as extended visiting at the natal village, foreground the permanence of a woman's ties to parents and to brothers. Vatuk's explicit critique of the emphasis on the lineal, corporate nature of north Indian kinship includes the argument that the "unbreakable bond" between a woman and her natal kin is related to the latter's obligation to supply her with gifts that ensure her security in her husband's home. And Dube, in her discussion of the production of women as gendered subjects in the Indian patrilineal milieu, points out that the particular contradictions within the kinship system produce an ambiguity surrounding women's transferal from natal kin to conjugal kin. While the life-long tie between brothers and sisters is emphasized in ritual and in everyday talk, young girls are nonetheless prepared for life in the husband's home by being told that a woman should be like water which, having no shape of its own, can take the shape of the vessel into which it is poured, or that she should be like soft and malleable clay that has no form until it is worked into shape by the potter. Thus, on the one hand, ritual perpetuates ties with the natal kin, while on the other, women are in many ways expected, as Dube points out, to discard their loyalties to natal kin, to be formed and shaped anew in the husband's family.[7] The more that women place themselves at a distance from their natal kin, the more vulnerable they may be to harsh treatment in the conjugal village; the natal place continues to be viewed as a place of refuge and of succor throughout a woman's life, and a husband may seek to place limits on a woman's ties to her natal kin, in order to enhance his own power over her (Raheja and Gold 1994, p. 76).

The poignancy of women's separation from natal kin is most vividly dramatized in north India at the moment of *bidāī* ("departure"), when a newly married girl first leaves her natal home in the company of her husband and his male kinsmen. Both men and women present at this time are apt to weep at the sight of the heavily veiled young woman being carried to a waiting automobile or water-buffalo cart, and the women of the bride's natal village sing "departure songs" (*bidāī gīt*) at the doorway as she leaves. Many of these songs reflect on the contradictory expectations concerning natal and conjugal relationships.

Departure Song 1

REFRAIN [Bride's natal kin][8]

Dear girl, today you've left your father's house, today you've become
    alien (*parāī*) to us.
The streets in which you spent your childhood have today become
    parāī.

[Bride speaking]

My grandfather cries, my grandmother cries, the whole family cries.
My younger brother cries, your sister "born from the same mother"
    (*mā jāī*) has left and gone away.

[Verses in which the bride speaks are repeated, using kin terms for father's elder brother, father's elder brother's wife, father's younger brother's wife, and so on.]

The second line of the refrain of this song ends with the words *parāī re*. The second line of the bride's verses ends with the word *mā jāī re*. The replication of the same sound pattern, the rhyme, in these two verses ironically foregrounds the dissimilarity in the meanings of the relationship enunciated by the bride's natal kin and by the bride herself. *Parāī re* and *mā jai re* share the same sounds, but this aural similarity serves to heighten the contradiction between the two representations of women in patrilineal kinship relationships, as "alien" to her natal kin because of the conventions of patrilineal kinship, yet "born from the same

156

mother" nonetheless. An ironic awareness of this contradiction lies at the heart of this song of departure.

Departure Song 2

REFRAIN [Bride speaking]

Don't let your mind be filled with sadness.
Mother, I'll meet you again.

I'll call my *dādas* (HFM) *dādī* (FM).
I'll call my *tāyas* (HFeBW) *tāī* (FeBW).
I won't remember my *dādī*, Mother I'll meet you again.
I won't remember my *tāī*, Mother I'll meet you again.[9]

[In the following verse of this song, the bride says that she will call her husband's mother "mother," her husband's sister "sister," and so on.]

This second song of departure expresses an ironic perspective on the same set of contradictions not by juxtaposing two contradictory perspectives, but by making utterances whose actual intended meaning is precisely the opposite of its conventional and literal meaning. The poignant irony of a bride saying "I won't remember my *dādī*, I won't remember my *tāī* " lies precisely in the fact that all of the women singing this song know that she will never forget, and though she may call her husband's father's mother *dādī*, as the ideology of *kanyā dān* enjoins her to do, her experience as she utters that word in her conjugal village is worlds apart from the experience of saying it in her own natal home.

Departure Song 3

Two water pots are on my head,
An ornament of gold hangs on my brow.
Call me back quickly, mother,
Beg with folded hands.
My heart is not here in my in-laws' house,
My heart is not here with this foreign man.
Call me back quickly, mother,
Beg with folded hands.
My friends still played with dolls together,
But I went off to my in-laws' house.
Call me back quickly, mother,
Beg with folded hands.

157

[First verse is repeated a number of times, changed only by the substitution of the names of other ornaments worn by married women.]

This third song of departure vividly portrays a woman's sense of belonging fully
neither to natal home nor conjugal home. The first two lines invoke conventional
and often recurring images of desire and fulfillment, and the pleasure of attracting
and pleasing one's husband; an image of a woman gracefully drawing water at a
village well often, in women's songs, precedes a happy flirtatious encounter, and
songs of conjugal happiness frequently include long lists of the ornaments worn
by a married woman that mark her body as sexual and pleasureful (Das 1988, p.
201; Raheja and Gold 1994). This song of departure begins with these images of
conjugal pleasures, but the desires and expectations are evoked but not fulfilled:
the husband is a "foreign man" and the bride cannot bear to stay. She has become
parāī to her own natal kin at the time of marriage, but the man to whose house
she has gone is a foreigner to her.

I spoke about these songs in 1988 with Simla, a woman who had been married
into Pahansu about twenty years before, and who had given birth there to four
children, one of whom was already married and about to give birth to Simla's first
grandchild. We talked about why so many women felt the poignancy of such
songs, and she said to me, very slowly and deliberately as she looked around the
house in which she had spent more than half her life: "You know, we never call our
sasurāl [husband's home] 'one's own house.' We only call our *pīhar* [natal home]
'one's own house.'" Simla's ironic tone speaks here to the fissure she seems to experience between the patrilineal convention that married women become "one's
own" to their husband's family and "alien" to their natal kin on the one hand, and
women's continual experience of "foreignness" in their *sasurāl*s and feelings of
longing for the natal kin on the other.

The acknowledgment of this fissure, the awareness of a contradiction within the
conventions of patrilineal ideology, is inserted into everyday speech and everyday
moral assessments through women's use of proverbs. A very commonly heard
proverb used by both men and women asserts the patrilineal idiom of the complete dissimilation of the woman from her natal kin: "Daughter, daughter's husband, and sister's son; these three are not one's own." Yet in speaking of the
emotional and pragmatic difficulties of this dissimilation and the assimilation into
the *sasurāl*, women frequently invoke a countervailing proverbial claim: "The
daughter and the son are one's own, and the daughter-in-law is 'other.'"

An ironic view of the substitutability of natal kin by the husband's kin found in
the second departure song is echoed in a very commonly heard women's proverb:

If a woman had sixty mothers-in-law and a hundred husband's sisters,
none could compare to her own mother.

Several Hindi proverbial couplets also point to women's experience of this contradiction in the patrilineal description of a woman's easy transferal from natal
home to conjugal home.

I have heard what you said, friend, and pondered it in my heart,
That after getting her married, a father doesn't keep his daughter in his
house.

In feigning surprise at the obvious fact that in north India a married daughter does
not remain in her natal home, this proverb, like the songs of departure, focuses on
women's complex experience of what appears, from the male perspective, as an
unproblematic transferal of women from one patrilineal kin group to another.

May the house of my mother-in-law be ruined, she who always creates
enmity.
May my natal house prosper, as long as the world endures.

Though the patrilineal ideology of *kanyā dān* enjoins a woman to abandon her
loyalties to her natal kin and see herself as "one's own" to her husband's kin, the
second rhymed couplet articulates a critique of that injunction. As it speaks of a
curse on the *sasurāl* and a blessing on the *pīhar*, this proverb, like the preceding
one, evokes a sense of the close and persisting ties to the natal kin, and a sense of
the shattered and incomplete solidarity a woman frequently experiences in her
husband's house.[10]

A second set of contradictions in north Indian kinship addressed in women's
speech genres concerns the relative valuation that is to be placed on the conjugal
relationship on the one hand, and on a man's ties to his own natal kin and the solidarity of that patrilineal group on the other. Marriage is deemed essential in the
social, ritual and emotional lives of both men and women. Many proverbs attest to
the common-sensical nature of this view.

A wife is sorrowful without her husband, like the body without food;
Her heart is burnt and heated like a field without rain.

A man without a wife is like a traveler on the road.

159

At the same time, however, the discourse of patrilineal kinship enjoins the wife to subordinate her desire for intimacy with the husband to his preexisting bonds of loyalty and affection with his natal kinsmen. Kakar (1978) suggests that, in this regard, the wife represents a pernicious threat to the unity and solidarity of the patrilineal unit, and her intimacy with him must not be allowed to disrupt or weaken his ties to his parents and siblings. Intimacy of all kinds, particularly sexual intimacy, is seen as dangerous to this solidarity; and attempts may be made to limit such intimacy if it does in fact come to threaten a man's other loyalties. The ideal wife, then, accepts without question the patrilineal assumption that her husband's natal ties take precedence over the conjugal relationship, and accepts, in consequence, her subordinate position in her *sasurāl*, her husband's family's house.

This dominant perspective concerning the valuation of men's natal ties over ties to the wife are exemplified in a number of proverbs that seem to be used primarily by men. The following is a particularly striking example:

> Whoever kicks his parents to strengthen his relationship with his wife,
> His sin will not go away even if he performs expiation in all the pilgrimage places.

Women's ritual songs, particularly the long narrative "dancing songs," offer a set of compelling critiques of this notion that women pose a threat to the unity of the patrilineal group, and of the consequent devaluation of conjugality and of the worth of women as wives. A dancing song sung at the festival of Tīj is typical of a great many such songs that I recorded.

Dancing Song 1, for the Festival of Tīj

[*Bahū* to *sās*][11]
Sāsū, someone has come selling fish.
Sāsū, everyone is buying some fish.
Sāsū, buy some fish and give some to us too.
You give us sweet pudding and fried breads every day, *sāsū*.[12]

Hearing of the husband's coming, a cup of poison.
She drank the cup of poison, and she felt so very sleepy.

[*Bahū*, who has just drunk the poison, to *sās*]
Tell me *sāsū*, where should I sleep?

[*Sās* to *baahū*]
Sleep on the top floor, *bāhū*, in the room with the red door.
Lie down and sleep on your bed, *bāhū*.

Away for twelve years, the beloved husband came home.

[Husband to his mother, the *sās*]
I see my mother, I see my sisters too.
But I don't see my wife, mother, the daughter of a gentleman.

[*Sās* to her son, the husband]
On the top floor son, in the room with the red door,
She's sleeping there, son, the daughter of a gentleman.

[Husband to the *sās*]
I called her once, mother, I called her twice,
But still she didn't speak, mother, the daughter of a gentleman.

[*Sās* to the husband]
Go into the garden and bring in a branch.
Hit her and wake her up, the daughter of a gentleman.

[Husband to the *sās*]
I hit her once with the branch, mother, I hit her twice.
But still she didn't speak, mother, the daughter of a gentleman.

The husband took off her veil, to have a look at her.

[Husband to the *sās*]
Is she dead or asleep, mother, the daughter of a gentleman?

[*Sās* to the husband]
Go to the garden, son, and cut some sandalwood.
Burn her body, son, the daughter of a gentleman.

He burnt her body, and he came back to the house.
The husband sat at the threshold, crying out with grief.

[*Sās* to the husband]
Why are you crying son, crying out so loudly?
I can have my son married four times.

Two fair brides, two dark ones,
I can have my son married four times.

[Husband to the *sās*]
You can throw all four down a well, mother.
I don't have that one, the daughter of a gentleman.

The husband spread out his scarf, and lay down to sleep.

[Husband, addressing his dead wife]
Come in a dream, fair one, and tell me all that happened.

[*Bāhū* speaking in the dream]
Husband, every day she gave bread and pudding.
She heard that you were coming, and she gave a cup of poison.
I drank the poison, and I felt very sleepy.
Where should I sleep, *sāsū*, tell me the place.
On the top floor, husband, in the room with the red door.

Go up to the roof, husband-lord, and shout out to everyone.

[Husband]
Don't listen, men, to your mothers and your sisters.
My mother and my sisters have laid waste to my home.

In this powerful song, we twice hear the voice of the husband resisting the assumption that a woman as wife is replaceable and indeed dispensable. When the mother suggests that her son can easily marry four more times if he wishes, the husband rejects this portrayal of the wife as an anonymous cipher, as either irreducibly "other" to her conjugal kin or as so assimilated to them that her own particular identity is dissolved. And finally, at the end of this Tīj song, as he climbs to the roof and proclaims that a man's loyalty to his natal kin must sometimes be subordinated to his loyalty to his wife, he subverts a fundamental tenet of north Indian kinship.

In many women's songs, men are represented as feigning adherence to these norms concerning the priority to be placed on patrilineal solidarities, while privately valuing intimacy and solidarity with the wife. In the following dancing song, public conformity to the requirements of these solidarities is at odds with a man's private subversion of them.[13]

Dancing Song 2

My mother-in-law is very cunning.
I am my husband's beloved.
I sat at the grinding stone, I ground the grain coarsely.
She rubbed the flour between her fingers, to see how coarse it was.
I am my husband's beloved.
When she rubbed her fingers together, she told her son about it.
I am my husband's beloved.
When she told her son about it, he brought a stick with knobs, and he
     beat me gently gently (*dhīre dhīre*).
When he beat me gently gently, I went into our bedroom.
I am my husband's beloved.
When I was sleeping in the room, he brought a *ser* of *laḍḍūs*.[14]
I am my husband's beloved.
When he brought a *ser* of *laḍḍūs*, I threw them back at him.
I am my husband's beloved.
When I threw the *laḍḍūs* back, he hand fed them to me and I ate one
     or two.
I am my husband's beloved.
When I ate one or two, I became very thirsty.
I am my husband's beloved.
When I became very thirsty, he brought some water to me.
I am my husband's beloved.
When he brought the water to me, I drank a drop or two.
I am my husband's beloved.
When I drank a drop or two, I became very cold.
I am my husband's beloved.
When I became very cold, he brought a red quilt to me.
I am my husband's beloved.
When he brought a red quilt to me, I became very warm.
I am my husband's beloved.
When I became very warm, he brought a red fan to me.
I am my husband's beloved.
When he brought a red fan to me, I waved it gently gently (*dhīre
     dhīre*).
I am my husband's beloved.

In this song, the husband makes a show of beating his wife to present a public image of acceding to his mother's claims on his loyalty, but he beats her "gently gently" and then in their own room, away from the scrutiny of his natal kin, he brings her food and drink and engages in sexual intimacy, as the last lines of the song strongly suggest. I have elsewhere suggested that embroidered fans (*bijna*) appear, for a number of reasons, in women's songs and in north Indian folk art as signs of sexual intimacy (Raheja, in press). The private sexual intimacy is read by the wife as a negation of the significance of the sham public beating. In this song, both the beating and the figurative sexual intercourse are done "gently gently" (*dhīre dhīre*). This rather prominent linguistic equation in the song might be read as an ironic commentary on another kind of equation that is often made in Hindi between beatings and sexual intercourse. A contemptuous way of describing intercourse is, in Hindi, *chūt mārnā*, literally "beating the vagina." *Mārnā* is the usual word for "beating," the one that is used in this song. But the equivalence between beating and sexual intimacy (both are done "gently gently") that is drawn in the song underlines the fact that a man's adherence to a public and "normative" devaluation of female sexuality and of women as wives may be only a cover behind which other perspectives are given moral credence, overtly by women, though perhaps covertly and furtively by men.[15]

There are a number of proverbs used by women that amplify the perspective voiced in these songs, proverbs that enunciate a negative judgment concerning the patrilineal norms that devalue conjugality and insist on the "replaceability" of wives.

> What is it to a man? He puts on a new shoe and takes off the old.

This particular proverb is sometimes heard in conversations in which women criticize a man (often with adverse consequences for him) who exhibits an attitude of disdain for his wife, or undervalues her in relation to his male kinsmen; he regards her as replaceable as a worn-out shoe.[16]

> He is hurt by the mountain and breaks up the grindstone.

Women sometimes use this second proverb as a commentary on men's tendency to unjustly place the blame for discord within the patrilineal group upon their wives, a tendency that places priority on the relationships among men while viewing the women as dangerous threats to male solidarity. Although the proverb can be invoked in a variety of situations of misplaced blame, its use by women in contexts in which kinship loyalties are at stake may represent a strategy of resistance to patrilineal values.

The third set of contradictions addressed in women's songs and proverbs concerns the tension women perceive between positing the patrilineal kinship group as a solidary unit on the one hand, and defining wives as both the upholders of the honor of that group and as its most subordinate members on the other. Women are expected to be devoted to their husbands even in the face of serious moral transgressions, and wives are enjoined to emulate the figure of Sita, the wife of Rama in the epic Ramayana, who remains steadfast in wifely devotion even as Rama unjustly banishes her from his kingdom. Kakar (1978, p. 66) speaks of a "formidable consensus" in India concerning the image of Sita as the "ideal woman." And the phrase "she is a second Sita" is, in northern India, a universally recognized appreciative acknowledgment of feminine virtue. Yet women's songs and proverbs from north India appear to challenge the values of unquestioned submission and self-sacrifice that Sita represents.

An extremely common theme in a wide variety of north Indian textual and oral traditions involves the banishment or scorn of barren women, of women whose husbands decide for one reason or another to take a second wife, and of women unjustly accused of engaging in sexual relations outside marriage. Representations of women's responses to such treatment, and the moral valuations of these responses, differ dramatically in the epic traditions, in popular north Indian folk dramas (*sāng* or *nautankī*) performed by and largely for males, and in women's narrative dancing songs from Pahansu and Hathchoya. I have elsewhere (Raheja and Gold 1994, pp. 136–142) described the way in which the epic texts and folk dramas portray the "ideal wife" as one who unquestioningly submits to such unjust banishment or scorn, and whose response is simply to wait for other male kinsmen—son or brother or father—to rescue her from her adversity and restore her to her husband. Despite the authoritative nature of these powerful images in north India, the narratives recounted in women's dancing songs set forth a strikingly different perspective on gender, agency and dependency in kinship relations.

Dancing Song 3, for the Festival of Tīj

From which direction did the rains come,
In which direction will it rain now?
Indar Raja comes down in the garden
The rains have come from the east,
And it's about to rain in the west.

[REFRAIN] Indar Raja comes down in the garden.[17]
   [*Bahū* speaking]
Mother-in-law, I heard a surprising thing,
That your son will marry again.
Mother-in-law, have I come from a bad family,
Or did I bring a small dowry?

165

[Mother-in-law]
No, *bahū*, you aren't from a bad family,
And you didn't bring a small dowry.
Your color is a little dark, *bahū*,
And my son wants a fair wife.

[*Bahū*]
Sisters, I went to ask my father-in-law,
Is your son to marry again?
Father-in-law, have I come from a bad family,
Or did I bring a small dowry?

[Father-in-law]
No, *bahū*, you aren't from a bad family,
And you didn't bring a small dowry.
You are a little dark, my *bahū*,
And my son wants a fair wife.

[These verses are repeated, changing only the kin term, as the wife
puts the same query to her husband's sister and her husband. She
then continues to question her husband.]

[*Bahū*]
Husband-lord, who will do the women's rites (*ṭehale*) at your
    marriage,
And who will sing the auspicious songs?

[Husband]
Wife, my mother will do the women's rites,
And my sister will sing auspicious songs.

[*Bahū*]
Husband-lord, who will send off the marriage party,
And who will bear the expense?

[Husband]
Wife, my brother will send off the marriage party,
And my father will bear the expense.

[*Bahū*]
Sisters, I went to the roof [to see the marriage party return, after the
    husband has married again].
And how many came in the marriage party?

Sisters, there were one hundred and fifty of them, without feet and
    hands,
And I couldn't count all the bald ones. [The wife is here reviling the
    men of the marriage party.]

Sisters, when I heard that the co-wife had come,
I got a fever right away.

Sisters, I went to see the new co-wife [to give a ritual gift]
A bent and worthless coin in my hand.

I went to the ritual feast for the co-wife,
Sisters, I made a rice pudding filled with poison.

Sisters, I heard that the co-wife died,
My fever went down right away.

Sisters, I went to the keen for the co-wife,
I veiled myself heavily [women veil while doing this ritual lament].

Sisters, outside I was keening, but inside I was laughing.
And my heart was joyful.

In this song, the wife is placed in a situation not unlike that of many of the wives who appear in the epics and the *sāng* dramas. Yet in contrast to the submissive posture assumed by the wives in the male-authored folklore genres, the heroine of this dancing song takes immediate and decisive action in the face of the threat to her position in her husband's house. The appeal made by the wife to "sisters," the women listeners who hear her tale, make it evident that the wife's actions are indeed valorized. It is not necessarily the violence, the poisoning of the co-wife, that is being extolled, but the ability to act decisively when one is treated unjustly. There is no talk of "fate" here, or of ineradicable ill-fortune, as is found in the *sāng* dramas. There is rather, in this dancing song, a definitive moral judgment, and an immediate and potent response to the injustice. And, as in many other women's songs, a woman is represented as having to struggle against the wishes and interests of her husband's natal kin in her efforts to establish and maintain intimacy with her husband and a nonsubordinate position in his home.[18] And finally, the heroine of this song does not wait for a son or brother or father to save her from her predicament; there are no such male rescuers in this text or in any of the songs I recorded in Pahansu or Hathchoya.

The critique of the patrilineal norm espousing unquestioned wifely submission evidenced in this narrative is not limited to the relatively narrow confines of ritual song. In this instance too, both the patrilineal norms and resistance to aspects of the dominant discourse are lodged in proverbs used in everyday speech situations as well.

> A proper wife feeds the household first,
> and saves only the leavings for herself.

This proverb plays upon several conceptions of familial well-being and familial hierarchy to reinforce the subordinate position of women within the kinship group. *Sulakkhnī*, translated here as "proper wife," refers literally to a woman "having propitious signs" or "auspicious." The auspicious wife, one who brings well-being to her husband's patrilineal household, is one who eats only the food left over after the men have eaten; this is a very common expectation for proper feminine behavior in north India. Precedence in eating is a potent marker of hierarchy in other arenas as well, and the eating of leftovers is a sign of very low status. The woman who accepts this subordinate position and who is ready to sacrifice her own well-being for that of others causes her husband's family to prosper.

While rural women do not totally repudiate this ideal of self-sacrifice and subordination, they do interrogate the discourse that proposes it as an unchallengeable and inflexible injunction. One women's proverb in particular appears as a direct response to the preceding proverb.

> A wife who is modest and shy always goes hungry.

In the dominant discourse of north Indian kinship, the possession of *śaram* (modesty, reticence, deference, "shame") is perhaps the most highly valued feminine attribute; one of the most devastating criticisms of a woman is that she is *beśaram*, without *śaram*. And yet, when they comment on the possession of *śaram* in this proverb, women cast a skeptical eye on this most Sita-like of qualities, and focus only on the deprivation that is often a consequence of its cultivation.

"Narrative Potency" and the Strategic Use of Speech

The songs and proverbs considered in this paper make visible the contradictions within a male-dominated discourse, and thereby envision that discourse as grounded not in a "natural" and unchangeable moral order, but in a vulnerable and perhaps transformable set of social conventions.[19]

The narrative potency of the stories told in women's songs is evident in the fact that the resistance to patrilineal ideology and the alternative perspectives on north Indian kinship found therein are not confined to intermittent ritual punctuations of social life, but are found in proverbial speech as well, a speech genre used in northern India as a form of everyday moral commentary. And beyond song and proverb, women may speak in ways that indicate the pervasiveness of these perspectives in more prosaic conversation as well. When in 1990 I naïvely asked several groups of rural women from the dominant landholding Gujar caste whether they aspired to be like Sita, the paragon of wifely virtue and self-sacrifice, my question was greeted with gales of laughter, and a plethora of anecdotes about outwitted husbands and independent strong-willed wives. No one is like Sita nowadays, they said, and they assured me further that no one has any desire to be a "second Sita." In their everyday lives, these women constantly behaved in ways that contradicted the norms that Sita represents, yet they did not view their actions as morally reprehensible.

And yet one must take into account the situations in which such utterances are made. When I posed the same questions to other women in the presence of their daughters-in-law, the responses tended to be evasive, or they were cast fairly unambiguously within the terms of the dominant discourse of subordination and dependency; a reply to the effect that women need not emulate the wifely virtues of Sita would perhaps, in those circumstances, diminish a mother-in-law's authority over her daughter-in-law, and women were obviously aware of this as they spoke.

A conversation I had with a Gujar woman and a woman of the very low Sweeper caste illustrates this sort of strategic self-presentation in a more complex fashion. This conversation took place in the company of an educated Gujar man, himself an anthropologist. I again asked about the desirability of emulating Sita, about deferring to one's husband, and about the importance of women's role in maintaining the honor of their husbands and brothers by cultivating the quality of *śaram*. This time my question elicited no laughter or mirthful repudiation of Sita, or subtle evasion of the question. Kalaso, the Sweeper woman, was extremely circumspect in answering my questions, insisting throughout the very long tape-recorded interview that women of her family and caste did indeed strive to model their behavior according to the image of Sita. The honor of one's husband and brothers was at stake, she maintained, as she used several proverbial phrases in constructing her argument about Sita and ideal womanly behavior. Kalaso made these assertions vociferously and at times almost angrily, as if the very question was a threat to her own honor and that of her family and caste.

169

Should we read the transcript of this interview as a token of Kalaso's unambiguous internalization of the image of Sita as the ideal woman, and of the dominant patrilineal perspective on kinship, gender, and agency and of the terms of her own subordination? Or should we remember that one of our interlocutors was a man of the dominant landholding caste, and that high-caste men, in the past and perhaps in the present as well, have often *expected* to find low-caste women who could be persuaded or compelled by force to disregard the value of sexual virtue that Sita embodies, and that Kalaso may have had this set of facts in mind as she angrily asserted her own adherence to the ideals represented by the heroine of the Ramayana? Was she perhaps not asserting her subservience so much as her defiance of a perceived expectation that she might possibly be viewed as subject to sexual coercion by a powerful male? And should we then regard Kalaso's words not as evidence of the circumscription of female subjectivity by the terms of the male discourse on patriliny, but as a strategic and indeed subversive presentation of self in a specific and highly charged social arena? Kalaso was asserting the validity of "traditional" discourses on kinship and gender not because she had internalized these in any unambiguous way. She made these assertions for quite a different purpose: to resist what she perceived as the possibility that a man of a landholding caste might regard her as a less "honorable" woman from a low and powerless caste and therefore as someone whose sexuality he might appropriate without expecting any repercussions from his own caste or from hers.

To understand such discourses on kinship, gender and "tradition," then, we must regard the words of our interlocutors not as fixed and reified and essentialized mirrors of consciousness, but as shifting and purposeful negotiations of identity and relationship that take different forms in different social contexts and before different audiences.

In this paper, a focus on the way in which proverbs insert the critical perspectives on patriliny found in women's songs into wider areas of social life permits us to regard aspects of women's speech practices in terms of such negotiations. In *The Practice of Everyday Life,* de Certeau reminds us that proverbs, like all discourses, are not inert objects whose meaning can be dissociated from the situations in which speakers enunciate them. They appear in speech as tools purposefully manipulated by their users (1984, pp. 18–21), who may at times play intentionally on the ambiguities of their speech to deflect the power of a dominant social order (1984, p. xiii). Kenneth Burke has also pointed to the strategic nature of proverbs in social life:

> Proverbs are *strategies* for dealing with *situations.* In so far as situations
> are typical and recurrent in a given social structure, people develop

170

names for them and strategies for handling them. Another name for strategies might be *attitudes*....The apparent contradictions [among proverbs] depend upon differences in attitude, involving correspondingly different choice of strategy. (1973, pp. 296–297)

Thus, proverbs and the diverse perspectives on kinship relationships embedded in them represent resources that speakers draw upon in framing their own social worlds. While north Indian women may at times speak in the terms set by the dominant discourse, they also interrogate and undermine the script of patriliny as their speech practices sketch a plural rather than monolithic moral discourse.

Notes

[1] Research upon which this paper is based was carried out in two villages of western Uttar Pradesh, northern India, from 1977 to 1979, and in 1988 and 1990. Fieldwork was supported by grants from the Social Science Research Council, the American Institute of Indian Studies, the Wenner-Gren Foundation for Anthropological Research, and a McKnight-Land Grant Professorship from the University of Minnesota. I thank Pamela Feldman-Savelsberg for helpful comments on an earlier version of this essay.

[2] On the positive valuation and auspicious nature of women's ritual song in north India, see Henry 1988, pp. 108–111.

[3] On the theoretical issue of the constitutive aspects of speech in social life, see Sherzer's (1987) explication of a discourse-centered approach to language and culture.

[4] See Raheja and Gold 1994, especially chapters 4 and 6, for examples of the sometimes quiet, sometimes flamboyant ways that rural women act in defiance of the kinship norms of wifely deference and submission.

[5] All of the songs translated for this paper were recorded in either Pahansu or Hathchoya (western Uttar Pradesh) in 1988 and 1990. I heard many of the proverbs in these villages, some in other places in northern India, and some are taken from two nineteenth-century compen-

dia of proverbs (Christian 1891 and Fallon 1886), and from William Crooke's *A Rural and Agricultural Glossary for the N.W. Provinces and Oudh* (1888). I found these three sources to be extremely useful. Fallon's text contains nearly all of the Hindi proverbs, on any topic, that I have ever come upon. Though I found translations and indications of usage contexts in these compilations to be sometimes misleading, Hindi texts for all the proverbs are provided in each case; when I have drawn on these works, I have therefore amended translations when necessary.

[6] The term *riśtā*, "relationship" is never used in connection with relationships within a "lineage" (*kunbā*); it is only normally used to characterize relationships through marriage. Thus, a woman's relationship with her own natal kin is characterized, from this perspective, in the same way as a relationship through marriage, because she has been assimilated to the affinal kin of her natal family.

[7] For discussions of the ritual ties between women and their natal kin, and the enduring gift-giving responsibilities entailed by them, see Raheja 1988, pp. 93–202 and in press, and Raheja and Gold 1994.

[8] All of the songs that I translate here are sung by groups of women without distinguishing, in the performance, the presumed "speakers" in the

conversation that is represented. I note in these translations the speakers that the women identified for me as I worked on the translations with them.

[9] These are anthropological conventions for noting kin relations. HFM is "husband's father's mother," FM is "father's mother," HFeBW is "husband's father's elder brother's wife," and FeBW is "father's elder brother's wife."

[10] There is also a male perspective on women's ties to natal kin, one that appears to respond to the critiques women pose in song and proverb. In the folk dramas performed in the *nautankī* popular theatre of northern India, a frequent theme is a husband's hostility to the wife's brother, and a fear and suspicion that the wife harbors powerful loyalties to her natal kin that could jeopardize his own power over her. But if a husband cannot fully trust his wife in these plays, brothers also frequently distrust their sisters because they have married into other families and have allegiances there (Hansen 1992, pp. 184–188). Two proverbs used almost exclusively by men attest to the suspicions harbored by husbands concerning their wives' brothers: "As niches weaken walls, so wives' brothers weaken the house"; and "The wife's brother eats special fried breads, while a brother's brother has only peas to eat," i.e., a wife will favor her own brother over her husband's kin.

[11] *Bahū* is a kinship term meaning "wife" or "son's wife." *Sās* (or *sāsū*) is "mother-in-law."

[12] These first lines of the song are not entirely clear to me. It seems apparent though that the mother-in-law is angered by the *bahū's* suggestion. The following line indicates that upon hearing that her son would soon return after a long absence, the *sās* poisons the *bahū*.

[13] My reading of this song owes much to Das's analysis (1976) of similar ambiguities in Panjabi kinship.

[14] A *ser* is a unit of weight, about two pounds. *Laḍḍūs* are sweets made from chick pea flour and sugar, often distributed in north Indian villages at weddings and other festive occasions.

[15] One tragic index of the limits to women's resistance is the fact that the heroine of this song must undergo a public beating, however "gently" it is administered, before she is able to speak up privately to her husband.

[16] The power of this particular male perspective is illustrated in "The Punishment," a short story by the Bengali writer Rabindranath Tagore, in which a husband unthinkingly utters the conventional sentiment "One can always replace a wife, but one can never replace a brother," with tragic consequences.

[17] The festival of Tīj is celebrated in the rainy month of Sāvan, hence the lines about the rains and Indar Raja (the god Indra) who presides over the monsoon rains. In north Indian oral traditions and pictorial art, the rainy season is represented as a time of erotic encounters and the reunion of lovers. (See for example Wadley 1983.) The repeated references to the rains in this song thus function in the same ironic mode as the references to the water pots in the third song of departure translated above; they create an expectation here of conjugal intimacy that is thwarted by the wife's realization of her husband's plan to marry again.

[18] A second set of significant limitations on women's resistance to the discourse of patriliny is evident in this song and in many of the others we have considered. In these songs, and frequently in everyday life as well, women's struggles are often directed against other women—co-wives, mothers-in-law, husband's sisters—and not against the men who perpetuate this discourse.

[19] Ann Grodzins Gold and I (Raheja and Gold 1994) use the term "narrative potency" to describe the way in which the stories women tell in ritual contexts enter into and transform their everyday lives.

References

Banerjee, Sumanta. 1989. "Marginalization of Women's Popular Culture in Nineteenth Century Bengal." In *Recasting Women: Essays in Colonial History*, ed. Kumkum Sangari and Sudesh Vaid, pp. 127–179. New Delhi: Kali for Women.

Briggs, Charles. 1988. *Competence in Performance: The Creativity of Tradition in Mexicano Verbal Art.* Philadelphia: University of Pennsylvania Press.

Burke, Kenneth. 1973. *The Philosophy of Literary Form.* Berkeley: University of California Press.

Chatterjee, Partha. 1989. "Colonialism, Nationalism, and Colonialized Women: the Contest in India." *American Ethnologist* 16, pp. 622–633.

Christian, John. 1891. *Behar Proverbs.* London: Kegan Paul, Trench, Trubner and Co.

Crooke, William. 1888. *A Rural and Agricultural Glossary for the N.W. Provinces and Oudh.* Calcutta: Superintendent of Government Printing, India.

Das, Veena. 1976. "Masks and Faces: an Essay on Punjabi Kinship." *Contributions to Indian Sociology* n.s. 10, pp. 1–30.

———. 1988. "Femininity and the Orientation to the Body." In *Socialisation, Education, and Women: Explorations in Gender Identity*, ed. K. Chanana, pp. 193–207. New Delhi: Orient Longman.

de Certeau, Michel. 1984. *The Practice of Everyday Life.* Berkeley: University of California Press.

Dube, Leela. 1988. "On the Construction of Gender: Hindu Girls in Patrilineal India." *Economic and Political Weekly*, April 30, pp. 11–19.

Fallon, S.W. 1886. *A Dictionary of Hindustani Proverbs.* Banaras: Medical Hall Press.

Flueckiger, Joyce Burkhalter. 1991. "Genre and Community in the Folklore System of Chhattisgarh." In *Gender, Genre, and Power in South Asian Expressive Traditions*, ed. Arjun Appadurai, Frank J. Korom, and Margaret A. Mills, pp.181–200. Philadelphia: University of Pennsylvania Press.

Gal, Susan. 1991. "Between Speech and Silence: The Problematics of Research on Language and Gender." In *Gender at the Crossroads of Knowledge: Feminist Anthropology in the Postmodern Era*, ed. Micaela di Leonardo, pp. 175–203. Berkeley: University of California Press.

Gluckman, Max. 1963. "Rituals of Rebellion in South East Africa." In *Order and Rebellion in Tribal Africa.* New York: Free Press.

Guha, Ranajit. 1983. *Elementary Aspects of Peasant Insurgency in Colonial India.* Delhi: Oxford University Press.

Hansen, Kathryn. 1992. *Grounds for Play: The Nautanki Theatre of North India.* Berkeley: University of California Press.

Henry, Edward O. 1988. *Chant the Names of God: Music and Culture in Bhojpuri-Speaking India.* San Diego: San Diego State University Press.

Jacobson, Doranne. 1977. "Flexibility in North Indian Kinship and Residence." In *The New Wind: Changing Identities in South Asia*, ed. Kenneth David, pp. 263–283. The Hague: Mouton.

Jeffery, Patricia, Roger Jeffery, and Andrew Lyon. 1989. *Labour Pains and Labour Power: Women and Childbearing in India.* London and New Jersey: Zed Books.

Kakar, Sudhir. 1978. *The Inner World.* Delhi: Oxford University Press.

Kumar, Nita. 1991. "Widows, Education and Social Change in Twentieth Century Banaras." *Economic and Political Weekly*, April 27: 19–25.

Mani, Lata. 1984. "The Production of an Official Discourse on Sati in Early Nineteenth-Century Bengal." In *Europe and Its Others*, ed. Francis Barker, pp. 89–127. Colchester: University of Essex.

173

———. 1989. "Contentious Traditions: The Debate on *Sati* in Colonial India." In *Recasting Women: Essays in Colonial History*, ed. by Kumkum Sangari and Sudesh Vaid, pp. 88–126. New Delhi: Kali for Women.

O'Hanlon, Rosalind. 1991. "Issues of Widowhood: Gender and Resistance in Colonial Western India." In *Contesting Power: Resistance and Everyday Social Relations in South Asia*, ed. Douglas Haynes and Gyan Prakash, pp. 62–108. Berkeley: University of California Press.

Raheja, Gloria Goodwin. 1988. *The Poison in the Gift: Ritual, Prestation, and the Dominant Caste in a North Indian Village*. Chicago: University of Chicago Press.

———. Forthcoming. "Negotiated Solidarities: Gendered Perspectives on Disruption and Desire in North Indian Expressive Traditions and Popular Culture." *Oral Traditions*.

———. In press. "Crying When She's Born and Crying When She Goes Away: Marriage and the Idiom of the Gift in Pahansu Song Performance." In *From the Margins of Hindu Marriage: New Essays on Gender, Culture and Religion*, ed. Paul Courtwright and Lindsey Harlan. Oxford: Oxford University Press.

Raheja, Gloria Goodwin, and Ann Grodzins Gold. 1994. *Listen to the Heron's Words: Reimagining Gender and Kinship in North India*. Berkeley: University of California Press.

Scott, James C. 1990. *Domination and the Arts of Resistance: Hidden Transcripts*. New Haven: Yale University Press.

Sherzer, Joel. 1987. "A Discourse-Centered Approach to Culture." *American Anthropologist* 89(2): 295–309.

Tagore [Thakur], Rabindranath. 1990. "The Punishment." In *Of Women, Outcastes, Peasants, and Rebels: A Selection of Bengali Short Stories*, ed. and trans. Kalpana Bardhan. Berkeley: University of California Press.

Trautmann, Thomas. 1981. *Dravidian Kinship*. Berkeley: University of California Press.

Vatuk, Sylvia. 1975. "Gifts and Affines." *Contributions to Indian Sociology* n.s. 5: 155–196.

Wadley, Susan S. 1983. "The Rains of Estrangement: Understanding the Hindu Yearly Cycle." *Contributions to Indian Sociology* n.s. 17 (1): 51–85.

Yang, Anand. 1989. "Whose Sati? Widow Burning in Early 19th Century India." *Journal of Women's History* 1 (2): 8–33.

This essay analyzes how Bangangté ideas about marriage and procreation reveal the gendered experience of kinship. Through her ethnographic research, Pamela Feldman-Savelsberg found out from Bangangté women how notions of procreative cooking are central to representations of children's double descent (that is, through both paternal and maternal lines). Even though women are "enclosed" at marriage in their husband's compound and his lineage, culinary images provide women with an alternative framework to the otherwise predominantly agnatic kinship ideology (that is, traced through the male line). Like the other essays in this section, Feldman-Savelsberg's demonstrates that kinship systems can look different from the perspectives within them.

9

Cooking Inside:
Kinship and Gender in Bangangté Idioms
of Marriage and Procreation

PAMELA FELDMAN-SAVELSBERG

Nâ Nda: Cooking Inside

While conducting fieldwork on infertility anxiety in Bangangté, a Bamiléké kingdom in the highland Grassfields of Cameroon, I was confronted with a puzzle.[1] The anthropological literature described Bangangté as a society whose members are drawn together and organized according to principles of patrilineal descent.[2] Bangangté citizens I spoke to themselves emphasized male inheritance when first questioned. The *mfən* (king) is the living representative of a patrilineal dynasty. Houses and land are passed from father to son in impartible inheritance. When asked to name one's village, all Bangangté say a child "belongs" to the village of their father.

But, by attention to cultural forms and constructs normally overlooked (the imagery of marriage and procreation), I noted that Bangangté talk about and use their kinship system in a more complex fashion. Three modes of corporate group organization (patrilineal, matrilineal and the uterine group *pam ntɔ́*) fulfill complementary functions in different spheres of Bangangté life. In their everyday conversations regarding children and childbearing, and through the metaphors with which they discuss procreation, Bangangté women tend to emphasize the multi-

Permission to publish given by American Anthropological Association.

plicity of their connections to different types of kin rather than focus on their husbands' patrilineages. Bangangté men seem to invoke these more complex ties mainly in situations of misfortune (requiring sacrifice) or risk (avoiding incest while seeking a bride). This concern with matrilineal and uterine ancestors is confusing to the anthropologist when s/he overlooks the complexities of Bangangté (and Bamiléké) kinship by misconstruing it as a patrilineal kinship system.

We can approach some of the complexity and relevance of actors' perspectives on kinship by analyzing the language Bangangté use to discuss marriage and procreation. The symbolism of marriage and procreation, shared by all Bangangté but elaborated and highlighted in the casual speech of (mostly married) Bangangté women, reveals the way gender shapes how individuals select, emphasize and invoke various aspects of their complex double descent system.[3]

This article is entitled "cooking inside" because it is organized around a key term, *nâ ndɑ* [pronounced naan'da]. *Nâ ndɑ*, the Bangangté expression for marriage, literally means "to cook inside." According to Tamveun, an elderly male informant:

> *Nâ ndɑ* is marriage. An unmarried woman cooks on the road, in the open where just anyone can smell the delicious aromas from her cooking pot. A married woman cooks *inside*, cooks inside her kitchen. Only her husband tastes her food, and sniffs the aroma from her cooking pot. Her husband builds her the kitchen. Then she does not have to cook on the road. Later her kitchen is full of children.

Tamveun's expression alternated between seriousness (in my husband's absence I should understand the importance that young married women only cook inside) and that twinkle in the eye that indicated his enjoyment of the double entendre of cooking food and sex. Tamveun's exegesis of the expression *nâ ndɑ* was shared by the rural women of all ages with whom I lived and worked during my fifteen months of fieldwork in Bangangté, Cameroon.[4] These women also shared his mirth at the thought of flirtatious cooking aromas contained in the marital kitchen. While making clear that they were also serious business, Bangangté women made cooking, sex and sharing food the basis of many jokes.

Nâ ndɑ refers to both the cooking of food and the cooking of sex and children inside the mud brick walls of the kitchen and the social walls of marital relations. The analysis of *nâ ndɑ* leads to a string of metaphors regarding marriage, women's roles, sex and procreation. The term *nâ ndɑ* contains two sets of idioms, one referring to mixing, cooking and eating (key symbols permeating Bangangté concepts of procreation, gender and the constitution of society), the other to social space and enclosure (representing marriage, and related to the cooking idiom through the kitchen). The use of these idioms reveals different perspectives on kinship and marriage within Bangangté society. These perspectives vary according to gender, the roles of husband and wife within the marital dyad, and differing and sometimes conflicting allegiances based on membership in different kin groups.

This essay explores how Bangangté ideas about marriage and procreation reveal the gendered experience of kinship and social belonging. The imagery of kitchens, cooking, and feeding emphasizes women's space and roles. While contained within it, this culinary imagery provides an alternative emphasis to a dominant ideology that highlights the enclosure of women and their children within the *husband's* patrilineage and compound. Most particularly, women's elaboration of culinary imagery in their everyday speech foregrounds the significance of uterine kin links. In Bangangté kinship ideology, notions of culinary skill, procreative cooking ingredients and vessels are integral to the complementary and sometimes conflicting demands that every person faces by belonging to both a matrilineage and a patrilineage.

Bangangté is one of over a hundred Bamiléké kingdoms in the Grassfields of Cameroon, a diverse country on the hinge between West and Central Africa. Bangangté subjects, while citizens of the Republic of Cameroon, owe allegiance to their king. Most believe the king's political and physical strength directly affects the incidence of plenty or hunger, business and scholastic success or failure, and a "full house" or infertility. As of 1986, some 46,000 Bangangté resided in the rural area of Bangangté Subdivision, and another 12,000 in Bangangté town, the capital of Ndé Division. Several hundred thousand people who identify themselves as Bangangté live in cities and plantations outside the kingdom's territory. The result of generations of labor emigration from Bangangté, this large population-in-exile figures prominently in the consciousness of rural Bangangté residents, who call them *exilés*. The movement of individuals and families between the kingdom and *exilé* communities, between natal compound and husband's compound, and between mother's kitchen and father's house initiates much discussion among Bangangté about inside and outside, a sociospatial dichotomy referring both to different kinds of social belonging and cultural authenticity. Here I concentrate on how Bangangté use the idiom of inside-outside to define gender roles in procreation and marriage and the different geography of matrilineal and patrilineal ties.

Bangangté imagery of marriage and procreation reveals a semantic web involving the locale, ingredients and skills of cooking. Bangangté is not unique in using cooking imagery to talk about reproduction and social organization. In other Grassfields societies, heat, cooking, feeding and commensality are closely linked to fertility and to the powers and rituals of kingship (Engard 1986; Goheen 1992, p.

392; Schmidt 1955). Elsewhere in Africa, the hearth, heat and cooking are key to understanding the symbolism of female initiation rites, birth and social order (Richards 1956; de Heusch 1980; Beidelman 1986). Culinary imagery, while not unique to double descent systems, helps us solve our puzzle regarding different perspectives on kinship.

Melon Vines and Rules of Descent

Let us return to Bangangté women's voices. What do they say about patrilineality and matrilineality? Simone, a thirty-two-year-old wife of king Njiké Pokam, with a tiny business as a seamstress, spoke to me about the joy of having two daughters:

> I have two daughters, aged eight and ten. They attend the *école primaire*
> at Batela'. Their praise name is So'nyu, that is, they are daughters of
> Bangangté. Their father is king of Bangangté, so all the kings of
> Bangangté are their *mɑ' ŋut ŋze'* ["melon vines" (pronounced ma ngut
> nzuh)], their ancestors.... I am happy that I have two daughters. I can
> tell you why. My own mother has only one daughter, and that is me. Of
> all my mother's children, only I am a girl. Only I can be her heiress. My
> brother is part of my *pam ntɔ* [uterine group (pronounced pam'to)]
> and also part of my mother's lineage. But only my children can contin-
> ue the *pam ntɔ*, and since they are girls, their children continue it too.
> Yes, my mother and her line, her ancestors, are also *mɑ' ŋut ŋze'* to my
> daughters. Everyone has two lines. *Pam ntɔ* is different from lines; it's
> not ancestors, but being from the same womb. That's why I am happy
> to have my two daughters.

Why is Simone thrilled to have only daughters in a society so often described as patrilineal? Exactly because Bangangté is not a patrilineal society. While Bangangté, in their conversations with inquisitive anthropologists, first list the property and titles they inherit from their fathers, they present a much more com-plex picture to those who listen further. Mothers of school-age children like Simone speak of the relation between their children and their ancestors, tied together through bonds of kinship the way that winding melon vines link the fruits on this earth to the deep roots below. Below the surface of the land, where the sun shines hot and the living light their cooking fires, lies the cool earth, the source of creation in which ancestral skulls are buried. When Simone spoke of these melon vine bonds of kinship, she indicated that her father, king of another Bamiléké kingdom, had plenty of male descendants. Her mother needed female descendants for her matrilineage and she, the only daughter, could provide them.

Simone referred to the two "lines" with which her daughters were affiliated, their two sets of ancestors. In anthropological terminology, these two sets of ancestors constitute Bangangté's system of double descent. Simone also mentioned a diffuse uterine group called *pam ntɔ*. The *pam ntɔ*, those from the same womb, is a corporate group consisting of persons related through uterine links. Bangangté believe members of their *pam ntɔ* share similar personality traits and either the presence or absence of a specific type of witchcraft substance in the intestines. In Bangangté customary law, a *pam ntɔ* relative is a valid legal substitute for the accused when judgments are made on the basis of oracles and poison ordeals. The *pam ntɔ* is thus a group of people who act as a single legal individual, but, unlike most patrilineal corporate kin groups, does not do so with regard to an estate in land.

Simone's account of ancestors and daughters, of two lines and *pam ntɔ*, illustrates that Bangangté can readily identify and put into practice rules of descent and uterine relation. Bangangté refer to these rules constantly to explain who they visit, who they marry, who they name their children after, and who they call upon in times of trouble.

Each individual Bangangté invokes his or her affiliation with a patrilineage and a matrilineage in different settings. Patrilineal ties determine rights to real estate and village belonging. Even an urban Bangangté citizen who has spent little time within the territory of Bangangté kingdom will say, "I come from Banekane [or any other Bangangté village], my father's village in Bangangté." Patrilineal kin are also believed to share physical likeness, but rarely personality traits.

Matrilineal ties and especially *pam ntɔ* determine rights to movable property and moral and legal responsibility. Just as *pam ntɔ* members may share the presence of witchcraft in their intestines "because they come from one womb," Bangangté believe that matrilineal kin pass on psychological qualities from generation to generation. Bangangté say these personality characteristics reside in the belly and are affected by both the womb they come from and whether the belly is well-fed, a maternal responsibility. Both matrilineal and patrilineal descent involve inheritance of titles and stewardship of ancestral skulls, with their attendant rituals for health, luck and fertility.

Because residence is virilocal (that is, brides move to the husband's home), Bangangté patrilineages are relatively localized, while matrilineages are dispersed. When Bangangté speak of "inside," they usually refer to an inside defined by patrilineal and virilocal principles: inside the kingdom characterized by allegiance to a patrilineal heir, inside one's village which is also the village of one's father, inside the compound where the only links among half-siblings are patrilineal, and inside the kitchen built to enclose a wife's cooking.

Bangangté matrilineages do not have the same association with place, and thus cannot have an inside. Only matrifocal households have a specific locality; they are centered around the hearth, the symbol of warmth, the womb and solidarity. In the context of the competition sometimes felt among half-siblings in a polygynous society, full siblings will explain their closeness by reminiscing about the stories and meals shared around their mother's hearth. The locality of these matrifocal households, however, is a kitchen within a larger compound held together by affinal and patrilineal ties.

Bangangté wives and children experience competing claims for allegiance and commitment from various groups of kin. The husband's kin want to be certain of a child's patrifiliation and thus membership in their patrilineage. They also demand commitment from the married-in wives, outsiders now enclosed in marriage who should socialize their children into identity with the patriline. The wife's kin expect continued allegiance, visits and food exchange from their daughter, and remind her of her filial duties through the symbolism of weddings; her relatives through her mother expect and give solidarity in times of crisis and in the period following childbirth. Bangangté talk about marriage and procreation using the culinary imagery of ingredients and cooking skills, all comments on the numerous types of belonging in Bangangté kinship ideology. The images of marriage and procreation also reflect current Bangangté gender roles and, to some extent, their changing economic circumstances.

Gender Segregation and the Division of Labor

The imagery of wives cooking inside (and men acting outside) is based on readily observable social relations in Bangangté. This separation of men's and women's activities is visually striking. A visitor's first glance at a Bangangté community catches the sexually segregated groups of people socializing and working together. Men and women cultivate different fields, and cluster in separate groups on public occasions and at market. Every polygynous compound has men's and women's areas. When women receive their own guests, they do so most often in their kitchens, or outside in the yard between their kitchen and the main house. This main house is the husband's realm. When men receive guests, serving food prepared by the wife, they do so in or in front of their main house. Much of the spatial segregation of men and women has its roots in the division of labor by gender.

The precolonial division of labor by gender has changed little, but the same types of labor have acquired new significance in the context of an international market economy. Men's tree crops now include the cash crops of coffee and cocoa;

their previous duties of fence-building, hunting and warring have declined or disappeared. New opportunities, such as commerce, taxi-driving and wage labor, allow men to acquire cash. Women grow the staples of maize, beans and peanuts on different types of soil in separate fields from their husbands'. Their food crops have become commercialized, giving them an independent source of income whenever they choose to sell their subsistence products. Women also sell prepared food on roadsides and at market, literally "cooking on the road." This allows them to buy the oil and salt their husbands often "forget," and to purchase the meat their husbands no longer hunt.

Wealth, titles and age have negligent influence upon this pattern of gender segregation and the division of labor in *rural* Bangangté. As elsewhere in Africa, divorce and male absenteeism due to labor migration affect the division of labor by increasing the repertoire of tasks and the burden upon rural women. While these exigencies do not change the ideology of the gendered division of labor in rural Bangangté, they have contributed to a rhetoric of complaint between genders. Bangangté discuss labor migration in an idiom of child loss, and appear to react to this loss by elaborating their visions of "how things should be."

Bangangté women continue to regard food and children as the two most important things they "serve up" or give to their kin and their world. In the ideal household economy, the husband provides his wife with meat, oil and salt to add to the culinary ingredients she produces herself (maize, beans and peanuts). The wife mixes these male and female ingredients to cook a final product, the meal. The imagery of measuring the ingredients of conception and the cooking of gestation mirror the gender roles of home economics in the realm of procreation. A married woman lives with her children, whom she has "cooked" through gestation and now nurtures inside the marital, procreative kitchen.

The division of labor, space and gender ideology are condensed in Bangangté culinary imagery of marriage and procreation. In Bangangté, a wife's kitchen is the basis of marriage. From the husband's point of view, marriage brings the wife—who comes from outside his village and outside his patrilineage—inside the husband's village, compound and the kitchen he has built. Marriage brings the potentially unruly unmarried woman into a socially circumscribed role. It also insures that the newlyweds' children will belong to the husband's patrilineage and village.

Viewed from the perspective of matrilineality, the kitchen and hearth emphasize woman as mother rather than woman as wife. The center of the kitchen is the mother's hearth, which also symbolizes her womb. A mother and her hearth are the center of every *pam ntɔ* group, whose members are all affiliated with the same matrilineage. The solidarity of these "one-womb" kin groups is based on the emotional warmth of the matrifocal household gathered round the mother's nurturing hearth and cooking pot.

In Bangangté gender ideology, the ideal woman is warm like her hearth. She is a mother, a preparer of food, sweating over her cooking pot and gathering her children around her to eat and tell stories. While many fathers dote on their youngest children, Bangangté generally describe fathers and husbands as cool, distant and authoritarian. Unlike in some East African societies, only women have hearths in Bangangté.[5] Men receive but do not serve food. *Nâ ndɑ*, to cook inside, expresses both the ideology and practice of a wife's incorporation as well as the gender segregation within the household, locating the "cooking" wife at her hearth.

When Bangangté men talk about kinship and gender, they tend to highlight the spatial symbolism of marriage. When women talk about kinship and gender, they tend to highlight the culinary symbolism of procreation. The symbolism of procreation reiterates the husbands' concerns with patrifiliation, but also forefronts the warmth and feminine skills that hold together matrilines and *pam ntɔ́* groups, insuring future cooperation in times of scarcity. Wives seem more aware than husbands that their food and children link people together in numerous webs of kinship affiliation.

The basic imagery of marriage and procreation is shared by Bangangté women and men, but contrasting emphases are part of subtle negotiations between men and women. Who shares food with whom, who feeds whose children, and who provides the parcels of land on which to grow the food all influence how people choose to affiliate with different groups of kin. While *nâ ndɑ* emphasizes capturing and enclosing a wife's allegiance and her children's affiliation within the husband's patrilineage, the extension of this culinary imagery in Bangangté notions of procreation provides an alternative to this largely agnatic ideology. The remainder of this essay is an analysis of the symbolism of marriage and procreation. We begin with a spatial idiom, the construction of kitchens through marriage.

Constructing Kitchens

Marriage establishes the procreative kitchen in which the cooking of food and offspring occurs. In Bangangté eyes, it is the contract which brings procreation under social control, preventing the new wife from "cooking on the road." The Bangangté concept of married womanhood refers to the cooking of food and offspring within the bounded, legitimized marriage relationship. Marriage, from the point of view of the groom and his patrilineage, assures the groom of eating, exemplified by the typical opening line of fiancés' appeal to their future fathers-in-law: "I have no one to cook for me." It also assures him of descendants, as children born in wedlock belong to the patrilineage of their fathers.

The symbols of cooking and measuring ingredients that permeate Bangangté imagery of procreation are evident in the marriage exchanges made over the period of betrothal and continuing after the couple is living together. The groom and his family bring gifts of palm oil, goats, firewood, blankets, clothing and cash bridewealth payments to the bride's family. The size of these gifts is clearly affected by market forces, and varies most particularly with the wealth of the groom and his family, but also with the wealth of the bride's family and the bride's skills and education. A ceremony, during which the bride asks her family's blessing, marks the bride's new status and change of residence to her husband's compound. The groom's family brings the elements necessary for a good kitchen—palm oil, meat, and firewood—to the bride's natal compound, which the bride's family *cooks* and serves as a meal to the entire assembly. Palm oil, mixed with camwood powder, is smeared on the bride's chest and feet by her father to insure her fertility. It is likened to blood, an essential ingredient of the *procreative* kitchen. The high point of the ceremony occurs when the bride serves her father palm wine, stating "this wine is poison in your stomach should I ever divorce." The daughter's horrifying patricidal oath is considered an encouragement to the longevity of the marriage.

The substances exchanged, cooked and manipulated in the family's blessing contain multiple layers of symbols of women and fertility. The lump of earth the bride receives from the ancestral skull house is the material in which women cultivate. Water used in cooking brings fertile moisture and is essential to conception. Oil is a symbol of peace and fertility, an ingredient of meals, and makes the woman soft and sexually appealing (Nzikam Djomo 1977, pp. 49–50). The new wife carries her gifts and the artifacts of her blessings to the kitchen her husband has built in his compound. Thus, the marriage ceremony establishes the procreative kitchen as a woman's space enclosed in a man's space, and imbues it with the many-layered meanings of culinary symbolism. Essential to the Bangangté conception of marriage (and sex unencumbered by potential supernatural sanction) is that the wife cooks only *inside* this kitchen.

Marriage, "cooking inside," literally encloses the newlywed wife within the walls of the kitchen her husband has built for her. In precolonial Bangangté, marriage also enclosed women within the palisade walls surrounding their husbands' compounds, protecting them from raids by citizens of neighboring kingdoms seeking slaves and wives. In polygynous compounds, a wife's kitchen is where she both cooks and sleeps, shares food and tells stories with her children, and receives her private guests. In monogamous compounds, the wife and her children may sleep in the main house, but the woman's daily activities center around her kitchen and her fields.

Bangangté marriage brings the woman inside in a number of figurative ways as well. Before marriage, the bride belongs to the patrilineage of her father and the matrilineage of her mother, both kin groups outside the groom's patrilineage. Marriage does not cut off the bride's kin ties, but contains her sexual and child-bearing services within the rights and duties of marriage. Norms governing marriage in Bangangté prescribe exogamy, forbidding marriage of both "close" and classificatory kin, and of descendants of people of the same village. Since post-marital residence is virilocal, the wife, formerly a stranger, has moved socially and geographically "inside" the husband's compound and village.

The movement from outside to inside so vividly depicted by the expression *nâ ndɑ* is a social process perceived from the point of view of the husband and his patrilineage. A wife will acknowledge that she has moved from outside to inside her husband's realm and the domain of his patrilineal relations. She has left her mother's kitchen and father's compound, but has never moved "outside" her important links to them as kin.

Enclosing Sex, Enclosing Affiliation

Bangangté bring the procreative powers of women, their potentially volatile heat and fire, under social control through institutions that regulate how pairs come together to make children, and under what conditions pregnancy and childbirth can occur. Bangangté are concerned with controlling sexual intercourse through norms regarding marriage and infidelity for two reasons: assuring patrifiliation and preventing affliction.

Controlling sexual intercourse by keeping it within the bounds of marriage insures that the child's patrifiliation is known and legitimate, and its kinship affiliations unambiguous.[6] Matrifiliation is made obvious by the act of birth, and mother-child bonds are strengthened through the child's care and socialization within the matrifocal household. Sharing this household with mother and full siblings fosters the child's identification with its matrilineage. The child's connection to its matrilineage is further strengthened through visits of its mother's sisters, mother's mother, and even more distant matrikin, starting with the care matrikin give the new mother and her infant. Patrifiliation, in contrast, is only made certain by the parents' submission to rules governing marriage choice and beliefs discouraging extramarital sexual relations. Importantly, patrifiliation determines the child's membership in a patrilineage, claims to inheritance, and village belonging.

In addition to assuring patrifiliation, keeping sexual intercourse within an approved marital union also assures the proper mix of the ingredients of a new being: the water and blood of appropriately paired parents. Bangangté are particularly concerned with issues of incest and adultery, expressed in terms of culinary ingredients. Using the right ingredients is necessary to keep the pot and its contents from spoiling, or in more prosaic terms, to prevent the misfortune of reproductive illness.

Bangangté women speak of a recent past when nearly all marriages were arranged between the parents of the betrothed. Marriages arranged by parents resulted in beneficial political and economic alliances for the parents. Arranged marriage also meant that the bride's and groom's genealogies were thoroughly checked, preventing risk of incest for the new couple. Arranged marriage was a way that parents contained the choice of mate, keeping alliances within their control.

Bangangté consider the sex which occurs in mismatched mariages, outside the control of elders, dangerous. Many Bangangté, including young women who wish for more choice for themselves as individuals, fear that the pairing of couples has escaped the regulation of their elders. They fear that marriage choice is no longer "inside," and that this increases the likelihood for such mishaps as incest, angering ancestors who then "seize" the kin group with the afflictions of illness and infertility. While either matrilineal or patrilineal ancestors can "seize" their descendants in their wrath, Bangangté most fear their matrilineal ancestresses who, they believe, are more sensitive and emotionally volatile.

In discussing this danger, Bangangté villagers often cited the case of the marriage of King Njiké Pokam and Paulette, his young wife who ran away in June 1986, never to return. When a pair rushes into marriage without allowing parents the honor or time to check and arrange, unwitting incest may be the result. In the case of the marriage between King Njiké Pokam and Paulette, Paulette's parents were completely uninvolved in her choice of husband. Only the pair's matrilineages were checked for kin relations. After the two had been wed, it was discovered that the king, as heir to Paulette's paternal grandfather, was his bride's classificatory father. By general understanding, the resulting incestuous marriage would never produce offspring.

In addition to incest, Bangangté believe that extramarital sex, especially that involving a married woman, can cause infertility, serious illness or death. Infidelity leads to a triangular relationship among the woman, her husband and her lover. If any of these three falls ill, and sees or is visited by any of the others, it is believed they will die. One wife of King Njiké Pokam, known to have had intercourse with a healer when seeking fertility enhancement medicine, was forbidden to visit her husband when he was hospitalized for cirrhosis in 1986. "It would be like murder," exclaimed the king's father's sister. Infidelity is particularly dangerous for women. They may be punished severely, such as when King Njiké II allegedly buried one of his wives alive after she had become pregnant by another man. Infidelity during pregnancy may cause fetal death, "when the two men's waters fight." It is also thought to lead to difficulties during childbirth.

In Bangangté notions of illness causation, even dreams and insinuations of infidelity, can lead to reproductive disorders. One prominent Bangangté healer treated a married patient whose fallopian tubes had been "plugged up" during a dream of having sex with her former foster father. And the royal wives believed that their unfortunate co-wife Paulette's honor and fertility had been compromised by the taint of "prostitution" and promiscuity adhering to a woman raised in Cameroon's largest port city, far from Bangangté. This belief added an additional layer to the story of Paulette's classificatory incest with King Njiké Pokam. Paulette eventually ran away, fleeing the same, gossip, and lack of economic opportunity she found in the royal compound.

With the exception of men who sleep with the king's wives, a heinous crime, only women are believed to commit adultery in Bangangté. In the context of polygyny, women are limited to a single partner, the only ones kept inside. Men not only can have many partners, they are also not sanctioned for sleeping with women other than their wives. Of course, this leaves their extramarital partners open to sanction. Women's sexual activity ideally is limited to their single spouse, because otherwise the father's paternity would be uncertain, and the child's kinship affiliation would be in doubt. Beliefs about the relation of infidelity to illness support social norms limiting the range of sexual partners any one person may have. Bangangté men and women say that keeping sex "inside" marriage is *prudent*, a way of preventing misfortune.

The Cooking of Procreation

Food production and preparation are women's tasks in Bangangté's sexual division of labor. In the ideal home economy of Bangangté households, both husband and wife contribute ingredients to the daily soup. In the figurative home economy of procreative cooking, husband and wife again both contribute the ingredients of conception. The wife's role in the *process* of procreation, however, is dominant. She is the cook who measures, stirs and adds ingredients, until the "food," the baby, is ready to be presented through the act of childbirth. In addition, the pregnant woman is both the fire and the cooking pot. The elaborate culinary imagery of procreation allows women to celebrate their skills and their uterine and matrilineal connectedness with their children and other kin, even while enclosed within the realities and rhetoric of the virilocal matrimonal kitchen.

Hearths, Heat and Sex

When Bangangté speak of sex, whether seriously describing "what needs to be known" to children and ethnographers or joking with sexual innuendos, their language is full of culinary imagery. Bangangté men and women, old and young, say that sex is hot and therefore contains both enormous transformative powers and danger. Sex is also hot in the same way that good music, a good joke or a freshly cooked meal one just cannot wait to taste is hot: "*ça chauffe!*" interject young Bangangté, borrowing slang from the pop music world. Bangangté men talk about sex and procreation using imagery of the cooking fire. When they impregnate a woman, they "cook" her. A woman who has conceived before marriage has not "cooked" in the proper way; she is called "oversalted," and her parents are given an oversalted meal by her affines (in-laws) (Nzikam Djomo 1977, p. 34). Men refer to repeated sex acts during the course of their wife's pregnancy as "tending the fire."

Women also talk about sex in terms of cooking, and stress *their* perception of cooking. Cooking and sex are work for rural women. Both recently married and elderly Bangangté women described sexual intercourse to me as one of the duties of wifehood. They sought it as the means to become pregnant. Their nonverbal behavior indicated that, while often work, sex could also be fun.

The Language of Cooking in Procreation

"Measuring" a Person

In sexual intercourse, the husband provides his wife with ingredients (water/semen and blood) to mix with her own water and blood to "cook" a child. Bangangté liken water or semen and blood to the water and red palm oil that are essential ingredients of all Bangangté soups.[7] Husband and wife "measure" these ingredients to procreate or conceive ("to measure a person"). Women are very familiar with measuring ingredients when cooking, part of their daily work. The "measuring" of procreation is expressed with the same verb denoting measuring cooking ingredients, distinct from the verb for measuring length or distance. Just the right amount of blood and water, and just the right amount of sex, are necessary for successful conception.

The Bubbling Pot

Both male and female Bangangté regard repeated sexual intercourse during the mother's pregnancy as the proper way to accomplish the continual mixing of good cuisine. We have seen that men refer to sexual intercourse during gestation as "tending the fire" (which in the sexual division of labor is women's work!). While the basic idiom is shared, women's speech, more than men's, elaborates the metaphor of cooking when talking about gestation and birth. Once the fire has been lit and the water put up to boil through sex and conception, Bangangté women view gestation as the continual, slow process of cooking a good sauce. The continual mixing of the central procreative fluids, water/sperm and oil/blood, is essential to produce a smooth and tasty meal, and for the proper gestation of the fetus. Bangangté women describe their feelings during pregnancy as swelling or growing, as maize meal expands when the woman cooks porridge. A mother in her twenties described the development of the fetus in terms of hearing noises in the belly, like a bubbling pot, to which the doctor then listens.

As an essential ingredient, Bangangté believe that the father's "water" (semen) fortifies and feeds the fetus.[8] In addition, when the mother has sex repeatedly with the child's father, the fetus "gets to know its father." Having sex with her fetus's father is a good deed the mother performs for her child, for it introduces or "names" the father to the child. The tone in which Bangangté women talk about sex when pregnant or not pregnant is striking. If the woman is not pregnant, the man asks for sex and the woman accepts. If pregnant, Bangangté women attribute more agency to themselves, considering it a woman's responsibility to have sex with her baby's father.

Bangangté women I spoke with assumed that difficulty in childbirth occurred when a child was conceived in an extramarital affair. The mother would fail to progress in labor because she had "named" the father neither to the child itself nor to the public. Many told stories of labors they had attended suddenly progressing after the mother confessed the name of her lover. These women also attributed dangerously small size and birth defects to the pregnant woman having had sex with someone other than the fetus's father; the "strengths" or "bloods" of the two men would fight over the fetus, endangering its health. This set of beliefs reflects Bangangté concern with verifying a child's patrifiliation. "Cooking inside" encloses the wife's sexual and childbearing activities within the bounds of marriage, and keeps her children inside her husband's patrilineage.[9] Even while celebrating their culinary skills at procreative cooking, my informants regarded cooking inside as an ideal standard. Their highlighting of women's work and uterine connectedness in procreation and kinship did not lead them to negate their children's patrilineal affiliations.

Serving the Meal

Before Bangangté women developed a preference for giving birth in hospitals and clinics, childbirth occurred at the woman's home in the husband's compound (Nzikam Djomo 1977, p. 69). This venue underscores the containment of the wife's sexual and childbearing duties within an area "belonging" to the husband's patrilineage. The procreative kitchen, however, is woman's space within that compound. Exemplifying the conflicting loyalties and demands on every Bangangté child and wife, the birthing mother was surrounded by other women—the neighbor-midwife or an experienced older woman, and, time permitting, a mother or sister, female members of her matrilineage. Men and children were not allowed to attend births which, like cooking, are still considered women's business.

Presently nearly all Bangangté women give birth in a hospital or clinic, where most nurse-midwives are men.[10] My informants considered hospital births the medically prudent choice, by no means a conscious withdrawal from their husbands' territory or control. In fact, husbands usually pay for their wives' hospitalizations. Bangangté mothers and their husbands identified hospital convalescence, typically one week, as more restful for the mother, who is removed from household duties and potentially argumentative co-wives.

Although they no longer give birth next to their cooking hearths, Bangangté women talk about the full-term fetus as cooked food, the final outcome of a long process of cooking. Once born, the baby is a "fresh person" (*mɛn fi*), no longer referred to as metaphoric food. Food and feeding, however, remain central in the care of the newborn and mother, serving as a medium to renew matrilineal and friendship ties among women, and as an expression of ethnic identity.

Infant Feeding and "Feeding" Infants

As soon as she returns from the hospital to her kitchen, the mother is surrounded by female neighbors, co-wives and kin, who nourish her with food they cook on *her* hearth. Bangangté women liken the period immediately following birth to *njα* (the pre-betrothal puberty rite). The mother is kept in semi-seclusion, fed special foods, takes special care of her bodily hygiene, and is not supposed to work. For up to two months, her female kin arrange their visits so that someone is always there to do housework and to bathe and admire the newborn. They bring or cook food for her, renewing ties through the exchange of food.

The placenta and umbilical cord are buried under a banana or plantain tree near the mother's kitchen within the child's patrilineal compound, even when the child is born hundreds of kilometers away in the hospital of one of the large cities. Mothers, concerned with the lure of the cities, remind their older children to "never forget where your placenta is buried." They admonish their children to remember the multiple affiliations signified by the place of burial: the compound of patrifiliation and the father's patrilineage; the kitchen of matrifocality, *pam ntɔ*, and matrilineal food exchange; and the "home" of one's village and kingdom, symbolic loci of cultural authenticity identified through kinship ties.

Infant care is the mother's responsibility, aided by the women and children who visit her during her convalescence. Mother's milk is considered best, being of the "same blood."[11] The mother is given special foods to help her lactation, and refrains from sexual intercourse until she has weaned the child in order to "prevent her milk from spoiling."[12] The infant is washed frequently, for water fortifies the child as the father's water fortified the fetus in the womb. For its first month, the child remains nearly continually in the procreative kitchen, within the walls that contained its mother's procreative and culinary arts. Gradually, the child's experiences expand from the "inside" of its mother's kitchen to the larger "inside" of its father's compound, and eventually to the "outside" world of neighborhood, school and work.

Double Descent, Double Ideologies?

This essay has pointed out the importance of idioms of marriage and procreation for understanding Bangangté society and, most particularly, for understanding the gendered experience of a complex kinship system. Cooking is a crucial form of expressing and maintaining matrilineal ties within Bangangté's double descent system. Culinary and spatial idioms describe procreation, marriage and kinship in Bangangté.

Cooking inside, *nâ ndɑ*, is only one point in a long process that brings individuals together to procreate and reproduce Bangangté society. Marriage, expressed as cooking inside, transforms social relations and highlights actors' complementary and competing kinship ties. The newly married woman is enclosed by her husband's compound and patrilineage; her claims upon her natal patrilineage persist but are weakened, and her matrilineal ties necessitate energetic work preparing and exchanging food. The activities associated with marriage, pregnancy and birth, undertaken to treat illness or to maximize reproductive chances, are based on Bangangté understandings of good cuisine. Referring to Highland New Guinea, Lindenbaum points out that, "indigenous theories of human reproduction contain within them an implicit recipe for social reproduction" (1987, p. 222). In Bangangté, this "recipe" may be understood even more literally than in New Guinea. Bangangté women put their metaphors into practice, using their experience in the kitchen to manage their social and sexual relations.

In Bangangté, the symbolism of marriage and procreation is key to decreasing our initial puzzlement regarding multiple perspectives on kinship. The four sets of lineages involved in any marriage (the patrilineages and matrilineages of husband and wife) use the sociospatial dichotomy of inside/outside, the first set of idioms contained within the phrase "cooking inside," differently when they represent and negotiate kin group affiliations. As in other parts of the world, this idiom of inside/outside is simultaneously a commentary on kinship ideology and gender concepts (Collier and Yanagisako 1987, p. 9), an image not only of lineage but also of the enclosure of otherwise potentially unruly women. The second set of idioms regarding cooking is central to Bangangté concepts of procreation. Cooking does a lot of representational "work" in Bangangté society.[13] Cooking and eating are crucial forms of expressing and maintaining matrilineal kin ties in Bangangté's double descent system, both via notions of physical relationship and through women's exchange of foodstuffs. Eating together also helps create ties formed through marriage via the symbolism of oaths, exchanges and ceremonies.

Bangangté not only use the many meanings of sex and cooking to understand and explain their kinship system, they also play with these meanings in frequent joking. Their humor indicates that the ways that men and women use the imagery of marriage and procreation involve subtle differences both of representation and of emotional tone. The distinction between the tone with which Bangangté men and women load their expressions is difficult to describe or demonstrate with verbal quotations. As pointed out by Karp (1987) and Giddens (1984), these attitudes toward kinship cannot be rendered as statements of propositional belief. Nonetheless, their very inchoateness may indicate the forcefulness of these emotional attitudes in everday experience.

The feelings Bangangté men and women have about marriage, procreation and their many forms of connectedness to kin are not the same every day and in every situation. Although these are tendencies, men do not talk *only* about the incorporation of wives and children into their patrilineages, and women do not talk *only* about their enduring relations with matrilineal and uterine relatives. The imagery of cooking emphasizes women's skill in providing food and offspring for three sets of kin groups; this cooking, nonetheless, is confined to inside the marital, procreative kitchen. The images project both a dominant agnatic ideology and an alternative vision of multiple forms of connectedness. When Bangangté women raise their eyebrows and laugh at the unspoken puns of the aromas and locales of cooking, they are playing with contradictions in their everyday experience, simultaneously expressing "official and unofficial ideologies" (Voloshinov 1973). The humor, and sometimes tragic irony, with which women invoke the imagery of marriage and procreation may be "subtle and powerful means of expression available to people whose communicative options are otherwise constrained by the social conditions in which they act" (Karp 1987, p. 138). The Bangangté women I grew to know recognized constraints on their actions while at the same time providing an alternative vision of the place they and their children took within a complex kinship system.

Cooking metaphors of procreation are contained within the dominant ideology of patrilineality, which is represented by cooking *inside* the husband-built kitchen. But women's *elaboration* of metaphors that represent their skill, and their material and symbolic action of exchanging food to maintain links with matrikin emphasize one side of a complex set of social relations, a side neglected by accounts of a dominant patrilineal ideology. Bangangté women reaffirm the importance of matrilineages within a double descent system through the way they use a common set of images in everyday speech.[14] They emphasize the daily practice of cooking, involving images of matrilineal and uterine ties, in their ideas about the very reproduction that makes agnatic as well as matrilineal kin groups possible in Bangangté.

Notes

[1] For a fully developed exposition of the ideas explored in this essay, see P. Feldman-Savelsberg, "Cooking Inside: Kinship and Gender in Bangangté Idioms of Marriage and Procreation," *American Ethnologist* (1995, vol. 22, no. 3). This article has benefited from the helpful comments of anonymous reviewers and of Don Brenneis, Gloria Raheja, Riv-Ellen Prell, Luise White, Ivan Karp, Gillian Feeley-Harnik, M.J. Maynes, Ann Waltner, Michael Herzfeld and Joachim J. Savelsberg.

[2] Anthropologists studying Bamiléké kinship disagree whether it is a patrilineal or double descent system, and most emphasize agnatic relations. See Pradelles (1986, 1994); Tardits (1960); Hurault (1962); and den Ouden (1987). Brain (1972) is the only scholar of the Bamiléké to emphasize maternal ties in his treatment of *atsen'ndia* uterine kin groups among the Bangwa-Fontem of Cameroon's Northwest Province.

[3] Other factors affecting perspectives on kinship include life-cycle changes, reproductive history, divorce, wealth and occasionally political party and/or church affiliation. The analysis in this article reflects mainly the views of married women. It thus reflects the experience of the majority of Bangangté women, and the ideals of most women. Those of my informants who chose separation, divorce or extramarital motherhood said they did so because the ideal of marriage did not work out for them. My pool of informants and the perspectives I heard were partly shaped by the ways my interlocutors defined me in the field—at times as a runaway wife, and, after my husband's first visit, as a newly married childless woman who needed instruction in the ways of marriage and childbirth. Through these differing perceptions of me, women's discourse on fertility and infertility and the metaphors of cooking and commensality described in this article remained remarkably constant.

[4] I conducted the fieldwork on which this essay is based in numerous villages of Bangangté Kingdom in 1983 and 1986. During 1986 I lived in the royal compound of Bangangté but participated in a wide range of activities throughout Ndé Division. I supplemented participant observation and interviews by collecting over 240 essays by school children, and eleven months of archival research in Cameroon, France and Germany.

[5] Bangangté men, excepting the temporary exigencies of widowers and students, neither cook nor huddle around a hearth. The only instance of male cooking occurs sporadically in ritual. The *bandansi*, men of the house of god (ritual specialists charged with maintaining the morality of the kingdom), "cook" raphia wine for litigants to use in oath-taking. The king is the only man with his own hearth, at which not he, but his wives, cook.

[6] Concern with patrifiliation is also central to the imagery of procreation in rural Turkey. (Delaney 1991).

[7] Blood is generally associated with women, while water/semen is associated with men. Nonetheless, Bangangté speak of the need to cleanse an infertile woman of bad water. Blood is a medium of inheritance. Bangangté describe parent-child resemblance in terms of which parent's blood is stronger, or in terms of a child "having the blood" of one of its parents.

[8] In other Bangangté contexts, and throughout the Bamiléké region, water is associated with fertility, often expressed as a distinction between moist and fertile versus dry and barren land. Water is used in therapy to strengthen or fortify as well as to wash or purify sufferers.

[9] While concern with patrifiliation is central whenever Bangangté discuss the ins and outs of marriage and procreation or "cooking inside," attitudes toward sexual relations during pregnancy are more varied among younger women. A slight majority of women among whom I conducted interviews approved of sex during pregnancy for the nourishment of the fetus, acquainting the fetus with its father, and opening the vaginal passage to ease childbirth. Others complained that sexual intercourse had a deleterious effect on the pregnant woman's energy or health, or that sex is unnecessary if one is already pregnant. Underlying this latter opinion is the general orientation among Bangangté women that the purpose of sex is to conceive. As one woman remarked regarding sex during pregnancy, "is it food?" (Bwoda', aged thirty-one, Bantoum).

[10] As early as 1937, there were few professional midwives in Bangangté (Egerton 1938, p. 236). I describe the health care alternatives available at different historical periods to Bangangté women in another publication (Feldman-Savelsberg 1990).

[11] Among the Bamiléké, being of the "same blood" as one's mother and her uterine kin is self-understood and highly valued. By contrast, among the strongly patrilineal Bambara and Mandinka of urban Mali, children are thought to inherit only their father's "blood." The process of breast-feeding, rather than breastmilk as a product, forms the kinship link between children and their mothers in urban Mali (Dettwyler 1988, p. 179). For a related discussion, see Gianna Pomata's essay in this volume.

[12] Some Bangangté women (especially the more experienced royal wives) stated that, while the "official" reason for abstinence during lactation was to protect the quality of breastmilk, sexual abstinence also prevented mothers of infants from becoming caught up in fights among co-wives regarding sexual access to the husband. Keeping the mother calm is considered best for her and her baby's survival chances.

[13] See also Karp on commensality and Iteso representations of social organization (1980).

[14] The social dynamics revealed by women's expressions is common to the contradictory position of wives in patrilocal and virilocal marriage regimes. Raheja, in her essay in this volume, uses women's songs and proverbs to demonstrate that, while heterogeneous, women's speech practices differ from men's in revealing the contradictions of a dominant discourse.

References

Beidelman, T.O. 1986. *Moral Imagination in Kaguru Modes of Thought.* Bloomington: Indiana University Press.

Brain, R. 1972. *Bangwa Kinship and Marriage.* Cambridge: Cambridge University Press.

Collier, J.F., and Yanagisako, S.J. 1987. "Introduction." In *Gender and Kinship: Essays Toward a Unified Analysis,* J.F. Collier and S.J. Yanagisako, eds., pp. 1–13. Stanford: Standford University Press.

de Heusch, L. 1980. "Heat, Physiology, and Cosmogony: *Rites de passage* among the Thonga." In *Explorations in African Systems of Thought,* I. Karp and C.S. Bird, eds., pp. 27–43. Bloomington: Indiana University Press.

Delaney, C. 1991. *The Seed and the Soil: Gender and Cosmology in Turkish Village Society.* Berkeley: University of California Press.

den Ouden, J.H.B. 1987. "In search of Personal Mobility: Changing Interpersonal Relations in Two Bamiléké Chiefdoms, Cameroon." *Africa* 57 (1): 3–27.

Dettwyler, K.A. 1988. "More than Nutrition: Breastfeeding in Urban Mali." *Medical Anthropology Quarterly* (N.S.) 2 (2):172-183.

Egerton, C. 1938. *African Majesty: A Record of Refuge at the Court of the King of Bangangté in the French Cameroons.* London: George Routledge and Sons.

Engard, R.K. 1986. "Bringing the Outside In: Commensality and Incorporation in Bafut Myth, Ritual, Art and Social Organization." Ph.D. dissertation, Anthropology Department, Indiana University, Bloomington.

Feldman-Savelsberg, P. 1990. "'Then we were many': Bangangté Women's Conceptions of Health, Fertility and Social Change in a Bamiléké Chiefdom, Cameroon." Ph.D. dissertation, Department of Anthropology, Johns Hopkins University.

———. 1995 "Cooking Inside: Kinship and Gender in Bangangté Idioms of Marriage and Procreation." *American Ethnologist* 22 (3) (in press).

Giddens, A. 1984. *The Constitution of Society.* Berkeley: University of California Press.

Goheen, M. 1992. "Chiefs, Subchiefs and Local Control: Negotiations over Land, Struggles over Meaning." *Africa* 62 (3): 389-412.

Hurault, J. 1962. *La structure sociale des Bamiléké.* Paris: Mouton.

Karp, I. 1980. "Beer Drinking and Social Experience in an African Society: An Essay in Formal Sociology." In *Explorations in African Systems of Thought,* I. Karp and C.S. Bird, eds., pp. 83–119. Bloomington: Indiana University Press.

——— 1987. "Laughter at Marriage: Subversion in Performance." In *Transformations of African Marriage,* D. Parkin and D. Nyamwaya, eds., pp. 137–154. Manchester: Manchester University Press for the International African Institute.

Lindenbaum, S. . 1987. "The Mystification of Female Labors," in *Gender and Kinship: Essays toward a Unified Analysis.* J. Collier and S. Yanagisako, eds. pp. 221–267. Palo Alto: Stanford University Press.

Nzikam Djomo, E. 1977. *Les rites relatifs à la naissance chez les Fe'e Fe'e de Babouantou (Pùàntù).* Yaoundé: Mémoire pour D.E.S., Department of Sociology, University of Yaoundé.

Pradelles de Latour, C.-H. 1986. "Le champ de langage dans une chefferie Bamiléké du Cameroun." Thèse du Doctorat d'État, Paris: École des Hautes Études en Sciences Sociales.

———. 1994. "Marriage Payments, Debt and Fatherhood among the Bangoua: A Lacanian Analysis of a Kinship System." *Africa* 64 (1): 21–33.

Richards, A.I. 1956. *Chisungu: A Girl's Initiation Ceremony among the Bemba of Zambia.* London: Tavistock.

Schmidt, A. 1955. "The Water of Life." *African Studies* 14 (1): 23–28.

Tardits, C. 1960. *Contribution à l'étude des populations Bamiléké de l'Ouest Cameroun.* Paris: Editions Berger-Levrault.

Voloshinov, V.N. 1973. *Freudianism: A Marxist Critique,* trans. I.R. Titunik. New York: Academic Press. Cited in Karp 1987, p. 142.

Part Three

"FISH WITHOUT BICYCLES"
GENDER AND THE PARADOXES OF KINSHIP

Barbara A. Hanawalt opens this section with an analysis of legal documents concerning provisions for widows and orphans among the propertied citizenry of late medieval London. She uncovers a variety of legal and institutional supports for widows, such as strong legal stipulations like the common law guarantee of a dower, and marriage contracts which established an economic partnership between spouses. Hanawalt's study of particular court cases, such as those involving women's claims to their dowries, illustrates the implementation of the laws supporting widows. Female prosperity at this stage of life was rooted in material resources and a legal system which allowed widows access to those resources. This case offers an interesting contrast to many of those which follow in this section of the book, for in many of these other milieux, as we shall see, the material or legal support for "women alone" was lacking.

10

Patriarchal Provisions for Widows and Orphans in Medieval London

BARBARA A. HANAWALT

The patricians and patriarchs of medieval London, as they evolved their laws concerning their widows and children, came to devise and enforce a set of rules that promoted the survival of the remnants of their conjugal families after their death. The laws and their interpretations, as we shall see, took into consideration every base motivation that their fellow men might have in taking over the wardship of their orphans or depriving their widows of their dowers. Being shrewd themselves, they had a lively imagination about how their survivors might fare among their fellow Londoners. In spite of their providential thought for their truncated families, their actions did not give enormous independence or prestige to their widows, nor did these actions serve to preserve their patrilineage, but their progeny were given the best possible chances of surviving in a home environment with their mother and with their patrimony still intact when they reached the age of majority. To presume a desire on their part for empowerment of widows or extension of a patriline, however, goes far beyond their own thinking about their laws or their concepts of social structure. That their foremost concern was the survival of their progeny and their fortunes, however, is an indication of their attitudes toward the responsibilities of patriarchy.

London Laws Protecting Widows and Orphans

The provision for a London widow of the propertied class was arranged at her marriage. In negotiating a marriage, the friends of the bride and groom agreed to the amount and terms of dower and dowry. Whether the marriage contract was oral or written, it established a "partnership" in which both partners and their families contributed capital and real estate to make a viable, familial, economic unit.[1] The presumption of marriage was that both parties would contribute not only property but also their labor and productive capacities to insure the survival of the household, including the rearing of children from their union. Family and friends assumed that both partners to the venture undertook their obligations willingly and regarded their partnership as binding. Announcement of the property exchanges and promises were made at the church door at the time of the marriage, so that a wide body of witnesses could assure the application of the terms.

The usual arrangement for a first marriage in London was for the husband to contribute property and perhaps a trade or business, while the wife contributed money and goods. The dowry capital that the wife's family or friends gave provided the liquidity for the new family to begin or expand business. The dower that the groom and his family and friends pledged was to provide for the wife should she outlive her husband. During the fourteenth century the age difference between husband and wife entering into first marriages in London increased. Young women were in their late teens when they married, but young men were over twenty-one in the fourteenth century and more likely to be in their late twenties or early thirties in the fifteenth century.[2] Because of the age differential, the wife usually outlived her husband, and might well have young children to raise after his death. The dower, therefore, insured that the husband's marital partner would receive a portion of his property that she could use during her lifetime.

London's law of dower or jointure followed that of English common law, in which the widow received one-third of the husband's property for her life use, and could even take it into another marriage. In London, widows received one-third if the marriage produced children, the children got one-third of the estate and the testator disposed of his third for the good of his soul. If the couple had no children, then the widow was entitled to one-half of the estate for life use. With the exception of the "free bench," that is the house in which the couple dwelled while they were married, the widow could take this property into a new marriage for the duration of her life. Only on her death did it revert to the male heirs of her former husband.[3] For the most part, the dower was real property—tenements and rents in London. The husband might make additional provisions in his will for movable property or even additional real property.[4]

The wife was compensated for her contributions to the marriage through a provision for her widowhood. She might also receive back her dowry, but that was more likely to be distributed to the children or subsumed into household and business expenses. The dower's advantage in terms of perpetuating the family unit was that it guaranteed that the widow would be able to support and rear the children of the union.

The widow was as financially secure as her husband's estate would permit. During her widowhood she could enter into contracts, sue and be sued, and generally enjoy both legal and economic freedom. She or her new husband could not alienate the dower property, but she could rent it and use it. The husband's male heirs could not control her use as long as she did not sell or otherwise alienate it.

Provisions for the care of orphans and their third of the father's estate also show the emphasis placed on protecting the children of the conjugal unit. In establishing their provisions for orphans, London citizens seemed to have had a tender concern both about their children and about what would happen to their inheritance.[5]

> A testator may bequeath guardianship of his son and his chattels to anyone he thinks fit: such guardians being bound to apply the proceeds of his inheritance to the use and advantage of such child until he comes of age. If arrangements are not made then the child is given to the side of the family from which his inheritance does not derive. If from the father, then the mother or nearest kinsman on the mother's side. If from the mother, then the nearest kinsman on the father's side.[6]

They required their mayor, aldermen and chamberlain to protect their orphans — both their bodies and their inheritance. They also expressed their doubts about the motives of their fellowmen when confronted with the person and estate of a vulnerable child.[7]

The law required that no one who would profit from the death of the child could serve as guardian. Thus, when a mother and her second husband came to claim the wardship of her daughter, Jakemina, the court said that, by city law, wardship of minors "ought not to be in the hands of a kinsman to whom the inheritance could descend." Since Jakemina had all her inheritance from her mother and none from her father, her wardship would remain with her paternal aunt, Prioress of Kelingburne.[8] Usually, however, the primary wealth of the family came from the father's estate rather than the mother's. Unless the dying citizen indicated other arrangements, the custody laws favored the mother or her kin.

The ward's marriage and even apprenticeship was put into the mayor's control, so that the children could not be married or placed below his or her rank or to the benefit of the guardian.[9] A typical case is that of Alice, daughter of William de Thele, who was granted to John de Gildeford provided he would "maintain, treat and instruct Alice as he ought, would not let her suffer disparagement [loss of social status] nor marry her without consent of the Mayor and Aldermen and of her parents [meaning friends]." When the child came of age, the estate would be returned to the orphan along with "2s. in the pound according to the custom," as "mesne profit."[10]

To insure that all surviving children and their goods be accounted for, it seems to have been customary to have the children physically appear before the mayor in the Guildhall. At least John de London, a barber, willed that "his said children be brought before the Mayor and Sheriffs of London for the time being at the Guildhall, so that the portion of each child may, with the assent of the said Mayor and Sheriffs, be delivered to some honest and sufficient person to keep in trust for them.[11]

London laws, therefore, potentially gave considerable economic advantage to the widow, especially one with minor children. When her husband died, the widow received one-third of her former spouse's estate, and was favored by law to have the custody of the children and their third of the inheritance until they came of age. The legal provisions, at least, indicated an intention that the conjugal family was to remain as a well-endowed unit.

Application of the Laws in Late Medieval London

Law and practice should coincide, but we have enough evidence to caution us about taking law books as evidence of reality. Did the widows actually receive their dowers, and did widows really gain control of their orphaned children and their inheritance to the exclusion of paternal kin?

Medieval records do not provide ready answers through census returns and parish registers, so we can only provide partial, albeit satisfactory, answers. The sources include a long run of court cases from the Husting Court of Common Pleas, which dealt with widow's claims for dower; the Letter Books, which recorded wardship cases coming before the mayor and aldermen; and a series of wills recorded in the Husting Court. While the vast majority of these cases concern Londoners who were citizens[12] and men and women of property, their statuses range from an occasional pauper through ordinary artisans and tradesmen to powerful merchants.

It is one thing to have a law providing for the widow, but another to say that she actually got her dower. Dower could be insured either by a marriage contract or by a recital of the provisions in the husband's will. When no contract or will was available, the mayor and aldermen undertook to divide the property into thirds and provide the widow with her property by law.

Since London did not have the strong notarial tradition that one finds on the Continent, a widow could find it difficult to establish firm claims based on verbal marriage contracts. One assumes that widows could be deprived of their dower because of lapses of memory or alienation of the property during marriage. The oral nature of the contract was partly protected by the reading of the contract before the church door. The court cases show that witnesses abounded, and came forward to testify to the terms of oral contracts. While it is impossible to know what percent of widows in London had a difficult time recovering their dower, fifty-three percent of those widows who did have to go to the Husting Court of Common Pleas were able to retrieve their disputed dower. When the widow's opponent was a son or member of her husband's family, she almost always regained her dower. In some cases the husband had been the villain himself and had promised to endow her with property he did not own on the day of their marriage.[13] If over half of the disputed dower claims ended successfully, we may assume that, for the most part, London widows received their dowers without hindrance.

We would like to know, of course, how many women became widows in a year, and what their age and condition were. In spite of the dangers associated with childbirth, women in the Middle Ages seemed to have outlived their husbands on the average.[14] In the London Husting Court wills, 1,743 out of 3,300 men's wills (fifty-three percent) mention a surviving wife.[15] We may assume, then, that the widow living on her dower was a common occurrence in late medieval London.

These London widows were well endowed with rents and property: eighty-six percent of the testators left their wives real property as well as goods. This property included tenements, rents, shops, gardens, taverns, breweries, wharves and land in the country. Only thirteen percent left goods and money alone, and one percent set up an annuity for their widow. Wills, of course, represent the upper end of urban status groups: those with sufficient land and wealth to make a will.[16]

London's wardship laws appear to have been as rigorously enforced in the fourteenth and fifteenth centuries as were the provisions for dower. The city had a special Common Pleader or Sergeant (usually the youngest attorney in the Mayor's Court) who took an inventory of the children's inheritance. The mayor and chamberlain could then assign the wardship of the orphan or orphans to either those designated in the citizen's will or those selected by the mayor and chamberlain. The court had a good idea about the wishes and wealth of the dead citizen, and so could make an informed choice of guardian. They took their charge seriously, and required the guardians to find sureties that they would protect the child and the property to be delivered when the child came of age. By the early fifteenth century, the city required the guardians to post bond for the children's wealth.[17]

The citizens seemed to have confidence in their law and in the mayor as its primary administrator. In the late medieval Husting Wills, only 210 men designated guardians for their children.[18] Their overwhelming preference (fifty-five percent) was for the mother to assume this role. After her, the testator looked to friends (twenty-seven percent), kinsmen (eight percent),[19] executors (six percent), and finally apprentices, servants, and churchmen.[20]

The mayor followed similar patterns when he selected guardians for the citizen's orphans in the 1,137 cases listing guardians in the Letter Books. The mother was the favored guardian: thirty to fifty-seven percent of the individual children were in the care of their mothers, either alone or with a stepfather. The low percentage included the plague years of 1350 to 1388, when a number of the mothers must have died of plague. The presence of so many stepfathers (seventeen percent in 1309 to 1348 and increasing to a high of thirty-four percent in 1389 to 1428) suggests that the combined wealth of dower and the children's inheritance had consequences not necessarily foreseen by the city patriarchs; a widespread remarriage of their widows. The father alone as guardian does not appear until the end of the fourteenth century.[21]

On the whole, the mayor and aldermen seem to have made an attempt to keep the children with kin. Until the onset of plague, sixty-one percent of children were placed with kin. The percentage fell to thirty-six percent in the worst of the plague years and only gradually recovered to fifty-four percent by the middle of the fifteenth century. Since some of the people in the nonkin category might have been distant kin or kin on the mother's side, the percentage of orphans who went into the household of someone they were related to must have been even higher.

London citizens came to rely increasingly on guild brothers or masters to act as surrogates in rearing their children. A small percentage of these were masters to children already apprenticed. The increasing reliance on guild brothers, from nine percent in 1309 to 1348 to twenty-three percent in 1429 to 1468, indicates that strong emotional bonds of trust and friendship had developed among the members.

Although maternal kin were favored over paternal kin, they did not enjoy a significant privilege. Testators could use their wills to empower kin to take an active role in rearing children. For instance, Nicholas de Halweford entrusted the money for his three sons to his brother, although his wife was to rear them. He also gave his brother and sister-in-law ten *marks* to take two daughters, Margaret and Matilda, into an apprenticeship. Matilda had an additional five *marks* toward her marriage.[22]

When little fortune and no immediate relatives could be associated with the orphan, the chamberlain took responsibility. Thus in 1320, when "Walter, son of Richard the cook, a vagrant orphan" came into the hands of the chamberlain, he appeared with the child before the mayor. His goods, such as they were, and his rearing were assigned to Andrew Horn, the chamberlain. If the child was truly destitute, the chamberlain might charge the city for expenses of custody.[23] No citizen's child, therefore, should have been without a home.

Care in granting of guardianship by dying fathers and civic officials appears to have been, on the whole, successful. To the extent that an orphan was a valuable market commodity, given the large inheritances, his or her well-being was at risk. The abuses included misuse of the orphans' funds, failure to produce the funds when the orphan came of age, marriage of the ward without the mayor's permission, and insufficient care in rearing the children. The Letter Book evidence indicates that only five percent of the 495 orphanage cases (a single case includes all children in one family) from 1309 to 1428 indicated some form of violation of the wardship arrangements. Most of the complaints were of diverting the orphans' funds and not repaying when they came of age, rather than marriage without permission. None involved the murder of a ward. While these figures certainly represent underreporting, nonetheless by far the majority of children in wardship must have not experienced misappropriations. Not only did the laws protect the persons of the orphans, they appear to have also generally preserved their wealth and material well-being.

London's laws protecting the integrity of the truncated nuclear family, including the mother and children, were carried out in practice. Widows apparently received their dowers or were able to go to court and pursue their cases to a successful closure. Mothers, being favored by London law and generally outliving their husbands, acted as guardians for their children. While the laws and their enforcement protected the interests of widows and children, they also had implications for the social structure of London.

Social Implications of the Laws and Their Enforcement

The evidence strongly suggests that in both the structuring and the enforcement of laws protecting citizen's orphans and widows, the patriarchs of London were highly successful. Their children and their fortunes were usually placed with the surviving mother or with kin or guild brothers. Close surveillance by the mayor also preserved the inheritances intact. Their property included real estate such as taverns, messuages (that is to say, dwellings and the adjoining land), houses and tenements. In addition, a certain amount of their inheritance included cash, plate, clothing and household goods.[24] Although the total value of the orphans' inheritances cannot be measured, that of the cash endowments can be calculated. The value of cash settlements was only £80 before 1348 but rose steadily in the period following the onset of plague to reach a high of £901 in 1429 to 1468. The change is partly due to the care in recording the orphans' property during the fourteenth century.[25] Better recording, of course, meant that civic officials were becoming even more responsive to citizen insistence on careful oversight and, therefore, the guardians would be less able to cheat their wards when they returned the property.

Amidst the success of the policies, a lone observer in the late fifteenth century, the printer and publisher, William Caxton, commented on what he thought was the failing of London's patricians. Writing a prologue to a book of advice modeled on the wisdom of Cato, he commented that London citizens left their children very healthy and wealthy, but that they did not produce great lineages, such as could be observed on the Continent. He lamented that only two in ten thrived and produced a lineage, while on the Continent lineages had endured for five or six hundred years. Caxton, of course, felt that the problem was a failure of moral fiber in the youth, and that if they read Cato they would realize the importance of establishing patrilineages.[26] What had happened, and did the matter disturb the London patriarchs?

The presence of so many stepfathers in the wardship records indicates the demand in which widows with children were held in London's marriage market. Widows with minor children were very desirable and remarried quickly, sometimes when they were still pregnant with a child by their former husband. Canon law did not require a period of mourning before remarriage.[27] Between 1309 and 1458, fifty-seven percent of the 212 widows who appeared before the Court of Orphans had already remarried. The proportion is very high, considering that in sixteenth-century England about a third of widows remarried.[28] Furthermore, the tendency for widows to remarry increased in the late fourteenth and fifteenth centuries. From 1309 to 1388 only thirty-six percent of the widows remarried, but from 1389 to 1458 seventy-three percent remarried.[29] A comparison of the growing wealth of orphans' inheritance with the increasing incidence of remarriage of widows suggests that London men were not insensitive to the considerable charms of manipulating the dower of the widow for her lifetime along with the inheritance of the minor children until they came of age (at sixteen for girls who married, and twenty-one for girls who had not married and for boys). While widows with only one child were more likely to remarry, the number of children did not make a substantial difference in widows' remarriage rate.[30]

An example will make the figures clear. A fifteenth-century London grocer married a widow with six children. Her dower was £764 and her children, of course, had an equal amount as inheritance (one-third of the total estate). In other words, he had the use of £1,528 until the children reached the age of majority, and still had the use of his wife's dower for as long as she lived.[31]

London patriarchs apparently had few qualms about the remarriage of their widows. In the London Husting Wills, only three percent of the husbands speci-fied that their wives not remarry. A husband actually might feel more comfortable about the welfare of his wife, his children and his business if his widow remarried. A skinner in 1403 left his business and apprentices to his wife along with her dower, specifying that she continue the business or marry someone in the trade within three years.[32]

From the patriarchs' viewpoint, we may offer several explanations about their lack of concern for establishing lineages. By putting a higher value on preserving their children and their wealth, rather than dwelling on future generations or col-lateral lines, they demonstrated that they placed their primary loyalties with their conjugal families, that economic and emotional unit they formed when they mar-ried. Aside from custom and even genuine emotion, several factors may have given rise to their preference. Mortality among children in London was very high, so that even hoping for survival of immediate progeny, let alone a lineage, was enough. Londoner patriarchs had reason to be concerned about guaranteeing the survival of children who lived through childhood diseases. About a third of the orphans died during wardship. To make up for the shortfall in the native-born population, London became a city of immigrants. Of the 536 apprentices registered in 1309 to 1312, only about a fifth were native Londoners. Furthermore, Londoners who made a comfortable fortune had a tendency to abandon the city and establish themselves as gentry in the countryside.[33] In this new capacity, they began to worry, like their gentry neighbors, about lineages rather than survival of their children.

Having preserved their offspring as best they could, London men had little con-cern that their wives might not strive to preserve their lineage, but instead remar-ry. London patriarchs increasingly valued their guild brothers, as we have seen, in assigning of wardship. These associations encouraged the strength of horizontal ties between guild brothers rather than vertical ones among kin. Such evidence as we have suggests that, in the selection of a new husband, London women seem increasingly to have turned to the same or a related craft or business. Sylvia Thrupp found that the mayor and aldermen, who had control over the marriage as well as the wardship of orphans, arranged for eighty-four percent of merchants' daughters to marry merchants. When widows remarried, the proportion was even higher. In thirty-seven cases from the fifteenth century, thirty-four widows chose husbands from the merchant class and twenty-two of these were from the same company as the former husband.[34] The same pattern may be observed for the crafts. Steve Rappaport was able to demonstrate that, by the sixteenth century, marriages within guilds were mandated, and widows even insisted on suitors joining their guild as a condition of marriage.[35]

We must also consider why widows who were so well endowed bothered to remarry. Why did they lack a sense of lineage, or a desire to remain on their own rather than risk further childbirths? In the urban environment, widows of London citizens became free of the city (that is to say, citizens in their own right), and as such could carry on their husbands' trades.[36] Although we do not have adequate guild records for the Middle Ages to determine how many women took this option, those from the sixteenth century indicate that very few women continued trades or businesses alone: under two percent of the apprentices worked for women.[37] Our contemporary viewpoint makes us want to place the emphasis on widows finally gaining independence from the legal and moral domination of men. But that perspective may not be one that a fourteenth- or fifteenth-century widow would share. Remarriage might have been preferable to having to deal with the problems a woman faced in a male-dominated work- and marketplace. Besides, remarrying widows could choose their husbands, and must often have married someone they already knew. Since they had the care of their children, their emotional and material bonds with the initial conjugal family would remain intact.

Assuming that the goal of London patriarchs, in generously providing for their widows and orphans, was to secure the best possible survival of their offspring, they succeeded admirably in the objective. Their widows were not destitute; their children's property was administered through the auspices of the mayor and chamberlain; their laws protected the property rights of both the widows and their children; and the mother was the favored nurturer in the event of the father's death. If widows chose to add the further protection of marrying within the guild structure, the patriarchs expressed few objections and some relief. The children of one's loins would survive, but the lineage was too abstract a concept to protect.

Notes

1 Barbara A. Hanawalt, *The Ties That Bound: Peasant Families in Medieval England* (New York: Oxford University Press, 1986), pp. 205–219.

2 Barbara A. Hanawalt, *Growing Up in Medieval London: The Experience of Childhood in History* (New York: Oxford University Press, 1993), pp. 205–206.

3 See Barbara A. Hanawalt, "The Widow's Mite: Provisions for Medieval London Widows," in *Widows in the Literature and Histories of Medieval Europe*, ed. Louise Mirrer (Ann Arbor: University of Michigan Press, 1992), pp. 23–25 ,for a more complete description of dower provisions in London.

4 Caroline M. Barron, "The 'Golden Age' of Women in Medieval London," *Reading Medieval Studies*, XV (1989), pp. 38–42, has a fine discussion of London dower customs.

5 Elaine Clark, "City Orphans and Custody Laws in Medieval England," *The American Journal of Legal History*, 34 (1990), pp. 168–187, has made this the major thrust of her very fine article on wardship in London and Bristol.

6 T. Riley, ed., *Munimenta Gildhallae Londiensis: Liber Albus*, I (London, 1859), pp. 95–96.

7 Reginald Sharp, ed., *Calendar of the Letter Books of the City of London*, I (London: John Edward Francis, 1912), pp. 220–221, restates the law explicitly in one case. The *Letter Books* will hereafter be cited with the appropriate letter of the alphabet.

8 A.H. Thomas, ed., *Calendar of Early Mayor's Court Rolls* (Cambridge: Cambridge University Press, 1924), p. 7.

9 *Letter Book K*, p. 93 (1428).

10 *Letter Book C*, p. 81, 82; *Letter Book E*, p. 121; *Letter Book G*, p. 91.

11 Reginald R. Sharpe, ed., *Calendar of Wills Proved and Enrolled in the Court of Husting*, London, A.D. 1258–1688, I (London: Richard Clay and Sons, Ltd., 1889), p. 377 (1332).

12 One could become a citizen by being born in the city of London, by serving out an apprenticeship and becoming a master in a London guild and thereby a citizen, or by redemption (that is, buying citizenship). By far the most common way to become a citizen was through apprenticeship.

13 See Hanawalt, "The Widow's Mite," pp. 27–32, for a complete discussion of court procedures and the success of widows. These cases are preserved in the Corporation of London Archives in the Common Plea Rolls.

14 Of the 326 wills of adult males I surveyed for fifteenth-century Bedfordshire, 235 (seventy-two percent) had a surviving wife. Bedfordshire Wills, 1480–1519, trans. Patricia Bell, *Bedfordshire Historical Record Society*, 45 (1966). *Bedfordshire Wills Proved in the Prerogative Court of Canterbury, 1383–1548*, ed. Margaret McGregor, Bedfordshire Historical Record Society, 58 (1979). *English Wills, 1498–1526*, ed. A.F. Cirket, Bedfordshire Historical Record Society, 37 (1956).

15 *Husting Court Wills*, 2 vols. Only medieval wills appear in this sample (until 1500).

16 The wills recorded in London's Archdeaconry Court are less detailed than those from the Husting Court (see note 11 above) from which the figures are taken. But they contain more wills of ordinary craftsmen of London. Of the 116 men who made provisions for their widows, only eighteen percent mention real property while sixty-five percent simply refer to the residue of their estate. Guildhall Library, Archdeacon's Court MS. 9051/1, 9051/2. Hereafter referred to as Archdeacon's Court and ms. number.

17 *Letter Book D*. Sharpe discusses the wardship procedures, pp. iv, xiv. *Letter Book G*, p. 79, mentioned the name of one of the Common Pleaders. For a general discussion, see Charles Carlton, *The Court of Orphans* (Leicester: Leicester University Press, 1974). Chapter 1 dis-

cusses the medieval foundation, and the rest of the book deals with the Tudor-Stuart period. *Letter Book K*, p. 93. The number of years was also limited.

18 *Husting Wills*, 1300–1500.

19 These included uncles or aunts of the child, grandparents, elder sons and a nephew.

20 *Letter Book G*, p. 95 (1358), records the terms of a will in a wardship enrollment. Thomas Bedyk gave to Simon Fraunceys, mercer, the wardship, custody and marriage of his son Henry during his minority.

21 The discrepancies between Clark's figures and mine represent a difference in years and categories that we used. Our basic results are the same. Clark, "City Orphans," p. 182.

22 *Letter Book E*, p. 9 (1318); in *Letter Book F*, pp. 248–249 (1350), an older brother became guardian to his young sister.

23 Betty Masters, *The Chamberlain of the City of London, 1237–1987* (London: Corporation of London, 1988), p. 11. Information from *Letter Book E*, pp. 135, 217, in which he presents his expenses for maintaining the child for 8 years. See also *Letter Book G*, pp. 320–321.

24 Of the 521 orphan families (sibling groups) in which a record exists of inheritance, forty-nine percent were left goods and fifty-one percent real estate.

25 Through 1368, only about a third of the cases recorded the value of the inheritance. Until 1438, forty to fifty percent of the cases registered the bequest. After that, almost 100 percent of the cases recorded the amounts. For some idea of the monetary values of the era, a loaf of bread, the dietary staple, cost one penny; a laborer earned between two and four pennies a day in the fourteenth century.

26 W.J.B. Crootch, ed., *The Prologues and Epilogues of William Caxton, Early English Text Society*, 176 (orig. ser., 1928), p. 77.

27 Michael M. Sheehan, "The Influence of Canon Law on the Property Rights of Married Women in England," *Mediaeval Studies*, 25 (1963), p. 121.

28 R.S. Schofield and E.A. Wrigley, "Remarriage Intervals and the Effect of Marriage Order on Fertility," in *Marriage and Remarriage in Populations of the Past*, ed. J. Dupaquier, E. Helin, P. Laslett, M. Levi-Bacci, and S. Sogner (London and New York: Academic Press, 1981), pp. 212, 214. Their figures are for small towns and villages rather than for London. David Herlihy and Christiane Klapisch-Zuber, *Tuscans and Their Families: A Study of the Florentine Catasto of 1427* (New Haven: Yale University Press, 1985), p. 217, found that widows seldom remarried in Florence.

29 Widows suing for disputed dower initiated their claims fairly quickly after the death of the husband and the probate of the will. The percentage of widows who were remarried at this time increased to fifty percent following the Black Death in 1348 to 1349 and reached a high point of fifty-three percent in 1374 to 1379, but then dropped again in the fifteenth century.

30 Barbara A. Hanawalt, "Remarriage as an Option for Urban and Rural Widows in Late Medieval England," in *Wife and Widow: The Experiences of Women in Medieval England*, ed. Sue Sheridan Walker (Ann Arbor: University of Michigan Press, 1993), pp. 141–164, for a complete discussion of remarriage of widows. Of widows with children who remarried, forty-five percent had one child, twenty-four percent had two children, seventeen percent had three children and fourteen percent had four or more children. Of widows who did not remarry, forty-three percent had one child, eighteen percent had two children, twenty percent had three children and nineteen percent had four or more children.

31 Sylvia L. Thrupp, *The Merchant Class of Medieval London* (Ann Arbor: University of Michigan Press, 1948), p. 107. Another man making a similar marriage controlled £3,000 in this manner.

32 Guildhall Archives, Archdeacon's Court 9051/1 105v.

33 Thrupp, *Merchant Class*, ch. 5.

34 Thrupp, *Merchant Class*, p. 28. Goldsmiths' widows seemed to have preferred goldsmiths.

Thomas F. Reddaway, *The Early History of The Goldsmiths' Company, 1327–1509* (London: Edward Arnold, 1975), pp. 275–321, has reconstructed biographies indicating marriages when known.

[35] Steve Rappaport, *Worlds Within Worlds: Structures of Life in Sixteenth-Century London* (Cambridge: Cambridge University Press, 1989), pp. 40–41.

[36] Barron, "The 'Golden Age' of Women in Medieval London," pp. 45–46, says that a widow was expected to continue her husband's business.

[37] Rappaport, *Worlds Within Worlds,* p. 41.

Maura Palazzi's examination of the situation of "women alone" in eighteenth- and nineteenth-century Bologna points to the changing impact of kinship norms on women's options for independence. Her focus is on records documenting women's work in industry and agriculture and on their place in the household at different points in their lives. She argues that patrilineality (which she sees as the prevailing logic of kinship rules in this context) is not incompatible with the presence of unmarried women. But "women alone" were marginalized because of their subordinate positions in the economy and in kinship. These hierarchies changed over time, however, with effects that varied in different social classes. Palazzi's study of these changes highlights both variability and mutability in balances of gender power in the family and the economy.

11

Work and Residence of "Women Alone" in the Context of a Patrilineal System (Eighteenth- and Nineteenth-Century Northern Italy)

MAURA PALAZZI

Attention to the work of "women alone"[1] in the context of a historical discussion of patrilineality raises two issues. First, it suggests how patrilineal systems[2] operate in the lower classes, where questions of patrimony and the social power of the family group are of little importance, at least in material terms. In this milieu, work activities rather than property constitute a vantage point from which to see how the division of roles and power between the sexes varies according to social class. Analysis of women's work shows how a customary system aimed at guaranteeing continuity and power to upper-class families ends up influencing the behavior of everyone.

Second, studying the work of "women alone" means focusing our analysis on those individuals who, in the framework of a patrilineal society, usually occupy the most marginal roles. We know that in societies where the task of guaranteeing family continuity is entrusted to men, the main social function attributed to women is ensuring a legitimate line of descent. Control by men of women's reproductive capacity is critical to maintaining the existing order, and not only gives rise to asymmetry in role divisions and power relations between the sexes, but also serves to institute an effective hierarchy among women themselves, based on marital status and childbearing. In European societies of the *ancien régime* (that is, before the French Revolution of 1789), the status of wife and mother was regarded as superior to that of the childless wife, widow or unmarried woman. "Unhappily wed" or separated women were particularly marginalized: it mattered little whether or not the woman was seen to be at fault. Children enhanced the position of the wife or widow if they were the offspring of a lawful marital relationship, but they inexorably worsened the circumstances of any woman if they were the result of sexual transgression, which was inevitably the case of the unmarried. Therefore, women alone occupied a marginal position in patrilineal societies, since they lived in conditions which were different from those decreed as normal and desirable for their sex. In these contexts an analysis of the work of women alone provides important keys with which to interpret the functioning of the overall kinship system.

But who are these "women alone"? This term can refer to very different situations which are too frequently grouped together. The common use of the term relates to legal marital status (in English, "single women") and defines female solitude in negative terms, as the absence of the nuptial bond. But "women alone," as I use it, includes both unmarried women and widows, as well as separated and divorced women, whatever form of residential arrangement they might have and whatever specific problems they might face.

An emphasis on residence is very useful for analyzing certain important historical problems, especially the degree of a woman's autonomy from family networks or her exercising roles and functions normally prohibited to women. Taking household form into account lets us see female "solitude" as not simply a function of marital status; it throws light on moments of living apart from men in the lives even of married women during stages when the normative division of family roles is suspended.

Analysis of women's residential arrangements, therefore, allows us to understand the limitations imposed by a patrilineal society on women, even when they are more or less independent from family authority and from subjection to a father, husband or other male figure of authority. These factors all affect the possibilities for female autonomy. The first part of this paper will provide an analysis of residence and work patterns of "women alone" in several Italian cities of the *ancien régime*, especially Bologna. The second part will examine family-based economies of rural areas in Northern Italy, especially day laborers' households.

In Italian cities of the *ancien régime*, a large number of women lived apart from any form of direct male family authority. For example, in the parish of St. Apollinare in Rome, with its high artisan population, the number of women who were heads of families (by this term, I mean both those living alone and those listed as a head of a household) was roughly twenty percent in the early eighteenth century.[3] At the end of the nineteenth century, in the socially different Milan parish of St. Stefano Maggiore, the proportion was sixteen percent.[4] Finally, in

216

fourteen parishes in Bologna, with a wide range of socioeconomic conditions, the proportion of households headed by women reached an average of 14.5 percent in the year 1797.[5]

In fact, it was in the popular quarters that the highest numbers of female heads of families were found. For example, in the Bolognese outskirts, home to the city's poor, who were forced to engage in activities on the brink of illegality in order to survive, one household out of five, sometimes out of four, was headed by a woman. As we move closer to the central urban areas, which were more socially diverse and on the whole characterized by higher living standards, the figures range from eleven percent to seventeen percent. Finally, in the heart of the city, with its proliferation of commercial and artisan activities, sources show fewer than ten percent of the household heads to be women.[6] Independent residence was particularly common for women of working class and poorer status. This is not to say that the phenomenon of female headship was entirely absent among the middle classes and aristocracy, but it was far less frequent.

These results suggest patterns of female solitude at different social levels in a society dominated by a patrilineal system of property transmission. My own research on female heads of households found in the records of fourteen parishes in Bologna has shown that, at the end of the eighteenth century, women living alone or heading households were typically widows over the age of fifty. Only four percent of these women were under thirty, and even fewer were married and on their own due to separation or an absent husband.[7] As in most cities of the *ancien régime*, the position of head of household was more widespread among lower-class widowed women, particularly those who were above a certain age; the death of the husband did not cause any apparent conflict over custody of the children, nor was there any patrimonial interest forcing the widow to return to her family. However, a woman's residential independence and her assumption of roles normally attributed to men did marginalize her. Even among the lower classes, we encounter only a very small number of independent unmarried women, for whom alternative solutions, such as residence with the family of origin or with that of other relatives, relegation to some charitable institution, or going into domestic service, were evidently considered preferable. Young widows were also very rare, a fact that can be explained by a variety of factors: the likelihood of becoming a widow increases in proportion to age and, in the case of young widows, there was also the opportunity of making a second marriage. However, my data reveal another interesting fact. In the richer classes, or in those classes that owned some property, independent female behavior threatened two kinds of family patrimony, the first material, the second symbolic (the honorable sexual behavior of the woman). In the working classes, only the second applied. I thus found two distinct resident patterns. The

217

autonomy of working-class women was problematic to families mainly during their childbearing years. In other phases of their life, many unmarried and especially many widowed women were freer from the family's control, but also of its protection. Their autonomy was limited not by the family, but by society more broadly: market and wage mechanisms prevented women from becoming economically self-sufficient, causing them to fall under the control of protection networks of public welfare institutions.

What was the domestic situation of households headed by women in Bologna? Almost one-third were women living alone, mainly elderly widows. Only six percent of these women were below the age of thirty; six percent of female heads were of the propertied or noble classes, but their "solitude" was obviously belied by a large number of servants. However, the largest group of female-headed households, more than forty-five percent of the total, included children. Some female heads lived with relatives (7.2 percent) or with unrelated men. But the most interesting are those defined in the sources as living "*a compagnia*" (8.2 percent): this refers to coresident groups of unrelated women of different ages and conditions. They include mothers with small children or adolescent daughters living with single women younger than themselves; or in some cases, sick or physically handicapped women living with others who worked or were registered as "poor." Living *a compagnia* appears to be one survival strategy aimed at partially alleviating the difficulties inherent in female solitude.[8] It was a choice involving the sharing of household tasks and many other aspects of day-to-day life. Because the sexual division of labor and pay discrimination did not allow lower-class women to live independently as household heads, they had to resort to more complex strategies. Thus, there appears to be an internal contradiction within the patrilineal model which is compatible with—one might even say, the cause of—the creation of a large number of households headed by poorer women, but economically structured without a guarantee of self-sufficiency. Unmarried lower-class men not living within the parental family found other ways of living: they usually became boarders in another family, that is, they exchanged money for board, lodging and domestic services, or they tried to have a woman living in their house—an unmarried or widowed sister, a daughter, their mothers, a servant.

The Work of Single Women

The problems faced by women alone are more easily understood in light of an analysis of female working conditions. We have already mentioned that the presumptions of the patrilineal system governed social practices. The characteristics of female work can be usefully interpreted in this light. The preeminence of the

Table 1. Percentage of men and women holding an occupation in four parishes in Bologna in 1796

Parish	Women		Men	
	a*	b*	a*	b*
St. M.delle Muratelle	62.1%	65.9%	87.7%	88.5%
St. M. Labarum Coeli	52.1%	58.7%	87.9%	88.1%
St. M. della Carità	73.9%	75.2%	89.6%	89.7%
St. M. della Ceriola	28.0%	46.3%	83.5%	83.7%

Note: All percentages refer to inhabitants over the age of 13.
a* = excluding domestic servants; b* = including domestic servants.
Source: A.S.B., *Archivio del Legato*, Censimento di famiglie distinte per parrocchie (ex notificazione 2 maggio 1796), parrocchie di St. M. delle Muratelle, St. M. della Carità, St. M. Labarum Coeli, St. M. della Ceriola.

female reproductive function did not mean that women did not work or undertake other activities outside the family sphere. It did mean, however, that such activities were assumed to be of less value, and this "devaluation" was expressed on many levels. First of all, work did not carry the same weight in defining the social identity of women as it did for men. For women, civil status was of greater importance, while for men, occupation was. This creates difficulties for historians attempting to determine the nature and characteristics of female work. Very often, sources such as parish records, which maintained a kind of yearly census of parish populations, recorded occupations for the male population, but provide information only about marital status for women.

Table 1 shows the percentages of the male and female population over the age of thirteen who were involved in work activities of some type in 1796 in four Bolognese parishes, each characterized by a different social composition. The percentages of men who worked varied relatively little from parish to parish. In the case of working women, the oscillations are enormous. The highest percentage of working women, not much different from the percentage for men, was to be found in the parish of St. Maria della Carità, the site of the town's main manufacturing activities, especially textiles. The lowest proportion of working women was in St. Maria della Ceriola parish, home of aristocratic families and members of the professional and mercantile classes. Here, very few women worked, and the majority who did were domestics in male-headed households.[9] Therefore, to a far greater extent than for men, paid work by women was linked to the family's social condition and, as expected, was more widespread among the artisan and commercial classes, and among the neediest sections of the population. In this context, the presence of working women was a sign of a family's economic and social marginality, and did not enhance a woman's social identity with positive connotations, although it may have partially shifted the power balance within the family. But the process of devaluation of women's work operated in two directions: if work did not enhance the social status of a woman, in some cases it actually led to a negative effect, since it distracted her from her fundamental tasks and made her behavior less subject to control.

Two further factors affected the working conditions of "women alone": pay discrimination and the stratification of female occupations according to marriage status. Discrimination between men's and women's pay stemmed from the fact that, according to the traditional social division of roles, it was the man who was responsible for family maintenance: it made no difference that many widows fulfilled this function.[10] Men's work was conceived to be the fundamental support of the family, while woman's work was seen as a minor extra contribution. This had an important economic impact on households headed by working-class women. A woman with the same work and household responsibilities as a man would in fact be in a far lower income bracket, crossing the threshold from poverty to destitution. The presence of many female heads of households in the poorest urban areas should therefore be viewed not only as the result of different family strategies among the lower classes, but also as the effect of the process of socioeconomic deterioration which struck families once they were deprived of the support of a man's wages. In the first year following a husband's death, many widows had to move to the poorest areas of the town.[11]

The list of "destitute persons" drawn up by the Bolognese police authorities in 1808 also provides some useful information. Here, it is not only the quantitative difference between men and women that is striking (the number of women is higher), but also the composition of each group. While destitute males tended to be either very old (more than fifty-six percent were over sixty years of age) or very young (under age ten), the females were of all ages (only thirty-five percent are over sixty years of age).[12]

In the 1796 city census, one out of three households in the Bolognese parish of St. Maria delle Muratelle was listed as poor. When the data for households not including married couples are looked at separately, we discover that the proportion of the poor is, in fact, far smaller in groups headed by men (fifteen percent), while it it is much greater for households headed by women (two-thirds of the total). Significantly, eighty-five percent of women living alone and eighty percent of those living *a compagnia* were registered as poor, destitute or dependent on charity. The vast majority of these women (two out of three) were employed, but evidently working did not allow them to transcend the poverty threshold. Only five percent of female household heads not in a state of poverty were listed as being without occupation: two of them were women of property and one was a countess.[13]

Women's Work in the Countryside

During the eighteenth and nineteenth centuries, the Italian countryside was a hodgepodge of different farm management systems, agricultural practices and farm sizes. Such variety affected the organization of the family and work, and produced a range of alternatives available to men and women. The number of rural "women alone" and their condition also depended on these differences. The economic function of the family farm and its structure were the most important factors.[14]

In areas where the land was divided into small family farms, the family constituted not only a group of cohabitants but also a work unit—a kind of corporation in which each person worked according to a division of labor based upon sex, age, civil status and relationship with the family head. Within this context, there was a close connection between family organization and production, and between residence patterns and work. The category of family farmer included small landowners, tenant farmers and sharecroppers, and also certain hired agricultural laborers, such as the *boari* (cattle hands),[15] whose contracts bound the entire family unit to live on the land and organize themselves as a work unit under the direction of the head of family. In these regions, generally in the north or center, rules of postmarital residence were strictly patrilocal: married men stayed on in the paternal household, while wives moved to that of the husband. When, on the other hand, the family was merely a unit of consumption and there existed no direct link between residential and work grouping—as was the case for the majority of poor southern peasants and the farmhands (*braccianti*) of the center-north—family groupings tended to be mainly nuclear or extended in typology.[16] I will analyze only the families of sharecroppers and hired agricultural laborers in central and northern Italy. Southern and insular areas, where the latifundium (large landed property) or an agricultural and pastoral economy dominated, are a different case.

The work of women in the countryside varied significantly according to the family economy. Where the family group a constituted a work unit, women's work did not affect parental control of female behavior. It did not foster female economic autonomy, because the head of the family was in sole charge of the family income. It did not allow for much latitude in behavior, because women were obliged to perform their duties in the context of the household, where their work did not undermine the internal hierarchy of family authority or the prescribed division of male and female roles. In such rural contexts, female work in the fields varied greatly, depending on marital status and norms about the distribution of women's work in the fields, in the house and in the courtyard.[17] Only the *reggitrice* (the woman who occupied the highest position in the female hierarchy), the widowed mother, the wife of the head of the family, or the wife of a brother of his did not work in the fields, because she ran the household and the courtyard. Unmarried women could become *reggitrici* only exceptionally and temporarily, in the absence of any other adult woman; theirs was the most marginal position within the family.[18] Women, when working in the fields, did all sorts of jobs: some were considered typically "women's work," but at other times women worked side-by-side with men. But it was men who always oversaw the work in the fields, since this was the main task of the head of family or of a son of his.

When the family was merely a unit of consumption, working in the fields meant both weaker parental control for women and, when the work was wage labor, the opportunity to earn an individual income separate from that of the family, even if the entire wage had to be handed over to the head of the family. In the central and northern regions of Italy, women often did work in the fields as farmhands, but their work had certain characteristics. First of all, women were never employed as hired laborers, but only as farmhands (*braccianti*) for the day. Their jobs were therefore the most precarious. Secondly, their wages varied between a half and one-third of those of men, and the average annual number of working days was much below that of men in the same work. Women were seldom employed in those activities which implied spending the night away from home.[19] Moreover, in work contracts, women were never referred to as direct contractors; they were never given an individual income separate from that of the head of the family who had drawn up the contract. At times, within the same contract, the men of the family appeared as regular hired laborers and the women as hired for the day: they were therefore paid only when the need for the work force was at its greatest.[20] In such contexts, what were the conditions of women alone?

Unmarried and Widowed Women in Sharecropping Families in Tuscany and Emilia-Romagna

In families constituting a work unit, the patrimony was held in a particular form of common property ("tacit family communion.") Adult male members of the family participated in this communion; women and certain disenfranchised men were excluded. This means that during the entire eighteenth and for most of the nineteenth centuries, women were not allowed a share of the two main elements of the family patrimony—neither the original contributions of the communion founder (the so-called "old patrimony"), nor the profits of the work of the whole family (the so-called "new patrimony"). The patrimony was shared among the members of the family grouping when the different genealogical lines composing the family grouping separated; contribution shares were established according to the laws regarding hereditary succession, which for the whole of the eighteenth century pertained almost exclusively to men (they were then gradually modified, and by 1865 sons and daughters were granted the same rights). "New patrimony" was divided according to local custom, once again to the detriment of women.[21]

According to inheritance rules, single women did not share their brothers' rights of succession, nor were they allowed any share in the new patrimony, in spite of the fact that they, too, had contributed to it with their work: this weakened their family position and, even more importantly, made their position radically different from that of men if they wanted—or had to—separate from the family. Only daughters who left the paternal house to get married received a dowry; others had no legal claim. Failure to recognize the work of women held important consequences for the genealogical line they belonged to: the patrimony was redistributed among those branches of the family in which male offspring prevailed. In fact, if two brothers had the same number of children old enough to work, the one who had more sons would be advantaged in the sharing. It was, then, more "convenient" to keep male children within the family (and the communion) rather than daughters. In the second half of the nineteenth century, when the rules regarding hereditary succession had already been reformed to give sons and daughters equal rights, in many districts the practice began to spread of granting women working in the fields a share of the new patrimony. However, in some areas women were not granted the right to share in the new patrimony until after World War II.[22]

The reasons for this lay in the failure to recognize and give any value to female labor. This fact was probably the cause behind the high rate of "masculinity" within sharecropping families, a widespread phenomenon during the eighteenth and nineteenth centuries.[23] Data are still incomplete, but they allow us to point to some noteworthy trends, especially in two sharecropping areas of central and northern Italy (Tuscany and Emilia-Romagna). Giuliana Biagioli[24] has shown how sharecropping underwent a severe crisis at the beginning of the eighteenth century. In order to avoid proletarianization, sharecroppers modified their marriage habits. They wanted more "arms" than "bellies," (more adults than children within the family). Therefore the number of sons and daughters who never married began to rise. In addition, family groupings grew more "masculine" since unmarried women were expelled. For example, in one parish where the number of sharecropping families was over ninety-five percent, the proportion of males rose from

47.6 percent in 1711 to 60.7 percent in 1800.[25] In the rural areas surrounding Prato, as noted by Marco della Pina, sex ratio in the sharecropping households rose to 130 men to every 100 women over the age of fifteen in 1786.[26]

Moreover, during the eighteenth and the nineteenth centuries, in those areas where sharecropping prevailed, the number of unmarried men was very high, while the number of unmarried women was much lower.[27] There was a place in the rural household for unmarried sons, but not unmarried daughters. When a surplus of labor existed, unmarried daughters were forced to find work outside the family farm more often than their brothers. Sometimes they became servants on other farms, but more often they moved to nearby villages and especially to cities. It is significant to note that, during the eighteenth and the nineteenth centuries in most Italian cities, the majority of the population was female.

On the other hand, widowed women were much more common than widowers in sharecropping units. This stemmed from a variety of factors: life expectancy; the greater likelihood for a widower to remarry; and the fact that husbands were generally older than their wives. We do not have any specific research on this point. However, the study of local custom seems to show that widowed women could occupy different roles. When the *reggitrice* became widowed, for instance, she could then retain her role of authority only when she was also the mother of the male members of the family, while she could see her function weakened if a sister-in-law was elected to fulfill her role. Moreover, we do not know anything about those widows who were not *reggitrici*, except that their position was very weak, especially when they had only young children, and above all when they had only daughters or no children at all. This fact made theirs a very weak role both in their husband's family and in their father's.

The number of widowed women heads of household in the hamlets and in the small towns near sharecropping areas indicates that these weak lines tended to secede from the sharecropping units. At Carpi, for example, an Emilia-Romagna center with about three thousand inhabitants, 18.8 percent of the heads of family were female in 1758.[28] Even in the Bolognese plain, the number of female heads of household is significant: in fact, it reached 10.5 percent.[29] So we may suppose that a certain number of widowed women, particularly those in the weakest positions, left the sharecropping units and moved to towns, where the prevailing activities were not agricultural but textile and clothing manufacturing.[30] Even in cases where women seceded from the familial household, then, they moved to a particularly difficult and generally poorer life.

A final point to consider regarding the sharecropping units is the possibility for widowed women to become heads of family. The data on this issue are very clear:

female heads of families are almost nonexistent within peasant households constituting work units, and even rarer among sharecropping units.[31] This is due to the fact that very often an adult man was available to replace the deceased head of family, and also to the fact that being the head of the family involved the running of a farm and the direction of a working group. Sharecropping contracts generally precluded female headship, except temporarily. For instance, in some cases the widowed wife was allowed to serve out the terms of a contract when there were no adult men available to substitute for her deceased husband. The women made heads of family under these circumstances were forced to abandon the holding in a short time if there were no son or other male relative ready to take over.[32]

Female Hired Laborers

Women could more easily become heads of household in family groupings that were primarily units of consumption. In such families, which were mainly nuclear and in which there was no farm to run, the death of the husband often led the wife to assume the role of head of family. Data on this point are scarce, but very meaningful. In St. Giovanni in Persiceto, in 1881, female heads of family constituted 0.3 percent among sharecropping families and two percent among the families of day laborers,[33] while in six villages in the hills surrounding Pisa, where there were no sharecropping groupings run by women, female day laborers who were heads of family constituted 3.1 percent of households.[34] Another interesting characteristic of such families is that, in the period we are analyzing, there were generally fewer bachelors and spinsters in comparison to sharecropping groupings.[35] The lower number of bachelors and spinsters is partially due to the fact that people could more easily marry, as parents had no need to keep adult workers for the farm, but probably also to the fact that children would more often leave the family when quite young, in order to find work.

Factors of Change

During the eighteenth and the nineteenth centuries, Italy underwent a process of profound transformation which signalled the end of the *ancien régime* and involved most forms of social organization, including those regulating family and work patterns. Within this framework, a gradual change took place in relationships between the sexes within the family and within society. Manifestations of the change appeared both in law and behavior. Important legislative reforms modified some of the principal rules governing the patrilineal system of transmission of material and symbolic property within the family. In addition, the economic and productive orders underwent a process of evolution such that women took on a totally new and strong self-identity as workers to a degree that had never occurred before.

From the legislative point of view, the first reforms were instituted by the Napoleonic Code and confirmed by the postunification Civil Code of 1865. These reforms granted full rights to adult daughters and, therefore, emancipation from parental authority; rights to succession were made the same for sons and daughters where legacies were not specified in a will; the granting of *patria potestas* to the widowed mother (guaranteeing her rights as guardian of her children) was no longer revocable but only limited in the event of her remarriage. Such legislation, while certainly not eliminating the disparities between men and women within the family, did reduce the asymmetries. However, this had little effect on the lot of married women who were still subject to their husband's authority; married women faced restrictions on their juridical freedom up until 1919.[36]

Conversely, unmarried women of the propertied classes acquired for the first time the right to a share of the family patrimony and the freedom to dispose of it as they wished. This is not to imply that the law led to an immediate and concrete change in behavior, but it did open up a new juridical possibility. For working-class women, the effects of the emancipation from family authority proved to be contradictory, at least in the short term. On the one hand, the acknowledgment of their freedom to act reduced the possibility of women resorting to the various forms of public assistance characteristic of societies of the *ancien régime*; such assistance came to focus on juveniles and elderly people. On the other hand, the law responded to the needs of the new labor market, which required mobile and flexible female labor, implying greater independence from family ties.[37]

In fact, one of the most important economic modifications in this period was the beginning of the industrialization process, in particular in the textile sector. This opened the way to female employment outside the house, which reduced both that typical control and protection on the part of the family where women worked as domestics. Unmarried women, in particular, parted from their families. These women, who now became holders of individual work contracts and whose income was clearly distinct from the family one, led a life in which control by, and protection of, the family was significantly weakened. This process was gradual: in the beginning employers built hostels next to the factories, in order to persuade the parents of working girls to allow them to leave the house.[38]

Not only did girls living in the cities begin to work outside the home, but so did peasants' daughters, as the land became insufficient for subsistence or when the family judged it useful for some members to work and earn outside the family household. Where this occurred, a deep transformation in the family balance of power became possible. The girls were often the only members bringing in a cash income, and therefore their position became less marginal. Girls tended to marry later, as the family wanted to profit from their income for a greater number of years.[39] Even when it was men who went to work in the factories, the family equilibrium would undergo a process of transformation, as women took over the direction of the work in the fields.[40]

In the northern rural areas, another relevant factor was the vast proletarianization process in agricultural work that took place in the Po Valley toward the end of the nineteenth century. There were many women among the masses of day laborers who worked in the rural areas. According to a 1908 survey, in some centers near Ferrara and Ravenna the number of female laborers was greater than the male. Their activities would take them far from the family for months at a time.[41] There are no studies available that allow us to evaluate precisely the composition of this work force according to marital status, but unmarried women undoubtedly represented a significant part of it. These women participated in the work force as relatively independent actors. They were also involved as protagonists in social protests and in struggles to obtain better working conditions, either side-by-side with men, or alone when engaged in strongly "feminized" occupations.

Finally, in many regions, especially in the southern ones, the emigration process, particularly the transoceanic one, followed by the agrarian crisis of the seventies, allowed women now alone because of the men's departure to experience new roles and functions. Emigration, primarily a male phenomenon, caused both an increase in the number of definitive spinsters in these regions and an enormous increment in the number of women who were temporarily alone (called "white widows" or "*vedove bianche*") who would take the place of their husbands by assuming the role of head of family.[42]

These changes, the consequences of which were far from linear, allowed large numbers of women to weaken parental control and to experiment with new roles within the family and society. Most notable were the "women alone," not only the unmarried women (even if they were perhaps the larger contingent) but also married women who were temporarily alone because their husbands were away for reasons of work. New female subjects were arriving on the social scene. While unmarried women were gradually, but inevitably, beginning to be less dependent on male family authority, the possibility for them to be fully autonomous continued to be limited by pay discrimination, unaltered until after World War II.

Notes

[1] This is an English translation of the Italian term *"donna sola,"* which, as denoted later in the text, refers broadly to women who live outside the marital bond, be they single, divorced, separated or widowed.

[2] For an excellent analysis of these problems see: Christiane Klapisch-Zuber, *Women, Family and Ritual in Renaissance Italy* (Chicago: University of Chicago Press, 1985). For an important discussion on the role of these themes in women's history, see: Gianna Pomata, "Storia delle donne: una questione di confine," in *Il mondo contemporaneo, X, Gli strumenti della ricerca, 2, Questioni di metodo* (Firenze: La Nuova Italia 1983), pp. 1137–1200.

[3] See Marina d'Amelia, "Scatole cinesi. Vedove e donne sole in una società di antico regime," *Memoria* 18 (1987): 58–80

[4] See Elena Armelloni, "Casa, famiglia e professione nella Milano di fine Settecento," *Archivio storico lombardo. Giornale della Sociéta storica lombarda.*

[5] Maura Palazzi "Vivere a compagnia e vivere a dozzina. Gruppi domestici comiugali nella Bologna di fine settecento," in Lucia Ferrante, Maura Palazzi, and Gianna Pomata (eds.), *Ragnatele di Rapporti 'Patronage' e reti di Relazione nella Storia della Donne* (Torino: Rosenberg & Sellier, 1988), pp. 344–380.

[6] Sources: Archivio Arcivescovile di Bologna (A.A.B.), *Status animarum* of the parishes of: S. Michele del Mercato di Mezzo (1797), SS. Cosimo e Damiano (1796), S. Michele dei Leprosetti (1797), SS. Gervasio e Protasio (1797), S. Marino (1797), S. Salvatore (1797), S. Michele Arcangelo (1797), S. Margherita (1797), S. Giacomo dei Carbonesi (1797), S. Maria al Tempio (1797), S. Cristina della Fondazza (1797), S. Cecilia (1797), S. Mamolo (1797) S. Nicola di S. Felice (1797).

[7] See Palazzi, "Vivere a compagnia, vivere a dozzina," pp. 353–361.

[8] See note 5, Palazzi; "Vivere a compagnia, vivere a dozzina," pp. 364–376.

[9] Source: A.S.B., *Archivi del Legato*, censimento di famiglia distinta per parrocchie (ex notificazione 2 maggio 1736). See also Maura Palazzi, "Tessitrici, serve, treccole. Donne, lavoro e famiglia a Bologna nel Settecento," in Cavaciocchi (ed.), *La donna nell'economia*. Atti della Ventunesima Settimana di studi dell' Instituto Internazionale di Storia Economica F. Datini (Firenze: Le Monnier, 1990), pp. 359–376.

[10] See Francesca Bettio, *The Sexual Division of Labor. The Italian Case* (Oxford: Oxford University Press, 1988).

[11] Maura Palazzi "Abitare da sole. Donne capofamiglia alla fine del Settecento," *Memoria* 18 (1987): 37–57.

[12] Archivio Storico Provinciale di Bologna (A.S.P.B.), Archivio della Congregazione di Carità, Casa di Lavoro, 1809, b.19, rubrica 7, "Elenco dei Miserabili degenti nel Circondario di Levante" e "Elenco dei Miserabili degenti nel Circondario di Ponente." See also Maura Palazzi, "Donne povere fra lavoro, assistenza e 'sigurtà,'" in Paola Nava (ed.), *Operaie, serve, maestre, impiegate* (Torino: Rosenberg & Sellier, 1992), pp. 202–236.

[13] A.S.B., *Status animarum* of the parish of S. Maria delle Muratelle, 1796.

[14] See Maura Palazzi, "Famiglia, lavoro e proprietà: le donne nella società contadina fra continuità e trasformazione," *Istituto Alcide Cervi, Annali* 12 (1990): 25–80.

[15] See Giorgio Giorgetti, *Contadini e proprietari nell'Italia moderna. Rapporti di produzione e contratti agrari dal secolo XVI ad oggi* (Torino: Einaudi, 1974); Franco Cazzola, "L'evoluzione contrattuale nelle campagne ferraresi del Cinquecento e le origini del patto di boaria," in *Il Rinascimento delle Corti padane. Società e cultura* (Bari: Laterza, 1977), pp. 299–337.

[16] See Marzio Barbagli, *Sotto lo stesso tetto. Mutamenti della famiglia in Italia dal XV al XX secolo* (Bologna: Il Mulino, 1984); David Kertzer, *Family Life in Central Italy 1880–1910. Sharecropping, Wage Labor and Coresidence* (New Brunswick, NJ: Rutgers University Press, 1984); Andrea Doveri, "Sposi e famiglie nelle campagne pisane di fine Ottocento. Un caso di matrimonio 'mediterraneo,'" S.I.D.E.S. *Popolazione, società e ambiente. Temi di demografia storica italiana (secc. XVII–XIX)* (Bologna: Clueb, 1990), p. 148.

[17] On the sharecropping family and the role division within it, see: Carlo Poni, *Fossi e cavedagne benedicon le campagne* (Bologna: Il Mulino, 1982), in particular chapter VI, "La famiglia contadina e il podere in Emilia-Romagna."

[18] In the records of the Giunta dell'Inchiesta Agraria, an enquiry into the agricultural situation, carried out by the Italian government in the postunion period, about Treviglio in Lombardy one can read: "The *reggitrice* is usually the wife of the *reggitore*, but in her absence it is the oldest married woman…and, if there are no married women, the oldest daughter." See "Atti della Giunta per la Inchiesta Agraria e sulle condizioni della classe agricola," vol. XI, X Circoscrizione (Roma, 1882), p. 592. In the same period there were some regions, as for example Tuscany, where the unmarried brother was to be preferred as *reggitore*. See "Atti della Giunta," vols. III, IX Circoscrizione (Roma, 1883), p. 436.

[19] See Ministero di Agricoltura, Industria e Commercio, *Relazione intorno alle condizioni dell'agricoltura nel quinquennio 1870–1874*, vol. III (Roma, 1877), pp. 92–132. See also the records of the enquiry into the agricultural situation, in particular "Atti della Giunta," vols. VIII, VII Circoscrizione (Roma, 1883), p. 591; "Atti della Giunta," vol. IV, IX Circoscrizione (Roma, 1883), p. 103.

[20] See "Atti della Giunta," in particular vols. III, XI Circoscrizione (Roma, 1883), p. 567; Maura Palazzi, "Nascita e sviluppo di un'economia agro-industriale. Città e campagna a Parma

negli anni Trenta," in "I comunisti a Parma," (Parma: STEP, 1986), pp. 23–28.

[21] All information on property division and family hierarchy is from the records of local customs. For the seventeenth century, see *Girolamo Calzolari, Consultazione legale del signor Girolamo Calzolari, bolognese, sopra la divisione de'Beni in comunione specialmente fra i contadini. Opera utile ai parrochi ed a tutte quelle persone che sono elette per arbitri nelle divisioni* (Bologna, 1709); Giovanni Fierli, *Delle divisioni dei beni contadini e di altre simili persone* (Firenze: Stamperia e Libreria di Antonio Brazzini, III ediz., 1804). About more recent times, see Carlo Frassoldati, "Consuetudini per le divisioni delle famiglie coloniche di Modena, Reggio Emilia, Parma," in *Archivio Vittorio Scialoja per le consuetudini giuridiche agrarie*, 1935; M.F. Rabaglietti, *Le divisioni delle famiglie contadine* (Bologna: Edizioni Agricole, 1948); Michele Giorgianni, Attilio Parlagreco, Antonio Palermo, *La comunione tacita familiare in agricoltura* (Roma: Bulzoni, 1971)

[22] See Poni, *Fossi e cavedagne*; Pier Giorgio Solinas, "La dot et la part. Transmission des biens, fils et filles dans le familles polynucleaires des métayers siennois," in G. Ravis Giordani (ed.), *Femmes et patrimoine dans les sociétés méditerranéennes* (Marseille: Editions du CNRS, 1987), pp. 169–188; Palazzi, "Famiglia, lavoro e proprietà," pp. 48–57.

[23] See Marzio Barbagli, "Formation system of families in Italy," in S.I.D.E.S. (ed.) *Popolazione, società e ambiente, temi di demografia storica italiana* (secc. XVII–XIX) (Bologna: Clueb, 1990), pp. 3–44.

[24] See Giuliana Biagioli, "La diffusione della mezzadria nell'Italia centrale: un modello di sviluppo demografico ed economico," in *Bollettino di demografia storica* (1986), pp. 59–66.

[25] Giovanni Maiardi, *La popolazione di una parrocchia della zona collinare imolese nel '700 (1711–1820)*, Thesis in Economics, University of Bologna, 1972–1973. Paolo Baldassarri, *La popolazione di Faenza nel 1812. Il forese*, Thesis in

Economic History, University of Bologna, 1968–1969.

26 Marco della Pina, "Le donne, la famiglia e il lavoro nelle campagne toscane: il caso pratese," *Istituto 'Alcide Cervi', Annali* 12 (1990): 99–112.

27 See della Pina, "Le donne, la famiglia, il lavoro," pp. 99–112; and Barbagli, "Formation System of Family in Italy," pp. 24–27.

28 See Lucia Armentano, *Storia urbana di Carpi (sec. XVIII)*, Thesis in Humanities, University of Bologna, 1991–1992.

29 See Barbagli, "Formation System of Family in Italy," p. 17.

30 See Aurora Angeli, "Mestieri, ruoli femminili, aggregati domestici in un'area mezzadrile," *Istituto 'Alcide Cervi', Annali*: 85–89.

31 See Palazzi, "Famiglia, lavoro, proprietà," pp. 38–48.

32 As regards the customs, these aspects are widely dealt with. It is said that in the Marches, widows may undertake managing responsibilities only "very seldom"; in the Bolognese area, this situation is purely transitory, and it lasts only the time required for the division. See Giorgianni, Parlagreco, Palermo, "La comunione familiare tacita," pp. 35 and 175.

33 Barbagli, *Sotto lo stesso tetto*, pp. 544–546.

34 Doveri, "Sposi e famiglie nelle campagne pisane," table 3a.

35 Barbagli, "Formation System of Families in Italy," p. 25.

36 See "Civil Code," *Manuale di legislazione universale* (Napoli: Tip. dell'Unione 1888: arts 371 et seq.); *Maria Vittoria Ballestrero, Dalla tutela alla parità. La legislazione italiana sul lavoro delle donne* (Bologna: Il Mulino, 1979), pp. 32–33; Palazzi, "Female Solitude," pp. 446–453.

37 See Palazzi, "Female Solitude and Patrilineage: Unmarried Women and Widows in the Eighteenth and Nineteenth Centuries," *Journal of Family History* 15 (1990): 443–459.

38 See Gianni Cisotto, "Donne in fabbrica fra '800 e '900. Il caso del lanificio Rossi," in *Deputazione di Storia patria per le Venezie* (Venezia: Archivio Veneto, 1983), pp. 74–107; L. Tilly and J. Scott, *Women, Work and Family* (New York: Holt, Rinehart & Winston, 1978), pp. 139–143; Tamara K. Hareven and Louise A. Tilly, "Solitary Women and Family Mediation in American and French Textile Cities," *Annales de Démographie Historique* 1981, pp. 253–271.

39 See Franco Ramella, *Terra e telai. Sistemi di parentela e manifatture nel biellese dell'Ottocento* (Torino: Einaudi, 1984), p. 46.

40 On this theme, there are some very interesting studies about the families in the mountains, where men had to emigrate for some months every year, because of the soil poverty, while women managed the agricultural economy. See Patrizia Audenino, "Le custodi della montagna: donne e migrazioni stagionali in una comunità alpina," *Istituto 'Alcide Cervi', Annali* 12 (1990): 265–288.

41 See Pubblicazioni dell' Ufficio del Lavoro della Società' Umanitaria, "La disoccupazione nel basso emiliano." Inchiesta diretta nelle provincie di Bologna, Ferrara, Ravenna (Milano: Ed. L' Ufficio del Lavoro, 1904). See also Maura Palazzi, "Rotture di equilibri tradizionali nelle relazioni fra i sessi. I nuovi ruoli familiari e lavorativi delle donne contadine durante la crisi agraria," *Istituto Alcide Cervi, Annali*, 14/15 (1994): 167–204.

42 On this theme, much information is found in *Inchiesta Parlamentare sulle condizioni dei contadini nelle provincie meridionali e della Sicilia* (Roma: Tip. Nazionale di Giovanni Berterio, 1909).

Eni de Mesquita Samara uses census material to document women's economic activities and their roles in households in colonial and postcolonial Brazil. Women, she finds, took part in a wide range of occupations in the domestic economy as well as "in public," despite norms that suggested that public activities were inapproproate for women. The important regional and chronological variations de Mesquita Samara has uncovered are also suggestive. Clearly, women's abilities to integrate themselves into active roles in the economy differed widely in more settled and frontier situations, and from one local economy to another. Her discovery of women in a wide range of places where in theory they were not supposed to be echoes Palazzi's findings about the economic roles of "women alone" in Bologna.

12

Heading Households and Surviving in a Man's World: Brazilian Women in the Nineteenth Century

ENI DE MESQUITA SAMARA

The world of colonial Brazil has always been considered a masculine space. The rough life of the tropics, the opening of new frontiers, relations with Indians and black slaves, all were part of a universe where women played a secondary role. Tenuous figures in conventional Brazilian historiography, with the exception of a few notable heroines, women rarely appear as significant historical agents. For many generations, stereotyped descriptions of the feminine condition, along with the omission of European women as participants in the colonization of Brazil, have contributed to the dominant image of the rigid and authoritarian "patriarchal family." This study concentrates on female heads of households in the nineteenth century, in a context where the expectation was that women would pass from the tutelage of father to that of husband, and that women all had aspirations centered on either marriage or religious life. How are we then to account for the presence of women in public and economic life? How can we come to understand single women forming families and living independently with their offspring? How did widows, transformed by law into "heads of nuptial couples," acquire state backing and come to manage slaves, property and businesses? It is when we encounter these women in the historical evidence that images become blurred and practices depart from the stereotypes.

Proud and valiant elite women embodied the spirit of colonization and its related social norms. As matriarchs of important families, these women headed families which bore their names. These matriarchs at times were more powerful than men in Iberian colonies. At the other end of the social spectrum, poor white, *mestiça* and black women lived in opposition to prescribed female roles. With dexterity and skill they confronted preconceived social norms while raising their children and grandchildren. In the absence of men, single women, widows and abandoned women formed a heterogeneous sector of the population, augmenting the labor force in many Brazilian towns and cities in the nineteenth century.

Many historians tell us of the problems they have encountered in researching the pasts of Brazilian women. They tell us about the "silence of the documents," "the secrets of the attics," and the need to "read between the lines" in search of references to the lives of women in both public and private spaces. The world of women and domestic life, the stage on which these "lesser powers" performed, has only recently been investigated and understood not as an anomaly but as evidence of a continual challenge to the prescribed social order. This applies equally to Brazilian families today: female-headed households in Brazilian cities today can be seen as an organized method of survival created by circumstances, rather than as a disintegration of "the family."[1]

These "women without history," whose past may be recovered through manuscripts and contemporary accounts, frequently penetrated what were considered masculine spaces, if we take literally the social roles prescribed for each sex. Men were associated with the public sphere, the control and support of the family, while women allegedly occupied the domestic sphere and were remitted to their husbands' custody. This has led many scholars to mislabel leadership and initiative as "virile attributes" when applied to the female personality. However, recent historical analyses have begun to identify the diverse social profile of colonial Brazilian women, distinguishing more clearly between social norms and practice. Obviously a considerable distance existed between formal discourse and the prescribed rules of the system of domination on one hand, and continually improvised, day-to-day social roles on the other.

Economy, Gender Relations and Household Structure in Colonial Brazil

At the beginning of the colonial period, during the sixteenth and seventeenth centuries, the economy of Brazil was based on the sugar plantations of the northeast. Next to these rural sugar mills, elite families lived in large mansions, surrounded by slaves and other dependents. In legally recognized marriages, men and women filled roles that were well defined by custom and tradition, and reinforced by law. Formal decision-making power belonged to the husband, as the protector of and provider for his wife and children. The wife was left to govern the household and provide moral guidance to the family. Legal power was explicitly linked to gender. The authority of the male head of the family was legitimized in the literature and documents of the period. This does not mean, however, that such prescribed roles were always practiced.

The first historical studies to demonstrate a divergence from the model of female idleness and submission are associated with a specific economic, geographic and chronological context, namely, the southern region of São Paulo at the end of the eighteenth and beginning of the nineteenth centuries. In this region, economic adversity, incipient urbanization and the migration of men to new areas led women to assume the role of head of the household.[2]

Economic shifts in the early colonial period had already begun to stimulate social change. The discovery of gold in the 1690s had acted as a magnet, drawing people away from the previous hub in the northeast, and establishing a southward pattern of colonization. With a more fully developed urban life, the region of Minas Gerais, rich in minerals, attracted those in search of wealth and adventure, even channeling the slave trade to the area during the eighteenth century. The society which emerged was one of mixed race and diverse origins, in which behavior was difficult to control, in spite of the efforts of the church and the Portuguese Crown. The number of unmarried people was high, and concubinage and illegitimacy were common. Many women engaged in economic activities outside the home, and single women with illegitimate children headed families.

In the eighteenth century, a similar situation existed in the poorer areas of the south, in the orbit of Minas Gerais and São Paulo. Economic operations were smaller in scale than in the sugar mills in the northeast, and fewer slaves were used. In this regime of reduced slave labor, impoverished free workers and their families worked the land, and often took in additional dependents in order to help provide for the household. In urban areas, petty trade and a broad range of provisioning services offered opportunities for those segments of the population who were not connected to the export sector. This less formal sector of the economy encouraged the work of women, who were ever present. While the colonial regime officially devalued the local production and commerce in foodstuffs, it nevertheless came to depend on this domestic-oriented economy for goods and services not provided by other occupational groups within this slaveholding society. Although their work was never officially recognized or valued, urban women, driven by the need to survive, and finding a market for their labor, slowly incorporated such informal economic activities into their daily routines. This economic development had the associated effect of eroding the surrounding patriarchal system and its rigid gender roles.

Working Women and Female Heads of Household in the Early Nineteenth Century

In early nineteenth-century Brazil, women ran the household economy and participated actively in commerce. In urban areas, rental slaves as well as poor white and mixed-breed women offered their services to the public. In 1822, the traveler Saint-Hilaire, admiring São Paulo from one of the windows in the Governor's Palace, described the commotion caused by a group of laundresses and women peddlers who brought their small surpluses to sell in the city, but refused to pay taxes on their profits, claiming that this was subsistence produce.[3] While travelers and chroniclers recorded female activities, the presence of women may be more fully recovered from official household censuses. In 1827, for example, Ana Rodrigues, a seventy-year-old white widow born in São Paulo, earned her living spinning cotton with the assistance of her two daughters, Maria and Gertrudes, along with three slaves. In another household, Gertrudes Maria, a white widow of sixty, was listed as a small farmer. Another female household head, Rosa Maria, a thirty-year-old *parda* (mixed breed), lived off the fruits of her labor as well. Since she did not have slaves and her children were still quite young, we may assume that at least part of the household income came from Gertrudes, an *agregada* (or, nonkin household member), also a *parda*, and a single mother of a two year-old son.[4] In the city of São Paulo, 144 of 492 households (29.3 percent) registered in the 1827 census had female heads, a category that included single women, widows and wives who had been abandoned by their husbands.[5] They represented several occupations, including planters, quiltmakers, seamstresses, spinners, weavers, dishmakers, subsistence and commercial farmers, and occasional laborers. Several of these occupational groups were almost exclusively female.

The 1836 census shows a similarly large proportion of female household heads throughout the São Paulo region. Of a total of 1,516 units counted, 542 (36.8 percent) were headed by women.[6] Kusnesof has separated these data into rural and urban areas, finding that women headed 39.3 percent of the households in urban areas as opposed to 31.4 percent of rural households.[7] Extended families were a minority in this region, a pattern which appears typical throughout southern Brazil.[8] A similar pattern emerges in Minas Gerais at the beginning of the nineteenth century. In the town of Vila Rica, in 1804, 764 adult women headed 45 percent of all households.[9]

According to the same census, the composition of households headed by women varied greatly. Many women lived alone or surrounded by slaves or *agregados*. Some had live-in relatives, while others, with illegitimate children, often incorporated women in similar circumstances into the household. In the absence of slaves and *agregados*, some women household heads depended on the assistance of their children and grandchildren to help them survive on a day-to-day basis. The most desperate and needy were the older women, who lived with *agregadas* who were children. As heads of households they assumed control over income and expenses, which guaranteed the survival of the group.

Men and women who lived alone lived primarily in the central areas of cities. In the 1836 census of São Paulo, they accounted for eleven percent of all households. Counting male- and female-headed households together, those who lived either alone without families or in nuclear families made up seventy-five percent of the registered population. The high frequency of households consisting of only one individual can be explained in part by economic hardship, the high cost of marriage, the lack of suitable partners, and the delay in formal marriage proceedings. At the same time, men complained about the duties and obligations brought on by marriage, preferring to live alone or with concubines. Such alternative families were quite common and it is possible that many women counted in the censuses as heads of households were, in fact, supported from a distance by white men of means. Illegitimate children, fruits of sporadic unions or publicly recognized concubinage relationships proliferated in towns.

Studies which focus on southern, export-oriented, mining regions, as well as on the agricultural fronts that opened with the decline in gold production also emphasize the complexity of household composition and female social roles during the first half of the nineteenth century. Ramos has exhaustively examined this phenomenon among people of diverse ethnic origins, social classes, marital status and age groups. He concludes that the presence of female-headed households is significant in all economic contexts analyzed, except in one area of late settlement and expansion. He also stresses that women developed their own survival strategies within a world formally dominated by men. At the mercy of fiscal and local authorities, these women became involved in commerce and artisanal activities. A smaller number were occupied in cattle raising and in mining. In some urban areas, such as São João del Rei, seventy percent of working women performed service-related activities.[10] In the struggle for survival, one possible path was to perform tasks vacated by slaves, which occurred among the free but most poverty-stricken population.

The results of studies such as Ramos's are quite consistent, and reflect the situation in southeastern Brazil during both the colonial period and the beginning of Independence, after 1822. Whether single, widowed or abandoned by their husbands, women of this region lived lives that foreign travelers either did not encounter or failed to mention in their accounts. Conventional images of veiled faces, rigid seclusion and fleeting appearances in the window, in effect, apply only to those women whose elevated economic status warranted this sort of protection.

Further inland, the female presence was less visible. In areas dedicated to agricultural production, particularly at times of frontier expansion, the presence of women among the total population was smaller, with proportionally fewer women appearing as household heads. Yet still, an average of one-third of the households in the interior were headed by women, including sugar mills or other estates with slaves. One of these was that headed by Anna Maria de Conceição, owner and resident of a property in Goiás, where she lived in the company of a single male slave. Another was Dona Gertrudes de Freitas, who bought a small farm measuring 1,500 *braças* (about 3,300 hectares), cultivated by her nine slaves. Other women owned small sugar mills, such as Dona Mariana Pereira, who purchased her estate and employed eleven slaves in agriculture.[11] Together, all of these findings counter the traditional image of a strongly patriarchal Brazilian family in the early nineteenth century, and the segregation of women inherent in that model.

Working Women and Female Heads of Households in the Late Nineteenth Century

If many Brazilian women headed households and were economically active during the first decades of the nineteenth century, how were they living in the second half? What changes or continuities may be observed over time? By the late nineteenth century, the south had become the economic center of the country. The independence of Brazil in 1822, the abolition of slavery in 1888 and the transformation of the Brazilian Empire into a republic in 1889 all brought major changes. The end of the slave trade brought free labor from Europe to the coffee plantations, although such immigration neither eradicated the residue of slavery, nor displaced the values and hierarchies nourished by a patriarchal system. Elite families continued to perpetuate customs originating in colonial times. As they became more modern and bourgeois, they sent their sons abroad to study, but they persisted in selecting fiancés for their daughters.

Nevertheless, the late nineteenth century also witnessed the beginnings of a feminist movement in Brazil, as well as legal and economic gains for women. Precocious feminist voices could be read in female-edited newspapers which appeared in the south-central regions of the country. Some of these publications called for changing women's legal status and for female suffrage. Simultaneously, women pressed for equal rights within the family, especially in connection with divorce. With urbanization and industrialization, new economic opportunities appeared for women. Some took advantage of new jobs, working outside the home as teachers, saleswomen, office workers and government employees. The majority of working women, however, continued in traditional, low-paying, female occupations. Access to education was limited to the very few; nevertheless, this offered a small but significant professional opportunity.[12]

There are few studies regarding the condition of women in Brazil in the second half of the nineteenth century, and none concerning women as heads of households. Obtaining statistical information is problematic, since the manuscript registers arranged by household and residents disappeared and were replaced by published summaries of general censuses. In these, statistical information is not very discriminating, and women's occupations are reported in broad categories.[13] In spite of these difficulties, it is still possible to extract some significant data about female headship.

In the northeastern cities, the number of women heading households approximated that of the south over the course of the nineteenth century. Twentieth-century studies point in the direction of an increase over time, especially in urban areas, due to the increase in poverty and difficulties of survival. In Fortaleza, Ceará, for example, the census of 1887 lists 17,533 persons who resided in 3,655 households. Of these, 29.84 percent were headed by women. However, family arrangements varied. For example, Teruliano Lourenço da Costa, age forty-three, had no occupation, while his twenty-six-year-old wife, Francisca Ferreira do Nascimento, starched clothes for a living. Some couples ran their own small businesses together. For instance, José Celestino de Araújo, thirty-four, and his wife Ana Maria de Araújo, thirty-one, were weavers. In other households, diverse activities were divided among the various members. This was the case of Vitolina Lopes da Silveira, age thirty-seven, no profession listed, who had seven children, among whom four worked: Maria da Graça, twenty, Maria do Carmo, eighteen, and Joana da Silveira, fourteen, were seamstresses, while Raimundo Nonato, sixteen, was a ship caulker.[14]

What is striking in this pattern is the great complexity in household composition, which stands in marked contrast to the contemporaneous southern pattern. In the north, children, *agregados*, relatives and servants were frequently included in these household listings. Frequently, employees of a given commercial establishment resided in the same house. Households were much larger and the relations within them were much more diverse than in the south. This pattern seems to confirm that the extended family model was more typical of the northeast.

The register of female occupations demonstrates that women participated actively in the labor market, and that multiple occupations were present in a single household. Among female household heads with declared occupations, we find the following diversity: three day laborers, fifty-four laundresses, one confectioner of sweets, thirteen domestic servants, 126 prostitutes, twenty-seven women who lived off the income from their properties, ninety-four seamstresses, ten cooks, twelve weavers, two public school teachers, four private instructors, twenty clothing starchers, one wholesale merchant, four lacemakers, one embroiderer, six merchants, nine peddlers, three florists, one woman who lived off a state pension, another who lived from occasional earnings, one midwife and one nurse. In addition to the 126 women registered as prostitutes, six seamstresses, eleven laundresses, one merchant and two weavers declared that they supplemented their income through prostitution. Similarly, women who were not household heads became involved in several new occupations while at the same time continuing their activities in traditionally female sectors of the economy. Most were domestic servants, but in contrast to the early nineteenth century, a few students and teachers began to appear among the lists of female occupations.

The 1872 Brazilian census points in the same direction as the findings for Ceará, concentrating the majority of women workers in domestic services: 98,497 of 194,617 in the free population, along with 8,239 slaves. The next professions listed were seamstresses, laundresses and textile workers, while teachers, midwives and artists were few in number.

Women, Work and Households in Brazil: Some Preliminary Conclusions

In spite of the poor quality of statistics for several regions of Brazil, it is possible to draw some preliminary conclusions about female-headed households and women's socioeconomic roles. First of all, the diversity of household arrangements in different regions is striking. The analysis of household units reveals less complexity in kinship ties and a greater reliance on economically motivated household relations in the south, especially in the slave regions. In day-to-day domestic relations, *agregados* and slaves appear more frequently than blood relatives. Significant numbers of widows, single women and illegitimate children are important aspects of family formation in Brazil. They should not be viewed as anomalies or symptoms of disorder, but as characteristic components of the system of family organization and of survival strategies dictated by circumstances. The recovery of information on female household heads is revealing in many ways, especially as a contrast to the model of exclusion and confinement held to be typical of patriarchal societies. Wider participation of women in the labor market and the development of alternative arrangements are suggestive of a greater flexibility in social roles, particularly in the Brazilian case. At the same time, these elements also point to the capacity of women to develop forms of survival in a male-dominated world.

Secondly, in the various areas examined, the number of women who headed households and managed the so-called domestic economies is significant, ranging between thirty percent and forty-five percent of all households. In comparing the southeast to the northeast regions over the course of the nineteenth century, we find some differences. For one, there were slightly fewer female heads of household in the north, according to the Fortaleza census of 1887. This perhaps suggests more rigid gender patterns in this area, even at such a late date, if we can accept this one example as representative of the entire region.

At the same time, the comparative focus also reveals differences in terms of the relationship between household heads and local economies. The evidence indicates that there were fewer female-headed households in areas of agricultural expansion, in contrast to urban areas in periods of economic decline, when male outmigration tended to be more pronounced and the number of women greater.

Thirdly, female participation in the labor force was extensive throughout the nineteenth century, though it was largely confined to specific sectors of the economy: petty commerce, artisanal activities and agriculture. Opportunities for women differed according to class, race and marital status and location. Single women had better chances in the cities. The primary difference between them and married women was that most single women worked outside their homes. Widows, when they were protected by law, received their half of inheritances and acted as guardians of their minor children. In their homes, women often ruled with a power that was denied to them by social convention. They took charge of their children, other dependents, slaves and *agregados* and secured the survival of the family unit. The inclusion of new occupational categories in recent studies has contributed to the revision of analyses concerning the economic systems that predominated in Brazil during this period. They question the concept of export-oriented economic cycles and the idea that local agriculture was exclusively for subsistence. Thus, the spectrum of Brazilian economic history has grown much wider, requiring us to assume a greater complexity of social relations, especially in the urban areas.

Surely the revision of conventional images entails a fundamental revision of our view of patriarchal societies such as Brazil. The re-insertion of women into the world of work and into the public sphere in the past has, of course, much to do with the current discussion of sex roles in Brazilian society. In terms of the public/private dichotomy, this work challenges the rigid models once thought to be valid for society as a whole and, setting aside regional and temporal variations, held to be essential to the understanding of a country like Brazil. Our new hierarchies are different, but equally the product of specific historical circumstances; historicizing Brazilian patriarchy contributes to the debunking of a myth as images are confronted with reality.

Notes

[1] About women's history in Brazil, see, among many others, Kusnesof, E.A. (1985). *Household Economy and Urban Development: São Paulo 1765 to 1836.* Boulder: Westview Press; Silva Dias, M.O. (1984). *Quotidiano e Poder em São Paulo no século XIX.* São Paulo: Brasilienese; Boxer, C.R. (1975). *Mary and Mysogyny.* London: Duckworth; Saffioti, Heleieth I.B. (1976). *A Mulher na Sociedade de Classes: Mito e Realidado.* Petropolis: Vozes; Hahner, J.E. (1990); *Emancipating the Female Sex.* Durham: Duke University Press; Nazzari, Muriel (1991). *Disappearance of the Dowry.* Stanford, CA: Stanford University Press; Metcalf, Alida C. (1992) *Family and Frontier in Colonial Brazil.* Berkeley: University of California Press; Samara, E.M. (1989). *As Mulheres, o Poder e a Família.* São Paulo: Marco Zero.

[2] Silva Dias, M.O. (1984). *op. cit.*

[3] Saint-Hilaire, A. (1974). *Segunda Viagem ao Rio de Janeiro, Minas Gerais e São Paulo* (1822). São Paulo: Editora da Universidade de São Paulo.

[4] Population registers (bundles) for São Paulo, 1827. *Agregados* are free individuals who establish themselves in another's house.

[5] The lists were searched for homes (*domicilios*), hearths (*fogos*) and houses (*casas*) as the basic units of reference; that is, individuals who lived under one roof.

[6] Population registers (bundles) for São Paulo, 1836.

[7] Kusnesof, E.A. (1985). *op. cit.*

[8] Samara, E. M. (1989). *op cit.*; Silva Dias M.O. *op. cit.*

[9] Ramos, D. (1990). "A Mulher e a Família e Vila Rica de Ouro Preto: 1754–1838." *História e População.* São Paulo: ABEP, IUSSP, pp. 154–163.

[10] Martins, A.M. (1990). "Século XIX: Estrutura Ocupacional de São João del Rey e Campanha." *Belo Horizonte. V Seminário Sôbre Economia Minera.* pp. 31–32.

[11] Census of Goiás, 1818.

[12] Hahner, J.E. (1990). *op.cit.*

[13] In order to complete this study, the following manuscript censuses were investigated: São Paulo, Capital, Population bundles 1827 and 1836; Minas Gerais, various locations, population lists of 1831, 1832, 1838 and 1840; Goiás, Riberia da Capela de Corumbá, 1818; Ceará, Fortaleza, Census, 1887 and also published works—Recenseamento Geral do Brasil, 1872.

Part Four

PARENTS, BREADWINNERS, PROVIDERS

FAMILY ROLES BETWEEN IDEOLOGY AND ECONOMICS

Norbert Ortmayr's comparative study offers an assessment of the possibilities and perils of unmarried motherhood in two different contexts—turn-of-the-century Austria and contemporary Jamaica. He combines the methods of the historical demographer with those of the ethnographer. Ortmayr suggests the variety of ways in which a phenomenon like widespread illegitimacy among economically marginal populations is generated and understood. For example, the cultural stigma attached to unwed motherhood in Austria, along with an employment system that forced illegimate children into foster homes, contrasts strongly with the more tolerant Jamaican culture. Ortmayr's comparison raises questions about the various aspects of illegitimacy—material and cultural—that contribute to the better and worse fates of "fatherless" children in different contexts.

13

Illegitimacy and Low-Wage Economy in Highland Austria and Jamaica

NORBERT ORTMAYR

Introduction

Highland Austria and Jamaica have one thing in common: high illegitimacy rates, in the nineteenth and twentieth centuries respectively.[1] Highland Austria experienced its peak in around 1900, when up to eighty percent of births were illegitimate.[2] Jamaica's rates rose from fifty-eight percent in 1879 to eighty-four percent in 1987. In Kingston, the "illegitimacy" capital of the Caribbean, ninety-three percent of births registered in 1987 were out of wedlock.[3] This paper compares present-day Jamaica with the Austrian highlands in the late nineteenth and early twentieth centuries, with the goal of developing a better theoretical understanding of the social forces behind Austrian and Jamaican illegitimacy, and distinguishing "family crisis" matrifocality (mother-centeredness) from matrilineality as that is usually understood. It shows connections between family systems which produced high illegitimacy rates and the political economy.

Highland Austria

Illegitimacy in Highland Austria followed a distinct pattern: moderate rates of illegitimacy (between ten percent and thirty percent) until the early nineteenth century, followed by a rapid increase over the remainder of that century, peaking around 1900 (between thirty-five percent and sixty-nine percent, and in some

Table 1: Ratio of illegitimate births in Highland Austria and Jamaica 1791–1970

Year	Highland Austria[a]	Jamaica
1791	20.4	
1822	33.8	
1836	50.9	
1855	64.7	
1871	70.0	58.9[b]
1900	81.0	64.4
1920	—	69.2
1940	—	69.7
1963	17.9	73.6
1970	22.6	77.5

[a]Data for 1791–1900: Mettnitz (district of St. Veit).
 Data for 1963–1970: district of St. Veit.
[b]1881/85.

Sources: Ortmayr, *Knechte*; Hartley, *Illegitimacy*, p. 387.

communities up to eighty percent). High rates persisted until World War II, after which there was a rapid decline (see Table 1).

The nineteenth-century rise in illegitimacy can be traced to particular forms of agricultural labor which accompanied the concentration of land into large peasant farms.[4] The postwar decline can be traced to changes in the postwar economy, notably the creation of better-paying jobs. Around 1900, approximately one million people lived in Highland Austria,[5] a predominantly rural region with very few small administrative centers and one mining district on the eastern fringe. To an outsider it would have looked like a very backward rural society, with few agricultural and infrastructural innovations compared to the more developed regions of central and northwestern Europe.[6] Its social structure had three characteristics which distinguished it from most other rural European societies. First, farming was predominantly large-scale. A few huge farmers controlled most of the land, bred cattle on the mountain pastures, grew corn and produced cheese for regional markets. Second, farm work was done by both family members and paid farmhands. The big mountain estates employed an average of six farmhands, both male and female, though the number could rise as high as forty. They were employed year round, were regarded as members of the employer's household and their wages were predominantly paid in kind (food, shelter, clothes, gifts). Cash wages were very low. Farmhands elsewhere in rural northwestern and central Europe were typically young and unmarried, and for them service was a life-cycle experience, usually ending with marriage in the mid to late twenties. But in nineteenth-century

Table 2: Proportion ever-married 1880 and 1960

Age Group	MALES		FEMALES	
	Highland Austria 1880[a]	Jamaica 1960	Highland Austria 1880[a]	Jamaica 1960
15–19	0	0.2	0.3	1.4
20–24	2.2	3.7	5.8	11.8
25–29	7.1	17.3	18.9	28.1
30–34	18.2	31.6	26.9	40.6
35–39	28.3	41.9	33.6	48.8
40–44	33.5	50.5	35.3	55.3
45–49	38.7	57.2	40.1	58.4
50–54	39.1	62.9	43.0	59.7
55–59	43.2	65.9	45.1	60.1
60+	53.0	71.4	45.7	63.3

[a]District of St. Veit)

Sources: Oesterreichische Statistik, Bd.2, 1882. West Indies Population Census, 1960..

Highland Austria, there emerged a new type of servant: the lifelong servant. This brings us to the third social structural feature of Highland Austria. Because it was unusual to hire day labor, there was no large class of cottagers or lodgers who worked seasonally on the large farm or at odd jobs. The absence of such classes held implications for the marriage opportunities of farmhands. Why? Day laborers and farmhands in rural Europe typically occupied different stages of the life cycle of the rural laboring classes: farm hands were young and unmarried and lived in the employer's household; seasonal or day laborers were married and had their own households. The typical lower-class lifecourse proceeded from childhood in a cottager or lodger household, through domestic service between the ages of twelve and twenty-five or thirty, to marriage and starting a new family as an adult cottager or lodger. When cottager and lodger positions were rare, so were the chances for farmhand marriages. This was the case in Highland Austria.

Diverse aspects of political economy, including ecological factors and the property concentration that accompanied industrialization in the nineteenth century, created a social structure based on very large peasant farms and a huge class of farmhands, who lived in the farmer's household and reproduced themselves mainly through illegitimate offspring. Many farmhands ended up serving not for only five or ten years before marriage, but over their whole lifetime. This is reflected in both the very late marriage[7] (between thirty and thirty-five for both men and women[8]) and low proportions of men and women ever marrying at all (see Table 2). Moreover, large numbers of unmarried adults spent their youth (and many their entire life) not in the household of their parents or foster parents but as nonkin members in the large farmers' households. Illegitimate offspring were a by-product of both the long time span between sexual maturity and marriage, and the reduced parental control because young people lived outside their parents' or foster parents' house. Moreover, these high rates of illegitimacy were associated with low percentages of female-headed households. After having given birth, the unwed mother did not head her own household, but remained a dependent in her employer's household. It is this factor which makes the Austrian case particularly interesting for comparative research on matrifocality. A final characteristic of the Austrian situation was that men fathered children but did not support them. Most of the fathers of illegitimate children were also farmhands, whose low cash income did not allow them to start an independent household and fulfill the normative role of breadwinner. Higher-status men (such as farmers) seldom fathered children with female farmhands. The pattern of master-servant sexual exploitation was typical for urban servants but not for rural ones. Marriage was out of the question in these rare relationships; the shortage of cash in rural society made economic support of a farmer's mistress off the estate difficult; moreover, social control through church and society was more rigid in rural than in urban areas.[9]

The society was also characterized by a high proportion of foster children (around a fifth of all children), many of whom were illegitimate. Typically, fostering in Highland Austria was nonkin fostering, highly unstable and inegalitarian. Illegitimate children of farmhands usually ended up in a higher-status foster home, generally in a farmer's household.[10] The ties between the child's mother and the foster parents were often patron-client ties rather than kin ties. Foster children ususally remained only three to four years before they were shifted to another foster home,[11] suggesting that these relationships were weak. Fostering in Highland Austria meant *traffic in children,* and made foster children the most vulnerable group in rural society. Foster children were the clear victims of Highland Austria's system of family and marriage. This can clearly be seen in oral histories and autobiographies of foster children, and is also reflected in statistics on disability: the Highland Austrian belt of high illegitimacy and frequent fostering coincides with regions of high levels of deafness and blindness.[12]

Foster children were not merely victims, however; they were also actors. Oral and written testimony shows in dramatic ways the survival strategies these children used to escape abuse and exploitation. Having been shifted around between foster homes and villages as babies, many of them rebelled when they reached the age of eight or ten; they turned into bed-wetters or ran away. Sometimes they contacted their mothers, complained to the local priest or the local schoolteacher. Sometimes conditions improved, sometimes they did not. Later, usually at the age of fourteen or fifteen, childen broke the chains of repression and exploitation, left their foster homes and started to work as farmhands on another estate.[13]

The next phase in the life cycle was experienced differently by men and women. Male farmhands in their twenties and thirties lived a life of freedom and little responsibility, in spite of hard work and relative poverty. Like their Jamaican counterparts, they "fooled around" with lots of women, fathering children here and there, but very rarely supporting them. Women also experienced years of relative freedom from family obligations, but very soon were caught up in a vicious cycle of pregnancy, recurrent hope of starting a family, and disappointment about failure to do so. Some women escaped this cycle and found a husband, and some never did, but most women usually had at least one child who looked after them in old age. Not so with the men; many of them ended up late in life poor and without adequate family support. Having failed to produce supportive family networks over their lifetime, they had to rely on community welfare when they were old, sick and unable to work. Community welfare for the elderly in Highland Austria meant a periodic shifting from one farm to the next. So child-shifting had its parallel in the shifting of old people.

Jamaica

In Highland Austria, illegitimacy rates of over fifty percent were a transitional phenomenon between the mid-nineteenth and the mid-twentieth centuries. After World War II, these rates dropped suddenly with the rise of a nuclear family system. This sudden change was facilitated by the shift from a low-wage to a high-wage economy, the disappearance of farmhand labor and the creation of new and high-paying jobs in industry and tourism. Such a shift did not occur in Jamaica. Jamaica, too, participated in the boom years of the Western economies after World War II. The years between 1945 and 1973 saw an enormous economic growth, mainly based in the discovery and exploitation of huge bauxite deposits. Bauxite brought enormous wealth to the country, but as a capital-intensive industry it did not employ a lot of labor.[14] Thus, industrialization in Jamaica did not transform the lower class. The main element of the preindustrial social structure—a huge lower class of low-paid casual laborers—stayed more or less the same. So did the lower-class family pattern: high rates of out-of-wedlock births (increasing since 1879 from sixty to eighty-four percent), low rates of marriage, large numbers of single mothers and female heads of households.[15] My argument here is that the existence of a low-wage economy explains to a very high degree the persistence of this type of family system.

I will now describe the elements of the current Jamaican lower-class family system. First, a tendency to bear illegitimate children changes over the life cycle; mothers under twenty have a ninety-five percent probability of giving birth out of wed-lock; mothers over forty-five only have a thirty-one percent probability. Among all mothers who give birth, approximately a third are single mothers, another third are living in consensual unions and a last third are married officially. When we break these statistics down by age of mother, we see that illegitimacy and single mother-hood are, in most cases, life-cyclic phenomena: *most* mothers have their first child as a single mother, but as they get older, more and more of them are in consensual unions of varying durations. Finally, the majority of the children born to women thirty-five and over have married mothers.[16] In addition, this pattern of illegiti-macy is a direct expression of the pattern of sexual unions. These typically start with casual relationships—since 1970 the census takers have called them "visiting relationships"—and become more stable in the older age groups. Formal marriage takes place relatively late in the life cycle, which means that marriage tends not to start but to cap childbearing.[17] This is the very general pattern, but a closer look at class and gender reveals important differences. First, the rich marry more fre-quently than the poor—not very surprising within the context of Western family norms. Second, men marry more often than women. The explanations of these dif-ferences lies in the nature of marriage as a class-specific status symbol, and in the marriage market, which favors men because of a surplus of women.

What statistics do not reveal is the high degree of multiple partnerships. Both married and unmarried men very frequently have more than one sexual partner, sometimes more than one family. The class difference is clear: rich men can afford to support them all; poor men cannot. In contrast to Highland Austria, higher-sta-tus men frequently father children with lower-status women in Jamaica. The rea-sons for this phenomenon lie, first, in the historic establishment of this pattern under slavery; second, in the fact that the lower class women know that they can never *marry* a higher-status man, but have a very good chance of getting economic support for their children from such men—usually a better chance than from a liaison with a poor man; and, finally, in the sex imbalance.[18]

Another characteristic of the Jamaican family system is that household forma-tion occurs late in life. Men are usually in their thirties when they form their own household. Moreover, Jamaica has a *dual system* of household formation. In con-trast to the Austrian case, men and women head households to nearly the same extent. Male-headed households tend to be smaller, and are more often single-per-son households than those headed by women. The male head is more likely to be married, and his household is more likely to be nuclear. Female-headed households tend to be larger, the head is less likely to be married and more likely never to have been married. Her household is more likely to be extended. The older the head gets, the more likely it is that grandchildren are members of the household: female heads over age forty-five have an average of between one and two grandchildren in their household.

Putting Jamaica in a broader international perspective, three main features of Jamaican (more generally, *non-Hispanic Caribbean*) family structure and house-hold formation deserve attention. First, the conjugal bond is weak, and the roles of father, husband and wife are underdeveloped.[19] When the conjugal bond breaks, people have to reactivate kin relationships to guarantee the continuity of the household and the support of the children. The most important of these relations is the one between mother and daughter. The maternal grandmother's role gets stronger when the father fails to support his children. About a third of all children (up to fourteen years) are raised in households headed by a grandmother or a grandfather; within the poorer social strata this rate goes up to nearly half of all children (56.9 percent within the age group up to two years, 34.8 percent within the nine to eleven group), whereas within the richest 10 percent of the households it drops to 12.8 percent. Children are raised in a great variety of living arrange-ments: about a third live with both parents; about forty percent with only the mother; and twenty percent with neither parent (two-thirds of the latter are raised in the grandmother's house and 5.9 percent in the father's house).[20]

Single-person households are very common. The rates of single-person house-holds (twenty to thirty percent of all households) are nearly the same as in con-temporary northwestern Europe and differ greatly from the much lower rates in southern Europe, Asia, Latin America and the Hispanic Caribbean (under ten per-cent). Contrary to northwestern Europe, however—where the typical single-per-son household consists of an elderly widow—the single-person household in Jamaica usually is an old man with a low income. In fact, like their Austrian coun-terparts, men in the Caribbean tend to live on the *periphery of the family* most of their lives. They live relatively free lives as young men, but very often have to pay the price for their "irresponsibility"—to use a label that their mates frequently apply to them—in old age, when many of them end up without adequate family support, and must rely on community welfare of some type.

Let us look more closely at households headed by women. In contemporary Jamaica, female-headed households are a common feature in all classes, but they are more frequently found in the very low and the very high-income groups. The female-headed household of the higher-income groups is best represented by the young professional woman; she usually holds a university degree or its equivalent, has a relatively well-paid job in public service or private enterprise, is independent, feels free from family supervision, is responsible for her own sexual and emotional life and does not regard marriage as a prerequisite for happiness and emotional sta-bility.[21] Her lower-class counterpart can be found in the ghetto areas of Kingston or in the sugar-belt regions of Jamaica. The poor woman heads her own household because she is forced to do so, because her mates are not able or not willing to be breadwinners of a family, but also because this style of family life has a very long tradition in Jamaica. People have learned to live with it, even though it produces a vicious cycle of poverty. Life stories of lower-class women reveal experiences that are shared by most of them. Let me offer an example.

Nicole is fifteen.[22] She lives in a sugar-belt area on the north coast of Jamaica, together with her mother and her five brothers and sisters. She never knew her father, who emigrated to the U.S. in search of a better life, just before she was born. The family lives in a single room and her mother scrapes together a living as a peddler, buying and selling fruits, sweets and drinks. The mother receives some money from two of her six children's fathers, and plants yams and potatoes on the family land, which she inherited from her mother. Nicole goes to school. She does not have any schoolbooks. Her mother can hardly support the family.

It is crop time. Many young men pour into the village and find work as cane cutters. They bring life into the village. They do not earn much, but what they do, they spend. It goes quickly on lodgings, food, laundry, alcohol and women. They prefer the younger women. Many of the older men have venereal diseases, and it is said that sex with virgins will rid them of their gonorrhea. One of them tries to give money to Nicole. Nicole hesitates, but finally she takes it to buy herself some new clothes. Sex for clothes is a common exchange in lower-class Jamaica. Over the years, Nicole has witnessed her mother's string of sexual partners. Sex is no big deal here on the plantation.

Nicole gets pregnant. She confesses to her mother, who flies into a rage, hitting Nicole and kicking her out of the house, not because of a moral outrage, but more because she sees another mouth to feed. Nicole finds refuge with her cousin. After a few days, they return to her mother, who has been thinking of her own remarkably similar first pregnancy. They talk, and all is forgiven.

Nicole moves back in her mother's house. She goes back to school. Shortly before her child is born, she leaves. For the first two years she stays at home with her child. Having no support from the child's father, at the age of eighteen she is forced to seek work as a domestic helper. She leaves the child to be raised by her mother. Having finished schooling early, Nicole had given up the hope of escaping poverty through education. But she still has not given up the hope of finding a good husband. She soon meets another man. She can only keep her new lover by also bearing him a child.

> Nicole gets pregnant. Again she hopes. Again she is ultimately disap-
> pointed. Men in Jamaica do not like to take on responsibility. Nicole is
> likely to go through the same cycle of pregnancy, hope and disappoint-
> ment several more times, until she will be the one looking after her
> daughter's children. Whether one of her daughter's children will escape
> this cycle of poverty and matrifocality will be decided not only by them
> but also by the cycles of the world markets and the decisions made in
> the world economic centers.

What social forces, then, lie behind this Jamaican pattern of family and illegitimacy? The interesting thing about Jamaican family history is that there is a high
degree of persistence in the domestic behavior of the lower classes. The basic elements of lower-class family structure—a weak conjugal bond, a strong mother-
child tie, a dual system of household formation, a high frequency of
grandmother-headed households and the pattern of higher-status men fathering
children with lower-status women—has stayed more or less the same since slavery.
Why was there no change in family behavior in spite of important economic
changes? My argument here is that the persistence of this family structure is closely
linked to the persistence of a low-wage economy, with a labor regime based on
unsteady jobs, seasonal employment, high rates of unemployed young men and
high rates of migration. Added to this is an ever-growing informal sector which
gives unmarried lower-class women possibilities for economic survival, but does
not produce a need for economic cooperation between men and women. This economic context is also influenced by a specific system of property transfer that does
not disinherit women and illegitimate children. Finally, there is a low degree of
institutionalization of marriage, as a direct result of the weak position of the
church in the British system of slave society. Low wages, unsteady jobs and seasonal
employment marginalize the lower-class man vis-à-vis households.[23] Such men
cannot provide reliable support. Instead they tend to remain dependent upon their
own family of descent. They hesitate to take over full responsibility for one family,
and prefer to live as temporary migrants between mates, families and jobs. When a
society is able to break this cycle of low wages, seasonal employment and poverty,
the family patterns usually change immediately afterwards.

This happened, for example, in Curaçao in the twentieth century.[24] Curaçao was
a slave society similar to Jamaica. After World War I, an oil boom and a shift to
higher wages were associated with a sudden drop in illegitimacy rates and the rise
of a middle-class nuclear family system. This also happened in Cuba.[25] For nearly
a century until the 1960s, Cuba had low marriage rates like those in Jamaica. Then
the marriage rate increased dramatically after Castro's social policy broke the old

sugar-industry-based cycle of seasonal unemployment and provided the men with steady incomes. This also happened in Austria after World War II.

But to make our argument less simplistically economic, two further factors have to be mentioned to explain Jamaican family patterns—namely, religious and legal factors. In Jamaica, unlike most Latin American countries with a strong Spanish Catholicism, the institution of marriage was never really strong. Lower-class people in Jamaica marry in old age to gain respectability, but not because marriage is regarded as a moral imperative. The Anglican Church in the British system of slavery never really had much of an impact on the slaves. The few priests on the island served mainly the European plantocracy.

In 1823, the Anglican Church strengthened the ecclesiastical establishment by appointing a bishop for Jamaica. Soon after emancipation, the British missionary societies again withdrew their missionaries from Jamaica, or did not send out new ones. British missionary activities in the second part of the nineteenth century were directed toward Africa and the East, not toward the Caribbean. Two structural problems continued to characterize the Jamaican churches throughout the nineteenth and twentieth centuries, namely the permanent shortage of priests, and the focus of the Christian ministers on the upper and middle classes. In 1869 the Governor of Jamaica estimated that out of a population of 500,000, the nonconformists counted 200,000 adherents, the Anglican Church 100,000, while no religious provision was made for 200,000. He added that this last group was the only one *increasing*. The Jamaican census of 1943 counted 382 priests to serve a total population of 1.2 million people, which equals a ratio of one priest for 3,238 inhabitants.[26]

On the legal side, in most countries marriage establishes legitimacy—that is to say, the right to inherit. Not so in Jamaica. Since 1976 children born out of wedlock have the same inheritance rights as children born in wedlock; moreover, even in the past, a common-law practice secured all children—regardless of sex and legitimacy status—a share on the family land, usually relatively small pockets of land which are not alienable.[27]

Matrilineality, Matrifocality and the Low-Income Economy

Highland Austria before and Jamaica after World War II represent two very different types of societies. Highland Austria was predominantly agrarian, scarcely urbanized and economically underdeveloped. Jamaica since World War II, on the other hand, is highly urbanized and industrialized, and has a lower class entirely dependent on wages.

In spite of these differences, one finds two commonalities in the economic system which, in turn, resulted in commonalities in family structure. First, as a direct result of the low-wage economy, lower-class men are marginalized. Second, women are not excluded from activities outside the home. On the contrary, both societies provide economic roles for unmarried women outside their families of origin. In both settings, people married late and many never married. Late age at marriage implies a long time span between sexual maturity and marriage, and therefore a high risk of extramarital births and single motherhood. Late age at marriage furthermore results in a large number of men whose family ties are weak. A high percentage of single men and a family system which offers little cohesion within the wider kinship system lead, moreover, to high proportions of older men whose familial links are precarious and who, in case of illness or inability to work, are relegated to communal welfare. But there are differences too. Most notably, the high rate of illegitimacy and single motherhood in Highland Austria did not result in a high proportion of female-headed households, as the single mothers were, for the most part, domestic servants who, after having given birth, remained dependants in the employer's household.

Single mothers in Jamaica, in contrast, formed their own households. The timing of household formation depends on their economic activity. Here, too, domestic service has the result of delaying the formation of an independent household, a time period which is commonly bridged by integrating the child into the grandmother's household. Matrifocal households can be found in both societies with varying frequency. In both of these case studies, however, matrifocal structures do not have anything to do with a matrilineal kinship system. On the contrary, both societies are characterized by bilateral kinship principles. The matrifocal households in Austria and in Jamaica are to be understood as "familial crisis" types.

What then is the difference between matrifocal families in Jamaica and families in matrilineal societies? Matrilineality means dominance of the mother's line in reckoning kinship.[28] Property as well as name are inherited through the maternal line. Descent is reckoned through the maternal line. Domestic arrangements in matrilineal societies vary, as is evident in several of the essays in this volume (see, for example, the studies by Alex Bolyanatz and Shanti Menon). In these societies, the mother's brother often plays a more formal and constant role in the lives of a woman's children than their father does.

Now, one also frequently finds the mother's brother in matrifocal families of Jamaica. Yet, this is not because of a cultural prescription but rather because the sons establish their own households very late or—as is often the case after the failure of a relationship—return to the household of their mother or their sister. In the societies of the Caribbean, the norm for living together toward which people strive seems to be the nuclear family. Matrifocal households come into being when the conjugal ties fail or were never formed. Therefore matrifocal housholds in the planters' societies of the New World rarely make up the statistical majority. The household structure, however, is characterized by a high degree of variety; nuclear families, extended families, single-person households as well as matrifocal households appear with varying frequency. Yet the matrifocal unit is often the most stable of these types.

How little societies in the New World have to do with matrilineal societies in Africa or India is illustrated by the fact that there is a distinction between legitimate and illegitimate children, even in the folk traditions of the New World. The popular-cultural distinction differs from the one noted in the church's baptismal records or official birth records. Legitimacy—in the state's definition and in canonical right—simply says that the mother was married at the time of birth according to the (then) valid law. The folk tradition's system of differentiation does not focus on the marital status of the mother as a point of reference, but rather starts out from the entire system of relations which mother, children and father form.[29]

To offer a Jamaican example, take a woman who cohabits with a man and has three children with him, as well as a child from a previous relationship. The latter is her "outside" child in reference to her conjugal tie at the time. Should she leave this man and move in again with the father of her first child, then the three younger children assume the place of "outside" children, while the previous "outside" child becomes the couple's own child. That is to say that there is a clear distinction between children who originated from the present conjugal union and "outside" children. The legal status of the conjugal union does not play any role whatsoever.

In strictly matrilineal societies such differentiations among children are missing. Illegitimacy as a category is alien to these societies. All children are the mother's children. Moreover, the transfer of property and name in Jamaica is neither strictly patrilineal nor strictly matrilineal. British law did not regulate explicitly what names were given to the children, but rather gave people room to manipulate naming. Illegitimate children could inherit the father's or the mother's name. Legitimate children received the father's name. The inheritance law prior to the legal reforms of the 1970s unequivocally discriminated against illegitimate children: they were excluded from the father's legacy. However, E. Clarke discovered in an ethnographic study of several Jamaican communities early in the 1950s that: "in contradiction to the law which recognizes the eldest son as the rightful heir where there is no testamentary disposition, we found the principle of joint inheritance by all the children generally recognized and it is by no means apparent that any discrimination is practised against illegitimate children."[30]

It appears most sensible to me to understand these matrifocal households—within a structural-functionalist tradition—as a familial adaptation to precarious economic conditions which require a high degree of flexibility on the part of historical actors. Matrifocal families in the New World are crisis families whose specific place within the political economy of these societies has to be understood precisely. The matrifocal family reproduces low-wage labor and a surplus work force. The mothers are exposed to double pressure; they carry the burden of both socialization and sustenance. This becomes especially apparent in the urban lower-class milieu, where children from matrifocal households often become victims of this system. Desperate mothers often send their children—usually boys at a very young age—out onto the streets to contribute to the family's survival through begging or theft. The boys soon constitute gangs as they engage in minor crimes; they also develop a lifestyle and survival strategies marked by drugs, weapons and demonstrative idleness. The deaf-mute of Austria thus finds his counterpart in the ghetto regions of west Kingston. In both cases they are the victims of a low-wage economy, and also of a society which accepts the inadequate reproduction of its surplus work force for the benefit of those who administer the political economy.

Notes

¹ Funding for research was provided by the Austrian Fond zur Förderung der wissenschaftlichen Forschung (Erwin-Schroedinger-Auslandsstipendien). Prof. George Roberts deserves special thanks for providing help on a day-to-day basis. Collin Williams, from the Planning Institute of Jamaica, did the special tabulations of the Jamaican survey on living conditions. Ian Cook helped with the translation. Helpful in discussing problems of interpretation were: Brian Allayne, R.T. Smith, Don Robotham, B. Chevannes, B. Higman, C. Levitte, Herman and Hermione McKenzie. Last but not least, the staff of ISER, Mona Campus, Jamaica, deserve special attention for providing me with wonderful working conditions during my fieldwork.

² Illegitimacy here refers to births to women whose sexual unions are not formalized by state or church. It would thus include births to women in consensual, stable unions that are not officially recognized as marriage.

³ S.F. Hartley, "Illegitimacy in Jamaica," in P. Laslett, ed., *Bastardy and its Comparative History* (Cambridge, Mass: Harvard University Press, 1980), p. 387; G.W. Roberts, *The Population of Jamaica* (Millwood, N.Y.: Kraus Reprint Co., 1977), p. 287; M. Mitterauer, *Ledige Mütter* (Wien: Bohlau, 1987), p. 23.

⁴ N. Ortmayr, ed., *Knechte. Autobiographische Dokumente und sozialhistorische Skizzen* (Wien: Bohlau, 1992); N. Ortmayr, "Späte Heirat," *Zeitgeschichte* 4 (1989): 119ff.

⁵ The entire range of the Austrian Alps did not have this pattern of high illegitimacy. The westernmost fringe (Western Tyrol and Vorarlberg) were characterized by low marriage rates, very low illegitimacy, and partible inheritance. The term Highland Austria, as I use it in the text, excludes this Western part.

⁶ Ortmayr, "Späte Heirat," pp. 121–125.

⁷ Ibid., p. 125.

[8] The estimate of age of marriage refers to the Singulate Mean Age at Marriage (SMAM), which is based on census distributions by sex, age and marital status. The original formulation of SMAM can be found in J. Hajnal, "Age at Marriage and Proportions Marrying," *Population Studies* 7 (1953): 130.

[9] N. Ortmayr, "Ländliches Gesinde in Oberösterreich 1918–1938," in *Familienstruktur und Arbeitsorganisation in ländlichen Gesellschaften*, ed. J. Ehmer and M. Mitterauer (Wien: Bohlau, 1986).

[10] Ortmayr, *Knechte*, p. 346.

[11] Ibid., p. 348.

[12] Ibid.

[13] Ibid.

[14] C. Stone, *Class, State and Democracy in Jamaica* (New York: Praeger, 1986), pp. 28–47.

[15] G.W. Roberts, *The Population of Jamaica*, p. 287.

[16] Ibid., p. 294.

[17] Ibid.

[18] R.T. Smith, *Kinship and Class in the West Indies* (New York: Cambridge University Press, 1988). A. Marino, "Family, Fertility, and Sex Ratios in British Caribbean," *Population Studies* 24/2 (1971): 163.

[19] The literature on the Afro-Caribbean family is abundant. A good starting point is N.L. Solien Gonzalez, *Black Carib Household Structure* (Seattle: University of Washington Press, 1969). See also Smith, *Kinship and Class*.

[20] Planning Institute of Jamaica, *Survey of Living Conditions* (Kingston, 1992).

[21] United Nations, *The Decade for Women in Latin America and Caribbean. Santiago de Chile* (1988).

[22] The life story was collected during a field research stay in Jamaica in Februrary 1992. The name Nicole is fictional.

[23] E. Miller, *Men at Risk* (Kingston: Jamaica Publishing House, 1991).

[24] A. Marks, "Institutionalization of Marriage and Family in Curaçao," in *Family and Kinship in Middle America and the Caribbean*, ed. A. Marks and R.A. Roemer (Willemstad: Institute of Higher Studies in Curaçao, 1975), pp. 113–143.

[25] L. Perez, "The Family in Cuba," in *The Family in Latin America*, ed. Man Singh Das and C.J. Jesser (Ghaziabad: Vikas, 1980), pp. 235–269. Cuba had relatively high marriage rates in the eighteenth century according to H. Klein, *Slavery in the Americas: A Comparative Study of Virginia and Cuba* (Chicago: University of Chicago Press, 1967). This rate dropped in the nineteenth century to 3.2 percent per thousand by 1862 (Census of Cuba 1862), and remained on about the same level until 1962, then rose suddenly to 13.4 percent per thousand by 1970. B.R. Mitchell, *International Historical Statistics. The Americas and Australasia* (Detroit, Mich.: Gale Research, 1983), p. 111.

[26] Inhabitants per priest (minister):

Jamaica (1800):	18,000
Cuba (1778):	168
Cuba (1860):	1,739
Mexico (1910):	3,398
Guatemala (1753/4):	1,164

R.W. Smith, "Slavery and Christianity in the British West Indies," *Church History* 19 (1950): p. 173; J. Van Oss, *Catholic Colonialism* (Cambridge: Cambridge University Press, 1986); Klein, *Slavery*, p. 98; Statistical Abstract of Latin America (1974), p. 59. *The Cambridge History of the British Empire*, vol. II (Cambridge: Cambridge University Press, 1961), p. 737; A. Caldecott, *The Church in the West Indies* (London: F. Cass, 1970), p. 89; Central Bureau of Statistics, *Census of Jamaica, 1943: Population, Housing and Agriculture* (Kingston, 1945).

[27] E. Clarke, *My Mother Who Fathered Me* (London: Allen & Unwin, 1957).

[28] Solien Gonzalez, *Black Household*, p. 14; A.R. Radcliffe-Brown and D. Forde, eds., *African Systems of Kinship and Marriage* (London: Oxford University, 1950), p. 73.

[29] Clarke, *My Mother*, 113.

[30] Ibid., p. 40.

Mary Jo Maynes turns to an unusual source—nineteenth-century European workers'
autobiographies—to assess what kinship maps look like in the framework of working-
class people in the midst of dramatic economic change. In the texts she examines,
fathers often appear marginal and problematic figures, compared with mothers. The
autobiographers' anger at their parents' failure to live up to normative expectations
persisted despite that fact that many working-class fathers did fail. The children the
memoirs resurrect appear as victims of a double injury—economic deprivation and
moral default. As in the situations in turn-of-the-century Austria or contemporary
Brazil described in other essays in this section, matrifocality may well have empowered
women within these European working-class families (relative to upper-class women),
but the economic and psychic costs of this form of empowerment hardly recommend it
as beneficial for women or children.

14

Women and Kinship in Propertyless Classes in Western Europe in the Nineteenth Century

MARY JO MAYNES

Introduction—Starting from One Story

Marie Sans Gène, the daughter of a carter and a laundress, was born in Danzig in 1853. She published her autobiography in 1906 at her husband's suggestion.[1] Her account maps a world of kinship and gender relations that was in many regards different from the one we know from sources pertaining to Europe's propertied classes of the era in which she lived. Sans Gène was able to commence her life story with a genealogy (at least that of her mother's side of the family). Her mother had come from the countryside around Danzig, and had seventeen siblings. Her mother's parents were farm servants. Sans Gène's maternal grandfather was the "natural child" of a servant maid seduced by a French army officer. All this, Sans Gène notes, was told to her by her grandmother (who eventually married this illegitimate child). Sans Gène notes that of all the family only she, her mother and her own daughters had inherited "foreign" traits from this illicit connection with the south—"black hair, big dark eyes, a dark complexion…a lively temperament."[2]

In Sans Gène's childhood memories—a tale of survival on the margins—her mother played the lead role. It was she who engineered the economy of make-do that held the family together. Like other working-class women of her times, she made her living through very public activities. No ideology of domesticity kept her

261

at home. Although the mother's primary work was as a laundress, she and the children found many ways to piece together a livelihood, especially when Marie's father was laid up with an illness that eventually killed him. They bought fuel wholesale and sold it retail in the streets of Danzig. They offered various services to the soldiers in the city's garrison: the children would go there before school to sell coffee; the mother took over the laundry of sixty soldiers; later she fed the same number through an arrangement with the commissariat—twenty at a time in three half-hour shifts. The kids did their part to keep her bid low by getting firewood for the cooking fire. They also washed the dishes between seatings. Mother and children resold fish and kept geese and other animals, which the children cared for and then sold at market. On occasion, claims upon extended kin—the mother's mother or one of her siblings—would bring emergency help, but the real story of survival centered on mother and children.

Sans Gène's story raises many of the themes I want to explore in this essay. As an empirical account of a quite specific milieu—in this case the propertyless classes of the Baltic port of Danzig in the second half of the nineteenth century—San Gène's autobiography calls into question many generalizations about family, kinship and gender in the European past that are based primarily on evidence about rural and propertied classes. Moreover, as an autobiography, Sans Gène's account also lends itself to interpretations of the cultural salience of various aspects of kin relationships—for example, the role that kin could play in the plot of a life story, or the clash between what the autobiographer had learned as an adult about normative kinship rules as opposed to what was recalled from childhood.

The study of kinship is a fairly recent development in the discipline of history. Except for the loving attention devoted to the genealogies of dynastic or aristocratic families, historical study of European kin relations largely postdates the emergence in the 1960s of "history from below," including family and demographic history.[3] While historical study of the European family initially centered primarily on demographic sources and questions, interest in kinship has expanded the terrain, and led to a search for sources that could illuminate social practices and meanings attached to kin relations in different periods and different classes.[4]

Historians have devoted particular attention to the relationship between the development of industrial capitalism and the displacement of the explicitly patriarchal forms associated with the early modern family, economy and state by more modern forms of class, gender and generational domination. But the nature of existing historical sources has sometimes led to the mistake of generalizing from elite attitudes, or of confusing prescriptions with practice. Alternative sources such as lower-class autobiographies bring with them their own interpretive perils but do offer, at least, a strikingly different perspective. I will turn now to these sources with the purpose of addressing questions about Europe's propertyless classes—people who lived by manual labor and petty commodity production—during the era of European industrialization. I want to explore how kinship worked where property and resources were minimal. And I am especially interested in the question of how *women* and *children* fared. I will discuss three particular themes relating to gender and kin relations in the propertyless classes: first, the "map" of salient kin relations the texts suggest; second, the nature of material resources transferred through kinship; and third, gender relations as reflected in control over children. Throughout this essay, I will note how the memories of lower-class parenting recorded in these autobiographies are the result of a complex of childhood experiences, norms (often contradicted by experiences) and later reflections or judgments.

The Sources

My work is based on evidence from published autobiographies. I have been collecting French and German lower-class autobiographies for many years now. My analysis in this article is based on about sixty of these—the ones that included adequate discussion of the kinship networks and arrangements in the milieux in which the authors grew up. In selecting texts, I aimed at broad regional and occupational variation. The geographic range covers French- and German-speaking areas of Europe. In terms of occupations, the coverage is also broad: autobiographers of landless peasant origins are rare, but represented; artisans and factory workers are well-represented; waitresses and domestic servants, miners and agricultural laborers, itinerant peddlers and railroad workers all have their place.[5]

What Resources Were Transferred through Kinship?

It is worth noting that, in a material sense, not a lot was at stake in the kinship groups the autobiographies record: this was an economy of make-do. Nevertheless, for the huge proportions of Europe's laboring population who, as late as the beginning of the twentieth century, continued to live on the margins of subsistence, even minimal resources meant the difference between survival and pauperization.[6] Proletarianization was converting Europe's poorest peasant and artisanal classes into wageworkers, beginning in the early modern period (roughly the sixteenth through eighteenth centuries). In earlier epochs, both artisanal families and poorer peasants held at least tenuous, if often meager, property rights. During the generations of proletarianization that accompanied the transition to capitalism, many families eked out a living by combining farming on a small plot with a small handicraft business or wage labor. This transitional status appears in many of the autobiographies. For example, Ulrich Bräker recounts his family's struggle to piece together a living through a combination of wool weaving, farming and herding; Agricol Perdiguier described his father as both a farmer and an artisan; Adelheid Popp's family initially made a living from weaving in rural Austria, but they later moved to Vienna, and various family members worked in factories or petty retail trades.[7]

The property held within the kin groups described in these autobiographical texts is modest at best. The resources that were sought after were those required for everyday life: food, rent and clothing, in that order. The autobiographers recalled with impressive detail and evocative phrasing this daily "struggle for existence," the literal "scramble" for the coins thrown from a pay envelope to buy food, the perpetual difficulties the mother faced "filling…hungry mouths," the mother who scrubbed the floor of an inn for "a sausage and a coffee," the reproach of "being fed to do nothing."[8] Raising the rent also produced its moments of drama; turns of fortune were often marked in life stories by moves to better or worse quarters. Again reflecting the closeness to subsistence of the milieux of interest here, in many autobiographies the failure of elders to provide shoes, school clothes, and confirmation or first communion suits represented both material deprivation and the symbolic humiliations associated with poverty.[9]

Since among poor families even the minimum for subsistence was not always assured, the kinds of intergenerational transfers of resources that were normative in propertied classes—particularly the dowries and inheritances by which the ties of kinship were traditionally manifested and reinforced—are all but unheard of in these texts.

Inheritance from the parental generation is mentioned in only one author's text. Marie Sans Gène, whose story introduced this article, described the breakup of her mother's household when the latter was forced by poverty to take up residence in a public home for the aged poor. Most of the household equipment was sold for the mother's sustenance. Marie, however, got "her mother's most valuable possession"—the mangle (ironing machine) which had been the basis of her laundry business. The one other mention of inheritance concerned a dispute over a small legacy left by Louis Lecoin's grandfather. His parents were deprived of a share in it because they had been too poor to contribute to the costs of the funeral![10]

Dowries are alluded to in only a few of the autobiographies. The Hamburg cigar-maker Franz Bergg's girlfriend was provided with one—basic household goods—at her insistence. The girl's parents had originally opposed the match, and only agreed to it when their daughter became pregnant. The dowry clearly was supposed to make the match honorable. But the wedding never happened, because Bergg was arrested for participating in a demonstration; the baby was born while

Bergg was still in jail. In another case, Frederic Mistral reported that his father, a very comfortable Provençal peasant, had made an appropriate first match. But since Frederic was the child of a second marriage, his mother, a gleaner, had had to earn her own dowry. She and her five sisters had all managed to marry well, Mistral noted, following the Provençal truism that "A pretty girl…wears her dowry on her face." Madeleine Henrey's father had decided against a "good" match with a widow who owned a café to marry the beautiful but dowryless woman who would become Madeleine's mother.[11] Two women autobiographers—Marie Sans Gène and the anonymous author of *Im Kampf ums Dasein*—also refer to the common lower-class practice of a daughter's earning her own dowry. Sans Gène complains that she has not been able to accumulate anything, while the latter author fears she is being sought in marriage for the sake of savings from her wages as a waitress.[12] These stories suggest that, even if the notion of dowry was not unknown in these classes, and may have carried some of the connotations concerning honor at marriage and "appropriateness" of match that it evoked among propertied classes, actual transfers of property from parents to daughter at marriage were not reported as "normal" in practice.

Beyond dowries and legacies, of which there is so little evidence in these memoirs, **parental investments in apprenticeship and/or schooling** are remembered occasionally among the somewhat better-off workers' families. Poor but ambitious parents sometimes found ways of putting together what was required to set their children up in what was seen as a better future. Prosper Delafutry recalled that his mother sacrificed and took in additional foster children to send her son to normal school. Madeleine Henrey's mother sent her daughter to her sister in England for education. Agricol Perdiguier's father, aided in turn by his father, paid for the school fees of Agricol and his brothers; Agricol's mother paid for the sister's fees from her market earnings.[13]

In the milieux the autobiographies describe, however, children were sent into the work force at the earliest possible moment, typically at the official school-leaving age (twelve to fourteen years) or younger. **Child labor**, in fact, represents the form of resource transfer between generations most frequently cited in the texts. This was a world, in other words, where the emphasis lay more on transfers up the generations than down. Around half of the authors explicitly recount earning wages as children or adolescents and turning them over to their parents, or dedicating them to the family income pool. This was seen by the autobiographers in most cases as a reciprocal transfer, a kind of repayment for the years in which parents had supported them as "unearning eaters," or an exchange for the services that the family continued to provide, although most of the authors seem quite aware that dominant norms of childhood regarded this kind of thinking as obsolete and even inde-

265

fensible. Significantly, family claims on adolescent labor were recalled differently by men and women. Whereas it was not uncommon for men to recount leaving home as adolescents, either as apprentices or unskilled laborers, the women left for employment rarely and ambivalently. Sons felt little obligation to send money home, whereas for adolescent daughters, their parents, especially their mothers, still commanded their loyalties and the greatest part of their wages.

Maps of Kinship

If the labor of children, at least older children, represented a resource, it was mothers who largely controlled it. From the point of view of working-class autobiographers recalling their years of growing up, the map of significant kin relations clearly centered on the mother. It was she who most directly and continually sustained the family group, who represented its emotional and material center in everyday terms, whose broader kin ties were most often called upon, and who controlled the children's daily world and made decisions that affected them. It should be noted here that an important feature of the group of autobiographers is their experience of what might be called family insecurity. The strikingly high proportion of single-parent families, especially as recalled by the German autobiographers, may perhaps signal somewhat atypical childhoods. Still, a comparison with national demographic statistics suggests that the experiences of the whole set of autobiographers mirror fairly closely what aggregate sources such as life tables would predict, even if the German accounts show slightly more and the French slightly less parental loss from death than would be expected. In this era of precarious existence, perilous working conditions and high levels of migration, it was a common fate for children to lose one or both parents.[14]

The mother's centrality in the memoirs was in no small part a result of the relatively common default of the father, who in law and in custom still supposedly held powers over his wife and children. Among the memoirists' fathers, thirteen had died early (before the end of the author's elementary school years) or suffered from a severe chronic illness; one had committed suicide; nine had either deserted the mother or not acknowledged paternity; two were blacklisted or exiled for political activities. At least a dozen authors indicated that their fathers had been at best unreliable providers who could not be counted on to turn over their pay envelope; most of these improvident fathers were "made tigers" by drink or, true to the Victorian melodramatic stereotype, had to be fetched from taverns on payday by their children. All told, nearly half of the fathers were recalled as being unable or unwilling to fulfill their basic paternal responsibilities, which were still, however, generally understood in a normative fashion. As Aurelia Roth put it, "in truth I couldn't forgive him for this even after his death, that he had never taken care of us *like a father*" (emphasis added).[15] In other words, the authors still thought that fathers should have behaved differently. But in the majority of these accounts, whatever should have been true, the mother is the dominant figure.

She is dominant because she stays with her children, for the most part. In contrast with the common tale of paternal death or abandonment, only a small fraction of these stories tell of absent mothers, mostly lost through death, although a few autobiographers told tales of being abandoned or put into foster care by their mothers. When the mother died, family life deteriorated, usually to the point of breakup of the household. A few mothers are recalled as being gratuitously cruel, even abusive, but most are tragically heroic figures.

The mother was remembered as *heroic* because she managed to "take care of everything and through her tireless hands support husband and children until even she couldn't do anymore," or because she "was proud because we could make it without the help of strangers," or because, despite her delicacy, it was she "who with her needle and agile fingers built a wall against misery."[16]

Her tragic character had two dimensions. First, the task was often too big for any mother. "Even with the greatest effort, the greatest frugality, it wasn't possible for her to pay for everything that was necessary for the family."[17] Second, perhaps more tragic, was the psychic cost attached to the mothers' survival strategies. Alfons Ger recalled that mothers of the mining village in which he grew up had been "hardened to the point of cruelty" by the grim poverty in which they lived; never having known happiness in youth, they in turn withheld all enjoyment from their own children.[18] Anna Maier remembered staring longingly out of the window at children playing, only to be recalled to her work by her mother's slap.[19] Fritz Pauk's mother went to work on distant plantations every summer, leaving him in the care of his aunt in exchange for thirty *pfennig* a day. He remembered that every spring "I would run after the wagon (she left in), until my little legs couldn't run anymore. Then I'd return, crying, to the village."[20] For Jean Guehenno, his memories of his mother were shaped by her constant activity and seemingly obssessive fear of waste:

> I see her always working, always running....She ran to "turn in" her work at the factory, because if she got there too late, she wouldn't get more piecework to do: the forewoman would put it off til the next morning and that would mean a night wasted. She would run back home because the chestnuts would be overcooked and that would be wasted gas. She was always running. "Wasted!" she never seemed to have any other word in her mouth. Everything was always at risk of being wasted—food, clothes, money, time."[21]

Guehenno and other authors who recall long-suffering mothers realize they came to understand only in retrospect why their mothers acted as they did. "Unfortunately we children had at the time too little comprehension of the values of the self-sacrificing wife and of the devotion to her children…of our good mother. We took it for granted." Rehbein wrote. Guehenno recalled his mother's anger at him for his inability to understand their poverty, for his refusal to "enter into her suffering," for his (and his father's) optimism in the face of her despair.[22] Obviously, all of the autobiographers were "survivors," but their stories reveal that the psychic cost of survival under the circumstance of poverty were very high indeed. The portrayal of the power and persistence of these mothers is darkened by these gnawing memories of their emotional failures.

The centrality of the mother is further revealed in the extended kin networks which surround the autobiographers as children. The stories themselves often begin with a genealogy, but with few exceptions, the knowledge about or salience of kinship roots goes no deeper than the grandparents' generation. Among those with peasant roots, family stories and kinkeeping made it possible to go further back. August Lange knew his family history back to the eighteenth century, and even knew the story of how the family property had been lost and the family reduced to living from sheepherding.[23] Marie Sans Gène, as we've seen, could trace her roots back three generations on her mother's side. But most of the stories, most of the maps of known kin, stop after looking back one or two generations, and a few cannot even trace their lineage that far.

But extended kin relations were nevertheless important to the autobiographers. More than half of them recall extended kin as significant caregivers or sources of support during childhood. The frequently mentioned relationships in this regard are grandparents and aunts and uncles. In fourteen stories, it is explicitly the mother's parents or siblings who care for or nurture: Lena Christ was raised through her early years by her maternal grandparents, and her grandfather was the strongest source of emotional support throughout her childhood. Philippe Valette was sent by his mother to her brother's family, where he recalled resenting the better treatment his aunt gave to his cousin. In only three or four stories do the significant nonnuclear-kin relationships originate on the paternal side, such as Agricol Perdiguier's paternal grandparents, who were his source of knowledge of Provençal tales and special patrons to his older brother, or the brother of Annaliese Rüegg's father, who acted as her guardian after the father's death (at times in contest with her mother). Another dozen memoirists attribute special significance to these same relatives, but do not identify them as maternal or paternal grandparents, aunts, uncles. René Bonnet, who spent his early years on his grandparents' farm while his parents worked in Paris, thought of his grandfather as "a kind of superhuman." Pierre-Jean de Beranger spent his later youth with an aunt who was an innkeeper, and whom he regarded as "his true mother."[24]

These examples point to the frequency with which children from poor families ended up spending a good portion of their childhood living with someone other than their parents. Of the three autobiographers who lost both parents in early childhood, one was raised by grandparents, one by a foster mother paid by the village and the third "in the hands of strangers." Most of the autobiographers who had at least one surviving parent did reside with a parent, but nearly a third, in fact, recalled spending substantial amounts of time apart from their parents. Of these, nine lived "with strangers" (either wet nurses or state-paid foster parents), six resided with grandparents and three with parents' siblings for periods of at least several years, usually when the parents' work demands made such arrangements preferable. Although many of these periods are recalled fondly, especially time spent with grandparents, there is a consistent note of anguish in the accounts of those sent to live with strangers when they know they have a living parent. The author of *Erinnerungen eines Waisenknabes* recalled his foster mother telling him that his biological mother must have been "thoughtless and heartless not to care for her own child"; Heinrich Dikreiter remembered not recognizing his father when he came to collect him from the orphanage where he had put him several years earlier when his mother had died; Angelina Bardin often wondered about the mother who had abandoned her as an infant, but she would never know why she had abandoned her—"they hadn't asked her." Madeleine Henrey's mother, who had sent her to a wet nurse in the country outside of Paris, told Madeleine she was jealous when Madeleine treated her like a stranger and called her wet nurse "Mamá!"[25]

Control over Children

Still, whoever children lived with, there is consistent evidence that, more than any other individual, it was the mother who was usually in charge of their fate. She made decisions about the child's treatment, work, schooling and future more often than anyone else did. About half of the stories, thirty in all, offer enough information about patterns of control over children to assess who was the primary decision maker.

In the households of widows and unmarried mothers, or in cases where mothers were married to a man who was not the father to all of her children, it is perhaps not so surprising that the mother was in charge of her children. Her control in several cases even permitted vetoes of plans made by her late husband's relatives. Annaliese Rüegg reported that her father's brother advised her mother after her husband's death to send her daughters out as farm servants where they could "earn their own bread." The mother refused, stating that "as long as she was healthy she would never send any of her children out of the house." Similarly, Lucien Bourgeois's father's family tried to have him and his brother placed with relatives after their father's death. But the mother refused, preferring to make a go of it on her own with the two boys in Paris.

But even in families where the father was alive, the power of the mother could be formidable. She was the one who assigned tasks to the children, often working alongside them. She decided whether to send them to school on a given day or keep them home to work. She was more usually the disciplinarian. This is not to suggest that there were no limits on her power. The father's "superior" power could manifest itself in the form of actual violence. Eight memoirists explicitly recalled their fathers attacking their mothers. The father also held more secure legal rights over the children. Madeleine Henrey's mother at one point fled her husband's brutality and went back to her own mother's home. But she knew the risk involved. Should he have wanted to, her husband could have sued her for desertion and taken custody of her child. Franz Bergg actually reported evicting his girlfriend from their room because she had left her hungry infant daughter, who was still nursing, in his care for four hours. Refusing to hear her pleas, he sent the child off to a wet nurse and refused the mother visitation rights. The limits were obviously there, but in practice, for most purposes of everyday life in most of the accounts in these sources, the mothers maintained control over the children.

Conclusions

The workers' autobiographies point to a kinship system that was matrifocal in tendency—centered on the mother-child relationship and buttressed typically by maternal kin. The centrality of mothers in practice counters generalizations about female subordination in dominant kinship norms and laws. At the same time, however, it cannot be denied that the resources available to these matrifocal groups were patently inadequate to the task of reproduction, and that economic marginality associated with this form of mother-centeredness apparently brought with it material deprivation and psychic repercussions. The damage to children that the autobiographies associate with poverty is refracted both through prevailing norms about what fathers and mothers were *supposed* to do (but did not) and through prevailing stereotypes—the long-suffering mother, the brutal father and so on. Moreover, their tendency to compute the effects of various survival strategies on the *remembered* child implies judgment—even condemnation—of the social structures that produce poverty but also of the individual agents of the child's personal drama, namely the parents who were remembered as agents and victims both.

It is possible to conclude that these stories testify to the operation of a kinship system among the propertyless that was quite distinct from the predominant one. But they also suggest that the authors were often responding to and judging the practices of that system by standards derived from dominant norms. Obviously, generalization would be premature. For one thing, I have not addressed important dimensions of variation among the stories—for example, the differentiation between the French and the German sources, or those that follow religious and regional lines.[26] Given our limited historical knowledge of the actual functioning of kinship, it is early indeed to begin comparative discussions that are even more ambitious. Still, the evidence suggests some parallels with nonnormative, mother-centered kinship systems in other geographic and chronological settings.

In their assessment of historical work on kinship, Hans Medick and David Warren Sabean have written that:

> An important limiting case is the role of the family and kinship in the survival strategies of propertyless and property-poor populations in emerging class societies. For highly divergent situations, such as those of Afro-American slave populations and their descendants, for contemporary immigrant town dwellers in Africa, Asia, and South America as well as for marginalized peasant groups and for the proletarian and sub-proletarian populations of Europe under emerging capitalism, the importance of kin relations beyond the nuclear family has been shown.... Much less research has been done into the nature of the specific structures and networks of kin mobilized for these purposes, and into the foundations of those expectations, obligations, and rights on which this mobilization of resources from kin rested.[27]

That we need more milieu-specific research is apparent. But the suggestion to look to parallels across times and cultures is also intriguing. It does appear to me that the kinship patterns I have found in these French and German workers' autobiographies resonate with accounts of kinship among certain impoverished populations on other continents and in other eras. For example, the analyses of matrifocality in this volume by Ortmayr and Scott, centering on more recent eras of economic transformation in Brazil or Jamaica, offer some analogies, even if the intense cultural condemnation of single mothers may be peculiar to Europe. Indeed, the systems described in these very different settings may come closer to offering clues to the kinship rules these autobiographies document than do

271

accounts of kinship among the contemporaneous propertied classes of Europe. The autobiographical evidence also echoes Maura Palazzi's argument that the "rules" and practices of kinship operate very unevenly across class as well as gender lines.

Notes

[1] Marie Sans Gène (Anna Hill), *Jugenderinnerungen eines armen Dienstmädchen* (Bremen: Friedrich Röver, nd [orig. 1906]). Sans Gène discusses in the Preface her motives both for writing her autobiography and for publishing it anonymously.

[2] Sans Gène, p. 13.

[3] There is a now a huge body of research on European family history. For a useful guide into it, and a good bibliography, see Michael Mitterauer and Reinhard Sieder, *The European Family: Patriarchy to Partnership from the Middle Ages to the Present* (Chicago: University of Chicago Press, 1982). Natalie Zemon Davis points out an earlier tradition of family history in her article "Gender and Genre: Women as Historical Writers," in P. LaBalme, ed., *Beyond Their Sex: Learned Women of the European Past* (New York: NYU Press, 1980). She notes that women's historical writings in the early modern period often centered on their own families.

[4] For discussions of the history of kinship, see Tamara Hareven and Andreas Plakans, eds., *Family History at the Crossroads* (Princeton: Princeton University Press, 1987); and Hans Medick and David Warren Sabean, eds., *Interest and Emotion. Essays on the Study of Family and Kinship* (Cambridge: Cambridge University Press, 1984).

[5] For a fuller discussion of the methodological issues involved in the historical use of autobiographies, see Mary Jo Maynes, "Autobiography and Class Formation in Nineteenth-Century Europe: Methodological Considerations," *Social Science History* 16:3 (1992): 517–537.

[6] This economy of make-do shares some of the characteristics of economically marginal groups in more contemporary settings. See, for example, Carol Stacks's study of African-American communities, *All Our Kin* (New York: Harper and Row, 1974).

[7] Ulrich Bräker, *The Life Story and Real Adventures of the Poor Man of Toggenburg*, trans. Derek Bowman (Edinburgh: University Press, 1970, [orig. 1789]); Agricol Perdiguier, *Mémoires d'un compagnon* (Moulins, 1914 [orig.1854]); Anonymous (Adelheid Popp), *Die Jugendgeschichte einer Arbeiterin. Von ihr selbst erzählt*, "Foreword" by August Bebel (Munich, 1909).

[8] Anonymous, *Erinnerungen eines Waisenknaben. von ihm selbst erzählt.* "Foreword" by Prof. A. Forel (Munich, 1910), pp. 106–107; Franz Rehbein, *Das Leben eines Landarbeiters*, ed. Urs J. Diederichs and Holger Rüdel (Hamburg: Hans Christians Verlag, 1985 [orig. 1911]), p. 17; Marie Sponer, "Aus Nordböhmen," in A. Popp, ed., *Gedenkbuch. 20 Jahren österreichischen Arbeiterinnenbewegung* (Vienna, 1912), p. 140; Charlotte Davy, *Une femme* (Paris: Eugene Figuiere, 1927), p. 37.

[9] This overriding concern with food and clothing also functions as narrative plot in countless fairy tales emerging from early modern European peasant milieux. For a discussion of this associated genre, see Robert Darnton, "Peasants Tell Tales: The Meaning of Mother Goose," in R. Darnton, *The Great Cat Massacre and Other Episodes in French Cultural History* (New York: Basic Books, 1984).

[10] Sans Gène, p. 207; Louis Lecoin, *Le cours d'un vie* (Paris, 1965), p. 16–17.

[11] Franz Bergg, *Ein Proletarierleben. bearbeitet und herausgegeben von Nikolaus Welter.* 2ter

Auflage (Frankfurt a. M.: Neuer Frankfurter Verlag, 1913), p. 159; Mrs. Robert Henrey, *The Little Madeleine* (New York: Dutton, 1925), p. 25; Frederic Mistral, *Mes origins, mémoire et récits* (Paris, 1906), p. 13.

[12] Sans Gène, pp. 179–180; Anonymous, *Im Kampf*, p. 170.

[13] Perdiguier, pp. 14*ff*; Prosper Delafutry, *Les mémoires d'un travailleur* (Paris, 1887 [orig.1886]), p. 35; Henrey, pp. 233*ff*.

[14] For a more detailed discussion of this point, see Mary Jo Maynes, "The Contours of Childhood: Demography, Strategy and Mythology of Childhood in French and German Lower-Class Autobiographies," in *The European Experience of Declining Fertility*, ed. L. Tilly, J. Gillis and D. Levine (New York and London: Blackwell, 1992).

[15] Aurelia Roth, "Eine Glasschleiferin," in A. Popp, ed., *Gedenkbuch. 20 Jahren österreichische Arbeiterinnenbewegung* (Vienna, 1912), p. 53.

[16] Sans Gène, p. 15; Henrey, p. 27; Annaliese Rüegg, *Erlebnisse einer Serviertochter* (Zurich, 1914), p. 23.

[17] Roth, p. 53.

[18] Alwin Ger(isch), *Erzgebirgisches Volk. Erinnerung von A. Ger* (Berlin: Vorwärts, 1918), p. 61.

[19] Anna Maier, "Wie Ich Reif Wurde," in A. Popp, ed., *Gedenkbuch. 20 Jahren österreichische Arbeiterinnenbewegung* (Vienna, 1912), pp. 107–109 .

[20] Fritz Pauk, *Jugendjahre eines Tabakarbeiters* (Jena, 1930), p. 7.

[21] Jean Guehenno, *Changer la vie. Mon enfance et ma jeunesse* (Paris: Bernard Grasset Editeur, 1961), pp. 78–79.

[22] Rehbein, p. 12; Guehenno, pp. 88*ff*.

[23] Heinrich Lange, *Aus einer alten Handwerksburschen Mappe. Eine Geschichte von Heimat, Werden and Wirken* (Leipzig, n.d.).

[24] Lena Christ, *Erinnerungen* (Munich: Albert Langen, 1921); Pierre-Jean de Beranger, "Ma Biographie." in P.-J. de Beranger, *Texts choisis et commentés* ed., S. Strowski (Paris: Librairie Plon, 1913); Marcelin Rene Bonnet, *Enfance Limousin* (Paris, 1954); Philippe Valette, *Mon village. Récit* (Paris, 1947).

[25] Anonymous, *Erinnerungen*, p. 106; Henrey, p. 28; Angelina Bardin, *Angelina. Une fille des champs* (Paris, 1956), p. 11; Heinrich Georg Dikreiter, *Vom Waisenhaus zur Fabrik. Geschichte einer Proletarierjugend* (Berlin: Vorwärts Verlag, n.d. [1914]), pp. 16–17.

[26] For a full discussion of the comparative dimension, see my book, *Taking the Hard Road: French and German Workers' Autobiographies in the Era of Industrialization* (Chapel Hill: University of North Carolina Press, 1995).

[27] "Interest and Emotion in Family and Kinship Studies," in Hans Medick and David Warren Sabean, eds., *Interest and Emotion*, p. 20.

Carmen Ramos-Escandon examines the social construction of motherhood in late nineteenth- and early twentieth-century Mexico. By studying legal codes, Ramos-Escandon shows how changes in family legislation in Mexico aimed to serve the state policy of promoting a nuclear family ideology and a modernized form of submission of women to male authority. Her analysis of popular periodicals suggest that there was little expression, even in these sources, of ideological alternatives, although in practice the official norms were continually violated, as is evident especially in the very high rates of illegitimacy and female-headed households that prevailed.

15

The Social Construction of Wife and Mother: Women in Porfirian Mexico, 1880–1917

CARMEN RAMOS-ESCANDON

El dia de la madre (Mother's Day, May 10) is one of the most important holidays in present-day Mexico; banks, schools and public offices are closed, and people often spend the day visiting their *cabecitas blancas* (the white-haired ones). Yet in spite of its enormous popularity, when viewed in historical perspective the holiday is a rather recent phenomenon. Offical celebrations of motherhood did not exist in colonial times or the nineteenth century. Indeed, the designation of an official day to celebrate motherhood dates only from the 1920s.

This new celebration of motherhood points to a change in the social relations among the sexes and the social construction of gender. It reflects the increasingly common equation of motherhood with womanhood. When I worked on an oral history project in Mexico in the mid-1980s, I often asked poor urban women what they thought about International Women's Day (March 8). A common response was: "What do we need Women's Day for? There is Mother's Day, it is the same thing."

In the following essay I will analyze the increasing legal and ideological emphasis placed on marriage and motherhood as the proper life course for Mexican women from the colonial period to the early twentieth century. I will follow the evolution of ideal motherhood through the Family Relations Law of 1915, and will stress the differences in meaning that "motherhood" had for women of different social classes. I draw primarily on how the roles of wife and mother were represented in Porfirian[1] family legislation (that is, dating from the period 1876 to 1911), in sociological essays and in newspaper articles for female readers. Although the historical study of social relations in late nineteenth-century Mexico is fairly well developed,[2] analyses that incorporate gendered as well as class and ethnic perspectives are still rare. While feminist scholars have documented the Victorian idealization of motherhood in Europe and the United States,[3] Mexican women's history has been far less explored. Most studies have come from feminist scholars whose analyses have not focused on motherhood.[4] This essay will analyze motherhood as a socially constructed paradigm for Mexican women.

Reconstructing Motherhood

Proper conduct for a woman in Porfirian Mexico was based upon the assumption that a woman's social value was equated with motherhood. A pronatalist discourse was central to Porfirian ideology, and was a key aspect of the process of gender construction. The outcome of the debate over *la cuestión femenina*, or woman question, can be easily summarized: women were allowed to work in occupations and trades that did not conflict with their role as mothers. Each individual had a specific role in society: women's proper place was in the family, and within it, as mothers.[5]

The importance of motherhood in Porfirian discourse was centered in the belief that mothers were critical as nurturers of future generations of workers. Thus woman's role as educator within the familial structure was paramount to the success of a "perfect family," which, in turn, would erase social tensions.[6] In fact, family life was seen as a remedy for social evils.

The analysis of gender ideology in Porfirian Mexico, however, must take into account the ethnic and social differences among women. The most obvious differences were between rural and urban women, and between indigenous and *mestiza* women on the one hand, and Westernized women on the other. Class, ethnic and regional distinctions had dramatically shaped women's experiences in colonial times, prior to independence in 1821. The colonial administration enforced a marriage policy that discouraged race mixture, and in effect fostered a caste system by imposing legal limitations on miscegenation.[7] On the other hand, the Catholic Church enforced freedom of marriage, and this inevitably led to contradictions.[8] While legal limitations on interracial marriages were no longer enforced in independent Mexico, this did not mean that the sharp social differences among women had disappeared.

When most late- nineteenth-century Mexican newspapers analyzed motherhood, their editorials frequently outlined different reasons for the need to promote motherhood for each ethnic group. Indigenous women were labeled poor mothers and blamed for letting their children die by ignoring hygienic practices. By contrast, upper-class women were blamed for having active and frivolous social lives that prevented them from taking motherhood seriously. In both cases, the emphasis on maternal care for the newborn was stressed, while sharp social differences among women as mothers were minimized. An 1892 editorial recommended that rich and poor women should get together to take care of children; class conflict was obscured in the observation that: "the misery of the peon's children could be remedied by feeding them at the kitchen of the hacienda owner." The article went on to laud maternal love, prizing it above medical care.[9]

It was not only in the discourse of magazines and newspaper editorials that new ideals of motherhood were promoted in Porfirian Mexico. Legislative changes at the time also reflect a major concern with motherhood. To evaluate these changes properly, we must first turn to a brief analysis of previous colonial legislation and its reform in the nineteenth century.

Nineteenth-Century Legal Reforms

Colonial legislation concerning women and women's rights within the family had been rooted in the Roman tradition of a *pater familias* whose descendants were accorded inheritance rights even if they were born out of wedlock.[10] This meant that a child, if recognized by a man as his offspring, could inherit his property or titles even if the child had been born while the parents were unmarried. In this type of legal structure, the role of the mother and her testimony in identifying the father of her child in cases of inheritance disputes was crucial. Thus, mothers had an important role in relation to their offspring's patrimony, and even when children were the product of an "illegitimate union" women could claim inheritance rights on their behalf.

Disparities often existed between legislation and real life; different types of family organization varied widely according to social class, region and ethnicity. Still, legislation can be said to represent the official ideological paradigm, and in this respect it is also an important indicator of the official construction of gender relations. For example, the interrelation between class, ethnicity and gender is clearly illustrated by variations in the legislation between Spain and New Spain. In Spain the institution of the *barraganía*, a monogamous and long term, but unofficial, union generally between a rich man and a poor woman, remained prevalent.[11] In New Spain, however, Charles III introduced in 1776 a more innovative perspective that instead encouraged actual marriages between individuals of different social classes and diverse ethnic and social origins.[12] His efforts were aimed at supporting the Western idea of monogamous family arrangements, at the expense of polygamy, a tradition in the New World in pre-Hispanic times.[13] Owing to the resulting miscegenation, family arrangements in the colonies varied enormously throughout the sixteenth and seventeenth centuries.[14]

After independence, Mexican family legislation was modified to reinforce and consolidate the nuclear monogamous family, with a single line of inheritance. The attempts to regulate the family and family life went hand-in-hand with the overall process of state consolidation in nineteenth-century Mexico. By mid-century, the traditional role of the church as the guardian of family values was challenged by the liberal state. The creation of the Civil Register in 1859 aimed to wrest family organization from church control.

This effort was in tune with a broader state policy: to gain control of civil society and undermine traditional church influence. In fact, the Ley Orgánica del Registro Civil (1859) declared that, in order to confirm independence between church and state, the latter could no longer trust the church to register its citizens births, marriages and deaths.[15] Furthermore, the state cancelled its agreement with the church whereby the church held the right to validate any marriage.[16] By doing so, the liberal government was claiming increased rights over the population. In colonial times, marriage had been considered a sacrament regulated by the church, while the liberal government considered it a civil contract to be regulated by the state. However, in relation to women in marriage, both the religiously oriented colonial legislation and the new liberal laws, such as the Ley de Registro Civil, promoted the idea that women's sexual purity was paramount for the preservation of morality. Both shared a common concern with the virtue of women, perceiving them as ethereal, fragile, dependent beings whose primary function was to reproduce within marriage.

Still, in a number of areas, liberal family legislation reiterated the colonial legislation it sought to replace. For instance, the colonial Catholic canon law declared marriage indissoluble, but allowed for the possibility of a separation whereby each spouse could live independently, although neither could remarry.[17] Similarly, the Ley de Matrimonio Civil (also passed in 1859) stated that marriage remained an indissoluble union, terminable only by death.[18] Separation did not dissolve a marriage, it only lifted some civil obligations.[19] Moreover, so-called divorce by mutual consent was not granted if the couple had been married for over twenty years or the woman was over forty-five.[20] Another form of suspending a marriage was the *separación de lecho y habitación* which involved separation by mutual consent, but could only be requested after two years of marriage. This was a temporary separation (not to exceed three years), and required the consent of a judge.

Both men and women could file for separation. In order to protect them from potential domestic violence, women could not be forced to remain with their husbands. The husband was understood, according to the new law, to be "the bread-winner, the lord of the house and the protector of his wife," and her obedience and submission to her husband was expected to be unconditional. The ultimate power of the father over his children was directly established in the law, since he was the only one allowed to name a guardian for his children in the event of his death. The wife had no say in certain areas that affected her children, and as a widow had to abide by the dispositions left by her husband.

In spite of its strongly patriarchal content, this law simultaneously strengthened the position of mothers with regard to *patria potestad*—that is, literally, the rule of the father. According to Justo Sierra, whose 1859 draft served as a blueprint for both the 1870 and 1884 Civil Codes, granting the *patria potestad* to women was a recognition of maternal or mothers' rights.[21] The 1870 Civil Code granted widowed mothers whose husbands had not left specific instructions, as well as single and separated mothers, both guardianship and *patria potestad* over their children. Grandmothers could also exercise both of these rights over orphaned grandchildren.[22] However, women could easily lose these rights if they remarried or lived scandalously.[23] Moreover, when a husband named his widow as his children's guardian after his death, the consensual authority of a counsellor, predesignated by the father, still limited the widowed mother's rights. The 1870 Civil Code justified this restriction as a means of providing assistance to the unprepared and unen-lightened widow.[24]

The 1870 Civil Code also established new regulations governing marriage. According to the new code, which reflected the 1859 Law, marriage was to be con-sidered not a sacrament but a civil contract into which each individual freely entered. According to its stipulations, men and women had a legal duty to be faith-ful to one another and to contribute to the marriage's primary objective: mutual help.[25] In addition, the union was to be regulated according to the rules of a civil contract, in which each one of the contractors would maintain "their own property rights independently." In practice this meant that both men and women, as parties to the marriage contract, would jointly agree upon which type of property-sharing arrangement they wanted for their union. They could choose between *separación de bienes*, separate ownership rights, or they could get married under the *sociedad conyugal* or common property arrrangement.[26] However, the 1870 Code imposed limitations on the legal status of women by prohibiting them from entering into legal contracts, undertaking litigation, or selling or buying property without their husband's written permission.[27]

If we therefore compare this liberal legislation to the colonial one, it becomes apparent that, in matters of property, the power of husbands increased at the expense of wives, since a woman's right to administer her property within marriage was diminished.[28] In effect, in the eyes of the law, a woman was considered a minor. On the other hand, an increased emphasis on the role of women as wives and mothers is evidenced in the detailed way in which their duties as married women were defined. A wife had to live with her husband, and was obliged to follow him whenever he changed his place of residence; she could not leave the common house without his explicit permission.[29]

A common cause for separation was adultery. It was considered in all cases that a woman's adultery brought dishonor upon the family and the husband. In contrast, male adultery was treated as a minor infraction, only periodically deemed grounds for separation and, in fact, was much more difficult to prove. In order for a wife to demonstrate her husband's adultery, she had to prove that the adulterous act had taken place within the home she kept with her husband. Additionally, a wife had to prove that she had been insulted by her husband's female lover and that this insult damaged her wifely reputation. Needless to say, such requirements proved difficult to satisfy. A more likely basis for a case for separation was domestic violence, not adultery.[30]

In a society where legal marriages had never been the norm and consensual unions were common, especially in rural areas, the new marriage legislation did not affect the high incidence of illegitimacy—documented by Francisco Bulnes at seventy percent of all births.[31] In fact, between 1895 and 1908, the proportion of all unions which were legalized marriages actually decreased.[32] It was within this context that legislation related to marriage and the family attempted to establish as a model a monogamous nuclear family, with a single line of inheritance. Accordingly, a woman's position in the laws was confined to a properly legitimized marriage, wherein motherhood emphasized her privileged role.

This model of a proper bourgeois family was blueprinted in the 1884 Civil Code which closely followed the 1870 one, with only minor modifications—mostly in relation to separation. Separation could now be granted if the woman bore an illegitimate child, abandoned the home or violated premarital agreements. By increasing the number of causes for separation, the 1884 Code made it easier for men to obtain one. This particular code aimed at narrowing the gap between legislation and real life.[33]

Although there was some variation between the 1870 and 1884 codes, the similarity in relation to women's rights is notable.[34] The new legislation was quickly enforced, and provoked some criticism. In 1891, a young liberal lawyer, Genaro García, published a short book, *Apuntes sobre la condición de la mujer*, in which he criticized women's legal position within the family as outlined in the new 1884 Civil Code. Although he was part of the Porfirian establishment, García's perspectives on women and motherhood were quite innovative. He challenged the notion that motherhood was a woman's natural inclination, and argued that marriage legislation was detrimental to the rights of women, because it presumed their inferiority in relation to men.[35] He further held that women's options in life should reflect their value as human beings, regardless of whether or not they were mothers. As he put it: "Pity women if all of them would have to become mothers."[36] For García, to advocate motherhood as a universal role for women was a mistake. He attacked specific provisions of the family law that disadvantaged women, including the prohibition that prevented women from testifying in paternity investigations. Such a proscription, García noted, worked against the mother and in favor of the father, whose reputation was protected by the law. He pointed out the inherent contradiction in the fact that men were granted legal protection against defenseless women on the grounds that the women could harm their reputation. However, García's criticisms were unique in the intellectual arena of Porfirian Mexico. He was a lone voice expressing concerns and opinions well in advance of the time. Moreover, his work in regard to women's rights remains virtually unknown even today.

Popular Discourses on Motherhood

Other sources, such as women's magazines and newspaper articles aimed at women, expressed different perspectives on motherhood. For instance, *El siglo XIX*, one of the most important Porfirian-era newspapers, devoted part of its Sunday issue to women, promoting domesticity and motherhood as women's only concerns. Home remedies, recipes and advice on hygienic practices for children and mothers alike were given. Such advice was reproduced in certain women's magazines, such as *El periódico de las señoras*, which in 1896 published a set of ten commandments in relation to motherhood. According to *El periódico*, the mother was to breast-feed the baby until the child had teeth, and frequent bathing and fresh air were recommended, along with sufficient sleep and silence. The most forceful recommendation to women in these commandments was to have children vaccinated as soon as possible.

In a country with a high rate of infant mortality, where women were "always pregnant, yet unable to see their offspring survive,"[37] hygienic advice was in fact greatly needed. Yet it is striking that such guidance was offered to women for the benefit of the child's health, never the mother's well-being. Indeed, women's health was not mentioned at all. Motherhood, then, was presented not as a source of satisfaction or pride for women, but as a national responsibility in a country that was attempting to increase its population through high demographic rates and immigration. Promoting motherhood was a way to promote population increase.

The role of women as the most responsible parent was emphasized. Women who did not take personal care of their children were censured. Mothers were designated the guardians of their children's health, and were obliged to sacrifice their own health in favor of their children's well-being. Responsibility for parenting was not equally shared between men and women, and the contrasting roles of the two sexes in relation to parenting reinforced the paradigm of the male as breadwinner and the mother as "angel of the home." Parenting was an important duty, yet the responsibility was not the same for both sexes.

Motherhood in the Postrevolutionary Era

Motherhood as the only legitimate option for women was emphasized even during the armed struggle of the revolutionary years (1910 to 1917), when children were an added burden for women who followed their men to the battlefield. With the termination of hostilities in 1915, the winning general, Venustiano Carranza, issued a new Civil Code. The new *Ley de Relaciones Familiares* sought to strengthen the patriarchal monogamous family even further. The responsibility of the man as breadwinner was stressed in Article 274, which established that within the marriage contract husbands should give wives a part of their earnings or possessions, even if the women did not contribute financially to the marital association.[38] The husband's duty to support the wife was chiefly established so that she could support the children, implied in a later article (277) as her foremost duty.

On the other hand, despite the emphasis on woman's role as mother, Carranza's new code did not necessarily recognize a woman's word as paramount in determining paternity, as had been the case in colonial times.[39] In fact, Carranza's *Ley de Relaciones Familiares* was very explicit in establishing two kinds of offspring: legitimate children and natural children. Legitimate children were those born within a marriage, while natural children were born out of wedlock. However, if a child was born after a marriage was dissolved, either by divorce, annulment or death of the husband, it was considered illegitimate, unless the mother could prove that the birth had taken place within three hundred days of the actual dissolution of the marriage (Article 143). The lengthy time period (since a normal pregnancy takes only 270 days) was probably aimed at easing the legitimation of numerous fatherless children who were the product of revolutionary times. Since divorce was also established as a legal option for women, in the event of a woman remarrying, a child born within 270 days of the new marriage was considered to be fathered by the second husband. If the child was born before that time, but still within three hundred days of the previous marriage annulment, it was to be considered the child of the first husband.

Although I do not have data on how this contradiction was actually solved in practical cases, my impression is that the emphasis on providing a legitimate father for the child was in fact beneficial for women, especially at a time when there was an increased number of children born out of wedlock. It was also a step forward from Porfirian legislation inasmuch as it allowed women to determine the status of their children and their rights.

This was not the case for natural children. A married woman could not recognize as a natural child a baby born before she had been married to her current husband (Article 43). So even the acknowledgment of the biological fact of a woman giving birth to a child was dependent upon her situation in relation to a man. If she wanted to acknowledge such child, it was necessary for her husband to consent (Article 215). On the other hand, fatherhood was much more easily established; a man could recognize a child as his natural offspring even when he was married to a woman who was not the mother of this particular child. The fact that a man was married, then, did not prevent him from recognizing as his own a child born previous to or even during his current marriage. Once again, motherhood was defined in relation to the subordinate position of women *vis-à-vis* men, and their children's rights were limited by men's will. Even in the postrevolutionary era, motherhood was thus constructed in a legal and social system in terms that did not recognize it as a woman's right but rather as a man's prerogative.

Notes

[1] Porfirio Diaz was president of Mexico between 1876 and 1880, and again between 1880 and 1911. The thirty-five-year period of his political control is referred to as the "Porfiriato" in Mexican history.

[2] See Bastian, Jean-Pierre, "La estructura social de México a fines del siglo XIX y principios del XX," *Signos* 2 (1989): 85–105.

[3] Showalter, Elaine, "Women Writers and the Double Standard: Victorian Notions of Motherhood," *Motherhood, a Reader for Men and Women*, ed. Susan Cahill (New York: Avon Books, 1982); Joyce Trebilcot, ed., *Mothering: Essays in Feminist Theory* (New Jersey: Rowman and Allanheld Publishers, 1984); Dixon, Penelope, *Mothers and Mothering: An Annotated Feminist Bibliography* (New York: Garland Publishing, 1991).

[4] For an analysis of women's history in Mexico, see Lavrin, Asunción, "La mujer en México, veinte años de estudio," *Memorias del simposio de historiografía Mexicanista* (Mexico: Comité Mexicano de Ciencias Históricas, 1990); Ramos-Escandon, Carmen, *Género e historia* (Mexico: Instituto Mora, 1992).

[5] Ramos-Escandon, Carmen, "Señoritas Porfirianas," *Presencia y transparencia* (Mexico: El Colegio de México, 1987), pp. 143–161.

[6] Guerrero, Julio, *La génesis del crimen en México* (Paris, Mexico: Vda. de Bouret, 1901); Roumagnac, Carlos, *Los criminales en México* (Mexico: El Fénix, 1904).

[7] Mörner, Magnus, *Race Mixture in Latin America* (Boston: Little, Brown, 1967).

[8] Seed, Patricia, *To Love, Honor and Obey in Colonial Mexico, 1574–1821* (Stanford, CA: Stanford University Press, 1988).

[9] González Navarro, Moisés, "El Porfiriato, vida social," *Historia moderna de México*, vol. 6 (Mexico: Editorial Hermes, 1957), p. 45.

[10] Ots Capdequí, José María, *El Imperio Español en las Indias* (Mexico: Fondo de Cultura Económica, 1946), pp. 115–140; Margadant, Guillermo, "La familia en el derecho novohispano," *Familias Novohispanas*, Pilar Gonzalbo, ed. (Mexico: El Colegio de México, 1991), pp. 25–56.

[11] Ibid.

[12] Margadant, 1991, p. 31. See "Pragmática sanción matrimonios," in Pérez y López, Xavier, *Teatro de la legislación universal de España e Indias* (Madrid: González, 1791–1798).

[13] Gruzinski, Serge, and Carmen Bernard, "Les enfants de l'Apocalypse: la famille en Meso-Amerique et dans les Andes," *Autres mondes, fait colonial et fait national* (Paris: Armand Colin, 1987), pp. 191–198.

[14] Malvido, Elsa, "Algunos aportes del estudio de la demografía histórica al estudio de la familia en la época colonial de México," *Familia y sexualidad en la Nueva España* (Mexico: SEP/INAH, 1982).

[15] "Ley Orgánica del Registro Civil del 28 de julio de 1859," *Legislación Mexicana o Colección completa de las disposiciones legislativas expedidas desde la independencia de la República*, Manuel Dublán, Jose Maria Lozano, eds. (Mexico: Imprenta del Comercio de Dublán y Chávez, 1877), vol. VIII, p. 696.

[16] "Ley del Matrimonio Civil 23 de julio de 1859," *Legislación Mexicana* (Mexico: Imprenta del Comercio, 1877), vol. VIII, p. 696.

[17] Arrom, Silvia M., *La mujer Mexicana ante el divorcio eclesiástico: 1800–1857*, pp. 13, 14.

[18] "Ley del Matrimonio Civil del 23 de julio de 1859," *Legislación Mexicana*, vol. VIII, p. 691.

[19] Ibid., Article 239, p. 49.

[20] Ibid., Article 247, p. 42.

[21] Sierra, Justo, *Proyecto de un Código Civil Mexicano formado de orden del supremo gobierno* (Mexico: Vicente G. Torres, 1861), p. iii.

[22] Arrom, Silvia, "Changes in Mexican Family Law in the XIX Century: The Civil Codes of 1870 and 1884," *Journal of Family History* 10 (1985): 308–22.

[23] *Código Civil del Distrito Federal y Territorios de Baja California* (Mexico: Aguilar e Hijos, 1870) Arts. 268, 271.

[24] Arrom, Silvia, "Cambios en la condición jurídica de la mujer mexicana en siglo XIX," *Memoria del Segundo Congreso de Historia del Derecho Mexicano* (Mexico: Instituto de Investigaciones Jurídicas/UNAM, 1988), pp. 811–822; *Código Civil del Distrito Federal y Territorios de Baja California* (Mexico: Agiular e Hijos, 1870), p. 227.

[25] *Código Civil del Distrito Federal y Territorios del Baja California* (Mexico: Imprenta de Jose Batiza, 1870), Art. 98, p. 45.

[26] Brena, Ingrid, "Los regimenes patrimoniales del matrimonio," *Memoria del IV Congreso de Historia del Derecho Mexicano* (Mexico: Instituto de Investigaciones Jurídicas/UNAM, 1988), vol. 1, p. 196.

[27] *Código Civil del Distrito Federal* (Mexico: Aguilar e Hijos, 1892), Arts. 196, 197.

[28] *Código Civil del Distrito Federal y Territorios de Baja California*, Art. 198, p. 45. On the similarities with colonial legislation, see "Supervivencia del derecho colonial en el regimén patrimonial de bienes en la codificación civil mexicana," *Memoria del cuarto Congreso de Historia del Derecho Mexicano* (Mexico: Instituto de Investigaciones Jurídicas/UNAM, 1988), p. 635.

[29] Ibid., Art. 199, p. 45.

[30] Gonzalez Montes, Soledad, "Violencia contra las mujeres campesinas," *Presencia y Transparencia*, Carmen Ramos, ed. (Mexico: El Colegio de México, 1987), p. 302.

[31] Bulnes, Francisco, *La verdad acerca de la revolución Mexicana* (New York: 1916), p. 302.

[32] The marriage rate was 4.5 in 1895 and 3.84 in 1908. Gonzalez Navarro, Moises, "El Porfiriato,

vida social," *Historia Moderna de México* (Mexico: Editorial Hermes, 1957), p. 320.

[33] Arrom, 1981, p. 509.

[34] Arrom, 1981, p. 495.

[35] García, Genaro, *Apuntes sobre la condición de la mujer* (Mexico: Cia. Limitada de Tipógrafos, 1891), p. 71.

[36] Ibid., p. 18.

[37] González, Luis, *Historia general de México* (Mexico: El Colegio de México, 1976), vol. III, p. 80.

[38] Carranza, Venustiano, "Ley sobre relaciones familiares," Mexico: *Diario Oficial,* 14 de abril de 1917.

[39] Seed, Patricia, "Las promesas de matrimonio y el valor del testimonio de la mujer en el México colonial," *Cristianismo y Sociedad* 102 (1989): 39–60.

Parry Scott uses ethnographic evidence from contemporary urban Brazil to address the question of what men and women gain from setting up households. Scott explores how men's attitudes, expectations and experiences shape their roles as fathers and providers in a setting where an ideology of male dominance counters a lived reality of matrifocal households. Men's economic marginality undermines patriarchal practice without apparently destroying the ideology. As in several other cases explored in this section, the relative power of women in this milieu is related to male economic disempowerment.

16

Matrifocal Males: Gender, Perception and Experience of the Domestic Domain in Brazil

PARRY SCOTT

> In all these cases we find the same combination of an expectation of strong male dominance in the marital relationship and as head of the household, coupled with a reality in which mother-child relations are strongly solitary and groups of women, daughters and daughters' children emerge to provide a basis for continuity and security. (Smith 1973, p. 129)

The principal objective of this paper is to understand how men and women perceive and live the "matrifocal" situation described by Smith (1973).[1] The term "matrifocality" identifies a complex web of relations constructed around the domestic group in which, even with the presence of a man in the house, the woman's side of the group is favored. This is evidenced in mother-child relations being more solidary than father-child relations, in the choice of residence, in the identification of known relatives, in exchange of goods and services, in visiting patterns and so on. All are stronger on the female side. It may also be expected that cultural and religious manifestations also emphasize the female role.

Permission given by the Fundação Carlos Chagas.

Smith alerts us against confusing "female headship" with matrifocality (Smith 1973, pp. 125–127). "Headship" and "focality" in the domestic domain are different ideas, and both have stirred much debate (see Aguiar 1984). The coexistence of patriarchal norms and matrifocal practices is a defining characteristic of Smith's matrifocal concept. Its cultural roots are historical and hierarchical, as Smith has made even clearer in his recent study of kinship and class in the Caribbean:

> Matrifocality arises from the way in which kinship and family life is practiced, and that practice is rooted in the cultural meaning of social life developed over several hundred years. It can and will change, not as a response to increases in the level of living, but only if, and when, there is a change in the structure of the social hierarchy and a change in the definition and meaning of sex roles. Matrifocality in domestic relations arises at the conjuncture of social hierarchy and marked sex role differentiation. (1988, p. 180)

Matrifocality may occur in different social classes, and, in fact, is historically rooted in such hierarchy. It is both in the relations among people within the household and with friends, relatives and others outside the household that observable matrifocality is constructed. The notion of the normality of this segregation of conjugal roles developed by Bott (1957) in a study of the English middle class leads her to the conclusion that "whenever there are no particular economic advantages to be gained from affiliation with paternal relatives, and whenever two or preferably three generations of mothers and daughters are living in the same place at the same time, a bilateral kinship system is likely to develop a matrilateral stress" (p. 137). These matrilateral groupings she describes as readily dissolved, and rarely lasting over several generations. In such a way, she recognizes that without property, substantial inheritance or other elements to maintain a privileged status for the father, the motherly role gains force and becomes the axis for the formation of the domestic group's family relations.

The concept of the developmental cycle of the domestic group, originally elaborated by Fortes (1958) and Goody (1972), argues that this group goes through the phases of formation, expansion and dissolution. This same sequence is described by Smith (1956) for Guyana, and is based on an ideal (although not obligatory) pattern of a lasting relationship between husband and wife.

Under conditions of urban poverty (evidence is abundant in Brazil, as well as in other countries) in households in the expansion phase of the domestic cycle, husbands are not able to contribute adequately to the household, and affective relations also are incapable of guaranteeing that most unions last (Merrick and

Schmink 1983; Woortmann 1987; Neves 1985; Quintas 1986; Barroso 1978; Kottak 1961; Scott 1986; Figueiredo 1980). The developmental cycle becomes repetitive, made up of almost "ephemeral" relations between men and women. Domestic groups change rapidly and constantly. Many authors working with the notion of matrifocality have registered the occurrence of visiting unions, where regular male participation is inherently limited, and not coresidential. Whether such unions are hierarchical or not, and whether they last for long periods or not, such relation-ships, in general, are imbedded in the history of each society (see Goody 1972 for an interesting cross-cultural study of concubinage). Even the more durable mother-child relations are placed in danger by precarious economic conditions, women having to give up their children, temporarily or permanently, in a process which Fonseca (1986, 1987) has called "circulation of children," and described, in some cases, as "special forms of internment."

Under these conditions the segregated conjugal roles characteristic of matrifo-cality flourish. The first relation to corrode is that between husband and wife. Sep-arations are constant, even if it is never very clear whether the husband abandons his wife or whether she kicks him out of the house. The colorful image of a Bahian woman who said that "in this yard the cock does not crow" (Woortmann 1987; Neves 1985) sums up this distancing of the male from the domestic domain. Along the same line, one might question how "not crowing in the yard" is seen by the men? Does it crush them? Does it free them? Does it do both (Scott 1986)? How-ever, another question precedes these: Do the actors involved agree about what the "yard" is?

Upon adopting a perspective which emphasizes a fundamental separation in gender roles, some points must be examined: (1) what does the home or household (that is, "the yard") represent for men and women, and (2) how is this space lived differently by men and women in their individual life cycles? This evidently leads to reflection on the articulation of gender relations, on the one hand, and to the establishment of different strategies of approaching the elapsing of the domestic cycle, on the other.

The solidarity between women and children is strengthened by a clear sexual division of labor which confers upon both an intense period of shared experience throughout childhood. The woman becomes the principal agent of biological and social reproduction, with the home as her stage. The man, often unable to fulfill his culturally ascribed role as provider, finds the economic "marginality" he suffers outside the home transformed into another marginality within the home. Tensions between husband and wife reinforce the segregation of conjugal roles, impeding the elaboration of explicit family projects such as those described for more eco-nomically stable working groups by Macedo (1979) and Bilac (1978). In the con-

289

text of constant tension among poor urban couples, it is no wonder that a pattern of "women's families" (Woortmann 1987) is sustained.

In these conditions, men are seen disparagingly by women as "slow and without initiative," representing and embodying their own failure outside the home. By contrast, women see themselves as "victims" (suffering through life and facing things alone) who are very savvy (initiators of essential activities to sustain the home). The home has become that "knot of individual interests" (Laslett 1985) where the context determines which interests will be outstanding at different moments. These interests take on different hues in accordance with the gender of the actors.

A weakened male role endures, since it is the fruit of historically established economic conditions which continue unaltered over the years. Even so, it is lived as something that is generalized for the group at the same time that it is transitory for the individual, different from his expectations or hopes. There is no preferential renouncing of marriage (legal or not) at the beginning of the family trajectory of each actor. Nevertheless, the combination of successive failures in attempted marriages and the coming of age of children make the renunciation of a live-in husband more of a rule than an exception (see Salem 1981, pp. 82–93, for an interesting discussion of this). As the cycle progresses, Smith's "economic and decision-making coalition" becomes a reality.

The exclusion of the male from the household is, partially, simply a manifestation of the cultural segregation of genders into very distinct spheres, justified socially as "traditional" and as "natural." The "home" (*casa*) is female, the "street" (*rua*) is male. Such a clear separation is part of a relational and cognitive reality, studied by Da Matta (1985); however, it should not hide the fact that women have to deal with the *rua* and men with the *casa*. It is interesting to note that Da Matta sets the division between *rua* and *casa* in another opposition—that of dominant/subordinate, declaring that "the dominant discourse is much more from the *rua* than from the *casa*. What comes from the *rua* comes with legal and juridical components. The speech of the subordinate is much more the language of the *casa* and of the family" (1985, p. 18). Legal and juridical components may be gained by women's incursions into the world of the *rua*. Recently much attention has been drawn to the evidence and implications of women's participation in the labor force (Aguiar 1984, and Nash and Safa 1986 are two edited collections which demonstrate the diversity of approaches to this subject).

The other side of the equation (of how men deal with the women's sphere of the home, the *casa*) has brought about much less study, and very little articulation among authors who approach the question from different perspectives. It is curious that, despite the voluminous criticisms and praise drawn from Gilberto Freyre's well-known works that document the patriarch's view of the family (1968, 1969), other authors have not taken the lead and developed the question of the relation between men and the home. The intensification of feminist approaches has brought about some study of men and the family which emphasizes domestic violence and other manifestations of machismo (Azevedo 1985; Drumont 1982; Oliveira and Prado 1981; Correa 1983). The male role can also be discerned in some works which focus on how men and women make family projects and survival strategies in specific conditions of labor market insertion (Bilac 1978; Macedo 1979; Rodrigues 1978; Motta and Scott 1983; Woortmann 1984, 1987). In most of these works, it is important to point out, the household is emphasized more than "gender relations."

There is still a lacuna in our understanding of that shantytown man, a potential patriarch, who mediates between the world of the *rua* and the world of the *casa*, but who must face his own incapacity to control the *rua*. What does he find in the *rua* to underwrite his exercise of power at home? How does he transport his experience as "dominated" (in the legal and juridical world of the *rua*) into an experience as a "dominant" figure at home? At home, his wife is the first one to accuse him of not playing his role adequately (see Salem 1981, and Barroso 1978). She says she is being the victim, just as Lopes and Silva postulated in their description of the effects of subordination (1981).

In a study in which Neves found high degrees of matrifocality, she explains the male's retreat as "attempting to minimize his participation in family life because he does not feel he has the authority to make certain decisions" (1985, p. 201). The larger problem involved here seems to be another one. One may ask, how do men see the sphere of home? What context for action is the *casa* for a male actor?

It is important to remember that, in most research on shantytown families, the informants are almost always women. Women certainly are easier to find at home, and they are also more willing to talk about the home. But not to have lent an ear to the men may have led to distortions in our perception about the formation of the domestic group, and especially about the man's role in it.

In this paper, it is argued that, in order to understand the role of the male in poor matrifocal households, it is necessary to adopt the point of view that the home, or *casa*, occupies different spaces in men's and in women's life strategies. Starting from this assumption, and keeping in mind the differentiated notion which results from its adoption, some considerations will be made about the articulation between analyses which focus on gender and analyses which focus on domestic groups.

Life Strategies, Gender and the Home

To register the existence of a strong sexual division of labor in relation to the home is only to repeat a fact recognized and investigated by generations of social scien-

291

tists (see Burton, *et al.* 1977, and Pouillon 1978 for a review of many of the arguments). What is emphasized here is that such a division of labor creates systematically differentiated representations and experiences of the reality of the home, whatever name is used to describe it.[2]

It is possible to describe one very basic difference in male and female strategies *vis-à-vis* the home. It is expected that the woman be *actively controlling* her home, and that the man present his home as *under control*, as something that has been solved. This is popularly recognized in often repeated comments that "that is Joao's house," but "it is Maria who runs it."

For most women in Brazil, the home is a fundamental part of female identity. It is in relation to her home that a woman constructs a self-evaluation of her status and of her articulation with the world of the *rua*. Generally, building a home is begun with the establishing of a more or less stable marital relationship with a man. Knowing that domestic tasks related to the preparation and reposition of the labor force (child care, food preparation, cleaning, and so on) will be theirs, women come to live and think of the home in an extremely active and critical way. The success or failure of a woman's life strategy hinges on her own, other women's and men's evaluations of the way in which she operates with the constituent elements of the home.

For men, the same is not true. With the overriding criterion for success located in the *rua*, the home becomes a domain which must be "*under control.*" It must be "unquestionable." In the same way that running a home becomes incorporated in the woman's identity, control over a woman, symbolized by his control over a home, must be "unquestionable" to be incorporated positively in the man's identity. The most devastating and violent insults to a man refer directly to his incapacity to control his own woman (*corno*—cuckold) or to his origins in a family in which the woman was not controlled (*filho de puta*—son of a bitch). The physical distance from home often demanded by work eliminates the possibility of active, personal watching over the daily home routine. Male discourse on the home is constructed on this reduced knowledge, but it is not a discourse whose importance is reduced. Once his discourse shows that his home is not *under control*, there is real danger that doubts will be cast on his performance as a man, doubts every bit as real as the direct admission of failure in his male role as "provider."

With these different bases to organize and perceive the home, men and women also see the development of the domestic cycle very differently. This can be seen by examining variation in household composition and income for men and women, and then examining the discourse of both about key moments in the development of the domestic cycle. The information was gathered through anthropological fieldwork carried out over several years in Coelhos, Recife.

A survey of the economic organization of families in the innumerable poor neighborhoods of Recife (Motta and Scott 1983) shows that 21.5 percent have their basic income earned by women, and that women's income is fundamental to sustain three of four households in the city. In the Coelhos neighborhood (1,347 houses; 5,298 people) focused on in this paper, the dependence on women is even greater. A statistical comparison of household composition and income (Scott 1990) demonstrated that men and women have quite different experiences. As a whole, men are part of homes with higher incomes. They form numerous solitary units, devoid of children and other dependents. They stay longer with their parents. And, of course, the majority of male adults in Coelhos are family fathers who are living with their wives. The majority of women (59.0 percent) also have resident husbands; however, there is a surprisingly high number of single female household heads. They run homes which usually include children and which have lower overall incomes. Despite the fact that girls leave home (to set up their own home) earlier than boys, they also return to live with their mothers in later moments of crisis. Much more so than men, as these women grow older they count on shelter in their children's homes. The "home," then, persists as a space which demands active controlling by women.

Gender and the Domestic Cycle

A comparison of male and female representations of how they live the domestic developmental cycle would rightly consider details of several key moments: leaving the parental home, joining with a spouse, the birth of children, joining other friends and relatives, separating from a spouse, excluding friends and relatives, death and the substitution of the domestic group. Such an extensive undertaking is beyond the scope of this paper; consequently, priority will be given to the moments of joining with and separating from a spouse, since they very transparently show the issue of gender in the making of a home.

"A woman without a husband is nothing." Many neighborhood women, and especially the younger ones, firmly believe in this declaration of a Coelhos woman. Having *a home* to care for is almost universally cited as an important reason for deciding to live with a man. Many factors must be weighed in choosing a husband whose qualities may contribute to the raising of the woman's status. Reputations, embodied in how one is talked about by the circle of acquaintances and neighbors, are brought into play with such a choice—both the woman's own reputation and that of her home of origin. One Brazilian cultural face-saving option is to elope (*fugir*). Rural patterns of elopement usually involve an initial visit or period of residence away from parental homes, but with or near other relatives. In such a way, all reputations are preserved, the woman's family avoids ceremonial expenses, and the woman herself goes from one home to another without having to go to the *rua*, where there would be no one to watch over her sexual activity, the principal symbol of her (and her home's) reputation. The new husband's relatives, often hosts to the elopers, provide a kin and domestic sanctioning for the new wife. She does not lose face. Some women from Coelhos, originally from the countryside, followed this pattern, but they are not the rule. The urban setting brings differences.

A great many women spent some time in their youth living and working in private homes, or else in boardinghouses and rented rooms. During this time, they "dated" (*namoro*) and had sexual relations with men. In this case, reputations, which were so carefully preserved with traditional elopement, must be earned some other way in the city's poor neighborhoods. Finding an adequate husband may represent the regaining of status as a "proper, respected woman" (*mulher direita e respeitada*). A secure, cohabiting sexual partner confers status. Here the regaining of a home is the regaining of a cultural identity which frees women from the dubiousness of the *rua*. The presence of a husband may be part of a strategy that does not necessarily depend on the question of material survival and increase of sources of income.

When young, many of the Coelhos women found sexual attraction to be of overriding importance in seeking husbands. A good "first experience" with a man, often met on festive occasions, naturally led to the setting up of a home. Generally, with the passing of the years, other elements become more important in the decision on whether a man should participate or not in the household.

Living together involves more than the establishing of a reputation and sexual attraction. Having your own home to care for is extremely important. The popular saying *quem casa, quer casa* ("those who marry, want a home"), in its very repetition of the word "home," strengthens the notion of such importance. Neolocal residence rules lead to a search for a separate physical space, whether near or far from relatives, where the new home can flourish. Her new home should be an uncontested locale where the woman can organize work and time, according to her own demands and to those of the relation with her husband. The noninterference of mothers, and even more so, mothers-in-law, is a significant gain.

A man with a secure income, a homebody who does not spend money on drinks or flings (which describes a minority of Coelhos men), often prefers that a woman give up her own income and work in order to care for him and for their home. *Their* home soon becomes *her* home. The term *dona de casa* is only suggestive of this. After a separation things become clearer—women keep the homes, whether as owners or renters.

Most women interviewed married more than once. The *home* thought of in second and successive marriages is no longer the physical space (which she commonly has already secured, even if precariously), nor is it the affirmation of her female identity through the gaining of her own stage of activities. Other factors become more central in "the economic and decision-making coalition" Smith described when characterizing matrifocality. The woman, with her own physical home space and with her responsibilities for children, transfers the weight of her evaluation of the new home into a questioning of the social relations implied in living with a man. Will he treat the children as if they were his? Just how much more work will she have to do if he moves in? And if she works, it is far less likely that she would be willing to give up her job for him. She has her own *home*, and it certainly would be inconvenient to take in a man who does little more than increase the work load.

In this context of urban poverty, staying with a husband is more the exception than the rule. Only six of twenty-eight women interviewed in depth in Coelhos are still with their first husbands. And five of these six are young and have had little time of marriage. From this fact, it is clear that any initial expectations that a first marriage would result in betterment are tempered by subsequent difficulties.

The first marriage generally does not meet the expectation that having a home will improve a woman's reputation. A husband and children require a lot of work. But the reputation is in constant danger, both because of the low and uncertain income and because of the recreational and amorous pursuits of married men. One woman said, in a tired tone: "I bought my husband with my sweat." After the first husband, women begin to weigh the work load which having a husband implies. Several women said that they did not permit their companions to move in, in order not to become slaves—of him, of his clothes, and of the stove. Some men who do not let their wives work end up spending their own money drinking and womanizing. Arguments and physical aggression increase. Many men go off to live with other women. It becomes evident that, with the passing of time, the presence of a husband who is poor, takes work to care for, and has no respect for his wife and home does more to hurt a woman's reputation than help it. To top it off, these women experience a decrease in sexual enjoyment. Separation is a foregone conclusion.

Men in Coelhos are in no rush to get married, but sexual initiation should be early. Women are first seen as sexual partners, and many men visit prostitutes. For most there is a clear separation between women of the *rua* (who are *fusacas*, for play only, and who participate in scoundrelry, *malandragem*) and proper women (*mulheres direitas*), the only ones who are marriageable. At dances, frequently held in Coelhos, the first category of women will certainly be present. In addition, often informally chaperoned, there will be some proper women. Many men who spent their youth in Coelhos met their first wives at a neighborhood dance. Many of those who have stronger ties to their rural origins make a point of excluding woman who go to these dances from the set of marriageable women.

However their first union started, most men declared that they were not thinking of marriage or a lasting union until the appearance of a pregnancy. For these men, then, the home does not present itself as part of an individual life project. It is more like a chance happening which resulted from amorous relationships. Many speak of parents advising them to set up their own household and take on the responsibility for a wife and children. Yet taking on the roles of husband and father is an increase in responsibility which frequently was not included in the immediate expectations of the man.

Those who take on longer periods of courting establish a fundamental condition for the women which becomes even clearer when they marry: they must be subordinate and under the control of the man. This discourse, paradoxically, is accompanied by frequent reference to the "equality" of both. As one Coelhos man said, "I believe in equal rights, I am not *machista*, but you cannot free the reigns" (Scott 1986).

This domination at home becomes a vigilance which always questions women going outside the home, even when it is to other people's homes. The men's most repeated complaint concerns their wives' flight from domesticity. "If she lives around other peoples' homes, she does not want her husband any more." A poorly run home, uncared-for children, unwashed dishes and so on are all signs that a man's home is out of control, and that he might do well to look for another wife. After all, a wife who does not have time for her own home must be using her time in some other manner.

Although women should stay at home and cannot run around, men do not believe that such demands should be reciprocal. Extramarital relations are frequent, and are a frequent reason for separations. First marriages in the neighborhood tend to be short, according to residents, ruined by low incomes and men's affairs. Data do not permit a statistical treatment of the average duration of marriages in Coelhos; however, of the fourteen men interviewed in depth, nine had a failed previous marriage and five did not have their own homes but lived with their parents, in rented rooms or in rapidly disintegrating successive marriages. Those men who do establish long-term relations after the first marriage tend to do so with women who have some income. Resistance to women working outside the home decreases in subsequent marriages. The man is less caught up in the ideal of *mulher em casa e homem na rua* ("woman at home and man on the street"). He perceives the importance of her income as well as the income of her children.

Most of the 16.7 percent of the men who have no wives live in rented rooms or ceded houses, and they say that they have no plans to form households or even to marry. They say that there is no lack of women, and that they prefer not to take on the responsibility of a home. These men feel that they are particularly shrewd in keeping themselves free of obligations (*desobrigados*). There are other ways to keep free of obligations, as in the arrangement of a forty-four year-old shoemaker who still lives with his wife and four children, contributing to their support, but "not having anything to do" with his wife, and hardly speaking to his children. He explains:

> I am not young any more, I'm tired and have worked a lot. Finding some young girl to live with won't work out. I know I will get mad. Why? Because I know that the majority of young girls nowadays are vain. I can't afford vanity. She wants to go to the club, to those things, and I don't want to any more. There is no lack of women around. You can always find one—but a woman to get my head hot, no way.

The male experience of the domestic cycle is very different from the female one. Based on the information presented, it is possible to isolate some key moments which illustrate important gender-related differences in strategies and perceptions. While women initially view their dating and having sex as strategies for establishing a home, men view these relations as an objective in itself, which incidentally may result in the establishing of a separate home. Both men and women believe that the failure of first marriages has to do with not being ready for them—being too young, having too little money and being unable to control the spouse's activity. After a separation, women normally emerge with an established home (at least children, and at times a house itself), while a man faces a decision between a life in which he renounces the idea of having a home, or establishing another relation with a woman who, if she also has separated, he will commonly allow, or even stimulate, to work. With this strategy he gives up his role as the only provider, and becomes integrated into a domestic group more equipped to face poverty with multiple strategies of making and managing income.

Some Suggestions for the Study of Gender and Domestic Groups

In the text, some conclusions were reached based on the data presented on poor Recife families, and there is no need to repeat them. These closing suggestions focus on how the approach taken here provides some clues for the understanding of the operation of gender in domestic groups.

First, it is important to register the usefulness of the notion of matrifocality, understood as the favoring of matrilateral relations in households where segregated conjugal roles, historically imbedded in social hierarchy, prevail. At the same

297

time it is emphasized that both male and female actions received attention. To restrict any analysis of the domestic group only to men or only to women would be to deal with only half the story. Observation and analysis should capture both sides.

Second, intimately related to the first point, upon adopting an approach which privileges the domestic cycle, it seems at first sight that it is free of the problem of gender. But that is an illusion. One of the most significant conclusions of this work is that the domestic cycle is lived and perceived in radically different ways by women and men.

Third, the *casa* and the *rua* are two parts of the arena which may be controlled by men and women when they set up a household. Gender relations are, as are all social relations, power relations. Both actors try to control part of the arena in order to influence the other's actions. The path of least resistance is to follow the culturally imposed dichotomy which attributes the home to the woman and the street to the man. The home becomes a resource, a part of the arena over which men and women construct strategies of interaction which they judge favorable to individual survival. In such a way, women *actively control* their homes, whereas men present their homes as *under control*.

If this discussion had focused on key moments in the domestic cycle different from those of joining with and separating from a spouse, other sets of meaningful relations would become salient. As an example, if focusing on the addition of children, the shifting weight of questions of "legitimacy" would gain more importance. In fact, this study concentrated on the question of the inclusion and exclusion of spouses in household formation strategies. A simple examination of the tremendous diversity of elements which make up the understanding of matrifocality listed in the beginning of this work, or of the list of other key moments in household formation strategies, shows that there is a rich field open for analysis to better understand other facets of how gender relations are constructed and given meaning in this context.

Notes

[1] This research received support from the Brazilian Association of Population Studies (ABEP), the National Research and Scientific Development Council (CNPQ) and the Carlos Chagas Foundation. An earlier Portuguese version was published as "O Homem na Matrifocalidade" in the *Cadernos de Pesquisa* (73): 38–47, May 1990, Fundação Carlos Chagas, São Paulo.

[2] We agree with authors who insist on an explicit differentiation between the notion of "family," more tied to ideas of kinship and ideology, and of "household," more tied to ideas of cohabitation and immediate economic cooperation; but for the argument here "home," "family," "household" and "domestic group," are used interchangeably, unless otherwise indicated. Most frequent reference will be made to the term "home" because of both its more popular usage and its polysemic qualities.

References

Aguiar, N. (ed.) *Mulheres na forca de trabalho na América Latina: analises qualitativas.* Petropólis, Vozes, 1984.

Almeida, M.C.L. "Em busca da igualdade: um estudo de casais de camadas médias urbanas no Recife." Recife, Antropologia-UFPe (Master's Thesis), 1988.

Azevedo, M.A. *Mulheres espancadas: a violência denunciada.* São Paulo, 1985.

Barroso, C. "Sozinhas ou mal acompanhadas: a situação da mulher chefe de familia," in *Encontro da associacao Brasileira de estudos populacionais, 1. Anais.* Rio de Janeiro, ABEP, 1978.

Bilac, E.D. *Familia de trabalhadores: estrategias de sobrevivencia; a organizacao da vida familiar em uma cidade paulista.* São Paulo, Símbolo, 1978.

Bott, E. *Family and Social Network.* London, Tavistock, 1957.

Burton, M.L, *et al.* "A Model of the Sexual Division of Labor." *American Ethnologist.* Washington, American Ethnological Society, pp. 227–51, 1977.

Correa, M. "Mulher e família: um debate sobre a literatura recente." *BIB* (18): 27–44, jul/dez, 1984.

———. *Morte em família: representações jurídicas de papeis sexuais.* Rio de Janeiro, Graal, 1983.

Da Matta, R. *A casa e a rua: espaco, cidadania, mulher e morte no Brasil.* São Paulo, Brasiliense, 1985.

Drumont, M.P. "O machismo como sistema de representações ideológicas recíprocas," in: Luz, M., *et al., O lugar da mulher: estudos sobre a condição feminina na sociedade atual.* Rio de Janeiro, Graal, 1982.

Durham, E.R. "A família e a mulher." *Cadernos do CERU.* São Paulo, Centro de Estudos Rurais e Urbanos. (18): 7–48, maio, 1983.

Farreira, A.B.H. *Novo dicionário da língua portuguesa.* Rio de Janeiro, Nova Fronteira. 1975.

Figueredo, M. "O papel socio-econômico das mulheres chefes de família numa comunidade pesqueira do litoral norte da Bahia." *Cadernos de Debate.* (6), 1980.

Fonseca, C. "Orphanages, foundlings and foster mothers: state intervention in the system of child circulation in a Brazilian slum." 1985 (mimeo).

———. "O internato do pobre: FEBEM e a organização doméstica em um grupo porto-alegrense de baixa renda." *Temas IMESC.* São Paulo, Soc. Dir. Saude, 4(1): 21–39, 1987.

————. "A circulação de criancas em grupos populares de Porto Alegre: um exame do processo jurídico de apreensão de menores, 1900–1926." *X Reunião de ANPOCS*. Campos de Jordao: mimeographed paper, 1986.

Fortes, M. "Introduction," in Goody, J., ed. *The Developmental Xycle of the Domestic Group*. Cambridge, Cambridge University Press, 1958.

Freyre, G. *Casa grande e senzala: formação da família brasileira sob o regime da economia patriarcal*. 14a edição, Rio de Janeiro, Graal, 1969. 2 volumes.

————. *Sobrados e mocambos*. 4a edição. Rio de Janeiro, José Olympio, 1968. 2 volumes.

Gerber, S.N., ed. "The Family in the Caribbean," in *Conference on the Family in the Caribbean*, 2. *Proceedings*. Rio Piedras, Institute of Caribbean Studies/University of Puerto Rico, 1973.

Gonzales, N.L. "The Consanguineal Households and Matrifocality." *American Anthropologist*. 67: 1541–1549, 1965.

————. "Towards a Definition of Matrifocality," in Whitten Jr., N.E. and Szwed, J.F., eds. *Afro-American Anthropology: Contemporary Perspectives*. New York, Free Press, 1970.

Goody, J. *Production and Reproduction: a Comparative Study of the Domestic Domain*. Cambridge, Cambridge University Press, 1972.

Greenfield, S. "Dominance, Focality and the Characterization of Domestic Groups: Some Reflections on Matrifocality in the Caribbean," in Gerber, S., ed. *The Family in the Caribbean*. Puerto Rico, Institute of Caribbean Studies/University of Puerto Rico, 1973.

Kottak, C.P. "Kinship and Class in Brazil." *Ethnology*. Pittsburgh: University of Pittsburgh, 16(4), 1961.

Kunstadtler, P. "A Survey of Consanguine or Matrifocal Family." *American Anthropologist*. Washington, AAA, 65(1): 56–66, March, 1963.

Laslett, P. "The Family as a Knot of Individual Interests," in Netting, R. McC. *et al.*, eds. *Households: Comparative and Historical Studies of the Domestic Group*. Berkeley, University of California, 1985.

Lopes, J.S.L. and Silva, L.A.M. "Introdução: estratégias de trabalho, normas de dominação na produção e subordinação doméstica de trabalhadores urbanos," in Lopes, J.S.L., *et al*. *Mudanças sociais no Nordeste: Reprodução da Subordinação*. Rio de Janeiro, Paz e Terra, 1981.

Macedo, C.C. *A Reprodução da desigualdade: projeto de vida familiar de um grupo operário*. São Paulo, Hucitec, 1979.

Merrick, T. and Schmink, M. "Households Headed by Women and Urban Poverty in Brazil," in Buvinic, M., *et al.*, eds. *Women and Poverty in the Third World*. Baltimore, Johns Hopkins University Press, 1983.

Motta, R. and Scott, R.P. *Sobrevivência e Fontes de Renda: Estratégias de familias de baixa renda no Recife*. Recife, Massangana, 1983. (População e Emprego, 16).

Nash, J. and Safa, H. *Women and Change in Latin America*. South Hadley, MA: Bergin and Garvey, 1986.

Neves, D.P. "Nesse terreiro galo nao canta: estudo do carater matrifocal de unidades familiares de baixa renda." *Anuário Antropológico 1983*. Rio de Janeiro/Fortaleza, Tempo Brasileiro/UFC, 1985.

Oliveira, C.F. and Prado, D. *Cícera, um destino de mulher: autobiografia duma emigrante nordestina, operária textil*. São Paulo, Brasiliense, 1981.

Pouillon, F. "A determinação de um modo de produção: as forças produtivas e a sua apropriação." In. _____ (ed.) *A antropologia econômica*. Lisboa, Edições 70, 1978, pp. 101_149.

Quintas, F. *Sexo e marginalidade: um estudo sobre a sexualidade feminina em camadas de baixa renda*. Petrópolis, Vozes, 1986.

Recife, Prefeitura. Empresa de Urbanização do Recife—URB. *PROMORAR: relatório*. Recife, 1981.

Rodrigues, A. *Operário, Operária*. São Paulo, Símbolo, 1978, (Coleção Ensaio e Memória, 2).

Salem, T. "Mulheres faveladas: com a venda nos olhos." *Perspectivas antropológicas da mulher*, 1. Rio de Janeiro, Zahar, 1981, pp. 49–99.

Scott, P. "Os maridos nas estratégias femininas de formação de unidades domésticas." Fortaleza: Seminário Relações de Trabalho e Relacoes de Poder (mimeographed paper), 1986.

———. "O Homem na Matrifocalidade" in the *Cadernos de Pesquisa* (73): 38–47, May 1990, Fundação Carlos Chagas, São Paulo.

Smith, R.T. *The Negro Family in British Guyana*. London: Routledge and Keagan Paul, 1956.

———. "Culture and Social Structure in the Caribbean: Some Recent Work on Family and Kinship Studies." *Comparative Studies in Society and History*. New York: Cambridge University Press, 6: 24–64, 1963.

———. "The Matrifocal Family," in Goody, J. *The Character of Kinship*. Cambridge, Cambridge University Press, 1973.

———. ed. "Introduction," in *Kinship, Ideology and Practice in Latin America*. Chapel Hill: University of North Carolina, 1984.

———. *Kinship and Class in the West Indies*. Cambridge, Cambridge University Press, 1988. (Cambridge Studies in Social Anthropology 65).

Woortman, K. "A família trabalhadora." Ciências Sociais Hoje. São Paulo, ANPOCS/Cortez, 1984.

———. *Marginal Men and Dominant Women: Kinship and Sex Roles Among the Poor of Bahia*. Cambridge, Harvard University. Ph.D. dissertation 1975.

———. *A família das mulheres*. Rio de Janeiro/Brasilia, Tempo Brasileiro/CNPQ, 1987.

Part Five

GENDER AND KINSHIP IN CHANGING POLITICAL ECONOMIES

Muriel Nazzari's study of colonial Brazil examines changing naming patterns among the Portuguese colonizers. She argues that new naming practices that emerged temporarily in this context reflected a shifting balance of power in elite colonial families in favor of women. Her explanation of this change centers on the history of intermarriages between European men and Brazilian-born women. Early Portuguese settlers had intermarried with native women, thereby creating a racially mixed colonial elite. But European presumptions about racial and color hierarchies led elite families in later generations, in the face of an exclusively male immigrant flow from Europe, to focus on daughters who could marry Europeans and thus "whiten" the lineage. Among the founding families of São Paulo, daughters (and their family names) thus become more prominent in family strategy. Nazzari's work describes a particular historical situation in which racial and class strategies undermined some aspects of patrilineal practice.

17

The Waxing and Waning of Matrilineality in São Paulo, Brazil: Historical Variations in an Ambilineal System, 1500–1900

MURIEL NAZZARI

In this paper I will describe changes in the patterns of surnames used by heirs of estates in seventeenth-, eighteenth-, and nineteenth-century São Paulo. I assume that the surnames of people carry a symbolic claim, related to lineage, and thus to status. In many societies law or strong customs determine what a child's surname or surnames will be, and any evaluation of the meaning of such practices holds implications for the norms and values of the whole society.[1] Such would be the case of a study of North American surnames of legitimate children, who, until a few years ago, always bore their father's surname. This suggests that North American society was, therefore, and undoubtedly still is, a society with strong patrilineal tendencies. In the case of Spain, and many Spanish-American nations, all children bear both their father's and mother's surnames. Those societies therefore show ambilineal tendencies with an underlying patrilineality that shows up in the names of grandchildren, who bear their father's and mother's *paternal* surnames.

In Portugal and Brazil, the system was much more fluid because custom allowed the family to choose a child's surname or surnames. Thus, the surnames people bore depended on the wishes of their parents or even on their own; dropping or adding surnames during the individual's lifetime was common.[2] The more general practice was for persons to use both their mother's and father's surnames, thereby, like the Spanish system, resulting in an ambilineal naming tendency, with an underlying patrilineality.[3]

In this paper I will study instances within this ambilineal/patrilineal naming system in which the Portuguese settlers in São Paulo and their descendants favored the mother's surname over the father's, thus stressing the matrilineal over the patrilineal. I will argue that this tendency toward matrilineality was due to considerations of status and of family, racial and class strategies, and that it was also connected to patriarchalism. In the seventeenth century, these strategies led to marriage strategies that emphasized daughters over sons and may have afforded individual women a certain power within marriage.

The Portuguese founded the first European settlement in Brazil in 1532, bringing with them Christianity and Portuguese law and customs. The cultivation and exportation of sugar took off in the northeast in the late sixteenth century, but it was not until gold was discovered in Minas Gerais (in the southeast) at the end of the seventeenth century that the Portuguese Crown started taking an active interest in the rest of its Brazilian colony, and strengthened its governmental presence there.[4]

The enormous size of the country, the long distances between settlements, and the very slow growth of government administration meant that it was the extended family, clan or kindred group that governed the colonies at the local and regional levels in most parts of Brazil.[5] The kindred acquired their power through struggles with other groups. For instance, in seventeenth-century São Paulo, the Pires clan, headed by the widow D. Ignez Monteiro, called the *Matrona*, had a feud against the Camargo clan that lasted over twenty years and included several assassinations, various full-fledged battles between members of both clans and their Indian troops, and continual vying for political control in the municipal council. At that time, the town of São Paulo had some seven hundred Portuguese or *mestiço* households, plus at least five or six thousand semienslaved Indians.[6] After the peace treaty signed at the conclusion of the war between the Camargo and Pires clans, marriage alliances between the clans forged one large kindred group with several branches, which controlled the administrative, judicial and commercial activities of the region, including the large slaving expeditions that brought back the Indian labor necessary for the settlers' prosperity.[7]

These clans were controlled by a patriarch or, occasionally, a matriarch such as D. Ignez; the patriarch's widow in some instances took over, instead of one of his sons or another male relative.[8] Brazilian patriarchs or matriarchs had much power, especially in the sixteenth and seventeenth centuries, precisely because the colonial government was relatively weak. Without a police force or a regular army, the clan's private forces, which, in São Paulo, included thousands of Indian archers, carried out punitive or defensive actions. Government administration at the local level was in the hands of the municipal council and local judges, all recruited from the clan currently in power, who carried out the clan's agenda. The patriarch had power over all the members of his clan, including his adult sons and sons-in-law. Some of the power over sons and sons-in-law was lost in the eighteenth century with the *de facto* independence from their fathers and fathers-in-law that men gained through geographic mobility.[9] In the nineteenth century, the power of the patriarch over the kindred declined, and the state acquired more political power at the local level, organized a regular army and a police force, and started taking over functions such as education, previously performed by the family. The decline of patriarchal power showed regional differences, since in remote frontier areas it persisted well into the twentieth century.[10]

The view of an extended patriarchal family as the Brazilian norm has been challenged, demonstrating that the extended patriarchal family existed only among the elite.[11] Demographic studies have also shown that even these elite extended families did not usually live in the same house. The household norm in colonial times was the nuclear family, with a sizable minority of female-headed households.[12] Censuses, however, describe residential patterns but not other links between households such as self-identification with a certain kindred or clan led by a patriarch, or matriarch, who made important decisions for the kindred or clan as a whole.

These powerful kindred, called *parentelas* or clans, played a vital part in the regional history of colonial and nineteenth-century Brazil. These clans defined themselves as kin through ties of blood from both mother and father, and also through marriage ties and fictive-kin ties. The *parentela* influenced who gained access to resources and power in the region, and, in the frequent cases of competing clans, went through alternating periods of greater or lesser power.[13]

It was precisely in these strongly patriarchal clans or kindred in São Paulo that a tendency toward matrilineality can be found in the realm of surnames. The fluid customs regarding surnames in Brazil meant siblings did not necessarily bear the same surname. For instance, let us consider the children of Captain Domingos Fernandes and his wife Anna da Costa in seventeenth-century Santana de Parnaíba, captaincy of São Paulo. Their children were Anastacio da Costa, Thomé Fernandes da Costa, Felippe Fernandes Cabral, Izabel da Costa, Anna da Costa, and Agostinha Rodrigues. Of the six children, only two sons used their father's surname, while two sons and two daughters carried their mother's. The two other surnames used, Rodrigues and Cabral, were probably the surnames of maternal or paternal grandmothers.[14] In some cases in seventeenth-century São Paulo, all siblings bore the father's surname; in others, the mother's. The most frequent pattern, however, was mixed, and many persons carried both their parents' surnames, or even three or four.

Table 1. Percentage of Children Having Father's, Mother's or Other Surnames

	Number and Percentage		
Surname	17th century	18th century	19th century
Father's	205 (60%)	257 (69%)	560 (81%)
Mother's	110 (32%)	138 (37%)	125 (18%)
Other's	71 (21%)	91 (24%)	126 (18%)
TOTAL SURNAMES	386	486	811
Average number of surnames per person	1.13	1.3	1.18

Source: Names of 341 heirs found in 48 estates settled in São Paulo between 1640 and 1651; 372 in 68 estates between 1750 and 1769; 690 in 178 estates between 1850 and 1869.[a]
Notes: All percentages rounded off.

To search for a pattern within this genealogist's chaos, I analyzed statistically the names of all the heirs to a São Paolo sample of estates.[15] The results are in Tables 1, 2, and 3. Studying Table 1, we see that there was a tendency for children to bear their father's surname, a tendency that was to increase substantially by the nineteenth century, from sixty percent in the seventeenth century to eighty-one percent in the nineteenth, demonstrating an underlying patrilineal naming pattern. A look at Tables 2 and 3, however, shows that the increase was mostly in the surnames of daughters; daughters went from only forty-five percent who bore their father's name in the seventeenth century to seventy-six percent in the nineteenth. Sons showed a relatively consistent use of their father's surname, going from seventy-eight percent in the seventeenth century to eighty-four percent in the nineteenth. In the seventeenth century, it appears, daughters tended to follow their mother's lineage and sons their father's. In the eighteenth century, there was a growing tendency to carry several surnames, and the proportion of children of both sexes who bore both parents' names rose. By the nineteenth century, there was a lesser ten-

Table 2. Surnames of Sons

	Number and Percentage		
Surname	17th century	18th century	19th century
Father's	122 (78%)	156 (81%)	347 (84%)
Mother's	36 (23%)	59 (31%)	69 (17%)
Other's	27 (17%)	45 (23%)	86 (21%)
TOTAL SURNAMES	185	260	502
Average surnames per son	1.18	1.34	1.22

Source: Males in above sample, 157 in seventh century; 192 in eighteenth century; 412 in nineteenth century.
Notes: All percentages rounded off.

Table 3. Surnames of Daughters

Surname	Number and Percentage		
	17th century	18th century	19th century
Father's	83 (45%)	101 (56%)	218 (76%)
Mother's	74 (46%)	79 (44%)	66 (23%)
Other's	44 (24%)	46 (26%)	40 (14%)
TOTAL SURNAMES	201	226	324
Average number of surnames per daughter	1.09	1.25	1.13

Source: Females in samples used in Table 1: 184 in seventeenth century, 180 in eighteenth, 288 in nineteenth.[b]

Notes: All percentages rounded off.

dency to use more than one surname, and it was the presence of more daughters carrying their father's name that increased the proportion of children with their father's name.

To seek an explanation for these changes, we must analyze more carefully the characteristics of seventeenth-century São Paulo. Despite the main patrilineal tendency in the pattern of surnames chosen, there was an observable tendency toward matrilineal naming that requires explanation. It is significant that twenty-two percent of sons and fifty-four percent of daughters did not carry their father's surname. The fact that forty percent of all children did not bear their father's name at all demonstrates that patrilineal naming was far from dominant.

The qualitative material on the São Paulo society of the seventeenth century provides an even clearer sense of a matrilineal tendency. Coming from a society in which all children bear their father's name, a twentieth-century historian of seventeenth-century São Paulo is first struck by the many families in which all children carried their mother's surname and not their father's, despite their father's presence and despite being legitimate children.

These families were in many cases the most important families in São Paulo. For example, there is the family of Manoel João Branco, a Portuguese merchant who married Maria Leme in the early seventeenth century; none of their children carried his surname. Their three children were Anna Leme, Izabel Paes (the maternal grandmother's surname), and Franciso João Leme. Another example is that of the Frenchman Estevão Forquim. He married Anna de Proença, who belonged to the powerful Leme and Taques Pompeo families, and did not herself bear her father's surname.[16] Their children were Maria Leite Proença (Leite was the maternal grandfather's name); Theresa Leite; Pedro Dias Leite (Dias was the maternal grandfather's name); Francisco Leite; Claudio Forquim Leite; Antonio Leite Proença; and

Bernando Forquim dos Santos. Neither of their two daughters carried her father's name, and only two of their five sons did, one of whom bore it together with Leite, the maternal grandfather's name that was chosen for the majority of the children.

Why was there such a tendency toward matrilineal naming in these powerful families? In the cases of Manoel João Branco and Estevão Forquim, it probably was because these men were Portuguese newcomers, while their wives belonged to prominent families of São Paulo, affiliated with the kindreds that governed the region, and whose patriarchs dominated the nuclear families that composed the clans. Parents must have chosen their children's surnames partly in consideration of the respective status of each side of the family.

The question is, then, why were there more mothers of high-status families than fathers, as naming patterns suggest. I will argue that this matrilineal tendency in seventeenth- and eighteenth-century São Paulo names was due to the racial history of the region, especially miscegenation or interracial sexual unions.[17]

The origins of European settlement in São Paulo go back to around 1510, when two Portuguese sailors were shipwrecked on the southern coast of Brazil. After crossing the rugged coastal mountains, João Ramalho and Antonio Rodrigues encountered tribes of Tupinikin Indians, who welcomed them and allowed them to marry their chieftains' daughters. When the Portuguese founded São Vicente, the first settlement on the Brazilian coast, Ramalho and Rodrigues became inter-mediaries between the Tupinikin and the settlers, and moved to São Paulo with their families after it was founded by the Jesuits in 1559.[18] All the prominent families of São Paulo descended from these and other Portuguese men who came early to Brazil and married Indian women.

Many of these families later traced their descent exclusively through the female line, especially during the first hundred years of colonization. For instance, a prominent seventeenth-century São Paulo priest, Dr. Guilherme Pompêu de Almeida, traced his ancestry back to João Ramalho through his mother, Ana Lima, the daughter of João Pedrozo and Maria de Lima, who was, he wrote, "the daughter of João da Costa, who had married the daughter of Domingos Luiz o Carvoeiro, who had married the daughter of Jeronimo Dias Cortes, who had married the daughter of Bartholomeu Camacho, who had married the daughter of João Ramalho" (who had married the daughter of Tibiriça, chief of the Tupinikins).[19] Though he mentions only male European names, he traces his ancestry exclusively through the female line. Each Portuguese father diluted further the Tupinikin blood.

Another example is in the following genealogy of Manoel Dultra Machado, who died in 1752 and traced his ancestry to another of the founding fathers, Pedro Affonso, again exclusively through the female line.[20]

Pedro Affonso == Tapuia Indian woman
(Port.) ||
Pedro Gomes == Isabel Affonso
(Port.) ||
Gaspar Nunes == Antonia Gomes da Silva
(Port.?) ||
Paulo da Costa == Pardua do Amaral
||
Manoel Dultra
Machado == Maria da Silva
(Port.) ||
Manoel Dultra Machado

I have concluded that this emphasis on descent through the female line came about because of the settlers' interest in whitening their lineage. They had brought to Brazil the Iberian concern with "purity of blood" and its horror of "infected" races, such as Jews or Moors. Because Jews and Moors were not Christian, this thinking originally had a religious component, but this became confused in time with biological race. After Jews were either expelled from Portugal or obliged to convert to Christianity, the Inquisition's concern with the survival of Jewish practices led to a distinction between "New Christians" (converts) and "Old Christians." All important privileges, titles or positions in the Portuguese Empire came to be bestowed only on those who could prove they were "Old Christians," which eventually required genealogical proof of their "purity of blood." These racial concerns were easily transferred in the Americas to attitudes toward miscegenation with Indians and, especially, with blacks.[21]

It is not surprising, therefore, to discover that, despite having married Indian women, sixteenth- and seventeenth-century Portuguese settlers appear to have been concerned with race. In 1561, for instance, the municipal council of São Paulo sent a petition to the crown asking that it "please send deportees who are not thieves to this town to help populate it, for there are many mixed-blood women here whom they can marry."[22] The fact that the settlers were willing to accept Portuguese men of the lowest class to marry their *mestiça* daughters and granddaughters means that race was more important to them than class. They were recruiting men who would whiten the succeeding generations to elevate them above the semi-enslaved Indians and the remaining *mestiças* and to continue their families' rule of the region.[23]

Even members of the church showed their concern for the reproduction of the white race. For example, Father Leonardo Nunes wrote to his superiors from São

Vicente in 1551, happily reporting that he had persuaded several single Portuguese men to leave their Indian mistresses and marry the daughters of white men.[24] If he had been concerned only with the men's morality, he would have had them marry their Indian mistresses. What must have made the daughters of white men better wives in his opinion is that they had a mixture of Indian and white blood, so that the children they had with Portuguese men would have much more European blood than would the children of pure-blooded Indian women.

The sons of white men, on the other hand, had almost no potential white brides, since, except for a handful of Portuguese couples who settled in São Paulo in the mid-sixteenth century, practically all European immigrants until the nineteenth century were male.[25] This fact gave the mixed-blood daughters of European men an advantage over their brothers. Only daughters could whiten the lineage through their marriages with European males, which explains why the geneology of important residents of São Paulo went back to the founding fathers through the female line. Each generation of daughters who married Europeans meant a whiter lineage, which, in a racist society, could more successfully compete for power.

This fact undoubtedly contributed to certain practices favoring daughters over sons in seventeenth-century São Paulo. Most daughters received in dowry much more than what their brothers would inherit many years later. And, if they had not married by the time the first parent died, daughters received large bequests that also gave them an economic advantage over their brothers.[26]

Though Portuguese husbands contributed the correct genes, many times they brought little else, so that, especially if the wife was from a prominent family and brought much more property to the marriage than her husband, it was only logical to choose to use her surname for their children more frequently than his. This was especially important when she belonged to one of the main clans or kindred, and bestowing one of the clan's names on her children meant their children's greater identification with it, with the concomitant access to power that that signified.

Moreover, the use of the mother's surname for most or all children in the seventeenth and eighteenth centuries may have been a reflection of the power of the patriarch, her father, over his son-in-law, especially true of the cases in which the wife's family was prominent and the husband was an unknown newcomer with no family of his own in the region. By the nineteenth century, as the power of the clan's patriarch over sons, sons-in-law, grandsons and nephews diminished, the patriarchal power of husbands within the nuclear family increased, and most children now bore their father's name.

Since the Portuguese man who married a woman from a prominent family of São Paulo in the seventeeth or eighteenth century received access to the clan's power through his wife, and usually also received all the property the couple owned from his wife, he was beholden to her. This fact undoubtedly gave such wives more power within the nuclear family than we would assume in such a patriarchal society. I have found evidence to support this view in a case in which a husband explicitly deferred to his wife's judgment.[27] There were also instances in which it was mothers, rather than fathers, who decided what property, or how many and which slaves or cattle would constitute a daughter's dowry.[28] Furthermore, in 1698 Governor Antonio Paes de Sande wrote that the women of São Paulo were "industrious, and more inclined to marry their daughters to strangers who would raise their status, than to local men who were their equals."[29] This confirms the importance of mothers in the arrangement of their daughters' marriages.

Another characteristic of São Paulo colonial society, which has been demonstrated by demographic studies, was a strong tendency toward matrilocality.[30] The tendency for couples to live near the wife's family may also be partly the consequence of the importance of the mother's family and of the large number of male Portuguese newcomers who had no parents near whom they could live.

The search for a whiter lineage also helps explain another practice of matrilineal tendency. I have found several families in which all sons entered the church, and only daughters continued the lineage. Father Guilherme Pompêo de Almeida is one example, an only son with two married sisters. Another is the family of Manoel Velloso, a Portuguese merchant who married in the early eighteenth century into the old Vieira family from São Paulo. Their four daughters married Portuguese immigrants, but of their three sons, two became priests and the third a monk.[31] Another such family is that of Maria Vieira da Cunha who married a Portuguese, Gaspar de Mattos, in 1706.[32] Their children were Frei Sebastião Maria Mattos, a Carmelite monk; Antonio Xavier de Mattos, who was sent to a university in Portugal, where he got into trouble and fled to Spain, becoming a soldier there and never marrying; Frei Francisco de Mattos, a Carmelite; José Vieira, a Jesuit monk; a daughter who died as a child from smallpox; and Maria Josepha de Mattos, who married a Portuguese.

We can only surmise why these and other families chose such a route for their children. It may have been due to the importance of religion in the eighteenth century. Not only was the Christian faith a vital part of society, but having relatives among the clergy was very prestigious. However, it is possible that, even as late as the eighteenth century, the families of São Paulo chose to continue their lineage through females who married immigrants as a means to whiten the lineage. Whether it was deliberate that the line was not continued through the male line, or just a chance result of the religious vocations of all sons, these cases certainly show that it was possible in this ambilineal society to continue one's lineage exclusively through women.

Class interests could also explain the tendency to matrilineality in São Paulo. The Brazilian ambilineal system, in which individuals and families were free to choose their surnames to emphasize one or the other lineage, made it possible for people to use descent through the female line to exalt their status, and to allow their own bloodline to be reproduced only through their daughters, in order to whiten their lineage. The racial aspect of this behavior had a class component to it, since the upper class was predominantly of mostly European blood. When people strove to whiten their lineage by having their daughters marry unknown Portuguese new-comers, they were therefore actually using a strategy to preserve or advance their class status. Moreover, within this class strategy it would be counterproductive for children to adopt their immigrant father's lowly name when they had a prestigious name available on their mother's side. Matrilineal names were therefore a strategy for class preservation or advancement. By the nineteenth century, when the issue of race was no longer important to the elite because there was a large pool of mar-riage partners of both sexes who were white, these matrilineal practices petered out. The change toward greater patrilineal naming tendencies was undoubtedly also furthered by the decline in the nineteenth century of the patriarch's power, especially over his sons-in-law, with the concomitant rise of the individual son-in-law's power over his wife and children.

That Brazilians have not entirely lost their matrilineal naming tendency can be seen in the case of the ex-president of Brazil, Fernando Collor de Mello, impeached in 1992. He carries the names of both parents: de Mello is his father's surname, Collor his mother's. He was known, however, as President Collor. This may well be because his father's family was not nationally known, whereas his matrilineal grandfather was a well-known politician of the 1930s.

Notes

[1] It can be argued that the surnames of mar-ried women also have symbolic meaning. For changes in usage of married women's surnames in São Paulo, see Muriel Nazzari, *Disappearance of the Dowry: Women, Families, and Social Change in São Paulo, Brazil* (Stanford: Stanford University Press, 1991), pp. 140–142.

[2] See Maria Luiza Marcílio, "Variation des noms et prénoms au Brésil," in *Annales de démo-graphie historique* (1972): pp. 345-353. For the same fluidity of naming in Portugal, see Antonio de Villasboas, *Nobiliaria portuguesa* (Lisbon,

1676), p. 164. He also shows that the Portuguese system was openly ambilineal regarding nobility which was transmitted by both father and mother; when only the mother had noble blood, children inherited it from her.

[3] Another difference with the Spanish system is that the Portuguese place the paternal surname last, whereas the Spanish place the maternal last.

[4] E. Bradford Burns, *A History of Brazil* (New York: Columbia University Press, 1980); Caio Prado, Jr., *The Colonial Background of Modern Brazil*, trans. by Suzette Macedo (Berkeley: Uni-

versity of California Press, 1969); Sergio Buarque de Holanda, ed., *História geral da civilização brasileira*, 7 vols. (São Paulo: Diffel/Difusão, 1981), vol. 1.

5 Linda Lewin, *Politics and Parentela: A Case Study of Family-Based Oligarchy in Brazil* (Princeton: Princeton University Press, 1987); and Charles Wagley, *An Introduction to Brazil* (New York: Columbia University Press, 1963), pp. 184–204. See Jenny Wormald, "The Blood Feud in Early Modern Scotland," in John Bossy, ed., *Disputes and Settlements: Law and Human Relations in the West* (Cambridge: Cambridge University Press, 1983) for a similar situation in Scotland. In *Politics*, p. 132, Lewin argues successfully that clans as such did not exist in Brazil, since clans by definition are formed by unilineal descent from a certain ancestor, and Brazilian kindred were ambilineal. I will, however, continue to use the word clan interchangeably with kindred, because it was frequently used by the actors themselves.

6 See Serafim Leite, *História da Companhia de Jesus no Brasil*, 10 vols. (Rio de Janeiro: Civilização Brasileira, 1938–1945), vol. 6, p. 290.

7 Luiz de Aguiar Costa Pinto, *Lutas de famílias no Brasil* (São Paulo: Brasiliana, 1980).

8 D. Ignez Monteiro was the matriarch who headed the Pires clan during the feud. When a truce was finally arbitrated by the Governor-General of Brazil, and accepted by a male delegate of the Pires clan, the Governor-General still felt the need to write to D. Ignez to solicit her full cooperation, stating, "I understand that you are the principal person on whose judgment depends the conclusion of peace that I attempt to bring about between the Pires and Camargos and which is so important to the stability of the captaincy of São Paulo." Pinto, *Lutas*, p. 89.

9 Nazzari, *Disappearance*, pp. 44–45.

10 For the decline of patriarchal power, see Antônio Candido, "The Brazilian Family," in T. Lynn Smith and Alexander Marchant, eds., *Brazil: Portrait of Half a Continent* (Westport, CT: Greenwood Press, 1972); also Nazzari, *Disappearance*, chapters 7 and 8. The first scholar to use the term "Brazilian patriarchal family" was Gilberto

Freyre, *The Masters and the Slaves* (New York: Knopf, 1956). Also Freyre, "The Patriarchal Basis of Brazilian Society," and Charles Wagley, "Luso-Brazilian Kinship Patterns: The Persistance of a Cultural Tradition," in Joseph Maier and Richard Weatherhead, eds., *The Politics of Change in Latin America* (New York: Praeger, 1964). Also Emílio Willems, "The Structure of the Brazilian Family," in *Social Forces* 31, No. 4 (1953) pp. 339–345.

11 A challenge to both Freyre's and Candido's arguments is in Mariza Corrêa, "Repensando a família patriacal brasileira," in Maria Suely Kofes de Almeida, ed., *Colcha de retalhos: estudos sobre a família no Brasil* (São Paulo: Brasiliense, 1982).

12 See Maria Luiza Marcílio, *A cidade de São Paulo, povoamento e população, 1750–1850* (São Paulo: Pioneira, 1974), pp. 105, 159, 163; Elizabeth A. Kuznesof, "Household Composition and Headship Rates as Related to Changes in Mode of Production: São Paulo, 1765–1836," in *Comparative Studies in Society and History* 22, No. 1 (Jan. 1980), pp. 86, 88; Donald Ramos, "Marriage and the Family in Colonial Vila Rica," in *Hispanic American Historical Review* 55, No. 2 (May 1975), pp. 200–225.

13 Linda Lewin, "Some Historical Implications of Kinship Organization for Family-based Politics in the Brazilian Northeast," in *Comparative Studies in Society and History* 21, No. 2 (April 1979), pp. 264–265.

14 Domingos Fernandes, 1653, vol. 27, *Inventários e Testamentos*, 44 vols. (São Paulo: Arquivo do Estado de São Paulo, 1921–1975), hereafter referred to as *IT*.

15 This sample, used in Nazzari, *Disappearance*, consists, for the seventeenth century, of all forty-eight published *inventários* (settlements of estates) in which the deceased had married daughters as heirs (or their descendants) for the period 1640 to 1651 in *IT*; for the eighteenth century, all sixty-eight manuscript *inventários* with married daughters as heirs for the period 1750 to 1769 found in "Inventarios Não Publicados" in the Arquivo do Estado de São Paulo (hereafter, INP, AESP); for the nineteenth century, all 178 manuscript inventários with married daughters

as heirs for the period 1850 to 1869 found in "Segundo Ofício da Família" in the Arquivo do Ministerio de Justiça.

16 See Pedro Taques de Almeida Paes Leme, *Nobiliarquia paulistana histórica e genealógica,* 3 vols. (São Paulo: Universidade de São Paulo, 1980), vol. I, p. 197.

17 Nazzari, *Disappearance,* pp. 31–34.

18 For the early history of São Paulo, see Richard Morse, *From Community to Metropolis: A Biography of São Paulo* (Gainesville: University of Florida Press, 1958); Frei Gaspar da Madre de Deus, *Memorias para a historia de São Vicente hoje chamada de São Paulo* 1797, reprint., (São Paulo: Martins, 1953), p. 122; Affonso d'E. Taunay, *São Paulo nos primeiros annos (1554–1601)* and *História da Cidade de São Paulo* (São Paulo: Melhoramentos, 1953).

19 See Nazzari, *Disappearance,* p. 33.

20 Source: Taques, *Nobiliarquia,* vol. I, p. 11; also Luis Gonzaga da Silva Leme, *Genealogia paulistana,* 9 vols. (São Paulo: Duprat, 1903–1905), vol. 9, under Dultra Machados.

21 See Charles R. Boxer, *Race Relations in the Portuguese Colonial Empire* (Oxford: Clarendon Press, 1963); and Evaldo Cabral de Mello, *O nome e o sangue. Uma fraude genealógica no Pernambuco colonial* (São Paulo, 1989).

22 Maria Beatriz Nizza da Silva, *Sistema de casamento no Brasil colonial* (São Paulo: T.A. Queiroz, 1984), p. 17.

23 Caio Prado, Jr., in *The Colonial Background of Modern Brazil,* pp. 123–124, tells how European travelers commented in the nineteenth century about the good life of Europeans who married in Brazil into families who wanted to "purify their blood," though in that century this wish was usually related to traces of black, not Indian, blood. For the importance of race in marriage in other parts of Latin America, see Verena Martinez-Alier, *Marriage, Class and Colour in Nineteenth-Century Cuba: A Study of Racial Attitudes and Sexual Values in a Slave Society* (London: Cambridge University Press, 1974); and Robert McCaa, "Calidad, Class, and Marriage in Colonial Mexico: The Case

of Parral, 1788-90," *Hispanic American Historical Review* 64, no. 3 (Aug. 1984), pp. 477-501.

24 Silva, *Sistema de casamento,* p. 18.

25 This is my conclusion after studying Silva Leme, *Genealogia.*

26 The inheritance of property was ambilineal or bilateral, not only because legal equally partible inheritance among all children meant both sons and daughters inherited, but because children inherited separately from their father and from their mother at the death of each. Since the inheritance of property was judicially controlled, it never deviated from the bilateral. Dowry was considered an advance on a daughter's inheritance, but in seventeenth-century São Paulo daughters who received greater dowries than their subsequent inheritance were not obliged to return the difference to their siblings. Testators could freely will only one-third of their estate. When a daughter received a bequest from that third, it was added to her legitimate share (equal for all siblings) to give her a great advantage. For the inheritance system, see Cândido Mendes de Almeida, ed., *Codigo philippino ou ordenaçes do reino de Portugal,* 14th ed. (Rio de Janeiro: Typographia do Instituto Philomatico, 1870), Liv. 4, Tit. 97 and Tit. 96, par. 12. For a description of the favoring of daughters, see Nazzari, *Disappearance,* Chapter 2.

27 See Nazzari, *Disappearance,* pp. 26–27.

28 See Nazzari, *Disappearance,* pp. 20–21; 26–27.

29 Maria Odila da Silva Dias, *Quotidiano e poder em São Paulo no século XIX: Anna Gertrudes de Jesus* (São Paulo: Brasiliense, 1984), p. 75.

30 For the matrilocal tendency see Elizabeth Kuznesof, "Clans, the Militia, and Territorial Government: The Articulation of Kinship with Polity in Eighteenth-Century São Paulo," in David J. Robinson, ed., *Social Fabric and Spatial Structure in Colonial Latin America* (New York: Microfilms International, 1979).

31 See Silva Leme, *Genealogia,* vol. 2, p. 474, and vol. 8, under Maciéis; also Manoel Velloso, 1752, AESP, INP #ord. 528 c. 51.

32 Taques, *Nobiliarquia,* vol. II, p. 39.

[a] See note 15 for definition of the sample used.

[b] The number of daughters in the nineteenth century is much lower in this table than that of sons in the former, because I did not include daughters who bore no surname. The nineteenth-century sample was different from the preceding ones because it included a large proportion of small proprietors whose wives and daughters were listed with no surname.

Jean O'Brien searches through sparse documentation for clues about how Native American women adjusted to colonial domination in New England. (Indeed, the scarcity of evidence about Native American understandings of kinship and gender relations is itself a product of the colonial assault on indigenous cultures and cultural memory.) This was a "shattered society" in which colonialism and the intrusion of the world market wreaked havoc with preexisting family and kinship practices. This essay highlights the links between kin and gender relations and modes of production, and demonstrates how kin relations were vulnerable to dramatic upheavals in the political economy such as those brought by European colonial settlement. These changes affected women, who traditionally worked the land, particularly adversely. Moreover, the economic activities of Native American men, who moved into military service and whaling as Indian land were taken over by Europeans, exacerbated the detrimental economic impact of colonialism by weakening kin ties.

18

Divorced from the Land: Accommodation Strategies of Indian Women in Eighteenth-Century New England

JEAN O'BRIEN

In 1624, Edward Winslow, Governor of Plymouth colony, observed about Native Americans that:

> The women live a most slavish life; they carry all their burdens, set and dress their corn, gather it in, and seek out for much of their food, beat and make ready the corn to eat and have all household care lying upon them.[1]

Winslow's use of the term "slavish" is instructive. The portrayal of the Native American woman as "squaw drudge" who toiled endlessly for her "lazie husband" was both a common English analysis of Native American division of labor in the northeastern woodlands and a commentary upon English expectations about gender roles.[2] Observers viewed Indian women as "slaves" because, unlike English women, they performed virtually all of the agricultural labor in their societies.[3] Indeed, most labor that the English would have regarded as male work was performed by Indian women.

The "squaw drudge" permeated early observations of Native Americans in the northeast. Two centuries later, different images of Indian women could be found in local accounts. Consider the following:

> The last Indian here was "Hannah Shiner," a full-blood who lived with "Old Toney," a noble-souled mulatto man.... Hannah was kind-hearted, a faithful friend, a sharp enemy, a judge of herbs, a weaver of baskets, and a lover of rum.[4]

This description, taken from a nineteenth-century history of Medford, Massachusetts, reflects not just the passage of time but also the extent to which relations, roles and expectations had changed on both sides of a sustained cultural encounter.

The juxtaposition of these two images reveals crucial changes in the circumstances of Indian women in New England. Three key structural changes differentiate the historical eras, and help explain the fundamentally different portrayals. First, Indian societies that were "tribal" and politically independent units prior to intensive colonization became effectively "detribalized" and politically encompassed by the late seventeenth century. By this time, most Indian individuals and families were incorporated into English communities, in small clusters that rendered Indians virtually invisible within the context of the dominant society. Second, the prosperity of Indian societies, based on diversified agricultural economies and intensive use of seasonally available plant and game resources, was undermined as Indians became almost entirely landless by the end of the seventeenth century. The central feature of subsistence was eliminated, requiring fundamental changes that resulted in the recasting of Native gender roles. Third, Indian societies that stressed communal values, sharing and reciprocity were thrust into a market economy with the advent of colonization.[5] These structural changes required massive adjustment, and produced a myriad of shifting and often contradictory responses.

In addressing these transformations, I will focus more directly on the issue of "gendered division of labor" than on the important problem of lineality in the northeastern woodlands. Use of the dichotomous construction of matrilineal/patrilineal obscures much diversity in means of delineating the ordering of families and descent, power relations and much more. Due to the paucity of early sources that provide detailed information on social organization, and the early occurrence of devastating epidemics throughout the region, there is much we will never know about the "precontact" shape of social organization in the northeastern woodlands. Indian peoples in early New England were concerned overwhelmingly with the survival of their shattered societies, and the devastation of early contact certainly must have obscured their previous shape at least to some extent. About all that is evident is that, by the eighteenth century, patrilineal naming practices predominated; whether this was the case because it had always been so, or because these were the rules by which the conquering society operated, is not so clear.[6]

About a gendered division of labor, much more seems to be clear. Most scholars agree that women performed most agricultural labor (except growing tobacco), built and transported bark or mat wigwams from place to place, manufactured baskets and pottery, gathered shellfish and wild foodstuff, processed hides, made clothing and raised children. Men also made some household tools and were the principal woodworkers: making canoes and fortifications, for example.[7]

By 1700, Native American groups in New England had a long history of encounters with Europeans. Imported diseases had decimated these societies, with many groups suffering demographic declines on the order of ninety percent. Military conquest followed quickly on the heels of epidemiological devastation. The last major war in southeastern New England ended in 1676, shattering those Native groups who had hitherto avoided total English domination. These events effectively terminated political independence for Indians in that region, and rendered many aspects of the aboriginal economy obsolete through massive displacement and dispossession. Amidst the tumult and permeating pain, Native peoples went about the process of rebuilding their shattered societies.

Missionary sponsorship had secured land bases for several Indian groups in the seventeenth century as part of their platform for change. Here, English expectations about gender roles structured Indian accommodations to the dominant society.[8] Indian groups were allowed to retain small plots of land in exchange for responsiveness to missionary messages about cultural change. They were expected to erect English-style towns, with men performing agricultural duties and women receiving training in "household skills," especially spinning and weaving. Indians were to adopt English work habits, individual ownership of land, English tastes in material culture, and values structured by a market economy. Some Indians did make fundamental transformations along these lines, but success in the market economy did not follow so easily. Many Indians were landless at the beginning of the eighteenth century, and they continued to lose land.[9] Many were encompassed within the flourishing English settlements, finding niches in colonial economies, performing agricultural and nonagricultural labor.

In some senses, Jacob and Leah Chalcom symbolized the transformation that was conceptualized by the English. He purchased land, established an English-style farm, and built a frame house in Natick, an important mission town established seventeen miles southwest of Boston. He was involved actively in the local land market, buying and selling small parcels as he strove to upgrade his farm. The cultural priorities of this family are visible in the ways in which they chose to raise their children. The Chalcom children were literate, and his daughters were given dowries upon their marriages to local Indian men.[10] After his death, Jacob Chalcom's estate included a thirty-acre home lot and "Buildings thereon," plus other lands, household goods and husbandry tools, a horse, a cow and books. After debts against his estate were discharged, fifty-two acres of land remained to be divided among his heirs.[11]

The women in Chalcom's family had made corresponding changes in their lifeways, including their separation from agricultural tasks. Leah Chalcom and her widowed daughters Esther Sooduck and Hepzibeth Peegun inherited land from from their husbands and their father. In 1759 they petitioned the Massachusetts General Court to sell their forty-six acres, arguing that "as your Petitioners [have been] brought up to Household business, [we are] incapable of improving said lands."[12] This created obvious problems for the three widows. They requested that their lands be sold and the money be put out to earn interest for their income and support, a strategy adopted by a number of Indian women. The implication is quite clear: these women were no longer farmers, and were thus unable to "improve" the land, except insofar as it represented a monetary resource. The mother and daughters recognized that English financial strategies could sustain them and prolong the nurturing functions of land from which they were effectively torn loose. Putting money "at interest" constituted one strategy for women who had maintained clear "legal" connections to the land.

The "Household business" to which Leah Chalcom and her daughters referred reflects the efforts of English missionaries to realign Native American gender roles. Biblical imperatives motivated them as they sought to train Indian women in English housewifery skills, and perhaps to contribute to cash income as well. In 1648, missionary John Eliot wrote that:

> The women are desirous to learn to spin, and I have procured Wheels
> for sundry of them, and they can spin pretty well. They begin to grow
> industrious, and find something to sell at Market all the yeer long.[13]

Some Indian women continued to pursue these tasks that had been pushed so vigorously in the early years of intensive English-Indian contact. Fifteen percent of inventories of Indian estates from Natick filed between 1741 and 1763 listed spinning wheels.[14] Ruth Thomas, who died in 1758, was described as a weaver in her probate docket. Esther Freeborn and Hannah Lawrence, sisters who both left wills, were described as spinsters.[15]

Esther Sooduck, also a weaver, died in 1778. Her probate documents vividly evoke the kinds of changes Indian women faced, even though very few accumulated and held onto material goods as successfully as Esther had.[16] Her house, described as "much out of repair," nonetheless contained an impressive array of furnishings, and sat upon thirty acres of land. Included among her belongings were a bed and bedstead, a rug, a table and two chairs, plus knives, forks and pewter. She read her two old bibles with "speticals." She owned two spinning wheels, as well as baskets and "Baskets Stuf."[17] Apparently merged in her economic pursuits were English skills (spinning and weaving) and Native American artisanal production (basket-making.)

Native American women displayed transformations in their work habits, material life, aesthetic emphases, and even their physical appearance. Hannah Lawrence owned several articles of clothing when she died in the 1770s, including several gowns and aprons (one of them linen) as well as quilted petticoats and a pair of shoes with buckles.[18] Cloth replaced animal skins, petticoats and gowns were substituted for breechcloths and leggings. These accommodations were rooted in more than a century of profound cultural change. Indeed, in the most fundamental sense they represent an *up*-rooting, a broken connection: English-style clothing signified the distance women had moved from their former way of life.

Indeed, Native American women in eighteenth-century New England were *divorced* from the land. English insistence upon cultural change meant for Indian women a stark separation: once the principal producers of the crucial agricultural element of subsistence economies, women were expected to sever the vital connection they had to the soil as its principal cultivators and nurturers. Though the English who insisted upon these changes may not have noticed, their models for transformation went well beyond a simple shift in the gendered organization of labor. On the practical level, knowledge and skills were altered drastically, and the content of material life was entirely recast. On the ideological level, less visible reverberations can only be imagined in individual and corporate identities, belief systems and other deeply rooted cultural values. Indeed, one possible explanation for the ultimate failure of Indian men as farmers in a market economy centers on their reluctance to engage in such "effeminate" pursuits as tending the crops—women's work.[19]

Leah Chalcom, Esther Sooduck, Hannah Lawrence—all of these women came from Indian-dominated towns. They all lived in Indian-dominated towns with their land ownership sanctioned by the English, at least in this nominal sense the beneficiaries of missionary endeavors.[20] Their relative success in emulating English ways was increasingly infrequent throughout the eighteenth century, as Indian landowners became steadily dispossessed. Other Indians were uprooted utterly almost from the beginning of their contact with the English. They adjusted to English invasion differently, mapping out alternative kinds of lifeways. After the 1660s, for example:

> The remnant of the Pocumtuck Confederacy, adopting in part the English costume, had gathered about the English in the valley towns.... Here they lived a vagabond life, eking out, as they could, a miserable

323

existence on the outskirts of civilization.… So hampered, their stock of
venison or beaver, with which to traffic for English comforts, was small,
and the baskets and birch brooms made by the squaws ill supplied their
place.[21]

This is a stark outline of the principal difficulties Indians faced in making the transition to landlessness within a society emphasizing the market. With the possibilities for hunting gone, and no land—what remained? Production of traditional
Indian crafts constituted one possibility for women, who remained important in
the economy, and maintained this traditional economic role which was possible
even when they were landless.

Craft production by Indian women constituted one of the crucial threads that
ran through the seventeenth, eighteenth and nineteenth centuries in New England.
Indian women in the eighteenth century were engaged especially in basket-making
as an economic activity, but other artisanal skills were added as well. In 1764, Abigail Moheag attested that she was "64 years of Age and…a widow [for] more than
fifteen years and hath…by her Industery in the business of making Brooms Baskets
and horse Collars; Supported her Self till about two years ago She was taken sick."[22]
The inventory from Hannah Speen's estate listed "baskets and barkes, brombs and
brombsticks."[23] Craftwork, including the production of "new" items like horse collars, moved from the periphery of women's economic activities to the center, as
Indian women became enmeshed in the market and were no longer engaged in
farming. For some women, craft production was fundamentally redefined. No
longer one activity in an integrated economy, artisanal activities became specialized and divorced from seasonal rhythms and a principal means to get a living.

Wage labor constituted another possibility for Indian women. It remains unclear
just what kind of work Indian women were doing, or what it was they received in
return. In 1755, the circumstances of some Indian women at Mattakeset were such
that "at present they live among White People, and work with them for a living."[24]
The formula in these situations may have involved the contribution of unskilled
and unspecialized labor, perhaps domestic work, in exchange for small wages or
some degree of basic sustenance. The existence of small clusters of Indians in virtually every Massachusetts town suggests that the lives of English colonists and
Indians were intertwined in ways we are only beginning to understand.[25]

Disruption of Native societies extended to every sphere, requiring their constant
adjustment. Marginal individuals, that is, those with few relatives or friends, Indian
or non-Indian, and little in the way of economic resources, suffered most. Prior to
Indian enmeshment in the market, caretaking and nursing constituted central kinship obligations. During the eighteenth century, as kinship networks thinned, fam-

ilies fractured, and involvement in the market made prosperity precarious at best, individuals could no longer count on thick networks of relatives to care for them when they were in need of shelter, sustenance or support. Nursing and caretaking became commodified and unreliable. These developments represented the cumulative effect of generations of demographic decline, military conquest, economic disruption and cultural transformation. Even when an intact family survived, taking on traditional obligations in this changed context could spell economic ruin. Abigail Speen reported to the General Court in 1747 that she had:

> by Reason of her great age & infirmities…been long and still is Unable to do anything to Support herself, & so having cast herself on Mr. Joseph Graves of S^d Natick [an Englishman] She has been kind entertained & Supported at his House now for near two years, & has nothing to recompense S^d Graves with nor to procure for her the Necessaries of Life for the time present & to come.[26]

This woman had land, and she liquidated the remainder of her estate in order to pay Graves. No doubt he realized that his "investment" was secured by that plot of land she owned. This replacement of Indian kinship obligations with market-driven social welfare occurred throughout New England, and accounted for much dispossession of Indian peoples who had little recourse remaining.

Just as Abigail Speen cast herself on Joseph Graves, Indian women cast themselves upon other Indian women, too. What differed in the eighteenth century was that these women were not necessarily relatives, and that nursing or caretaking was often given in exchange for monetary compensation. The administrators of the estate of Elizabeth Paugenit, for example, allowed nearly two pounds to Hannah Awassamug "for nursing."[27] Sarah Wamsquan was cared for by Eunice Spywood, among others. Englishman John Jones petitioned the General Court in 1770, setting forth Sarah's pitiful story, and begging: "let something be done that Shall Speedily relieve the poor person that has her—or they will perish together."[28] Town authorities did not always countenance such arrangements. In 1765, when "Sarah Short a molatto woman Last from Wrentham [was] Taken in by Esther Sodeck," Natick selectmen feared she would become a town charge and warned her that she should leave town.[29]

Banding together just to survive, these women struggled within a radically changing world, their situation complicated by complete dislocation from land and community. One response was to move constantly in search of a niche. As landlessness accelerated, a pattern of Indian vagrancy emerged: this pattern, accepted by the dominant society as natural, was also an accommodation strategy. An Englishman of Dorchester petitioned the General Court in 1753 as follows:

> An Indian Woman called Mercy Amerquit, I think Born Somewhere about Cape-Cod, but had no settled Dwellingplace any where,… Strolled about from one Town & Place to another, & sometimes she wrought for Persons that wanted her work[. She] came to my House…and desired liberty to tarry a little while, and your Pet^r condescended, expecting that she would go some other place in a little time (as their manner is) and what work she did for your Pet^r she was paid for as she earned it.[30]

It is clear from this passage that English observers expected Indians to "wander." Their semisedentary existence had always been regarded most simplistically as nomadism. In the eighteenth century this translated into constant movement, "from one Town & Place to another…as their manner is." In this case, an arrangement seems to have been negotiated which involved Mercy Amerquit performing labor for wages as well as her temporary residence with the narrator. He expected her to "go [to] some other place in a little time," and the arrangement was regarded as rather unexceptional. The only reason this relationship was documented at all was because the woman died while in the petitioner's residence and he sought to recover money for her burial.

The story of Mercy Amerquit was by no means unique. An Englishman from Roxbury reported to the General Court about sixty-year-old Hannah Comsett, who became ill at his house:

> She informs that her Mother was born at Barnstable, she at Scituate, and that for 30 years past she has been [strolling] about from Town to Town geting her living where she could but never lived During that time the space of one year at any Town at any time.[31]

Though Hannah Comsett's mobility seems rather astounding, there are so many similar stories available that it is certain it was not an aberration.

The mechanisms behind Indian vagrancy were complex. Prior to the arrival of the English, Indian societies in New England enjoyed abundant economies that depended upon the extensive use of resources and a semisedentary lifeway. Scheduled mobility lay at the center of this system. In the eighteenth century, Indian migrations may have been scheduled, but if so, they were motivated by very different priorities and they were not governed by Indian communities. Probably kinship ties and some knowledge of labor markets entered into movements, but for women like Mercy and Hannah, there was nothing particularly patterned about their shifting about. Instead of relying upon community knowledge of seasonally available resources, perhaps it was the hope of locating a charitable English settler that spurred on the solitary and needy Indian woman. One important element that differentiated earlier migratory practices from new patterns was their largely individual nature; this new "vagrancy" drew upon older patterns and places, but was not necessarily kin-group sponsored movement with planned, deliberate ends in mind. At the heart of the problem lay landlessness, whether from military conquest in the seventeenth century, or from failure in the market economy in the eighteenth. "Divorced" from the land initially when their economic role was redefined along English lines, a much more literal separation had been accomplished for most by the middle of the eighteenth century.

The situation of these women hints at two recurrent themes regarding Indian women in eighteenth-century New England. First, transiency is graphically described in a manner consistent with the emerging problem of landless poverty in New England more generally. The "wandering Indian" had much in common with the "strolling poor."[32] The extent to which these are stories of women alone, or mostly alone, is the second theme, and it is most striking.

Where were the men? The evidence suggests that, despite the missionary model of settled agriculture performed by men on family farms, transiency also remained characteristic of even landowning Indian men. Most Indian landowners lost what they had over time, and the tendency for Indian men to enter service in two areas— military service and the emerging whaling industry—contributed to a grossly distorted sort of transiency.[33] As a result of their participation in these activities, Indian men were absent for extended periods of time, engaged in dangerous pursuits that seriously jeopardized their lives and well-being and compromised their ability to function effectively within the English-dominated society. Whaling, in fact, fostered the same sort of debt peonage that proved so devastating in fur trade relationships.[34] These orientations contributed to uncertainty and instability for Indian families, and also reduced the number of Indian men available and desirable as spouses. Interpretations of the involvement of Indian men in the military and in labor at sea have stressed continuity in skills and culturally determined priorities that they offered.[35] One might also read into this context an element of escapism; evidence may be found in scattered narratives of Indian men "absconding" as difficult circumstances evolved into insurmountable economic and legal problems. Such was the case for Eunice Spywood, whose "Husband Some Years Ago Absconded and left her in very distressing Circumstances, and he…never returned."[36]

Whatever the underlying motivation, Indians of both sexes suffered through periods of devastating demographic change as a direct result of participation of Indian men in military service, especially. The impact of the Seven Years War on Indian enclaves in New England was enormous. In 1756, a cluster of Indians at Mettakesett in Pembroke, Massachusetts, pleaded to the General Court:

327

> that Several of us [have] in the late Warrs, lost our husbands & Sons, & Some of our Sons [are] yet in S^d Service, & that some of us are old, blind, & bed rid & helpless poor Creatures, Many of us [are] old Women & want help.[37]

Indians of Eastham and Harwich in Barnstable County, Massachusetts complained many of their men "Have Died in ye Service & left their Squa & Children in Distressing Circumstances."[38] In 1761, Ezra Stiles visited Portsmouth, Rhode Island. He reported that "4 Ind. Boys [had] enlisted in the service...only one Boy more in Town, & he [is] about 10 y. old. I can't find...any Ind. Men in Town,...but several Squaws, perhaps 8 or 10." At Milford, Connecticut, the population shifted from twenty male Indians in 1755 at the beginning of the Seven Years War to, in 1761, "not one: but 3 or 4 Squaws."[39]

Even when they did return, many Indian men were rendered incapable of working to support themselves or their families as a result of war-related disabilities. Thomas Awassamug complained to the General Court in 1761 that

> he having been engaged...as a Soldier...for more than thirty years past, has indured inexpressible hardships, and fatigues and thereby brought on him the Gout, and many other ailments.... And [he has] no means of support.[40]

Awassamug sought to stir compassion by describing in detail his "deplorable Circumstances" and reminding the magistrates that he had "jeopardized his life in so many...very dangerous Enterprizes against those of his nation who remain Savage, and in behalf of his friends, the English." The General Court allowed a small sum to be paid out of the public treasury for temporary relief.

No comprehensive evidence is available to investigate the precise dynamics of demographic change for Indians in eighteenth-century New England. Several censuses gathered by Ezra Stiles in his journeys through the region are suggestive, however. Stiles compiled detailed lists of residents by household from three Indian communities he visited in 1761 and 1762, in addition to his more random observations. He found widows constituted heads of households in proportions ranging from twenty-nine percent (Mashantucket Pequot, Groton, Connecticut) to fifty-two percent (the "Potenummekuk" Indians, Eastham and Nauset, Massachusetts). These figures suggest that the tribulations outlined above were not idle and unconnected complaints.[41]

One solution to the problem of unbalanced sex ratios and insufficient numbers of Indian men was for Indian women to locate African-American spouses. The dynamics of intermarriage between Indians and African Americans are difficult to map precisely from the evidence. Impressionistic evidence does exist. Stiles observed in 1761 that "At Grafton [Massachusetts]...I saw the Burying place & Graves of 60 or more Indians. Now not a Male Ind. in the Town, & perh. 5 Squaws who marry Negroes." A nineteenth-century history of Needham, Massachusetts noted that there was "a colony of negroes, with more or less Indian blood, dwelling along the south shore of Bullard's Pond (Lake Waban)."[42] Clearly, intermarriage did occur, as yet another kind of accommodation for Indian women and an important demographic shift for native populations of the northeast.

Equating "Indianness" with "blood quantum" (the perceived importance of "pure" blood lines) in rigid ways, English observers failed to understand the demographic and cultural changes that enabled the Native population of New England to survive. Some vaguely grasped the complex pattern of vagrancy and intermarriage that were so central to eighteenth-century accommodations even if their cultural blinders remained intact, rendering them incapable of analysis. In 1797, the minister at Natick observed that:

> It is difficult to ascertain the complete number of those that are now here, or that belong to this place, as they are so frequently shifting their place of residence, and are intermarried with black, and some with whites; and the various shades between these, and those that are descended from them, make it almost impossible to come to any determination about them.[43]

In the end, the migratory pattern and complexities of intermarriage left the impression that the native population was simply and inevitably melting away.

In truth, monumental adjustments spanned the entire colonial period, and stretched into the nineteenth century. Both precontact Native American societies in the northeast and early modern European societies were organized according to tightly defined gender roles. In New England, Indian women were responsible for most agricultural tasks, for gathering wild foods, building houses, most craft production, and child-rearing. Men were warriors, diplomats, hunters and fishermen, and they aided women in agricultural production by clearing fields. This way of organizing society came into direct conflict with English expectations, and the ability to maintain a basic economic organization that reflected Native gender roles ran into the hard realities of changing circumstances. The loss of political independence and the massive displacement of Indians within their homelands brought tremendous changes that affected Indian women and men in different ways. Hunting and fishing became marginal, diplomacy became obsolete, and military involvement evolved into economic activity. Agriculture was enormously altered in technique and organization, it became predominantly if not exclusively a male activitiy for Indian landowners, a diminishing element of the Indian economy as they lost land throughout the eighteenth century.

English insistence upon altering the gendered Indian division of labor structured interactions between Indians and settlers, and missionary platforms encapsulated most fully the norms the English expected Indians to adopt. Even when missionary fervor calmed considerably, these expectations remained. In many ways, the accommodation strategies of Native American women in the eighteenth century can be evaluated by the extent to which they complied or did not comply with these expectations, and indeed, by the extent to which they could or could not comply.

How does all of this connect to Hannah Shiner? The manner in which she is portrayed in the nineteenth-century account that I began with can be compared to how she might have been described in the seventeenth century. This Indian woman is not described generically, as most Indian women were when regarded as members of a tribal unit, but as an individual with an Anglicized name. She is categorized as an Indian based on the observer's judgment of her (pure) genealogy. And her husband is seen as a "mulatto," probably with some African-American heritage. Hannah Shiner was assigned several traits, including two ("judge of herbs" and "weaver of baskets") that were associated in the public imagination with "Indianness," and especially with Indian women. They also suggest trades, or means of support, based on traditional activities. Hannah Shiner symbolized the tumultuous changes experienced by Native peoples in seventeenth- and eighteenth-century New England. Indian people survived the catastrophe of English colonization, and rebuilt their shattered societies. Men and women experienced fundamental transformations in their lifeways in different ways. Divorced from the land, many women displayed characteristics visible in this brief description of Hannah Shiner. Apparently accepted and incorporated as an individual member of the community of Medford, Massachusetts, Hannah Shiner represents a particular kind of transformation, though not of the sort English missionaries had in mind. Marginal and a bit exotic, she was in some senses portrayed as a bit of local color, a tangible tie to what seemed to be an increasingly distant Indian past.

Notes

I would like to thank the following individuals for invaluable assistance in preparing this essay: Ann Waltner, Mary Jo Maynes, Louise Edwards, Lisa Norling, Kathy Brown, James Merrell and Margaret Rodgers.

[1] Quoted in Howard S. Russell, *Indian New England Before the Mayflower* (Hanover, NH: University Press of New England, 1980), p. 96.

[2] William Wood, *New England's Prospect* (1634), as quoted in James Axtell, ed., *The Indian Peoples of Eastern America: A Documentary History of the Sexes* (New York: Oxford University Press, 1981), p. 119; see Rayna Green, "The Pocahontas Perplex: The Image of Indian Women in American Culture," *The Massachusetts Review* 16 (1975): 698–714, for an analysis of Pocahontas as literary convention and national symbol, and how Native American women have been conceptualized according to the dichotomy between "princess" and "squaw."

[3] Women's labor accounted for well over half of Indian subsistence in most northeastern woodland cultures. Agricultural production alone contributed approximately sixty-five percent to the diet. See M.K. Bennet, "The Food Economy of the New England Indians, 1605–1675," *The Journal of Political Economy* 63 (1955): 369–397.

[4] Charles Brooks, *History of the Town of Medford, Middlesex County, Massachusetts* (Boston: Published by James M. Usher, 1855), pp. 80–81.

[5] William Cronon, *Changes in the Land: Indians, Colonists, and the Ecology of New England* (New York: Hill and Wang, 1983).

[6] Scholars of this region have argued positions with regard to social organization across a wide spectrum: as matrilineal or patrilineal societies, or as bilateral, or some blend of these general rules. Lewis Henry Morgan, "Systems of Consanguinity and Affinity of the Human Family," *Smithsonian Contributions to Knowledge* 218 (Washington, D.C.: Smithsonian Institution, 1870), and Lorraine Williams, "A Study of 17th Century Central Community in the Long Island Sound Area," Ph.D. dissertation, New York University, 1972, are most often cited by those who argue for the matrilineality of southeastern New England groups. William S. Simmons and George F. Aubin, "Narragansette Kinship," *Ma in the Northeast* 9 (1975): 210–231, argue for the patrilineal reckoning of political leadership and tribal identity, and suggest that exogamous matrilineal clans may have existed to regulate marriage. In general, Kathleen Bragdon agreed. ("Another Tongue Brought In: An Ethnohistorical Study of Native Writings in Massachusett," Ph.D. dissertation, Brown University, 1971). Elise Brenner suggests that a bilateral kinship system was in place ("Strategies for Autonomy: An Analysis of Ethnic Mobilization in Seventeenth Century Southern New England," Ph.D. dissertation, University of Massachusetts, 1984). Those who argue for patrilineality or a bilateral system focus on the lack of evidence for matrilineality from the seventeenth century. Dean R. Snow, *The Archaeology of New England* (New York: Academic Press, 1980), and William A. Starna, "The Pequots in the Early Seventeenth Century," in Laurence M. Hauptman and James D. Wherry, eds., *The Pequots in Southern New England: The Fall and Rise of an American Indian Nation* (Norman: University of Oklahoma Press, 1990), pp. 33–47, have argued that the inconclusive nature of the evidence might signal differences in degree, and/or be the result of the chaotic conditions surrounding conquest which required flexible social responses and the at least periodic appearance of matrilineal or bilateral kinship systems. I am indebted to my research assistant, Margaret Rodgers, for helping me sort out this literature.

[7] Snow, *Archaeology of New England*; Neal Salisbury, *Manitou and Providence: Indians, Europeans, and the Making of New England, 1500–1643* (New York: Oxford University Press, 1982); and William Cronon, *Changes in the Land*. Debate over

gender roles in this region centers on the permeability of the boundaries between women's and men's work, and implications of the meaning of gendered division of labor for the relative power and status of women and men in these societies.

[8] See Theda Perdue, "Southern Indians and the Cult of True Womanhood," in Walter J. Fraser, Jr., R. Frank Saunders, Jr., and Jon L. Wakelyn, *The Web of Southern Social Relations* (Athens: University of Georgia Press, 1985), pp. 35–51.

[9] The process of gradual loss of individually owned land in one missionized Indian town is documented in my thesis, "Community Dynamics in the Indian-English Town of Natick, Massachusetts, 1650–1790," Ph.D. dissertation, University of Chicago, 1990.

[10] Massachusetts Archives, vol. 31, Document 175, 1730, hereafter cited MA, then Vol.: Document, Year. MA, 32: 417–418, 1753.

[11] Middlesex County Probate Docket #4124, Jacob Chalcom, Admin., 1756, hereafter cited MCP).

[12] MA 33: 106–176, 1759.

[13] Thomas Shepard, *The Clear Sun-shine of the Gospel Breaking Forth Upon the Indians in New-England* (London: Printed by R. Cotes for John Bellamy, 1648), reprinted in *Collections of the Massachusetts Historical Society* ser. 3 4 (1834): 59. Hereafter cited as MHSC.

[14] O'Brien, "Community Dynamics," p. 365.

[15] MCP #22411, Ruth Thomas, Admin., 1758; Esther Freeborn, Worcester County Probate Docket #22322, 1807; Hannah Lawrence, WCP #36457, 1774.

[16] Probate documents for several hundred Native American estates in Massachusetts were filed throughout the eighteenth century and have been preserved in county court records. Probate procedures seem to have been followed most vigorously when English creditors to Indian estates sought payment. The majority of Indians died intestate; divisions of Indian estates then almost always followed English estate law quite closely, with provisions made for "widow's thirds," a double share given to the eldest son, and equal shares to other children.

[17] Esther Sooduck, MCP #20860, Will, 1778.

[18] Hannah Lawrence, WCP #36457, 1774.

[19] This is a common theme. See especially Anthony F.C. Wallace's classic work, *The Death and Rebirth of the Seneca* (New York: Alfred A. Knopf, 1970), as well as a critique offered by Diane Rothenberg, "The Mothers of the Nation: Seneca Resistance to Quaker Intervention," in Mona Etienne and Eleanor Leacock, eds., *Women and Colonization: Anthropological Perspectives* (New York: Praeger, 1980), pp. 63–87.

[20] Indian women could obtain title to land as individuals within the landholding system of Massachusetts, but most Indian women gained access to land as wives and children, as heirs to estates. In the process of dividing land in early eighteenth-century Natick, Massachusetts, nineteen individuals were designated proprietors, with principal rights to all of the land within the town. One of these was a woman, the rest were men. O'Brien, "Community Dynamics," chapter four.

[21] George Sheldon, *A History of Deerfield, Massachusetts* (Greenfield, MA: Press of E.A. Hall & Co., 1895), vol. I., p. 71.

[22] MA 33: 300, 1764.

[23] Hannah Speen, MCP #21027, Will, 1742.

[24] MA 32: 675–676, 1755.

[25] See, for example, John A. Sainsbury, "Indian Labor in Early Rhode Island," *New England Quarterly* 48 (1975): 378–393. Sainsbury found that "35.5 percent of all Indians in [Rhode Island] were living with white families in 1774; and if the Indians still living on the Charlestown reservation are excluded, the figure rises to 54 percent." He suspected they were "rent-paying lodgers." (Quotations are from p. 379.) In examining vital records from all over Massachusetts to identify Indians who were connected to the town of Natick, I located at least one Indian in each of 113 towns. Taking eight very distinctive surnames of Natick Indians, I located individuals with the same surnames in twenty three towns. O'Brien, "Community Dynamics," p. 426.

[26] MA 31: 529, 1747. Speen was petitioning the General Court for permission to sell all of her remaining land so that she could reimburse

Graves for caretaking. Massachusetts erected a system of oversight for Indian land that required General Court permission in order for Indian individuals to sell land to non-Indians.

[27] MCP #17057, Elizabeth Paugenit, Will, 1755.

[28] MA 33: 513, 1770.

[29] Natick Town Records, First Book of Records for the Parish of Natick, 1745–1803, Morse Institute, Natick, Massachusetts.

[30] MA 32: 375–376, 1753.

[31] MA 32: 230, 1751–1752.

[32] Douglas Lamar Jones, "The Strolling Poor: Transiency in Eighteenth-Century Massachusetts," *Journal of Social History* 8 (1975): 28–54; and Jones, "Poverty and Vagabondage: The Process of Survival in Eighteenth Century Massachusetts," *New England Historical and Genealogical Society Register* 133 (1979): 243–254.

[33] Richard R. Johnson, "The Search for a Usable Indian: An Aspect of the Defense of Colonial New England," *Journal of American History* 64 (1977): 623–651; Daniel Vickers, "The First Whalemen of Nantucket," *William and Mary Quarterly* 3rd ser., 40 (1983): 560–583; Laurie Weinstein, "'We're Still Living on Our Traditional Homeland': The Wampanoag Legacy in New England," in Frank W. Porter III, ed., *Strategies for Survival: American Indians in the Eastern United States* (Westport, CT: Greenwood Press, 1986), p. 91.

[34] Vickers, "The First Whalemen of Nantucket."

[35] See the works cited in Note 33.

[36] MA 33: 204, 1762.

[37] MA 32: 710, 1756.

[38] MA 33: 10, 1757.

[39] Franklin B. Dexter, ed., *Extracts from the Itineraries and Other Miscellanies of Ezra Stiles, D.D., LL.D., 1755–1794* (New Haven: Yale University Press, 1916), pp. 117, 149.

[40] MA 33: 170, 1761.

[41] Stiles, *Itineraries*, p. 170 ("Potenummekuk"), p. 130 (Nyhantic, Lyme, Connecticut—47 percent widow-headed households); and Stiles, "Memoir of the Pequots," in *MHSC* 10 (1834): 102–103.

[42] Stiles, *Itineraries*, p. 203; George Kuhn Clarke, *History of Needham, Massachusetts, 1711–1911* (Cambridge, MA: University Press, Privately Printed, 1912), p. 558. Determining the degree of intermarriage between Indians, African Americans, and whites is problematic because of the lack of vital records that systematically note the race of the individuals. Even when race is designated in vital records, labels such as "colored" and "mulatto" only indicate that intermarriage had occurred at some time in the past. Clerks did not necessarily use these labels consistently, either. Certainly intermarriage had been occurring between Indians and African-Americans over the course of the eighteenth century. Intermarriage with the English was proscribed by legal statute. See Jack D. Forbes, "Mulattoes and People of Color in Anglo-North America: Implications for Black-Indian Relations," *The Journal of Ethnic Studies* 12 (1984): 17–62.

[43] Stephen Badger, "Historical and Characteristic Traits of the American Indians in General, and Those of Natick in Particular, in a Letter from the Rev. Stephen Badger of Natick, to the Corresponding Secretary," *MHSC* 1st series, 5 (1790), p. 43.

Kiran Cunningham offers us an ethnographic study set in a Mende village in contemporary Sierra Leone. Her study centers on postmarital residence patterns and their impact on gender relations and female power. From a methodological point of view, Cunningham's study highlights the negotiation process that is involved in decision-making about where to set up a household, and uncovers the different stakes men and women have in the decision. Wives who live in their natal communities, Cunningham argues, enjoy a greater degree of autonomy and respect than wives who live in their husband's communities. She also finds evidence of deliberate attempts on the part of women to stay closer to home, in particular as economic conditions shift in a way that disrupts previous patterns. Her study adds a political-economic dimension to the analyses of female positionality common to the essays in this section.

19

Let's Go to My Place: Residence, Gender and Power in a Mende Community

KIRAN CUNNINGHAM

This article analyzes the relationship between postmarital residence, gender relations and power among the Mende of Sierra Leone.[1] I had not initially intended to study kinship and residence during my stay in a Mende village. The literature stated that the Mende were patrilineal and patrilocal, so I saw no need to pursue the issue any further. However, my attention turned to residence and gender after I had administered the demographic interview and noticed a wide variation in patterns of postmarital residence, and then reconstructed the village genealogy and noticed what appeared to be a trend toward increasing numbers of marriages with wives from outside the village. Moreover, I observed that gender relations in the households with wives native to the village were quite different from those in the households with wives from outside. These differences called to mind Karen Sacks's well-known distinction between sisters and wives.[2] Sacks argued that women's primary identity changes from sister to wife with the transition from a kin-corporate society to a class society. My research, however, was suggesting that women *within* kin-corporate societies could be sisters or wives, depending on their postmarital residence. In households with native wives, the women appeared to have the rights Sacks associates with "sisters," while in households with wives from outside, women's positions seemed to be as "wives."

Although the relationship between residence and gender relations has not formed the centerpiece of any study, it has been alluded to by some. Richards,

Schlegel, and Coontz and Henderson, for example, all suggest that residence is an important factor in influencing women's position in a society *vis-à-vis* men.[3] However, because these studies are either theoretical treatises on the roots of male dominance, or comparative studies of several societies, the specifics of how residence affects women's day-to-day lives remain unclear. The distinctive nature of kinship and postmarital residence that I encountered in my fieldwork allowed for such an analysis.

Women, Men and Postmarital Residence

My research was conducted over a twelve-month period in 1988 and 1989 in Kpetema, a Mende village in Moyamba District of southern Sierra Leone. Kpetema has a population of roughly 350 people, and has a land base of approximately six square miles. Almost all of the fifty-six households are involved in farming, with rice being the staple crop. Farms are made in the uplands, and more recently in the surrounding swamps as well. Men and women divide up the farm work, with each contributing equal amounts of labor.

In Kpetema, descent groups, or *kuwuisia*, are not unilineal, and, therefore, not "lineages" in the strict sense of the term. Rather, a *kuwui* is a descent-based kin group with membership in the group determined either matrilaterally or patrilaterally.

Residence, like descent, is flexible in Kpetema. While much of the ethnographic literature describes the Mende as a patrilocal society, I found a lot of variation in postmarital residence patterns both within and across marriages.[4] A couple may live in the husband's village for a while, then, for any number of reasons, move to the wife's village, and vice versa. In addition, a woman may marry a man from the outside, live in his village, divorce him, marry another man, and move back to Kpetema with him. In one case, for example, a woman married a man in Kenema and lived with him there. After he died, she married his brother and they moved back to Kpetema. Where a married couple ends up residing is, however, of utmost importance. As land is held by the *kuwui*, every household must affiliate with a *kuwui* in order to obtain land on which to farm. Both men and women have land rights in their natal *kuwuisia*, so a couple can farm the land belonging to the *kuwui* of either the husband's mother, the husband's father, the wife's mother, or the wife's father. Upon marriage a couple must decide with whom they will affiliate.

Initially, the decision on where to settle and with whom to affiliate will likely be made by the husband, particularly if it is the first marriage for the wife. While it is difficult to pinpoint the exact source of a man's decision-making power, his seniority in age, his payment of bridewealth, and the general cultural assumption that men

Table 1. Distribution of *Kuwui* Affiliation for the 44 Conjugal Households in Kpetema

Kuwui Affiliation*	N	%
Wife's mother's	8	18%
Wife's father's	2	5%
Husband's mother's	8	18%
Husband's father's	15	34%
Neither	11**	25%
TOTAL	44	100%

*Indicator of affiliation is whose land the household farms.
**These households farm land belonging to neither the husband nor the wife. Seven of these are "stranger" households in which both the husband and wife are from the outside, and four are households which, for one reason or another, do not want to farm the husband's or wife's *kuwui* land.

have the power in the household, all contribute to the husband's privileged position in the negotiations about postmarital residence. Thus, if economic opportunity, particularly quality of land and accessibility of labor, is the same in both his and his wife's village, he will probably choose to settle in his village, where he has land rights, and obtain land from the *kuwui* with which his parents are currently affiliating. While the wife may not have much overt power in the initial decision of where to reside, she certainly can and often will attempt to change her husband's mind. Fully aware that her position is more secure politically and economically in her natal village, a woman will attempt to persuade her husband that life would be better in her village, or otherwise try to coerce him into moving there. One woman tried to persuade her husband that his village was unsafe because people were bewitching her children, and that for their children's sake, they should move to her village.

Table 1 shows *kuwui* affiliation in Kpetema at the time I was there. Of the forty-four conjugal households, twenty-three percent affiliate with the wife's *kuwui* and fifty-two percent affiliate with the husband's. In the former group, most affiliate with the wife's mother's *kuwui*, while in the latter group it is most common to affiliate with the husband's father's *kuwui*. An interesting pattern not shown in the table is that nine of the twenty-three households affiliating with the husband's side contain wives who are also from Kpetema. None of the households affiliating with the wife's *kuwui* contain husbands from the village. Thus, in all households with both husbands and wives from the village, couples affiliate with the husband's *kuwui*. I will argue, however, that actual *kuwui* affiliation is not as important for women as whether or not they are residing in their natal villages.

In sum, postmarital residence varies over time, and from household to household, and is the outcome of a good deal of strategizing on the part of both men and women, although men clearly have the upper hand in the initial decision. In the following analysis, I will look at the implications of the outcomes of these decisions for women and gender relations. It is important to keep in mind, however, that the residence pattern I observed reflects only one moment in time. That is, it reflects only one moment in an ongoing process of negotiation between men and women, husbands and wives.

Women, Independence and Economic Resources

For my analysis of residence patterns, I initially divided the thirty-seven conjugal households with at least one spouse from Kpetema[5] into three categories based on where the husbands and senior wives[6] were from: (I) households in which the wife was from Kpetema and the husband was from outside (ten); (II) households in which in the husband was from Kpetema and the wife was from the outside (eighteen); and (III) households in which both the husband and wife were from Kpetema (nine). I collapsed Categories I and III because variation in gender relations seemed to be more associated with whether or not the wife was natal to the village. Women's power seemed to be associated with the presence of her kin, and varied independently of where her husband was from. Thus, Category I includes the nineteen households with wives from Kpetema, and Category II comprises the eighteen households with wives from outside the village. In the following, I will compare these two categories of households in terms of women's access to a variety of important resources, and discuss the implications of access or nonaccess for gender relations and power.

Land is probably the most important economic resource for the people of Kpetema. Not only does the farm provide the bulk of the household's food, the marketing of crops provides the main source of income for both men and women. While people do not have direct ownership over the land, anyone from Kpetema, male or female, has assured access to the land belonging to their descent group. Outsiders, on the other hand, must "beg" for land from one of the descent group heads, or obtain rights to the land through marriage. Obtaining rights through marriage, however, leaves the outsider vulnerable, given the fragility of marriage in Mende culture. Thus, while women from Kpetema have assured access to land, regardless of where their husbands are from, women who marry in have no inherent right to land, and must rely on their husbands to obtain it for them.

The implications for gender relations of this difference in access to land are clear. Women from Kpetema are less dependent on their husbands. They know that, whatever happens in their relationship with their husband, they can always have land to farm. In one household, for example, the husband and wife, both from

Kpetema, were having marital problems, and he refused to make an upland farm for her. The wife, wanting a farm, secured a small piece of her *kuwui*'s land, teamed up with an older man and made her own farm. This would be difficult for a woman from the outside to accomplish. As she has no inherent rights to land and no kin group to support her efforts, there would be little chance of her getting her own farm independent of her husband. Women who marry in are thus clearly at a disadvantage.

In addition to affecting access to land, residence has a very strong impact on women's control over money from the sale of upland vegetables. It is from the petty trading of crops like cucumber, squash and cassava that women often get the money needed for foodstuffs and small things for themselves and their children. I asked the senior wife in each household who sells these crops, who gets the money from the sale, and who decides what to do with that money. There was little variation across residence categories in the answers to the first question: women almost always sell the crops. A significant difference, however, appeared in the answers as to who decides what to do with the money. Seventy-seven percent of the women in Category I households said they, not their husbands, were the ones to decide how the money from their sales was spent, while only forty-three percent of the women in Category II households said they controlled the money.[7]

Some women also obtain income from the intravillage sale of kerosene, medicinal tablets, homemade soap, palm nut oil, snacks and foodstuffs such as onions, pepper, dried fish and salt bought at Moyamba Junctions and resold within the village. Two-thirds of the women selling these items married into the village, which would be expected, given their more limited access to upland vegetables. Of the twelve women in Category I households who participate in this trade, 83.3 percent control the money from the sale of these items, while only sixty percent of the women in Category II households have full control over the proceeds from their sales. While the difference between the two kinds of households is not as significant as it is with the sale of upland vegetables, the same pattern is evident. The marketing of these items, however, is clearly a strategy that women not from Kpetema have for earning the money needed for household expenditures.

As was the case with access to land, this relationship between residence and control over marketing proceeds has significant implications for gender relations. West African women are known for their economic independence from their husbands, and Mende women are no exception to this pattern. They tend to have their own income independent of their husbands', the most important source of which comes from marketing upland vegetables. While most of both incomes may well go to supporting the well-being of the household in the end, the economic independence a woman obtains from having her own income ensures her a degree of independence from her husband. As the data indicate, however, women from the village are much more likely to maintain control over that income. Women from the outside, on the other hand, are more likely to have to ask their husbands for money, placing them in a more dependent position.

Women, Power and Political Resources

An important source of political power for many African women, especially West African women, is female group membership. In Africa, as in other parts of the world, membership in such groups has provided women with both economic and political power, as well as basic support networks for their day-to-day activities.[8]

Probably the best-known of the West African women's associations is the Bundu, or Sande, Society in Sierra Leone, to which roughly ninety-five percent of all Sierra Leonean women belong.[9] Much of the power behind the Bundu Society is rooted in its religious legitimacy. Backed by the supernatural, the Bundu Society guarantees women respect from all members of Society,[10] and plays a significant role in women's relationships with men:

> Bundu law enhances the status of all women by protecting them, for example, from degrading acts such as male voyeurism. Should a man fail to make a warning noise as he approaches the place where women bathe, he will be charged for his offence. Should he make sexual advances to an uninitiated girl, he risks illness and death unless he goes to the Bundu leader, confesses, pays a fine, and submits to a ritual cleansing. Husbands are wary of offending their wives in marital disputes. There is always a chance that the abused wife, or her mother, will use "medicine" known to Bundu women to harm him, especially to render him impotent.[11]

Membership in the Bundu Society, then, provides important benefits to women, not the least of which is a deterrent to mistreatment by their husbands. These benefits, however, are much stronger for active participants, particularly those who hold positions in the Society. One man, who has two wives, one from Kpetema and the other from outside, told me how he has to be especially careful not to do anything to his Kpetema wife that could be deemed abusive, as she is a *ligba* (assistant to the Society leader), and great harm could befall him.

In Kpetema, leadership and participation in Bundu activities appear to be related to residence. While all women in Kpetema are members of the Society, all seventeen Society leadership positions were held by women native to Kpetema, and

Kpetema natives were far more active in Society activities. The window on my veranda overlooked the entrance to the Bundu bush, so I often watched who was coming and going. On one day of particularly heavy activity, I noted nineteen women coming or going from the Bundu bush (the area of forest adjacent to the village associated with the Bundu Society) during a twenty-minute period. Of those nineteen, eighteen were from Kpetema. This difference could be due in part to the bond created between women initiated "in the same bush," that is, those initiated at the same time. Even Kpetema women who were not initiated in the same year have been together in the Society for years. Outsiders, however, do not have the intimate past with the other members. One woman who married into Kpetema told me that she does not enjoy participating in Society activities, and only does so when it is required of her as a Bundu member. She spoke with great elation, however, about Society activities in her own village.

Another explanation of the lack of participation in Bundu activities by women from outside Kpetema may involve the stratification that exists within the Bundu Society.[12] Bundu leaders often exploit subordinate women. By initiating girls into the Society, Bundu leaders essentially build a constituency of clients. As "strangers," women from outside Kpetema are considered subordinate. As these women do not have relationships rooted in allegiance to the leaders of the Kpetema Bundu chapter, they choose not to place themselves in subordinate positions by simply not participating.

Whatever the basis, this difference in participation in Society activities between women from Kpetema and those from outside has clear implications for gender relations. Women who actively participate in Society activities have more immediate access to the Society as an important political resource. They have more support from the other women, many of whom, due to their prominence in the Society, have a great deal of political power and authority in the village. Thus, while these women may be clients of the Bundu leaders, they receive political backing from their patrons, the powerful Society leaders. Moreover, simply being a Bundu member guarantees a woman respect. That respect and the concomitant deterrent to abuse from others, however, is greater for those who are active participants, the vast majority of whom are women native to Kpetema.

Another important political resource more available to women from Kpetema is politically influential kin. Invariably, politically influential villagers, such as lineage heads, members of the Town Council, and heads of the secret societies, are natives of Kpetema. Women from Kpetema, then, are likely to have kin in positions of authority who can defend them during marital disputes. Women who marry in, however, do not have politically influential kin in the village, although their husbands probably will. Thus, in marital disputes, the woman from outside is much more likely to lose. Indeed, a woman in a patrilocal household will rarely take her husband to court for abuse, because she knows she stands little chance of winning.

I know of only one exception to this, namely a household in which the man's first wife was from the outside and his second wife was from Kpetema. While there was rarely any kind of abuse in this household, on one occasion the husband hit his first wife on the shoulder with a long stick, claiming she had been abusing him by singing while he was talking to her. She immediately left the house and took the case to the Town Chief. He refused to hear the case, however, telling her she should take it to her husband's father, who was the Court Chairman of the chiefdom. She knew she probably stood little chance of getting anywhere with her father-in-law, but she respected him as a judge, and went to him anyway. She told her father-in-law what had happened, and said she wanted to leave her husband for a while, take their three children, and return to her own village. Moreover, she said that her husband should give her the money to go. (Typical of patrilocal households, her husband maintained control of all the money she earned, so she had only the little bit that she managed to sequester, not nearly enough to pay for transportation to her village.) Her father-in-law sympathized with her plight, and agreed that it was very wrong of her husband, his son, to beat her. Nevertheless, he encouraged her to return to the household, citing the children as the reason that she and her husband should remain together. He verbally reprimanded her husband for beating her. Later, she and I were talking about the incident, and she told me grudgingly that her husband never would have done what he did to her co-wife, Adama. "He's partial to Adama," she said. "She has her people here, so he wouldn't beat her. My people, though, are far away."

This incident illustrates two points relating to the issue of residence and politically influential kin. First, the significance of having politically powerful kin is clear: the woman's father-in-law was a man with much political authority, and when she took the case to the Town Chief, he told her to go to the Court Chairman because he was the father of one of the parties involved in the case. This is quite common. Rather than taking the case to an objective third party, it is customary to have the case heard by the kin group first, a practice clearly favoring the individual from Kpetema. Second, the example highlights the differential treatment, or at least the perceived difference in treatment, of wives from Kpetema and wives who marry in. The abused wife knew that the fact that she was not from the village was part of the reason she, and not the other wife, was beaten. Thus, politically influential kin are important in cases involving physical or emotional maltreatment, and, more significantly, like Bundu Society membership, they are deterrents to abuse in the first place.

Women, Security and Social Resources

The family of origin is a very important resource for people in Kpetema. Even after one has moved out of the parental household, one's parents and siblings continue to be a source of both material and emotional support. For women in particular, having access to one's family is a definite asset. It can provide a place of refuge in times of trouble, and a resource center in times of need. For example, a woman lacking money to buy the ingredients for the day's sauce often turns to her siblings or parents for a loan, rather than asking her husband and becoming indebted to him. Similarly, food is frequently exchanged among family members.

In addition, a woman may turn to her parents or siblings for support when she is having problems with her husband. Indeed, she may even stay with them for a while, until the tension in her own household eases. Like politically influential kin, not only do family members provide an important support group in marital disputes, but their presence can often deter mistreatment. In one household, for example, there were four wives, only one of whom, Nancy, was not from Kpetema. Nancy was the second wife, and should have had seniority over the third and fourth, but the latter often got away with shirking some of their responsibilities, passing them on to Nancy. Quite often when I went to visit this household, Nancy was working, while the other wives were sitting idly by, or engaged in simple tasks like picking stones from the rice. I asked my assistant why Nancy had to do so much of the work, and she said, "She doesn't have any people here." The husband, who realized the inequity among his wives, was reluctant to intervene, not wishing to anger his other wives and risk ruffling the feathers of their prominent families.

Similar to the presence of the immediate family, simply being in one's own community is important. For Mende villagers, being a stranger in the community has definite drawbacks. A Temne man from the north, for example, brought his family to live in Kpetema over ten years ago. While I was there, someone stole all the cassava from his upland farm during the height of the hungry season in August, when cassava is all there is to eat. He was very upset, but never took the case to the Town Chief, or even to the head of the *kuwui* with which he was affiliated. I asked him why he did not pursue the matter, and he said, "I am a stranger here. I will never be compensated for the stolen cassava." "Strangers," including spouses who marry into the community, are at a definite disadvantage. In disputes, the party from the outside has little chance of winning, as the villagers will tend to back their "brother" or "sister."

Two issues came up again and again in this analysis of residence and women's access to resources. The first concerned women's autonomy and independence from their husbands. Women who married into the village had less autonomy, due to not having guaranteed access to land, being less likely to maintain control over the proceeds from their market sales, and not having their immediate family available as a backup source of both emotional and material support. By contrast, women who remained in their natal village had access to all of these resources, and were thereby able to maintain a greater degree of autonomy from their husbands.

The second issue that figured prominently in my discussion concerned deterrents to mistreatment. Active membership in the Bundu Society, the presence of politically influential kin, and, again, the availability of the immediate family, are all important deterrents to the physical or emotional abuse of a woman by her husband. These resources, too, are more available to women from the village. Clearly, women who remain in their natal villages after marriage have economic, political and social advantages over their sisters who live in their husbands' villages. The latter are much more economically dependent on their husbands, and more subject to abuse in the absence of deterrents provided by the presence of their kin.

Women, Resistance and Changes in Residence

The significance of this disparity is intensified, given the trend toward increasing numbers of households with wives from the outside. After collecting routine kinship data on Kpetema's population, and tracing descent back to the village founders, I noticed that, in the past, couples with wives from the village and husbands from the outside had been more prevalent. In order to analyze this trend, I divided the current population into three age groups and looked at the residence patterns of each group. Then I looked at the residence patterns of each group's parents.[13]

Table 2 shows that in the current population, less than thirty percent of the marriages in each age group fall into Category A (the wife from Kpetema and the husband from outside). In the parental generations, however, over sixty percent of the marriages were Category A. Furthermore, of the founding generation, seven out of the nine marriages, or over seventy-five percent, were Category A. Thus, over the past three generations, Category A marriages have diminished from seventy-five percent to less than thirty percent of all marriages. At the same time, there has been an increase in the frequency of marriages with husbands from the village and wives from the outside (Category B). Women, in other words, are increasingly likely to live in their husband's village rather than in their own.

This trend may be at least partially explained by changes in patterns of male outmigration over the past twenty years. Ever since the early part of the century, Mende society has been characterized by high rates of male outmigration as men left their villages to work in the gold and diamond mines in the eastern part of the

Table 2. Residence Category of Current and Parental Generations by Age of Household Head

Age of Household Head	Wife Native; Husband from Outside		Husband Native; Wife from Outside		Both Native	
	Current Gen.	Parental Gen.	Current Gen.	Parental Gen.	Current Gen.	Parental Gen.
20–40	28.6%	62.5%	50.0%	31.2%	21.4%	6.3%
	(4)	(10)	(7)	(5)	(3)	(1)
41–60	27.8%	61.5%	50.0%	30.8%	22.2%	7.7%
	(5)	(8)	(9)	(4)	(4)	(1)
61+	20.0%	71.4%	40.0%	28.6%	40.0%	0.0%
	(1)	(5)	(2)	(2)	(2)	(0)
	10	23	18	11	9	2

NOTE: Data for the parental generation were determined as follows: for each of the 37 household heads, I determined whether their mother, their father, or both were from Kpetema, and placed that marriage in the appropriate category.

country. During this time of male out-migration, women remained in their natal villages rather than staying in their husband's village. The years since the late 1970s, however, have seen a decline in the mining industry. The economy of the country in general has virtually collapsed, leaving very few economic opportunities outside the village. In response to this crisis, there has been a trend toward returning to the village, where one can at least farm and be guaranteed food to eat.

The sex ratio of Kpetema today, compared with that of a nearby town twenty years ago, attests to this phenomenon. Isaac, in his 1968 study of Bambara Chiefdom, found that in a subsample of sixty male-headed households with a population of 344, there were 145 adult women and only 116 adult men.[14] Today, however, the sex ratio in Kpetema is even, reflecting a return of adult males to the village.

As men returned to Kpetema to farm, a few brought wives with them. More commonly, though, they married upon their return, either someone from Kpetema or a woman from a nearby village. Because he was returning to make a living, a man would prefer to be in his own village so that he could be assured of the resources needed to do so.

This trend, however, is not being met without resistance. Women are fully aware of the advantages of living in their own village. They know that a woman who marries into a village as a stranger has a greater chance of being abused by her husband

345

and less chance of winning a case against her husband in court due to the absence of "her people." While a woman may not have much say in where she lives at the time of her first marriage, she can make life difficult for her husband once they are married, in an attempt to persuade him to move to her village. More frequently, however, women return to their natal villages on their own, by either divorcing their husbands or simply leaving for an extended visit with their family.

I know of three women who were trying to return to their villages, of which two eventually succeeded. I also know women who at one time married and lived in their husbands' villages, but have since divorced their husbands and returned to Kpetema. Some of these women are remarried to men from Kpetema; others remain single.

Discussion: Residence, Sisters and Wives

At the beginning of this article I mentioned Karen Sacks's work, in which she makes the critical distinction between women's identity as sisters and their identity as wives.[15] Comparing kin-corporate societies (such as the Mende) and class-based societies, she argues that women in the former have equal access to the means of production (that is, lineage land) as sisters, an identity she claims they retain even as wives in their husbands' villages. In the latter, however, they only have access as wives (and sometimes daughters) of male property owners. As a result, she says, women in kin-corporate societies maintain a greater degree of autonomy from their husbands, while women in class-based societies are more likely to be in positions of subordination.

While I accept her argument, my research suggests that the distinction she makes between women as sisters and as wives can also be found *within* kin-corporate societies. I would argue that, while women in most kin-corporate societies do indeed have the rights as sisters that Sacks describes, only when they are in their natal villages can they fully exercise those rights. Once they leave for their husbands' villages they become wives. Sacks acknowledges this fact,[16] but claims that wives "were often able to enforce something resembling sisterly autonomy when they carried out their daily wifely work as part of a female collectivity."[17] However, perhaps because she drew her examples only from patrilocal societies, and did no fieldwork in Africa herself, she could not appreciate the real difference between actually being a "sister" in one's natal village, and being a "wife" in one's husband's village. In Kpetema, for example, gender relations in households with native wives were more characteristic of those Sacks described for kin-corporate societies. In comparison, gender relations in households with wives who married in from outside more closely approximated those she described for class-based societies.

Clearly, postmarital residence will be more significant in societies in which women really are "sisters" in their natal village, in the biological sense and in the sense of having economic and political rights to the means of production. Among the Gusii of East Africa, for example, women do not retain economic and political rights in their patrilineage after they marry.[18] In societies such as these, postmarital residence would be less consequential than in societies in which women remain sisters in their natal kin group throughout their lives. This does not mean that residence is not important for women in such societies, however it may have less bearing on women economically and politically. The distinction may be more between daughter and daughter-in-law, as in much of India,[19] than between sister and wife.

While the significance of residence for women in Kpetema is quite apparent, due to the flexible rules governing postmarital residence and related issues of resource accessibility, this does not necessarily mean that residence is not significant in societies with, for example, strict rules of virilocality and/or strict prohibitions against divorce. Residence in such societies may be just as significant in determining women's access to key resources. Comparative work needs to be conducted in societies with various forms of descent, marriage payments and postmarital residence patterns to further determine how and under what circumstances residence relates to issues of gender and power.

Notes

[1] This research could not have been conducted without the people of Kpetema, the moral support of Russell Rhoads, Susan Abbott, and John and Tenneh Soriba, and the financial support of the National Science Foundation.

[2] Karen Sacks, *Sisters and Wives: The Past and Future of Sexual Equality* (Westport, CT: Greenwood Press, 1979).

[3] Audrey I. Richards, "Some Types of Family Structure amongst the Central Bantu," in A.R. Radcliffe-Brown and D. Forde, eds., *African Systems of Kinship and Marriage* (London: Oxford University Press, 1950); Alice Schlegel, *Male Dominance and Female Autonomy: Domestic Authority in Matrilineal Societies* (New Haven: Yale University Press, 1972); Stephanie Coontz and Peta Henderson, "Property Forms, Political Power and Female Labour in the Origins of Class and State

Societies," in Coontz and Henderson, eds., *Women's Work, Men's Property: The Origins of Gender and Class* (London: Verso, 1986).

[4] Kenneth L. Little, *The Mende of Sierra Leone* (London: Routledge and Kegan Paul, 1967); Carol P. Hoffer, "Madame Yoko: Ruler of the Kpa Mende Confederacy," in M. Rosaldo and L. Lamphere, eds., *Women, Culture and Society* (Stanford: Stanford University Press 1974); Sylvia Boone, *Radiance from the Waters* (New Haven: Yale University Press, 1987).

[5] I omitted the seven households in which neither the husband nor the wife were from Kpetema; in all seven cases both husband and wife were Temne.

[6] In polygynous households, which constitute 12 of the 37 households, I focused on the senior wife, as her situation more clearly reflects the hus-

band-wife dynamic. The position of junior wives, on the other hand, tends to be influenced by their subordinance to the senior wife.

[7] The fact that the key is whether or not the woman is from Kpetema as opposed to whether or not the man is from Kpetema is clear in terms of control of resources. In households with native wives and husbands from the outside, 77.3 percent of the women reported that they controlled the money; in households with native wives and husbands from Kpetema, the corresponding figure is 80 percent. Thus, as long as the wife was from the village, it did not seem to matter whether or not her husband was from the village.

[8] Audrey Wipper, "Women's Voluntary Associations," in Margaret J. Hay and Sharon Stichters, eds., *African Women South of the Sahara* (New York: Longman, 1984); Kathryn March and Rachelle L. Taqqu, *Women's Informal Association in Developing Countries* (Boulder, CO: Westview Press, 1986). Sanday found that the existence of female solidarity groups correlated closely with female political participation, and was an indicator of high female status, see Peggy R. Sanday, "Female Status in the Public Domain," in M. Rosaldo and L. Lamphere, eds., *Women, Culture and Society* (Stanford: Stanford University Press, 1974).

[9] Hoffer, "Madame Yoko," p. 173.

[10] Hoffer, "Bundu," p. 155.

[11] Ibid., p. 162.

[12] Bledsoe discusses how relations between Bundu women are far from egalitarian. See Caroline Bledsoe, "Stratification and Sande Politics," *Ethnologische Zeitschrift* 1 (1980), 143–49; and id., "The Political Uses of Sande Ideology and Symbolism," *American Ethnologist* 11 (1984), 455–472.

[13] I determined the residence pattern by looking at whether the husband, wife, or both came from Kpetema or from outside.

[14] Barry L. Isaac, "Economic Development and Subsistence Farming: The Case of the Mende of Upper Bambara Chiefdom, Sierra Leone," *Central Issues in Anthropology* 4, vol. 1 (1982), 7. Clarke shows a similar phenomenon in his map depicting excesses of males and females by chiefdom in 1963. According to his data, Fakunya Chiefdom had an excess of roughly 1,000 females. See Johne Innes Clarke, *Sierra Leone in Maps* (London: University of London Press, 1969), p. 45.

[15] Sacks, *Sisters and Wives.*

[16] Sacks, *Sisters and Wives*, p. 119.

[17] Karen Sacks, "An Overview of Women and Power in Africa," in J. O'Barr, ed., *Perspectives on Power* (Durham, NC: Duke University, 1982), p. 3.

[18] Thomas Hakansson, *Bridewealth, Women and Land*, Uppsala Studies in Cultural Anthropology 10 (Stockholm: Ahnquist Wikesll International, 1988), 51*f*, 191–192.

[19] *Dadi's Family* (Film), Odyssey Series (Waterton, Me: Documentary Educational Resources, 1981).

References

Bledsoe, Caroline. "Stratification and Sande Politics." *Ethnologische Zeitschrift* 1 (1980), 143–149.

———. "The Political Uses of Sande Ideology and Symbolism," *American Ethnologist* 11 (1984), 455–472.

Boone, Sylvia. *Radiance from the Waters.* New Haven: Yale University Press, 1987.

Clarke, John Innes. *Sierra Leone in Maps.* London: University of London Press, 1966.

Coontz, Stephanie, and Peta Henderson. "Property Forms, Political Power and Female Labour in the Origins of Class and State Societies." In Stephanie Coontz and Peta Henderson, eds., *Women's Work, Men's Property: The Origins of Gender and Class*, London: Verso, 1986, pp. 108–155.

Dadi's Family (Film). Odyssey Series. Waterton, ME: Documentary Educational Resources, 1981.

Hakansson, Thomas. *Bridewealth, Women and Land.* Uppsala Studies in Cultural Anthropology 10, Stockholm: Ahnquist Wiksell International, 1988.

Hoffer, Carol P., "Madam Yoko: Ruler of the Kpa Mende Confederacy." In M. Rosaldo and L. Lamphere, eds., *Women, Culture and Society.* Stanford: Stanford University Press, 1974, pp. 173–188.

———. "Bundu: Political Implications of Female Solidarity in a Secret Society." In Dana Raphael, ed., *Being Female: Reproduction, Power, and Change.* The Hague: Mouton, 1975, pp. 155–164.

Issac, Barry L. "Economic Development and Subsistence Farming: The Case of the Mende of Upper Bambara Chiefdom, Sierra Leone." *Central Issues in Anthropology* 4, no.1 (1982), pp. 1–20.

Little, Kenneth L. *The Mende of Sierra Leone.* London: Routledge and Kegan Paul, 1967.

March, Kathryn, and Rachelle L. Taqqu. *Women's Informal Association in Developing Countries.* Boulder: Westview Press, 1986.

Richards, Audrey I. "Some Types of Family Structure amongst the Central Bantu." In A.R. Radcliffe-Brown and D. Forde, eds., *African Systems of Kinship and Marriage.* London: Oxford University Press, 1950, pp. 207–251.

Sacks, Karen. *Sisters and Wives: The Past and Future of Sexual Equality.* Westport, CT: Greenwood Press, 1979.

———. "An Overview of Women and Power in Africa." In J. O'Barr, ed., *Perspectives on Power.* Durham, NC: Duke University, 1982, pp. 1–10.

Sanday, Peggy R. "Female Status in the Public Domain." In M. Rosaldo and L. Lamphere, eds., *Women, Culture and Society.* Stanford: Stanford University Press, 1974, pp. 189–206.

Schlegel, Alice. *Male Dominance and Female Autonomy: Domestic Authority in Matrilineal Societies.* New Haven: Yale University Press, 1972.

Wipper, Audrey. "Women's Voluntary Associations." In Margaret J. Hay and Sharon Stichter, eds., *African Women South of the Sahara.* New York: Longman, 1984, pp. 59–86.

Bill Maurer's study examines how lineality and descent are constructed in law and political discourse in the contemporary British Virgin Islands. His discussion centers on current debates about citizenship and competing views about how citizenship ought to be legitimated. Maurer shows that even discourses that critique orthodox views are often based in naturalizing presumptions. For example, Virgin Islanders who protest narrow definitions of citizenship based on the citizenship status of fathers still conceive of birthplace as the basis of their alternative notion of national belonging. The compelling political problem he addresses—who does and does not "belong" to a nation and how such "belonging" is established—echoes as a contemporary problem of global political economy far beyond the boundaries of his study.

20

The Land, the Law and Legitimate Children: Thinking through Gender, Kinship and Nation in the British Virgin Islands

BILL MAURER

Introduction: People, Place and Nation

Anthropologists have been taken to task recently for too readily assuming a necessary or natural link between culture, people and place.[1] Like nationalist discourses, anthropological ones often "present associations of people and place as solid, commonsensical, and agreed-upon, when they are in fact contested, uncertain, and in flux."[2] This essay is about a place where questions of belonging are currently hotly debated. To understand the competing claims of participants in this debate, it is necessary to pay attention to the specific ways in which the different sides claim their association with the "national territory." Although all the people involved in the argument about national belonging naturalize their connections to the national space, they do so in subtly different fashions. The two camps I describe in this essay both establish claims to the national territory based on ideas about lineage and kinship, but in doing so they prevent any easy reading of what "kinship," "lineage" or "territory" might be.

Mindie Lazarus-Black has recently demonstrated that understanding family and kinship in the Caribbean requires an examination of the legal codes and processes Caribbean peoples have used "to define family and to achieve the rights and duties that belong to kin."[3] Understanding how law and kinship intersect in the

351

Caribbean is furthered by attending to issues surrounding land, and taking the time to look at land allows us to see more clearly the role of kinship and gender in the production of Caribbean nationalisms and the development of nationalist political discourses. The connections among ideas and practices centered around land, gender, kinship and law are central to the the construction of nationalist discourses and the various inequalities they engender in Caribbean national contexts.

The British Virgin Islands (BVI) are a self-governing British Dependent Territory consisting of about forty islands, and populated by about 18,000 people of African and European descent.[4] Nearly half of the people living in the BVI are not citizens. Most are migrants from other Caribbean islands and Guyana who have been coming in increasing numbers since the 1960s to work in jobs created by a boom in high-class tourism and offshore banking. At present, there are more jobs available than there are people to fill them.

I begin this discussion by showing how the official discourse of nationalism emerges from the intersection of citizenship and land-ownership laws. I then examine the challenges to this discourse, and conclude by discussing the place of gender, kinship, land and law in the construction of nationalism.

The Official Discourse of National Belonging

The 1981 British Nationality Act laid down the principles by which citizenship rights were to be conferred in the dependent territories of the United Kingdom, including the British Virgin Islands. The Act itself is quite straightforward. In part II, section 15, the conferral of citizenship is laid down for the British Dependent Territories, thus:

> A person born in a dependent territory…shall be a British Dependent
> Territories citizen if at the time of his birth his father or mother is—(a)
> a British Dependent Territories citizen; or (b) settled in a dependent
> territory. (British Nationality Act 1981, II §15[1])

The Act's definition of "settlement" is somewhat tautological: to be "settled" in a dependent territory is to be subject to no residence, employment or immigration restrictions (V §50[2]). In other words, one is "settled" if and only if one is a "citizen," so in clause (b) above, one is a citizen if one's mother or father is a citizen.

The citizenship of one's mother or father then, is key to one's own citizenship. And "father" and "mother" are specifically and narrowly delimited by the Act:

> For the purposes of this Act—(a) the relationship of a mother and child
> shall be taken to exist between a women and any child (legitimate or

illegitimate) born to her; but (b)…the relationship of a father and child shall be taken to exist only between a man and any legitimate children born to him; and the expressions 'mother,' 'father,' 'parent,' 'child,' and 'descended' shall be construed accordingly. (British Nationality Act 1981, V §50[9])

Prior to 1981, citizenship rights were passed along "patrials," or lines of descent traced through legal and nonlegal fathers. Under this earlier system, women could not pass their citizenship rights to their children. The 1981 Act was seen by some as affirming the "natural" bond between mother and child, as women who were citizens were for the first time able to pass on their citizenship. For men, on the other hand, the Act shifted emphasis from "patrialty" to "legitimacy."[5] Now men who are citizens only pass on citizenship rights to some of their children—the legitimate ones born to noncitizen mothers or the legitimate and illegitimate ones born to citizen mothers. The 1981 British Nationality Act thus denies "belonger" status—as BVI citizenship is popularly termed—to children born in a nonlegal union of a belonger father and a non-belonger mother.[6]

The emphasis the law places on the legitimacy of children born to non-belonger mothers fits neatly into local land laws and practices. By law and in practice, land frequently is inherited by groups of relatives in common.

Since at least the 1740s, when Quaker settlers on Tortola freed their slaves and granted them perpetual rights to the land on which they lived, women and men have both had access to property through inheritance. Groups of siblings, both male and female, have tended to inherit property of their mothers and fathers in common tenure. As a result, over time, increasing numbers of relatives have had the ability to lay claim to relatively small plots of land. Until the early part of this century, and in many cases into the present day, land plots remained undivided, and people would share the land to which they had common rights instead of dividing it up into separate "shares." A person with claim to the land generally would need the permission of all the other people with any claim on it before building or farming on it, or selling a piece of it to another person. Historically, however, the only people consulted have been those actually living on the land. At the turn of the century, however, as a class of British Virgin Islander civil servants and lawyers began to emerge, British common law was increasingly brought to bear on BVI common tenurial traditions. These laws did not interfere much with local tenures (many of which, after all, had their basis in the common law brought by the Quaker settlers), but in land disputes they did tend to disfavor the claims of widows of landowning men who had not provided their husband with "issue." In addition, before 1926, the law favored first-born sons over their mothers and other siblings in disputes over inheritance. After 1926, however, the rights of the first-born son as heir-at-law were abolished, and British land law again approximated the BVI traditional pattern of even distribution to surviving relatives, whether under common tenure or under a system of evenly divided shares.[7]

Long-standing BVI property laws and common courtesy, thus, at present require that all persons with claim to a piece of land be consulted before any party holding a claim begins construction or development on the land. Although this frequently results in conflict, most British Virgin Islanders cite this pattern of land ownership as giving rise to their sense of "independence" as a people and a "nation." As one informant put it, everyone has "a piece of the rock" she or he can go back to in time of need. One elderly man held that the main difference "in character" between British Virgin Islanders and other peoples of the Caribbean is their independent-mindedness, based on their history of land ownership: "We have always been an independent people. It was different from St. Kitts, Antigua because they were always dependent on plantations [even after Emancipation]. [But] we are not servile, and [so] we should not sell it [our land]."

While at the turn of the century conflicts over land inheritance involved British Virgin Islanders exclusively, today the conflicts foremost in peoples' minds involve the divide between citizens with "rightful" claims to BVI land and immigrants and their children with what are perceived to be "legitimate" claims. This is because of the changes in citizenship law. Illegitimate children of belonger fathers and non-belonger mothers cannot make legitimate claims to their fathers' land and, more importantly, cannot participate in the sense of independence that comes with it. Non-belongers must petition the government for a "Non-Belonger's Land Holding License" before they can purchase land. This involves an application stating the potential buyer's development plans for the land, along with a commitment to complete any proposed development within three years of the time of purchase. Land so purchased cannot be sold to or inherited by another non-belonger with-out application for another such license.

According to popular tales, the Virgin Islands were so named by Christopher Columbus after the legendary British martyr, Saint Ursula, who with her eleven thousand attendant virgins, was murdered by the Huns sometime in the third century A.D. Columbus, sighting the islands for the first time, apparently thought they looked like countless dead virgins. Today, the eleven-thousand-and-one marytrs live on in the metaphorical uses to which the territory's name is put. Almost with-out exception, punning and wordplay invoking the "virginity" of the islands take place in discussions about the land and the presence of immigrants on it. For many older BVIslanders, the land takes on deeply religious meanings. One elderly man told me that, before the rapid development of the 1960s and increasing immigration, "Tortola was a garden! Fruit on every tree, fresh water from the springs, fish would jump into your boat!" And an elderly woman farmer asked, "Where did God put Man? In a Garden! We are descended from farmers—Abraham, Isaac and Jacob!" Saint Ursula's Day, meanwhile, is a national holiday.

The land occupies a central symbolic place in discussions about the rapid development of the BVI. Perennial conflicts born out of patterns of land inheritance helped convince the territory's leaders of the need to reclaim land from the sea when planning the development of the capital city, Road Town, in order to make the territory more attractive to investors and tourists. British Virgin Islanders continually point to this new land as a symbol of the islands' progress. They also discuss how, in keeping foreigners localized on this new space, reclaimed land helps protect the "virginity" of the rest of the islands. And indeed, these protectionist policies have checked uncontrolled foreign development, and have helped the British Virgin Islands avoid the "Miami syndrome" blighting their U.S. Virgin Island neighbors.

BVIslanders frequently describe the islands' "virginity" as under siege by marauding migrants. The interconnectedness of three distinct themes of "legitimacy"—of birth, of rights to citizenship and of claims to land—comes to the fore in belongers' statements about certain recently arrived groups of migrants. Belongers describe immigrants from Guyana as "hoarding and destructive of the environment." They are also seen as "clannish" and "crafty," and thus a threat to belongers' businesses. One belonger states:

> Our parents taught us not to pick fruit until it is mature, and to throw back little fish. They come and gather immature fruit, and take all sizes of fish, and scrape tiny snails off the reefs. They move onto your land without permission.

Another belonger maintains:

> They are greedy and want to save even the rust from the pennies! And they eat, eat, eat! Everything in sight! They would clear the land of all the plants just to eat!

Recently, significant numbers of Dominicans have arrived in the British Virgin Islands. Some of these people are second- and third-generation descendants of British Virgin Islander men who went to the Dominican Republic in the beginning of this century to work on sugar plantations. In the past five years, they have started to petition the government for conferral of the citizenship status they feel is rightfully theirs. One belonger woman, describing the situation to me, said:

> Dominicans have been coming in droves recently. There is communication now, by air, so no real problems in their coming here. But they cannot claim property unless their father wills it to them or gives it to them because they have no rights, because they are illegitimate.

She continued:

> The people who are coming are children of BVIslander fathers. It seems there were two brothels the men used to go to. But I suppose the fathers would have died by this time, so the people we are seeing are their grandchildren.

This informant, and others, articulates the three themes of legitimacy—of birth, citizenship and land claims—when discussing Dominican migrants, and connects these with sexual morality. By implication, she holds Dominican women to be whores. She does so in accordance with the widely held belief among belongers that Dominican prostitutes brought AIDS to the islands, and are therefore not only dirty and amoral, but a profound threat to the nation.

The official discourse of national belonging rests thus on the threefold nature of "legitimacy" as encoded in law and in cultural practice and belief. Just as Guyanese (purportedly) do not respect the land or fair business practices, Dominicans (purportedly) do not respect moral convention or personal hygiene. Both violate "legitimacy" in its various aspects. And both are therefore systematically excluded from full participation in the nation as citizens.

As the official discourse stitches together the three threads of "legitimacy," it prescribes sexual morality in fabricating a sense of the nation and those who "belong" to it. Children born to non-belonger women are citizens (and landowners) only by virtue of their mothers' virtue. Illegitimate offspring of non-belonger women are stateless, because the state needs to protect itself from illegitimate incursions lest its "purity" be stained.

The Counterdiscourse of National Belonging

Of course, in a territory in which half of the residents are classed as noncitizens, alternative discourses of nationhood and national belonging are bound to arise and gain popularity. On August 3, 1991, Benji V, a man from St. Kitts living in the British Virgin Islands, was crowned Calypso King at the annual Miss BVI beauty contest. His winning song, entitled "Where We Born Is Where We From," made an explicit challenge to the official and legal discourse of national belonging by invoking U.S. and Canadian citizenship policies. I will quote from the lyrics at length; note that Benji V adopts the subject position of a belonger man:

> They say if me girlfriend get my baby in my country,
> the baby can't have the same rights like me.
> How come when anybody go to Rock City[8] to get their baby
> the baby can have the same rights like Farrelly?[9]
> Where a baby first is born, that country must be their own;
> they must have the rights like anybody born in the same region.
> So if the mother born in Antigua and she children born in Tortola—
> Where we born is where we from.
>
> We could born in St. Lucia, and live in Grenada;
> We could born Dominica;
> Well, we could have green card for the States, and born in Bermuda;
> We could live in England for years, that's not the answer;
> Where we born is where we from.
>
> If a woman from England goes to Canada
> Born a baby, that baby is a Canadian.
> But the baby still have rights in his mother's land,
> And if he needs a birth paper, he have to get one in Canada
> Because where foreign man get birth paper in foreign land?
> They have to get it in the land where they was born.
> And if a child need a passport he should achieve one without a storm,
> Because where we born is where we from.
>
> What's wrong if a woman gets a child in a next man's land?
> That is something a lot of us can't understand.
> But it could be land, sea or even in the air
> All our babies, they have to born somewhere.
> A child never know where his mother will put him out.
> He is innocent, he doesn't know his whereabouts;
> Until he reach to a stage that he could understand, he will say
> Where we born is where we from.[10]

The challenge to official policy and discourse could not be clearer. And Benji V brought the house down. Where official policy emphasizes the "natural" connections among marriage, mother, child and nation, Benji V focused on the "naturalness" of the connection between place of birth and child. His counterdiscourse thus skirts the issue of legitimacy altogether. It ties a child directly to the nation-state in which it is born; there are no intermediaries—such as parents, legal strictures surrounding kin and land ownership, and so forth. Where the official discourse relies on the conjuncture of three themes of legitimacy to establish the nation, Benji V simply links national identity and the rights associated with it to place of birth. And for Benji V, the nation is a naturally given piece of territory.

The kind of move Benji V is making in establishing challenges to the official discourse of national belonging is echoed throughout the territory. The August 8th, 1991, horse races at Sea Cows' Bay on Tortola featured Prospect versus Kentucky, two horses which, according to the commentator, were "born of foreign parents right here in the BVI, so they're local horses." Of course, were they *people* they wouldn't legally be "local" at all. But like Benji V's song, the message is that birth in a territory should be the basis of citizenship in that territory-cum-nation, regardless of legitimacy.

The counterdiscourse is subject to multiple readings, and like the official discourse, it ends up denoting and defending a particular character of nationhood. A contestant in the Miss BVI beauty contest stated during the competition that her one wish for the BVI would be "to build better incentives for local businesses, keep money in the country." A *non*-belonger woman who works for a *foreign*-owned rental car agency expressed agreement with the contestant's statement and, with the rest of the crowd, rose to her feet, cheering. Although she has no "legitimate" claims to citizenship (or land), her economic standing depends on the BVI's continued prosperity, and so she supports protectionist land, labor and citizenship policies.[11] Non-belongers' support of protectionism is not paradoxical given their sense of being "of" the nation in which they were born, whether or not they have "legitimate" claims to it. In recent years, youths have taken to using the term "born here" to designate their status as members—albeit, as far as the state is concerned, "illegitimate" members—of the nation.

The "born here" category, and the particular kind of nationalism it represents, has the effect of excluding some non-belongers from the counterdiscourse of national belonging. The day after Benji V's performance, an elderly belonger reprimanded a Trinidadian residing in the BVI—but *not* born there—by stating, "Hey, where we born is where we from, and you're from Trinidad" [that is, "shut up!"]. The Trinidadian was disciplining a child in the older man's care, and the latter was invoking the counterdiscourse not quite politely to tell the younger man to butt out.

The counterdiscourse has other implications as well, especially in the wider Caribbean context. Even before decolonization (which, for the BVI and other colonies has still not been realized), Caribbean peoples had been deeply ambivalent toward their affiliations to larger communities such as nations. Intra-Caribbean and transatlantic migrations have further encouraged this ambivalence, and it is not uncommon for people to identify more strongly as people of the "Caribbean" than as members of a particular island nation. The ambiguity of national affiliation is played out particularly sharply in the BVI, where relative prosperity and national pride have gone hand in hand with increased immigration and the nationalist discourses inspired, in part, by the 1981 British Nationality Act.[12] For example, two days after Benji V's performance, the local band Caribbean Ecstasy led a crowd through Road Town as part of annual festival celebrations. One of the band's songs contained the refrain "It don't matter where you're from," and then extolled members of various national communities to "jam" and "jump" (as in, "It don't matter where you're from; Antigua posse ready to jam. It don't matter where you're from; St. Kitts posse ready to jam"; and so on.). At the Miss BVI contest, one of the contestants included in her talent number a speech invoking "the days of Emancipation" while she quoted the theme of Festival 1991: "Don't fret, let's fete; All o' we is one in 1991." In the same spirit, a minister from Guyana spoke at a public event of the happy day when she would carry a passport stamped "Citizen of the Caribbean."

In contrast to the official discourse of national belonging, the counterdiscourse eliminates mediating factors—such as kin or land ownership—from the "fact" of belonging to a nation. The foundation of the counterdiscourse—that *place* of birth alone should confer national identity and citizenship rights—is taken further in expressions of pan-Caribbean solidarity. I think there is a logic linking "where we born is where we from" to "it don't matter where you're from." When citizenship rights and national identity become a matter between an *individual* and her or his place of birth, inequalities based on legitimate birth and land ownership cease to affect an individual's legal rights as a citizen. This is the ideal of liberal civil emancipation. As all individuals become equal individuals in the new liberal political milieu, "where you're from" just does not matter anymore—except outside your "own"—that is, your "natural"—national context into which you were born. The difference between Benji V's nationalism and the pan-Caribbean one of Caribbean Ecstasy is merely that of defining the limits of the "nation" in terms of its territorial borders; the underlying politics of birth and nation are the same.

Conclusion

Both the official and counterdiscourses of national belonging in the British Virgin Islands take the nation as a natural and necessary fact of life. Both end up excluding different groups of people from the nation. The official discourse locates national belonging in legally defined kin relations based on the "natural facts" of gender difference and reproduction. The counterdiscourse, holding forth the liberal ideal of individualism, maintains birth in a particular territory as a central event, naturalizes divisions of territory into "nations," and elevates the birth of individuals as the basis of national belonging. Both thus rest on particular config-urations of land, gender, kinship and legal discourse.

In both the official and counterdiscourses, the land, the place of the nation, is cen-trally important to one's claims to "belong." BVIslanders trace lineages and cite land ownership to prove their place as sons and daughters of the "virgin" soil. Non-belongers claim rights to the territory in which they were born. This counterdis-course in particular should lead us to examine the naturalization of nation and birth in other Western models of citizenship, kinship and gender. As Carole Pateman, Dipesh Chakrabarty and others have argued,[13] the Western notion of liberal civil emancipation is predicated upon a notion of autonomous individuals connected in predetermined national communities. The nation alone gives birth, as it were, to its citizens. For the nation-state to be imagined as a collectivity of atomistic individu-als all "born there," connections among individuals must be denied. This goes together with the "self-evident" divisions of the land masses of the earth into "nations," and the congruence of feeling and interest they are held to engender.[14] According to this logic, people do not make nations; rather, nations make people.

The essentialism of the official discourse lies in its concern with kinship, defined almost exclusively in terms of paternity and legitimacy. It has the effect of policing the sexuality of women, both citizen and alien. The essentialism of the counterdis-course—strategic or otherwise—meanwhile promotes the kinds of inequalities more familiar in places like California: "Where you're born is where you're from" echoes the same deeply conservative and protectionist sentiments expressed by many Anglo-Americans on the U.S.-Mexico border, with the same potential to increase surveillance of pregnant noncitizen women who, it is feared, might bear their children in the "wrong" place. Unlike their compatriots in London, New York or other diasporic contexts,[15] the Caribbean peoples living in the British Virgin Islands are rapidly beginning to *assert* rigid demarcations of land masses, cultures and peoples.[16] These national terrains are being reconfigured in a field of meaning and power fundamentally implicated in the construction of gender, kinship and land. They are being enacted in cultural practice, and formalized in state law.

Notes

[1] This paper has benefited greatly from the careful readings of Jane Collier, George Collier and Stefan Helmreich. I would also like to thank Colleen B. Cohen, Michael O'Neal, the editors of this volume and the participants in the "Gender and Kinship" roundtable at the Minnesota conference. Special thanks to Nan Enstad and Birgitte Soland.

Research for this paper was conducted in the summer of 1991 and from July 1992 to July 1993. It has been supported by grants from the Tinker Foundation through the Center for Latin American Studies at Stanford University, the John D. and Catherine T. MacArthur Foundation through the Center for International Security and Arms Control at Stanford, and the National Science Foundation, Law and Social Sciences Program (SES–9208273). I am most grateful for these sources of support. I would also like to thank the British Virgin Islands Community College and the British Virgin Islands Public Library.

[2] Akhil Gupta and James Ferguson, "Beyond 'Culture': Space, Identity, and the Politics of Difference," *Cultural Anthropology* 7 (1992): 6–23. Some earlier work in anthropology also problematized, rather than assumed, the connections both "analysts" and "natives" make between place and sense of identity or belonging. See, for example, Martin Silverman's ethnography of "displaced" Banabans, *Disconcerting Issue: Meaning and Struggle in a Resettled Pacific Community* (Chicago: University of Chicago Press, 1971); and Andrew Strathern, "Kinship, Descent and Locality: Some New Guinea Examples," in Jack Goody, ed., *The Character of Kinship* (Cambridge: Cambridge University Press, 1973), pp. 21–33. Note especially Strathern's discussion of how ideas about shared substance ("blood") and ideas about shared locality ("land") intersect in forming a sense of belonging or identity. I would like to thank the editors for bringing this literature to my attention.

More recently, Liisa Malkki has traced out the bonds between "blood" and "land" as grounded in arboreal metaphors in western and other nationalist discourses; see her "National Geographic: The Rooting of Peoples and the Territorialization of National Identity among Scholars and Refugees," *Cultural Anthropology* 7 (1992): 24–44.

[3] Mindie Lazarus-Black, "Why Women Take Men to Magistrate's Court: Caribbean Kinship Ideology and Law," *Ethnology* 30 (1991): 119–133.

[4] The principal islands are Tortola, Virgin Gorda, Jost van Dyke and Anegada.

[5] A point of clarification: prior to the 1981 Nationality Act, technically only "legal" fathers passed citizenship rights down patrials. In practice, however, and especially in the Caribbean with its high rates of "illegitimacy," the requirement that the father be "legal" was often ignored. Furthermore, prior to 1981, one could legally establish a claim to citizenship if one could prove that a direct male ancestor had been legally born to a citizen father; in other words, if one's grandfather had been a legitimate child of a male citizen, one had a legal claim to citizenship.

I will not rehearse the body of literature on the high rates of "illegitimacy" in the Caribbean. Richard Price provided an apt critique of the framing of the "problem" by North American social scientists in his "Studies of Caribbean Family Organization: Problems and Prospects," *Dedalo* 14 (1971): 23–59. See also Ortmayr, and, in general, the essays in Part IV of this volume, as well as Rose Brewer's "Matrilineality and Patrilineality" conference paper, "African-American Family Formation: Adolescent Fathers, Mothers and Kin." "Legitimacy" is bound up with Western traditions (and monotheistic ones; see Eilberg-Schwartz in this volume, as well as Carol Delaney, *The Seed and the Soil: Gender and Cosmology in Turkish Village Society*, Berkeley, CA: University of California Press, 1991), which place primacy on "fatherhood" as opposed to "motherhood" for ascribing status, identity and so forth. The irony of the 1981 Nationality Act for Caribbean kinship is that, whereas the Act was intended to ensure a means of mothers passing on their citizenship rights to their children, in practice it reconstructed and reinvigorated "fatherhood" (via notions of "legitimacy") as centrally important to citizenship.

6 "Belonger" and "non-belonger" are legal terms which refer to landholding and employment rights; legally, they are not immigration or citizenship categories. However, since the passage of the 1981 Nationality Act, BVIslanders and immigrants have used "belonger" and "citizen" (and "non-belonger" and "noncitizen" or "foreigner") interchangeably. In this essay, I use the terms "belonger" and "non-belonger" in their popular (i.e., nonlegal) senses, to mean "citizen" and "noncitizen," respectively. I have explored the shifts in the popular and legal meanings of belonger and citizenship statuses and identities in 'Belonging,' Citizenship and Flexible Specialization in a Carribbean Tax Haven," PoLAR: Political and Legal Anthropology Review 16 (3): 9–18, 1993.

7 Jean Besson has explored in great detail the "family land" phenomenon and forms of common tenure in the Caribbean. She argues that land ownership in the Caribbean is symbolically central to ideas about autonomy and individual liberty conceived as against or resistive to a cultural memory of plantation slavery. Common tenure arises, she maintains, because of the overall scarcity of land available for individuals to lay claim to as they establish their autonomy. I would suggest that Besson perhaps does not take her analysis far enough. There seems to me to be no necessary contradiction between individual autonomy and ideas about "scarcity" of resources—the weight both concepts carry in liberal political and economic discourses suggest that both are central to the market- and state-building projects of modernity. See Jean Besson, "Symbolic Aspects of Land in the Caribbean: The Tenure and Transmission of Land Rights among Caribbean Peasantries," in Malcolm Cross and Arnaud Marks, eds., Peasants, Plantations and Rural Communities in the Caribbean (Surrey: Department of Sociology, University of Surrey), pp. 86–116; Jean Besson, "Family Land and Caribbean Society: Toward an Ethnography of Afro-Caribbean Peasantries," in Elizabeth M. Thomas-Hope, ed., Perspectives on Caribbean Regional Identity (Liverpool: Centre for Latin American Studies, 1984), pp. 57–83; Jean Besson and Janet Momsen, eds., Land and Development in the Caribbean (London: Macmillan Caribbean, 1987); Jean Besson, "Agrarian Relations and Perceptions of Land in a Jamaican Peasant Village," in John S. Brierley and Hymie Rubenstein, eds., Small Farming and Peasant Resources in the Caribbean (Winnipeg: Department of Geography, University of Manitoba), pp. 39–61. For a detailed discussion of the family land phenomenon in the British Virgin Islands, with special reference to its changing gender, kinship and legal dimensions, please see my Recharting the Caribbean: Land, Law and Citizenship in the British Virgin Islands, Ph.D. dissertation, Stanford University, 1994, chapter 2.

8 "Rock City" is slang for the island of St. Thomas in the United States Virgin Islands (USVI).

9 Farrelly was Governor of the USVI when Benji V sang his song.

10 Lyrics copyright © 1991, Vanclair Benjamin.

11 I would like to acknowledge Colleen B. Cohen for making this point.

12 See Paul Gilroy, "There Ain't No Black In The Union Jack" (Chicago: University of Chicago Press, 1987). Gilroy discusses how British citizenship laws have relied implicitly on ideas about a perceived racial community needing to be preserved for "true" Britons. Indeed, the British Nationality Act effectively denied British citizenship to the children of immigrants from independent Caribbean nations. In the BVI, however, the Act was greeted by many belongers with pleasure, especially as political turmoil in the Dominican

Republic and Guyana brought more and more immigrants from those countries, and as the BVI achieved one of the highest standards of living in the Caribbean. BVIslanders found themselves reluctant to share the spoils of their economic prosperity, even with their "long-lost" Dominicano cousins.

[13] Carole Pateman, *The Sexual Contract* (Stanford: Stanford University Press, 1988); Dipesh Chakrabarty, "The Death of History? Historical Consciousness and the Culture of Late Capitalism," *Public Culture* 4 (1992): 47–65.

[14] See Akhil Gupta and James Ferguson, "Beyond "Culture': Space, Identity, and the Politics of Difference," *Cultural Anthropology* 7 (1992): 6–23. See also Benedict Anderson, *Imagined Communities* (London: Verso, 1983); and Partha Chatterjee, *Nationalist Thought and the Colonial World: A Derivative Discourse?* (London: Zed Books, 1986).

[15] This is in contrast to the situation Dick Hebdige, Stuart Hall and Paul Gilroy have described for the Atlantic diaspora of Caribbean peoples. See, in addition to Gilroy's work cited above, Dick Hebdige, *Cut 'n' Mix: Culture, Identity and Caribbean Music* (London: Methuen, 1987); Stuart Hall, "Cultural Identity and Diaspora," in Jonathan Rutherford, ed., *Identity: Community, Cultural Difference* (London, 1990), pp. 222–237. See also Stefan Helmreich, "Kinship, Nation, and Paul Gilroy's Concept of Diaspora," *Diaspora* 2(2): 243–247, 1992.

[16] My assumption in this conclusion, of course, is that immigrants to the BVI and their children will, eventually, be successful in obtaining citizenship rights or in forcing a redefinition of the legal statuses "belonger" and "nonbelonger." The intent of my conclusion is to sound a cautionary note, however, on the kind of community that might be designed after this becomes the case. The counterdiscourse demands we come to grips with the contradictions of liberal political theory and its ethics of freedom, individuality and choice. For a discussion of these dilemmas for feminist practice, see Jane Collier, "Negotiating Values: 'You Can't Have It Both Ways," in Patricia Lyons Johnson, ed., *Balancing Acts: Women and the Process of Social Change* (Boulder: Westview Press, 1992), pp. 163–177. See also Kath Weston's "Matrilineality and Patrilineality" conference paper, "Forever is a Long Time: Friendship and Enduring Solidarity in Gay Kinship Ideology."

Index

Contributors

ALEXANDER H. BOLYANATZ is a social anthropologist who recieved his PhD from the University of California, San Diego in 1994, where he currently holds a teaching position. Recent publications include "Legitimacy, Coercion and Leadership among the Sursurunga of Southern New Ireland," (*Ethnology*, 1994) and "Matriliny and Revisionist Anthropology" (*Anthropos*, 1995).

HOWARD EILBERG-SCHWARTZ is Associate Professor of Jewish Studies at San Francisco State University and a Guggenheim Fellow. He is the author of *The Savage in Judaism* (Indiana) and *God's Phallus and other Problems for Men and Monotheism* (Beacon).

PAMELA FELDMAN-SAVELSBERG is Assistant Professor of Anthropology in the Department of Sociology and Anthropology at Carleton College. Her recent publications have appeared in *Social Science and Medicine* (1994) and *American Ethnologist* (1995).

LUCIA FERRANTE teaches in the Political Science department of Bologna University. She is one of the founders of the Italian Association of Women Historians.

BARBARA A. HANAWALT is a professor of history at the University of Minnesota. She has published *Crime and Conflict in English Communities 1300-1348* (1979), *The Ties that Bound: Peasant Families in Medieval England* (1986) and *Growing up in Medieval London: The Experience of Childhood in History* (1993).

CHRISTIANE KLAPISCH-ZUBER is a professor at the Ecole des Hautes Etudes en Sciences Sociales, Paris, where she teaches the historical demography and anthropology of medieval Italy. She is editor of *A History of Women*, vol.2 *Silences of the Middle Ages* (1992).

BILL MAURER is a Lecturer in the Department of Anthropology. Stanford University. His recent publications appear in the *Law and Society Review*, *Nieuwe West Indische Gids*, and *PoLAR: The Political and Anthropology Review*.

MARY JO MAYNES is a historian of modern Europe at the University of Minnesota. She is the author of *Taking the Hard Road: Lifecourse in French and German Workers' Autobiographies of the Industrial Era* (Chapel Hill: UNC Press, 1995).

SHANTI MENON has just completed a dissertation on Women and Schooling in Kerala, South India, at the department of Cultural Foundations of Education, Syracuse University.

MURIEL NAZZARI is associate professor of history at Indiana University, with a concentration in Latin American history. She has published *Disappearance of the Dowry: Women, Families and Social Change in São Paolo Brazil (1600-1900)* (Stanford, 1991).

JEAN O'BRIEN has been an assistant professor in the department of history at the University of Minnesota since 1990. She is the author of *Dispossession by Degrees: Indian Land and Identity in Natick, Massachussetts, 1650-1790*, forthcoming from Cambridge University Press.

NORBERT ORTMAYR has been a Lecturer in the Department of History of the University of Salzburg since 1986. He has published many articles and the recent book *Knechte* (Male Servants) (Vienna: Boehlau Verlag, 1992).

MAURA PALAZZI teaches economic history at the University of Bologna. She is the editor, together with Gianna Pomata and Lucia Ferrante of the volume *Ragnatele di rapport. `Patronage' e reti de relazioni nella storia delle donne* (Webs of Relations: `Patronage' and Networks of Relationships in Women's History) (Torino, 1988).

GIANNA POMATA teaches history at the Universities of Bologna and Minnesota. She is the author of *La promessa di guarigione: Malati e curatori in antico regime* (Rome, 1994), an English translation of which is forthcoming from Johns Hopkins University Press.

GLORIA GOODWIN RAHEJA is Associate Professor and Chair of the Department of Anthropology at the University of Minnesota. She is the author of *The Poison in the Gift: Ritual, Prestation and the Dominant Caste in a South Indian Village* (University of Chicago Press, 1988).

CARMEN RAMOS ESCANDON is Associate Professor of History at Occidental College in Los Angeles. In 1987, Dr. Ramos founded the first seminar on Women's History Research at the Interdisciplinary Program on Women's Studies at El Colegio de Mexico in Mexico City. Her most recent articles include "Genderizing History in Latin America: the Mexican Case" in Liz Dore ed. *Gender Cross Currents in Latin America* (forthcoming, Routledge, 1996).

ENI DE MESQUITA SAMARA is a Professor of History at the University of São Paolo, Brazil. She is the author of many articles and books, including *A Familia Brasileira* (São Paolo, Brasiliense, 1984) and *As Mulheres, o Poder e a Familia* (São Paolo, Marco Zero, 1989).

R. PARRY SCOTT is a professor of Anthropology at the Federal University of Pernambuco in Recife, Brazil, with an MA in Latin American Studies and a PhD. in Anthropology from the University of Texas at Austin. He has been a visiting scholar in Demography at Georgetown University (1983) and in Anthropology at Harvard University (1992, 1993).

BIRGITTE SOLAND (cand. mag. from the University of Aarhus and PhD from the University of Minnesota) teaches European women's history at Ohio State University. She is currently completing a manuscript on Danish women in the 1920s, and is also researching gay and lesbian partnership legislation in Denmark.

ULRIKE STRASSER is a doctoral candidate in Early Modern European and Comparative Women's History at the University of Minnesota. She is currently working on her dissertation which explores the impact of the Counter-Reformation on women's lives in Germany, and compares findings on the changing parameters of marriage, sexuality and piety in Germany to research on Counter-Reformation Italy and Ming China.

ANN WALTNER is an associate professor in the department of history at the University of Minnesota. She is the author of *Getting an Heir: Adoption and the Construction of Kinship in Late Imperial China* (Hawaii, 1990)